Cyrus Lakdawala

The Trompowsky Attack

move by move

EVERYMAN CHESS

www.everymanchess.com

First published in 2014 by Gloucester Publishers Limited, Northburgh House,
10 Northburgh Street, London EC1V 0AT

British Library Cataloguing-in-Publication Data
A catalogue record for this book is available from the British Library.

ISBN: 978 1 78194 177 5

Distributed in North America by The Globe Pequot Press, P.O Box 480,
246 Goose Lane, Guilford, CT 06437-0480.

All other sales enquiries should be directed to Everyman Chess, Northburgh House,
10 Northburgh Street, London EC1V 0AT
tel: 020 7253 7887 fax: 020 7490 3708
email: info@everymanchess.com; website: www.everymanchess.com

Everyman Chess Series
Chief advisor: Byron Jacobs
Commissioning editor: John Emms
Assistant editor: Richard Palliser

Typeset and edited by First Rank Publishing, Brighton.
Cover design by Horatio Monteverde.

About the Author

Cyrus Lakdawala is an International Master, a former National Open and American Open Champion, and a six-time State Champion. He has been teaching chess for over 30 years, and coaches some of the top junior players in the U.S.

Also by the Author:
Play the London System
A Ferocious Opening Repertoire
The Slav: Move by Move
1...d6: Move by Move
The Caro-Kann: Move by Move
The Four Knights: Move by Move
Capablanca: Move by Move
The Modern Defence: Move by Move
Kramnik: Move by Move
The Colle: Move by Move
The Scandinavian: Move by Move
Botvinnik: Move by Move
The Nimzo-Larsen Attack: Move by Move
Korchnoi: Move by Move

Acknowledgements

Many thanks to my ever-encouraging editor, GM John Emms, to IM Richard Palliser for the final edit, and to Nancy for both proof reading and her tea kettle turning-oning each morning. May your Tromps take on the attitude of a mischievous child who pulled something over on the unsuspecting adults.

Contents

Series Foreword

Move by Move is a series of opening books which uses a question-and-answer format. One of our main aims of the series is to replicate – as much as possible – lessons between chess teachers and students.

All the way through, readers will be challenged to answer searching questions, to test their skills in chess openings and indeed in other key aspects of the game. It's our firm belief that practising your skills like this is an excellent way to study chess openings, and to study chess in general.

Many thanks go to all those who have been kind enough to offer inspiration, advice and assistance in the creation of Move by Move. We're really excited by this series and hope that readers will share our enthusiasm.

John Emms,
Everyman Chess

Bibliography

Dealing with 1 d4 Deviations, John Cox (Everyman Chess 2007)
Fighting the Anti-King's Indians, Yelena Dembo (Everyman Chess 2008)
Play the London System, Cyrus Lakdawala (Everyman Chess 2010)
Playing the Trompowsky, Richard Pert (Quality Chess 2013)
Secrets of the Trompowsky, Vol.1, Julian Hodgson (Hodgson Enterprises 1997)
Starting Out: The Trompowsky Attack, Richard Palliser (Everyman Chess 2009)
The Modern Defence: Move by Move, Cyrus Lakdawala (Everyman Chess 2012)
The Scandinavian: Move by Move, Cyrus Lakdawala (Everyman Chess 2013)
The Torre Attack: Move by Move, Richard Palliser (Everyman Chess 2012)
The Trompowsky, Joe Gallagher (Chess Press 1998)
The Trompowsky, 2nd edition, Nigel Davies (Everyman Chess 2005)
Winning with the Trompowsky, Peter Wells, (Batsford 2003)

Electronic/Online
Chess Today, with annotations by Viktor Moskalenko
ChessBase 10, with annotations by Alex Finkel and Julian Hodgson
ChessBase Live database
ChessPublishing.com, with annotations by Eric Prié and Aaron Summerscale

Introduction

I see the bad moon arising. I see trouble on the way.

The Trompowsky: Dispenser of Abstractions

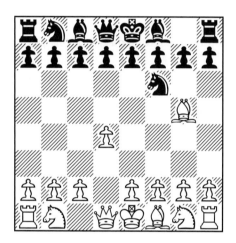

The DNA of every person on earth is virtually identical. Yet infinitesimally slight differences in our species give birth to the vast array of ugly and attractive, cruel and compassionate, idiotic and wise, those who take and those who give, evil and holy. A chess game is the same way. The tiniest shift gives rise to destinies as varied as winning, drawing and losing. The Trompowsky is an opening very much like this as well, where we reach hair-trigger positions which alter our destiny with one seemingly trivial inaccurate or accurate move.

In most openings, the positions we reach are like one of those dreams where the landscape always remains the same, no matter how far your dream character travels. But most certainly not in the Trompowsky, a paradoxical byway and an inexhaustible font for originality, a reality where 'normal' fails to apply and the solution to our problems is often a paradox within a paradox. It's difficult to label that which lacks an abiding identity and in the Tromp, accidental happenings – both terrifying and joyful – have a way of unexpectedly shaping our futures.

Yet our opening is not a case of ambition outweighing rationality. Deep down, we sense a stratum of rationality behind what appears to be purely irrational. On our second move, our not-so-subtle message blares, as we issue the ultimatum: Play in my backyard, or else!

Our bishop arises from nowhere, just itching to create unrest. Almost instantly, we withdraw recognition of opening theory's intimidating authority and incite rebellion. 2 ♗g5 stands outside the terms of a 'normal' opening's contract. Be warned: the Tromp is an opening of wild fluctuations and our games rarely flow smoothly, in a consistently upward trajectory. We enter a realm where measurement of known quantities isn't so easy. The positions often defy physical laws and we find ourselves faced with paralyzingly difficult over-the-board choices and compromises.

People of cautious nature tend to live long lives, while graveyards are filled with optimists. The Tromp, I'm afraid, falls under the latter category. I tend to engage the Tromp when desperate for a win and unafraid of loss. For three decades the opening has been my not-so-secret weapon of choice in critical, must-win games. The Trompowsky is a very difficult opening system to play with a degree of skill. Play it without full understanding and familiarity, and we risk sounding like a Mozart symphony performed and assassinated by a high school orchestra. I originally took up the Trompowsky with a dreamer's natural aversion to mathematical measurement. Today, 30 years later, all this has altered, and the opening originally intended to dodge theory is now encircled by reams of it.

There are few things more depressing than the realization of your long labours having been rendered null and void. In a way we do just this to our booked up opponents, by engaging the Tromp. For King's Indian, Grünfeld, Nimzo-Indian, Queen's Indian, Slav, Queen's Gambit players, their theoretical knowledge – and more importantly, the experience accumulated from these lines – virtually vaporizes after our second move. With our second move we may disarm a normally well-armed theoretician and toss him or her into a world of partially-formed images, murky speculations, half-recollections of positions which shift in and out of focus into writhing, alien configurations.

Each time I begin a book, it feels as if I am about to build the Great Wall of China and have placed but a single stone. For all my anti-theory rhetoric, this book will be an exceedingly difficult task for the reader to absorb, from a theoretical standpoint, mainly because the positions reached are so bafflingly alien and the convoluted variations so difficult to remember. Misunderstand one slight shift, or forget a single move in a variation, and we risk flipping a '+-' into its dreaded opposite, '-+'.

The logistical challenges of the Tromp remind us of Noah's woes, when he had to work out a way to fit a pair of every animal on earth into an ark, 300 cubits in length – rather a tight fit. Luckily he didn't have to worry about the fish. Also, I quite reasonably ask: why did he bring along mosquitoes, wasps and venomous snakes?

Frustratingly many of the Tromp variations we contend with are like ones in a dream, the memory of which fades to oblivion upon awakening. If this is the case for our side, then I argue: how much more so for our opponents, who I'm guessing, don't spend all that much of their study time on the Trompowsky?

Saying this, in our opening, the ability to retain one's bearings within the unfamiliar is perhaps every bit as important as memorizing and then spewing out opening theory and its offshoot equations. But we must also recognize our limitations. The human brain is incapable of housing and storing so much data, unless your FIDE rating happens to exceed the 2700 mark. So prepare yourself to get tossed into indecipherable situations where we play by feel, rather than logic. And why not? When we were children, we all understood that the only way to blow the Deathstar to smithereens was to feel the Force and disengage the autopilot. Gaze at the vistas we may visit:

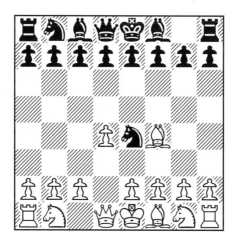

This innocuous-looking position, from Chapters One and Two often leads to head-spinning complications. Black's ambitious knight often lives with a guilty feeling of intrusion on its advanced square, since it grows vulnerable to various undermining devices and f3 tempo-gains.

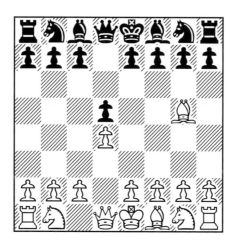

The Pseudo-Tromp (actually, technically the Levitsky Attack) can also be played on double queen's pawn games, where Black has a tempting array of second move responses:

a) 2...♘f6 gets us back to Chapter Four.

b) 2...c6 intends ...♕b6, attempting to punish us for our early bishop jump by going after b2.

c) 2...f6!? 3 ♗h4 ♘h6 can lead to head-spinning complications.

Trompowsky Gambits

If we keep a full grown tiger as a pet, we had better make certain it is well fed, or it may regard us as the next meal. The Trompowsky represents the blurred synthesis of a player from Morphy's era and one from the present. It is an opening conducive to extremes and some of our lines look a bit like a guy in a bar, having had one too many, warning another patron next to him, twice his size: "Look at me like that again and I'll take your head off, buddy!"

Sometimes in the Tromp we conduct business on a cash-only basis, and are required to pay up front. I speak of gambits, that altered reality where the heart rules the head, where b- and e-pawns are given away like candy at Halloween. It's always a surreal feeling when we spontaneously deviate from the predictable habits of a lifetime. I am not a gambiting kind of guy in any of my other openings. Yet there are several lines of the Tromp, which seem to hold a seducer's sway with my chess personality, in which I am willing to do just that. Even though every gambit in this book can't be endorsed as a construct of 100% unimpeachable soundness, I'm pretty certain they reach the 99% mark.

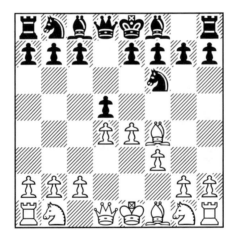

Here is the Reversed Blackmar-Diemer Gambit (a full move up for our side), Lakdawala-Ivanov, from Chapter Two.

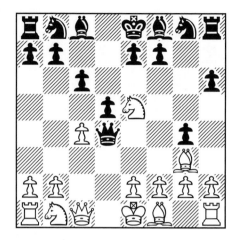

This is a gambit we offer in Chapter Seven, Hodgson-Lalic. White gets a development lead and a loosening of Black's structure in exchange for a pawn.

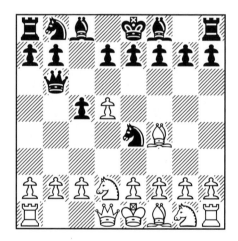

This is Gareev-Mikhalevsky, from the final chapter, where Gareev offered b2 to a fellow grandmaster.

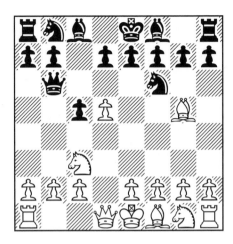

The diagrammed position, Vaganian-Jansa, is from the dangerous – for White and Black! – and is known as the Vaganian Gambit.

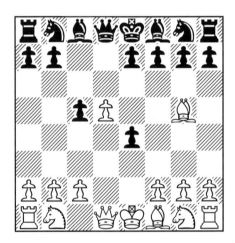

In Hodgson-Roeder we reach a Reversed Albin Countergambit, but a full move up since we get it as White, not Black.

The Contamination Factor

A few tiny granules of sand are enough to clog a system of vast machinery. One interesting feature of the Trompowsky is that we reach positions which look like other systems, but with a contaminated alteration sneakily inserted. This can play havoc on a rigid opponent who relies upon a theory-prescribed counter – except it doesn't apply, since we are not in his or her theory.

When chaos begins to morph into recognizable geometries, clearly some hidden organizing principle is at play behind it. These significant alterations have the power to render a confused opponent vectorless and directionless, a drifting chunk of debris, floating in outer space. For example:

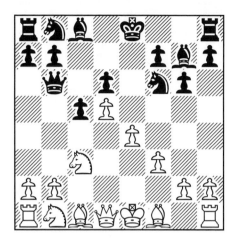

In Nakamura-Lie we see a kind of drunken Benoni, with a pair of modifications:

1. Black's b6-queen is misplaced since she gets in the way of the queenside pawn majority.

2. White's g1-knight usurped c3. This allows White to later play a4 and ♘a3, seizing control over c4, and also clamping down on Black's ...b5 and ...c4 breaks.

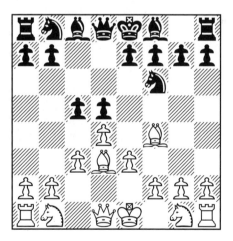

Lakdawala-Bruno reached a rather placid London System position, except White is up a full move over a normal London, since Black took three moves to play his knight to f6, while we only used two for our bishop to reach f4.

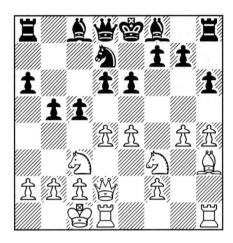

Finegold-Benjamin. Have you ever been this far ahead in development in an Open Sicilian? White's scary development lead probably means more than Black's bishop-pair and queenside attacking chances.

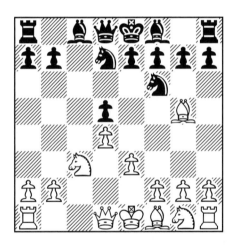

Hodgson-Del Mundo. We reach an Exchange Slav with Black's knight on the inferior d7-square. And here is the best part: Black probably intended to enter a Queen's Gambit Declined.

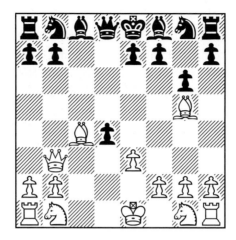

Lakdawala-Bruno. Have you ever been in a Grunfeld which looks like this? ...♕a5+ would pick off my hanging g5-bishop, except for the fact that White threatens f7.

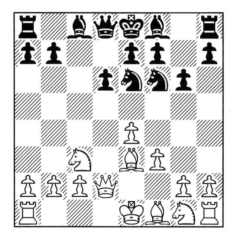

Lakdawala-Cuarta. It's a Dragon; well, sort of, with Black's knight lured to e6, rather than its normal c6-square and White's knight remains on g1, rather than on d4. Also White looks further ahead in development than in a normal Dragon, and therefore retains the superior chances.

King Julian the First
Our opening was first played by Stepan Levitsky in the early 1900's, but is named after the Brazilian Champion Octavio Trompowsky, who bewildered opponents with it in the 1930's and 40's. Then our opening fell into unused disrepair for decades, until it was revived in the 80's through GM Julian Hodgson's amazing interpretation of an obscure opening scheme, which he single-handedly turned into a deadly and fully accepted theoretical

weapon. Today, the once rarity is commonplace, with super-GM Hikaru Nakamura's use of it in his repertoire.

Hodgson's games are the benchmark, against which all other players' Trompowsky skill throughout history will be compared. In fact, the opening really should be named after him, since he was the first GM to employ it exclusively with the white pieces. Hodgson's chess nature is not one to lend itself to conciliatory gestures and I would describe his style as never-back-down absolutism. At times his interrogative attitude borders on open bully-ism. This book is a virtual Hodgson-fest, loaded up with his always-entertaining games.

Here is a whopper of a homework assignment for any reader brave enough to under-take it: fire up your database, and call up and study every Hodgson Trompowsky (in case you were wondering, I did this in preparation for this book). To start you off on this monu-mental project, here is a classic Hodgson win with his opening:

Game 1
J.Hodgson-J.van der Wiel
Amsterdam 1994

GM Aaron Summerscale writes of this game: "The Hodgson Legacy: Julian Hodgson has done more than anyone to revitalize the Tromp. For anyone learning this exciting opening, his games are a treasure trove of interesting and entertaining ideas. The following game highlights Hodgson's creative approach to the Tromp, as he happily sacrifices material for a fierce initiative."

1 d4 ♘f6 2 ♗g5

Bye, bye King's Indian; adios Nimzo-Indian and Queen's Indian; au revoir Old Indian; godspeed Grünfeld...you get the picture. On our second move, we politely ask our oppo-nents to leave their theoretical knowledge at the door, wipe their feet, and enter our home: The Trompowsky.

2...c5

For the record, here is the earliest Trompowsky game in my database: 2...g6 3 ♗xf6 exf6 4 c4 ♗g7 5 ♘c3 0-0 6 e3 d6 7 ♗d3 f5 8 ♘ge2 ♘d7 9 ♕c2 ♘f6 10 0-0 c6 11 b4 ♖e8 12 ♖ab1 ♕e7 13 b5 with a position remarkably similar to ones we look at in Chapter Six, S.Levitsky-A.Burn, Breslau 1912.

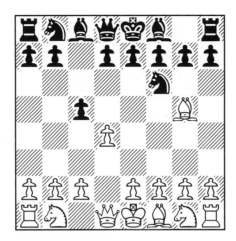

3 ♗xf6

> *Question:* Don't we cover 3 d5 and the Vaganian Gambit in this book?

Answer: Correct. I had no room for the variation Hodgson played in this game (the normally easy-going folk at Everyman view your undisciplined writer with enraged, bloodshot eyes of menace whenever I surpass a book's space quota – which is pretty much every book I write), and decided to sneak it into the book's introduction.

3...gxf6

> *Question:* Why not recapture with the e-pawn, as Black does in Chapter Four?

Answer: This position is very different than the Chapter Four version, since Black already tossed in ...c5. Let's look: 3...exf6 4 e3 and now if Black follows logically with 4...♕b6 5 b3 (5 ♘c3!? ♕xb2 6 ♘d5 cxd4 7 ♖b1 ♕xa2 8 ♘c7+ ♔d8 9 ♘xa8 dxe3 10 fxe3 ♗c5 actually looks at least equal for Black, since he eventually picks up the a8-knight) 5...cxd4 6 exd4 ♘c6 7 c3 d5 8 ♗d3 ♗d6 9 ♘d2 ♗e6 10 ♘e2 0-0 11 ♘f1 ♕a5 12 ♘e3 b5?! (Black later pays for this move strategically) 13 0-0 ♖fd8 (13...b4 14 c4 favours White) 14 a3 g6 15 f4 f5 16 ♕e1 ♘e7 17 b4! ♕b6 18 ♘c1! (heading for c5, which nullifies Black's would-be pressure on c3) 18...♖ac8 19 g3 ♔g7 20 ♘b3 ♘g8 21 ♘c5 White stood clearly better, since a4 follows, with queenside pressure, Y.Zherebukh-A.Hambleton, Athens 2012.

4 d5 ♕b6

Our Achilles heel in the Tromp: b2, which we often sacrifice.

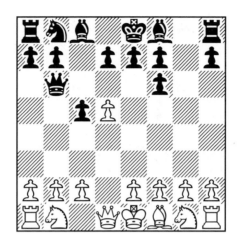

5 ♕c1

But not this time.

5...♗h6

Black utilizes a deflection device. He can also try the calmer:

a) 5...f5 6 c4 ♗g7 7 ♘c3 d6 may be Black's best line. The unopposed dark-squared bishop makes up for White's space. An example: 8 e3 ♘d7 9 ♕c2 ♕a5 10 ♘h3 ♘b6 11 ♗d3 ♗d7 (also possible is 11...♗xc3+ 12 bxc3 ♕a4 13 ♕b3 e5 14 f3 with approximate equality) 12 0-0 ♗xc3 13 bxc3 e6 14 dxe6 fxe6 15 e4 fxe4 16 ♗xe4 0-0-0 17 ♘g5 ♖hg8? (necessary was 17...♖df8 18 ♘xh7 ♖f7 19 ♕d3 d5 20 cxd5 exd5 21 ♗g6 with great complications) 18 ♘f7 (forking d8 and d6) 18...♘xc4 19 ♘xd8 ♕xd8 failed to offer Black enough compensation for the exchange, L.Van Wely-E.L'Ami, Wijk aan Zee 2013.

b) 5...♗g7 6 g3 (what a loathsome feeling to clearly see a path and then not take it out of cowardice; I wish I had the courage to jump through the flaming hoop with 6 c4) 6...d6 7 ♗g2 f5 8 c3 ♘d7 9 ♘d2 ♘f6 10 ♘h3 h5 11 ♕c2 ♗d7 12 a4 h4 13 ♘f4 hxg3 14 hxg3 ♖xh1+ 15 ♗xh1 0-0-0 16 ♘c4 ♕a6 17 ♕d3 ♖h8 18 ♗g2 ♔c7!; ...e5 is in the air and Black already stood slightly better, C.Lakdawala-H.Nakamura, US Championship, La Jolla 2004.

6 e3 f5 7 c4

The safer 7 g3 prevents the coming firestorm and ruins the fun for both sides.

7...f4!? 8 exf4 ♗xf4!?

Overloading White's queen, whose services are required to cover b2. The parties draw near to the inevitable collision course. We sense that Hodgson feels restless and uneasy, a corralled horse before an approaching storm, since Black's last move fails to mollify White's attacking ambitions.

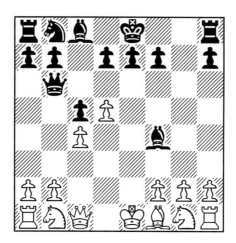

9 ♕xf4!?

Everyone wonders if White's queen may soon require the services of a tailor, to measure for a straitjacket. Clearly the new regime makes for fewer allowances for insubordination than the old one. The greatest offence you can give to a person of imperious nature is to challenge her authority. White's queen does just that with her b6 sister. The feeling of constraint which hung over White now vanishes, to be replaced with reckless abandon. But this is to be expected, since the Tromp's nature is one which veers to extremes.

> ***Question:*** Wait a minute! You just said "overloading White's queen, whose services are required to cover b2", didn't you?

Answer: Those words don't ring a bell, but having reviewed the transcripts, I see that you may be right. In this case, Hodgson accepts the dare, offering a full exchange and pawn for a massive development lead and dangerous attacking chances.

No one has tried 9 ♕c3 ♖g8 10 g3 ♗h6 11 ♕c2 d6 12 ♘c3 ♘d7 13 f4 ♔f8 14 ♘f3 ♗g7 15 ♗d3 h6 16 0-0 when I actually prefer White's space and attacking chances over Black's bishop-pair and dark-square control.

9...♕xb2 10 ♘e2

The beginning of a dual purpose plan to trivialize Black's offside queen and also unravel White's kingside.

10...♕xa1

The queen realizes she sinned, thinking: "Ah, yes, that pesky eighth commandment – that one about stealing...I keep forgetting. Oh, well, I will be forgiven." Unfortunately, she is mistaken in her theory.

11 ♘ec3

Because of chess computers and databases, we now live in an age of miracles, where 12-year-olds memorize theory into the middlegame. This is all book so far. Be careful though. There lies a great divide between the theoretical and actual performance of a task. Such positions should first be practiced against the comps, before they are tried out against human opponents. After all, would you hire a bodyguard if he had a black belt in jujitsu, earned by a correspondence course? So test such ultra-sharp positions first, before engaging them in tournaments.

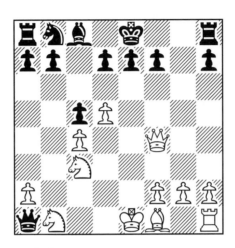

Question: White remains down a massive amount of material. Didn't he wander past legitimacy's borders and shouldn't he be thinking about resigning here?

Answer: Not quite, although an enraged *Houdini* insists that Black is winning. It certainly appears as if Hodgson courts his own destruction. Upon closer inspection, we find that White actually accumulated enormous compensation for the exchange:

1. Whenever we deliberately violate a principle, we essentially plead (to ourselves) extenuating circumstances. In this instance Black violated the E=MC squared of principles: don't fall behind in development.

2. Black's queen, who comes across as a bit of a half-portion when compared to her powerful sister, takes an eternity to return to relevance.

3. If White is allowed to play d6, he generates serious attacking chances along the devastated dark squares.

4. White scores 60.3% from this position – a higher average than most white opening lines.

Conclusion: Let's ignore the nay-saying comp's assessment and test this gambit, which looks sound to a human, like your writer. In fact, I think this line is more than sound, and prefer White's side.

11...♕b2!?

Van der Wiel, fearing for his queen's life – since ♕d2 may trap Black's queen – decides to get her out while he can, but at high cost to his king.

11...d6! is the true test of White's speculation: for example, 12 ♕d2 (threat: ♗d3, 0-0 and ♘a3, trapping Black's wayward queen) 12...♖g8 13 g3 ♖g4?! (13...a6 looks safer) 14 f4 and I still prefer White's attacking chances over Black's material, N.Vitiugov-D.Dubov, Khanty-Mansiysk 2013. At this stage *Houdini*, getting cold feet about its earlier assessment, claims the position is now in White's favour.

12 d6!

This move punctures the dark squares around Black's king, who endures trial by ordeal in order to pay dues for past unpunished transgressions.

12...♘c6?

In such hair-trigger positions, even a seemingly trifling deviation from the exact sequence brings with it fatal consequences. This knight is the awkward best man who desperately searches for the misplaced ring, while the entire wedding party awaits in expectation. It was awarded an exclam by Summerscale, but Black's position is so precarious that I think it may be a losing move (although I must confess: sometimes when I criticize a player for a move or plan, I suffer a guilty twinge, realizing that I may well have followed exactly the same incorrect plan over the board; sometimes criticism applies equally to the critic):

a) 12...♕c2?? (a paroled ex-convict, when faced with freedom's temptations, sometimes forgets her promises to her old jailers) 13 ♕e3! and Black is busted. 1-0, P.Wells-A.Shirov, Gibraltar 2006.

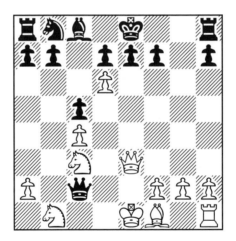

Question: I wonder if you care to elaborate on your outrageous claim? Why didn't Shirov spiel on when up so much material?

Answer: Upon review, Black's position fails the examination with multiple unsatisfactory elements. Black's last move was a blunder. White wins since Black can't unravel and basically plays without the use of 80% of his army: for example, 13...♘c6?! 14 ♗d3 ♕b2 15 0-0 b6 16 ♗e4 (threat: ♗xc6, followed by ♕xe7 mate) 16...e6 17 ♗xc6 dxc6 18 ♕g5 (threatening mate on the move) 18...♔f8 19 ♕h6+ ♔g8 20 ♖e1 f6 (20...a5 21 ♖e2! ♕b4 22 ♖e3 forces mate) 21 ♕xf6 h6 22 ♕d8+ ♔g7 23 ♕e7+ ♔g8 24 ♘e4 ♖h7 25 ♘f6+ and Black must hand over his queen.

b) 12...♖g8! may be Black's best move: 13 ♗e2! ♖g6 (13...♖xg2?? 14 ♕e4 ♕c1+ 15 ♗d1 ♕g5 16 ♔f1! wins the rook) 14 0-0! ♖xd6 15 ♗h5 ♖f6 16 ♕e4 d6 17 ♘d5 ♕e5 18 ♘c7+ ♔d8 19 ♕xe5 dxe5 20 ♘xa8 and *Houdini* claims chances are even while I like White. It isn't so easy for Black to trap the a8-knight.

13 ♗d3 exd6

An old landmark which turned into an eyesore, is finally taken down. Gulp! *Houdini* assessment: +11.92 – completely resignable for Black. However, Black can't survive 13...e6 14 0-0 ♖g8 15 ♕h6 b6 16 ♗xh7 ♖f8 17 ♕g5 ♖h8 18 ♘d5! ♔f8 (18...exd5 19 ♖e1+ ♔f8 20 ♕h6+ ♕g7 21 ♖e8+ forces mate) 19 ♘f6. The threat of ♕h6 costs Black his queen after 19...♕xf6 20 ♕xf6 ♖xh7 21 ♘d2 when he has no chance to survive White's coming assault.

14 0-0

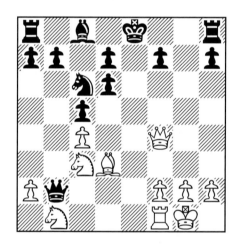

No rush. 15 ♖e1+ is a horrendous threat. A key element of martial arts is that at certain stages of combat, the martial arts expert yields, rather than resists, in order to throw the opponent's equilibrium off balance. Hodgson utilizes this strategy with a calm move, increasing his development lead.

14...♘e5

It isn't easy for Black to retain defensive bearings while under a fusillade of threats, both real and imagined.

15 ♕f6

The black king begins to look exceedingly uncomfortable. Even more crushing is the simple 15 ♖e1 f6 16 ♘d5 0-0 17 ♘xf6+ ♖xf6 18 ♕xf6 when there is no good defence to the coming ♗e4, transferring to d5.

15...0-0

The beleaguered king clutches at his f8-protector in a fervour of gratitude. Black gets annihilated after 15...♖g8 16 ♖e1 ♕b6 17 ♘d5 ♕d8 18 ♕xd6 f6 19 ♘xf6+.

16 ♘d5

Threatening mate on e7.

16...♖e8 17 ♕g5+ ♘g6

17...♔h8 (Black's king, not feeling so well, notices an uncharacteristically bitter after-taste to his morning cup of tea; even more disconcerting is the fact that his ambitious sister on g5 seems to be watching him with unusual attention this morning) 18 ♘f6 ♘xd3 19 ♕h6 is decisive.

18 ♘f6+

White begins the final assault, driving Black's king to the centre of the board.

18...♔f8

The king is forced to emerge from his hermitage, to face the dangers of the outside world.

19 ♕h6+ ♔e7 20 ♘d5+

Of course this knight is worth a lot more than Black's rook.

20...♔d8

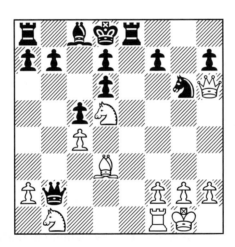

Exercise (planning): White's attack flows with one mind, as a single unit, free from independent parts or interrelated components of any kind. One glance tells us that all is not well in Black's world. We sense a knockout, but where in the name of Alekhine is it?

Answer: Removal of a key defender/Interference.

21 ♗xg6!

The black king's depleting and weakly-armed garrison soon gets whittled down to zero.

21...hxg6 22 ♘bc3! 1-0

Shutting out the black queen's influence over f6. Attackers stare in cold cruelty at

Black's king. There is no reasonable defence to 23 ♕h4+ or 23 ♕g5+: for example, 22...f6 23 ♕g7 ♖e6 24 ♕f8+ ♖e8 25 ♕xf6+ ("well, well, well, what have we here?" gloats White's queen, as she discovers Black's king cowering within a secret chamber; the queen voices popular sentiment when she apologetically informs the king: "we took a vote and it was unanimous: we all want you dead") 25...♖e7 26 ♕xe7 is mate. With the fall of the final defender, the black king's isolation is rendered absolute.

Black played the entire game without the help of his a8-rook and c8-bishop, so in effect, it was White, not Black, who was up material the entire game.

Summary: The exchange and pawn sacrifice looks completely sound for White – at least to your writer's Tromp-biased eyes!

Cyrus Lakdawala
San Diego,
February 2014

Chapter One
Quasi-Benoni Lines

1 d4 ♘f6 2 ♗g5 ♘e4 3 ♗f4 c5

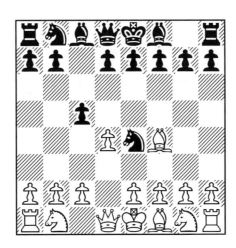

In this first chapter, the top diagram soon morphs into the one below after **4 f3 ♕a5+ 5 c3 ♘f6 6 d5 ♕b6 7 ♗c1**.

In this position, both parties flagrantly violate a key opening prohibition: Don't move the same piece more than once in the opening. One would never guess that White's c1-bishop already moved three times in order to reach its original square, c1, and that Black's queen moved twice while his f6-knight took three moves to reach f6.

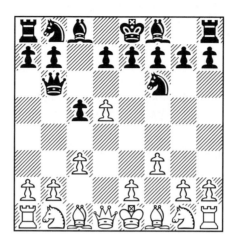

After **7...e6 8 e4 exd5 9 exd5 d6 10 c4** we reach one of our key tabiya positions of the chapter, a strange-looking Benoni, where White recaptured with exd5, rather than the traditional cxd5.

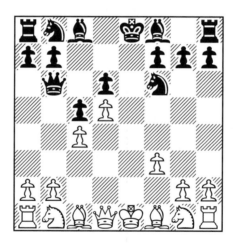

On the surface it appears quite decent for Black, due to his developmental lead, yet I believe this represents merely a symbolic gesture. In my research, I concluded that the parties don't suffer problems of parallel degree, and the accumulation of evidence trends in White's favour. Black's main predicament is lack of a target, and the 'free' queen's move to b6 constitutes a liability rather than a benefit since she blocks Black's thematic ...b5 break. In the games of this chapter, we observe White slowly building for a kingside assault, based on our space advantage.

At the end of the chapter, we reach real Benoni positions (sort of!), with a few hallucinatory changes, like White's g1-knight usurping the c3-square from his b1-brother, and also Black's familiar, 'free' ...♕b6. In this case as well, I prefer our Trompowsky version over normal Benoni lines. Since this introduction has grown too long, I suggest we examine the games of this chapter to determine if the writer's claims are true.

1 d4 ♘f6 2 ♗g5 ♘e4

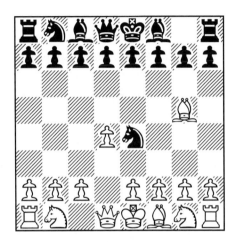

With this move, Black agrees to play in our Trompowsky backyard. An important transpositional note to be aware of is 2...c5 (we cover this move in Chapter Four) 3 d5 ♘e4 4 ♗f4 ♕b6 5 ♗c1 and if 5...e6 6 f3 ♘f6 7 e4 exd5 8 exd5 d6 9 c4. We reach the same position we get in most of the games from this chapter.

3 ♗f4

Question: Do we cover the 3 ♗h4 line in this book?

Answer: I used to play this line in the 80's, and loved the disorienting positions which arose. Then as theory progressed, it felt as if the line grew more and more shady, and quickly became the semi-criminal cousin who inflicts unwanted visits from time to time. Today, the vast majority of Trompers go with the sounder 3 ♗f4 line. I would love to cover 3 ♗h4, if just for fun, but we don't have room to cover both branches.

3...c5

Next chapter we look at 3...d5. More rarely played third move alternatives are:

a) 3...d6 4 f3 ♘f6 5 e4. We reach either a Pirc or Philidor style position with White having the free move ♗f4. This is because White's bishop moved twice to reach f4 and Black's knight moved three times to reach f6. However, the 'free' part goes away if Black regains the tempo with an eventual ...e5: for example, 5...♘bd7 6 ♘c3 e5 7 ♗e3 ♗e7 8 ♕d2 0-0 9 0-0-0!? c6 10 g4 b5 11 ♔b1 b4 12 ♘ce2 with a sharp mutual attacking position most Trompers would enjoy as White, C.Bauer-Z.Kozul, Istanbul Olympiad 2012.

b) 3...e6 4 f3 ♗d6 (4...♘f6 5 e4 d5 6 e5 ♘fd7 7 ♗e3 transposes to a position we examine in Chapter Two) 5 ♗xd6 ♘xd6 (Black's knight makes an odd impression on d6) 6 e4 f5 7 e5 ♘f7 8 f4 d5 9 ♘f3 0-0 10 ♗d3 b6 11 c3 ♗a6 12 ♗c2 g5? (Black should be satisfied with a slightly inferior position after 12...c5) 13 g4! fxg4 14 ♘xg5 ♘xg5 15 ♕xg4 saw White regain his piece with interest and Black was busted in N.Vitiugov-A.Deszczynski, Warsaw 2008.

c) 3...g5!? (I love it when Black treats our Trompowsky with utter disdain and tosses in weakening moves like this) 4 ♗c1 (threat: f3 and ♗xg5) 4...h6 5 f3 ♘f6 6 e4 d6 7 ♘c3 ♗g7 8 ♗e3 ♘bd7 9 ♕d2 and we reach a Pirc position where Black likely comes to regret the rash ...g5 decision, C.Lakdawala-C.Milton, San Diego (rapid) 2007.

d) 3...g6 4 f3 ♘f6 5 e4 d6 6 ♘c3 ♗g7 7 ♕d2 ♘bd7 (hoping to regain the tempo with ...e5 next, which White's next move cheats him out of) 8 ♗h6 0-0 (maybe Black should try 8...♗xh6 9 ♕xh6 c5) 9 0-0-0 left White up a valuable move in a Pirc opposite wings attack situation, F.Peredy-C.Nwachukwu, Caleta 2012.

4 f3 ♕a5+

We examine 4...♘f6 5 dxc5 in the final chapter of the book.

5 c3 ♘f6

Amazingly, there are four games in my database with 5...g5??. In three of them, White found 6 ♗xb8! which won a piece.

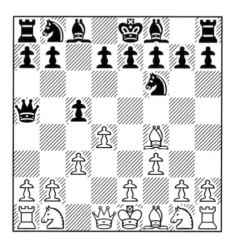

6 d5

Sharpest and, in my opinion, best. Let's stick with this line for the book.

Question: Why aren't we covering 6 ♘d2?

Answer: I thought about it and decided not to dilute the chapter. I actually played this way

all my Tromp life (until I wrote this book and became ever so much wiser). Black gets dynamic equality in a variety of ways in this opening/ending, the best of which may be:
6...cxd4 7 ♘b3 ♛b6 8 ♛xd4 ♘c6! 9 ♛xb6 axb6 10 ♘d4 e5! (this pawn sacrifice took all the fun out of the ending for White) 11 ♘xc6 dxc6! 12 ♗xe5 ♗e6 when Black's massive development lead easily compensates White's extra pawn, N.Nguyen-T.Radjabov, Khanty-Mansiysk Olympiad 2010.

6...♛b6

The main line and Black's best move. The attack on b2 is annoying and forces a concession from White. The following two lines can have independent significance if Black refuses to play ...♛b6:

a) 6...d6 7 e4 g6 8 ♘d2 (heading for c4) 8...♗g7 9 ♘c4 ♛d8 10 a4 (note that Black lacks easy access to ...e6 or ...b5 counterplay ideas) 10...0-0 11 ♘e2 ♘a6 12 g4! (planning a King's Indian Sämisch-style attack with ♘g3 and h4) 12...♘c7 13 ♘g3 b6 14 ♛d2 ♗a6 15 h4 ♘d7 16 h5 and White effortlessly built up a potent attack, since Black lacks either central or queenside counterplay, H.Nakamura-V.Daskevics, Oslo 2010.

b) 6...e6 7 e4 exd5 8 exd5 (8 e5 ♘h5 9 ♗c1 also may come under consideration; I prefer to avoid the e4-e5 adventures and recapture on d5 whenever possible) 8...d6 9 ♛d2 (cited as best by IM Richard Pert in *Playing the Trompowsky*) 9...♗e7 10 c4 ♛xd2+ 11 ♔xd2 (White achieves a slight yet nagging endgame edge due to his extra space) 11...♘h5 12 ♗e3 f5 13 ♘c3 0-0 14 ♗d3 ♘d7 (maybe Black should bite the bullet, hand over e4 and play 14...f4!?) 15 f4! ♘df6 16 ♘ge2. White's space edge continues to nag Black, who has yet to fully equalize, J.Hodgson-P.Wells, York 2000.

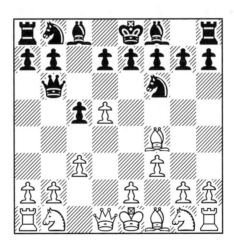

7 ♗c1!

White's best scoring move in the position and a clear theoretical challenge for Black. Now I realize that this undeveloping move increases provocation levels, which would incite Gandhi, Mother Teresa and the biblical Job to clench fists and froth at the mouth, if they played the black pieces.

Question: Why not cover the b-pawn some other way?

Answer: The trouble is the other ways fail to challenge Black. For example:

a) The logical looking move 7 ♕d2? is actually a blunder. Black exploits the overworked queen with 7...♘xd5!. Now if we take the dare with 8 ♕xd5? ♕xb2 9 ♕b3 ♕xa1 we are following A.Fernandes-A.Vasques, Amadora 2010.

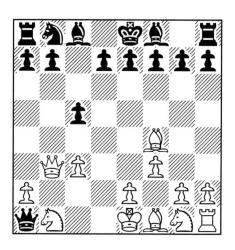

Question: Isn't this winning for White?
There must be some way to trap Black's queen.

Answer: The comps, who all hold PhDs in material grabbing, say it's too slow: for example, 10 ♗c1 (or 10 e4 ♘c6 11 ♘h3 e5! 12 ♗e3 b5! 13 ♔f2 – 13 ♗xb5 ♘a5 14 ♕c2 ♖b8 wins – 13...♖b8 14 ♗e2 c4 15 ♕c2 b4 and Black extricates the queen) 10...♘c6 11 e4 b5! (White can't afford to take the pawn either way) 12 ♘h3 ♖b8 13 ♗e2 b4 14 ♕c2 g6 15 ♗c4 (threatening ♗b2) 15...bxc3 16 ♘xc3 ♘d4 17 ♕d2 ♗h6! 18 f4 d5! 19 exd5 ♗xh3 when White can't recapture due to the fork on f3 and his position collapses. This is involved stuff, but all we need to really remember is that 7 ♕d2? fails.

b) 7 b3 is playable, but just strikes me as limp and unchallenging to Black after 7...e6 8 e4 exd5 9 exd5 ♗d6!. This exchange is desirable for Black, who gains time. Following 10 ♗g5 ♗e7 11 ♘e2 d6 12 c4 Black reaches a position superior to the ones he reaches in this chapter, A.Moiseenko-A.Volokitin, Kharkov 2004.

7...e6

Black's most critical response, playing on the principle: open the position and create confrontation when leading in development. We examine 7...g6 in the last two games of the chapter.

8 e4

At the time of this writing, this move is generally considered to be White's best shot at an opening edge. We won't have room to look at White's other main branch 8 c4 exd5 (also critical is 8...♕b4+!? 9 ♘c3 ♕xc4 10 e4 ♕b4 11 ♗d2) 9 cxd5 c4! which I believe offers Black full equality.

8...exd5 9 exd5

In my opinion, superior to 9 e5 ♕e6 10 ♕e2 ♘g8 11 ♘h3 ♘c6 12 ♘f4 ♕xe5 13 ♘xd5, H.Nakamura-D.Gormally, Internet (blitz) 2008. I don't believe in White's full compensation after 13...♗d6!.

9...d6

We look at 9...♗d6 later in the chapter.

10 c4

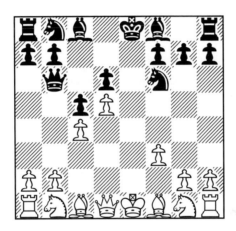

One of our tabiya positions of this chapter. We arrive in a Benoni-like position, but with White recapturing on d5 with the e-pawn, rather than the c-pawn.

> **Question:** You say the position is Benoni-like, but don't we reach a favourable Benoni for Black, who leads in development?

Answer: I don't think so. Optically, Black leads in development. When we look closer at his queen on b6, we may need to re-evaluate, since it is poorly placed, getting in the way of thematic ...b5 breaks. This means that Black must at some point move the queen, costing time. When you play through the games in this chapter, keep watch on the disassociated black queen, who somehow just can't seem to fit in.

10...g6!

I actually feel that fianchettoing here is Black's best bet in this Tromp line. Black, justifiably doesn't like the looks of e7 for the dark-squared bishop and seeks to claim a Benoni birthright on g7. We take a look in the next few games at the more popular ...♗e7 development scheme, and will probably come to the realization that Black's position is terribly passive. However, there is a cost to the fianchetto plan.

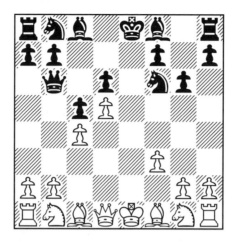

Question: What cost?

Answer: Please see White's next move.

11 ♕e2+!

This disruptive move costs Black more time than it does White. White can also bypass the check with 11 ♗d3 ♗g7 12 ♘c3 0-0 13 ♘ge2 ♘bd7 14 b3 ♕d8 (ah ha – this is what I was talking about: Black's queen, realizing she isn't needed or wanted on b6, retreats with loss of time back to her home square) 15 ♗g5 h6 16 ♗h4 ♘e5 17 ♗c2 g5! (otherwise at some point, White plays h3 and f4) 18 ♗f2 ♘h5 19 ♕d2 ♗d7 when Black's piece activity on the kingside compensates for the slight weakening of his king, D.Boros-V.Kotronias, Hungarian League 2008.

11...♔d8!

11...♗e7?! 12 ♗h6 leaves Black wondering just why he weakened his dark squares with ...g6.

12 ♕c2

White's queen quickly exits from her precarious perch on the e-file. I would play the untried 12 ♕d1!? to stay clear of ...♗f5. I prefer to avoid a potential swap of light-squared bishops to keep Black cramped. After 12...♗g7 13 ♗d3 ♖e8+ 14 ♘e2 ♔e7! (Black's king is safer on the kingside) 15 ♘bc3 ♔f8 16 0-0 ♘bd7 17 b3 (in order to meet ...♘e5 with ♗c2, without hanging the c4-pawn) I prefer White, who can leisurely build for a kingside attack. There is nothing really wrong with Black's position, except a marked absence of an active plan.

12...♗g7

Black's light-squared bishop is traditionally a problem piece in Benoni structures, so perhaps he should toss in 12...♗f5 13 ♗d3 ♗xd3 14 ♕xd3 ♘bd7 (C.Correa de Almeido-L.Alfredo, correspondence 2010) 15 b3 ♔c7 16 ♘e2 ♖e8 17 ♘bc3 ♗g7 18 0-0 ♔b8, although

I still prefer White, who plays for an eventual ♖b1, a3, ♔h1 and, at some point, b4 plan.

13 ♗d3 ♘a6!?

GM Eric Prié offers the line 13...♖e8+ 14 ♘e2 ♘bd7 15 0-0! (15 f4 ♘g4 offers Black enough counterplay) 15...♘e5 16 ♘bc3 ♘xd3 17 ♕xd3 ♗f5 18 ♕d2! (trying to recover some harmony after the loss of the important light-squared bishop) 18...♔e7 19 b3 ♔f8 20 ♗b2 ♔g8 21 ♘g3 ♗d7 22 ♘ce4 with a violent dark-square assault for White.

14 a3

Preventing ...♘b4; for a while, at least.

14...♖e8+

14...♘d7 15 ♘e2 ♘e5 16 ♘bc3 ♗d7 (16...♘xd3+ 17 ♕xd3 ♗f5 18 ♘e4 ♖e8 19 0-0 looks promising for White, who follows with ♘2g3) 17 0-0 ♔c7 18 ♗e3 ♖he8 19 ♗f2 ♖ac8 20 b4 ♔b8 21 ♖ab1 was K.Muukkonen-U.Maffei, correspondence 2009. In such opposite-wing situations, both sides invest heavily in being faster than the other. *Houdini* says even. I don't buy it though and prefer White due to the pressure down the b-file and c6.

15 ♘e2 ♔e7!

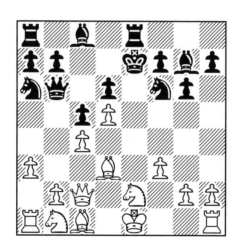

Black's king seeks to escape a Dostoyevskian destiny on the queenside, and into one of normalcy on the kingside. Kotronias correctly perceives that the walk over to f8 constitutes a sound tempi investment, since his king run hobbles White's queenside attack at its inception.

16 ♘bc3

A new move in the position. 16 0-0 ♔f8 17 ♔h1 ♕d8 (once again we observe Black losing time with the queen) 18 ♘bc3 ♘c7 19 ♘g3 ♔g8 was A.Girish-G.Akash, New Delhi 2010. I would continue 20 ♘ge4, intending ♗f4 or ♗g5, with an edge for White.

16...♔f8

The king survived today and dares tomorrow to do its worst.

17 0-0 ♘b4!?

Consistent, yet the venture proves to be economically lacklustre, yielding no benefit for his labours. If we chart Black's collapse, it begins with this move, which hopes to transform a vice into a virtue by ridding himself of the problem knight. In the end, Black's game slightly worsens through this exchange.

18 axb4 cxb4+ 19 ♔h1 bxc3 20 ♘xc3 ♘d7 21 ♗d2

21 ♘e4 also looks tempting.

21...♘c5?!

Black has better chances of holding the balance with 21...♘e5! 22 ♘e4 a5 (22...♘xd3 23 ♕xd3 clearly favours White since b2 is untouchable) 23 b4 ♕d4 24 ♗e2 ♗f5 25 ♗c3 ♕e3 26 ♖xa5 ♖xa5 27 bxa5 ♗xe4 28 fxe4 ♘d7 29 ♗b4 ♘c5 30 ♗f3 ♗e5. It feels to me like Black's dark-squared play may offer compensation for the pawn.

22 ♘b5!

Threat: ♗a5. The black queen's unfortunate placement, along with the weaknesses of b6 and d6, are ineradicable evils, which prove impossible to fully expunge.

22...♘xd3 23 ♕xd3

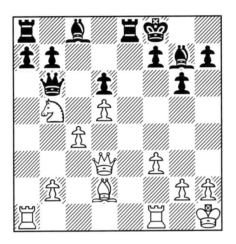

23...♗d7

Cautious.

Question: Can Black get away with 23...♗xb2?

Answer: White retains an edge, and more importantly, Black's coming moves look exceedingly difficult to find. *Houdini's* analysis runs: 24 ♗a5 ♕e3 25 ♕d1. White threatens to clip d6 and ♘c7 wins an exchange as well. Now *Houdini* wants the nuclear option: 25...♗xa1!? 26 ♕xa1 ♕e5 27 ♗c3 ♕f4 28 ♗b4 ♔g8 (greed has its limits as shown by 28...♕xc4?? ! 29 ♕h8+ ♔e7 30 ♕e5+! ♗e6 31 ♕xd6+ ♔f6 32 ♗c3+ ♔g5 33 ♕e5+ ♗f5 34 ♗d2+ ♔h5 35 g4+ ♔h4 36 ♕g3) 29 ♘xd6 ♗h3! (the only move; not 29...♖e2?? 30 ♘e4 ♖xe4 31 fxe4 ♕g5 32 ♕d4! f6 33 h3, covering the back rank when Black's detritus and rubble-strewn kingside structure isn't a pretty sight) 30 ♘xe8 ♖xe8 31 ♖e1! (certainly not 31 gxh3?? ♖e2) 31...♗d7

32 ♖xe8+ ♗xe8 33 ♕e1 and White holds all the chances, since Black's king will never be safe with the unfavourable opposite-coloured bishops remaining on the board.

24 ♗a5! ♕e3

Alternatively, if 24...♕c5 25 ♘c7 ♖e3 26 ♕d2 ♖c8 27 ♗b4 ♕d4 28 ♗xd6+ ♔g8 29 ♕xd4 ♗xd4 30 ♖fd1 ♗b6 31 ♗f4 ♖b3 32 d6 when I like White's chances.

25 ♕xe3

Escape from the black queen's company is out of the question, so White's queen heaves the tolerant sigh of one who must make allowances for the behaviour of a boorish relative, now a permanent fixture, who overstays her welcome and refuses to go home.

25...♖xe3 26 ♘xd6

White commandeers d6 to black's consternation.

26...♖b3

26...♗xb2 27 ♖ab1 ♗a3 28 ♖xb7 ♗xd6 29 ♖xd7 leaves White up a pawn and winning.

27 c5! ♖xb2 28 ♖ac1!

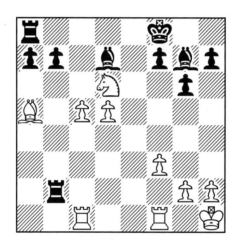

White's plan is clear: ram the c-pawn down as far as it will go.

28...♗b5

Black decides to stage a protest, without much effect, but if 28...♗e5 29 ♘c4 ♖e2 30 ♗b4 ♔g8 31 ♖fe1 ♖xe1+ 32 ♖xe1 ♗f6 33 ♘d6 ♖b8 34 ♗a3 and the coming ♖b1 will be decisive.

29 ♖fe1 b6

After 29...♗a6 30 c6 I doubt Black can hold the position together.

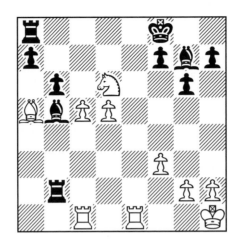

Exercise (combination alert): With 29...b6 Black offered a pawn to break up White's central passers. How does White continue?

Answer: The scalpel gives way to the bludgeon. White ignores the threat and keeps pushing, after which there is no way around the impenetrable mass of central passers.

30 c6!

The hanging a5-bishop hopes to get through the war with all body parts intact.

30...♗a6?

The experiment in tenacity abruptly comes to a conclusion. This makes matters worse. The bishop approaches coverage of c8 with the mournful air of resignation of a soon-to-be-bathed dog. Black had to try 30...bxa5 31 c7 ♗d4 (if 31...♗d7?? 32 c8♕+ and the interference move mates in two moves) 32 ♘xb5 ♖xb5 33 c8♕+ ♖xc8 34 ♖xc8+ ♔g7 35 ♖d1 ♗e5 36 ♖c6 ♖b7 37 d6 ♖d7 38 ♖d5 ♔f6 39 ♖xa5 ♔e6.

31 c7!

The c7-pawn tells Black's rook and bishop: "You may be higher ranked than me now, but at the end of the game, we all get put away in the same box."

31...♗h6

Or 31...bxa5 32 c8♕+! (interference) 32...♗xc8 33 ♖e8 mate.

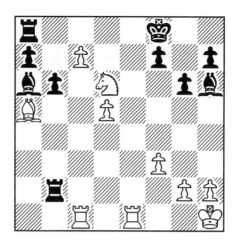

Exercise (combination alert): Find White's knock-out blow.

Answer: Attraction/interference/skewer.

32 c8♕+! 1-0

It is the nature of misfortune that it always arrives in torrents and rarely in a single drop. Whether this is a trap or a cheapo probably depends on which of the players you ask. 32...♗xc8 33 ♖e8+ ♔g7 34 ♗c3+ ends resistance.

Summary: Let's take our chances in the quasi-Benoni territory of 6 d5 and bypass the slower 6 ♘d2 line.

Game 3
S.Martinovic-E.Dizdarevic
Sibenik 2009

1 d4

Compare 1 e4 ♘f6 2 e5 ♘d5 3 d4 d6 4 c4 ♘b6 5 exd6 exd6 6 ♘c3 ♗e7 7 ♗d3 ♘c6 8 ♘ge2 0-0 9 0-0 ♗f6 10 b3 ♖e8 11 ♗e3 to what we get in our Trompowsky position after 11 moves. I think we Trompers get the better deal and our advantage is more substantial than White's in the symmetrical exchange variation of Alekhine's Defence.

1...♘f6 2 ♗g5 ♘e4 3 ♗f4 c5 4 f3 ♕a5+ 5 c3 ♘f6 6 d5 ♕b6 7 ♗c1 e6 8 e4 exd5 9 exd5 d6 10 c4 ♗e7?!

Nothing fancy. Black decides he doesn't have the luxury for a fianchetto and develops the bishop rapidly to a less active square.

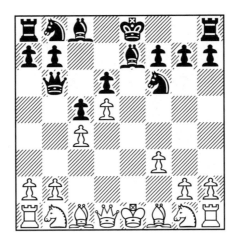

Answer: Just because something is popular doesn't automatically make it wise. We examine the popular e7 development scheme in this and the next game. Going over these games, we come to realize that Black's lifeless, counterplayless position hands White a sustaining, safe advantage.

Answer: Your move does activate a traditionally problem piece, but with a hitch: After 11 ♗d3 (White's most common response; I would actually play 11 ♘c3 ♘bd7, as in A.Smirnov-R.Heimrath, Bad Wiessee 2011, and at this point White can try 12 g4!? ♗g6 13 ♘ge2, intending ♘f4 and h4, going after Black's g6-bishop) 11...♗xd3 (11...♗g6 is unplayed, but also possible; White will only swap on g6 after Black castles kingside) 12 ♕xd3 (now Black gets stuck with a bad remaining bishop) 12...♗e7 (12...g6 13 ♘c3 ♘bd7 14 ♕e2+ sees White disrupt the fianchetto plan, whereupon 14...♗e7 15 ♘h3 0-0 16 0-0 ♖fe8 leaves Black solid but cramped, as in the game) 13 ♘e2 ♘bd7 14 b3 0-0 15 ♘bc3 ♖fe8 16 0-0 ♗f8 17 ♘g3 g6 18 ♗f4 ♗g7 19 ♕d2 a6 20 ♖ae1 ♖xe1 21 ♖xe1 ♖e8 22 ♘ce4 ♘xe4 23 ♘xe4 (Black's difficulties in defending d6 induce a concession) 23...♗e5 24 ♗xe5 dxe5 (if 24...♖xe5 25 f4 ♖e8 26 f5! ♖e5 27 f6 ♕b4 28 ♕c1 h5 29 h3 when Black's king may be in serious danger) 25 g4 White's protected, passed d-pawn gives him a clear edge, S.Olsen-O.Sande, corrrespondence 2011.

11 ♗d3 ♘bd7 12 f4!

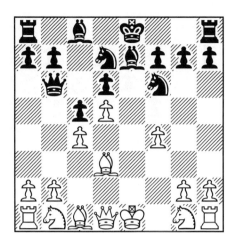

Oh, no you don't! White cancels any ...♘e5 plans.

12...♕d8

In this variation, Black's queen tends to play the role of the fairy tale innocent, the princess duped into drinking the drugged potion.

Question: I very reasonably ask: did Paul Morphy lie to us about the benefits of rapid development? What motivated Black to retreat?

Answer: Black felt his queen played a less-than-useless role on b6. We take note: ...♕b6 and ...♕d8 turn out to be two wasted moves. In fact in this line, both parties routinely violate the principle which states avoid moving the same piece more than once in the opening:

1. White's bishop took three moves to undevelop to c1.
2. White's c-pawn took two moves to reach c4.
3. Black's knight took three moves to reach f6.
4. As mentioned, Black took three moves to get his queen to d8, its original square.

In the end, it tends to be a wash, with neither side gaining or losing time.

Black has a comp-like possibility with 12...♕b4+!? 13 ♘c3 (nobody has had the nerve to try 13 ♗d2! which I think is an improvement – as long as you are willing to sac: 13...♕xb2 14 ♘c3 ♕b6 15 ♖b1 ♕c7 16 ♘f3 with space, a development lead, an open b-file and attacking chances for the pawn; I prefer White's chances and would be willing to gambit this way if given the chance) 13...b5! (Black's disruptive point) 14 a3 ♕a5 15 cxb5 ♗b7 (15...♘xd5 16 ♗d2 ♘5f6 17 ♘d5 ♕d8 18 ♘xe7 ♕xe7+ picks off the bishop-pair) 16 ♘f3 (16 ♗d2! looks more accurate) 16...♘xd5 17 ♗d2 ♕b6 18 ♘xd5 ♗xd5 19 ♗c3 ♗f6 20 ♕e2+ ♔d8 21 0-0-0!? ♗xc3 22 bxc3 ♖e8 23 ♕b2 a6 24 ♗e2 ♘f6 25 ♘g5 h6 was C.Cruzado Duenas-M.Sadowski, correspondence 2009. Now White can try 26 ♘h7!? ♘xh7 27 ♖xd5 ♘f6 28 ♖dd1 with a totally unclear position.

13 ♘c3 0-0 14 ♘f3 ♘e8!?

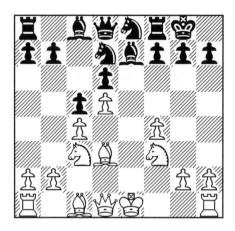

A new move, but clearly no improvement.

Question: Why would Black retreat an already developed piece?

Answer: Black felt constricted and probably wanted to activate his dark-squared bishop via f6. After 14...♖e8 15 0-0 ♘f8 16 ♕c2 a6 17 a4 ♗d7 18 b3 White enjoys a space advantage on both wings and it's difficult to come up with a constructive non-waiting plan for Black, Z.Papp-M.Csikos, Szeged 1997.

15 ♕c2 g6?!

Consistent and probably incorrect. Black creates dark-square weaknesses, for which he later pays. He avoided 15...♘df6 since he had plans for his bishop on the square, but this looks like a better try than the game continuation. Black can play for an eventual ...b5 break with ...♘c7, ...a6, ...♖b8 and ...♗d7.

16 f5!?

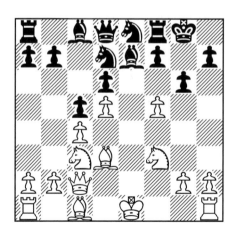

White hands over e5 to grab even more kingside territory. 16 0-0 is the safer alternative.

16...♘g7

Question: If Black's entire strategy revolved around activating his dark-squared bishop on the a1-h8 diagonal, then why not occupy it now?

Answer: The trouble is the bishop gets chased with 16...♗f6 17 ♘e4 ♗g7 (*Houdini* suggests the inhuman 17...♘e5 handing over the dark squares; it assesses at equal, but later on apologizes and gives White a clear advantage after 18 ♘xf6+ ♕xf6 19 ♘xe5 ♕xe5+ 20 ♕e2 ♗xf5 21 ♕xe5 dxe5 22 ♗xf5 gxf5 23 ♗h6 ♘g7 24 0-0 f4 25 g3! fxg3 26 ♖f6! ♖ae8 27 ♖e1 ♔h8 28 hxg3 ♘h5 29 ♗xf8 ♘xf6 30 ♗xc5 with a clean extra pawn) 18 0-0 b5 19 ♗g5 with a dangerous initiative for White.

17 g4!?

An attacker past the point of no return must destroy in order to exist. White ignores the prodding, stubbornly refusing to relinquish f5. I'm not so sure about this move. White decides the moment is ripe to colonize the kingside, rejecting the safer and probably stronger 17 0-0, after which White gets to attack without much strategic investment.

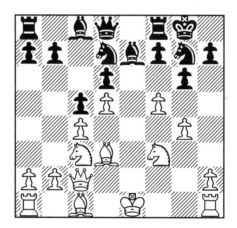

17...♗h4+?!

Black finds the narrative not to his liking and hopes to radically alter it, by press-ganging the once dormant bishop into service in a dubious venture. Disruption of castling doesn't bother White and Black loses more time later moving the bishop from the danger zone. Black's best hope is to disrupt, even at the cost of his precious dark-squared bishop, with 17...♗f6 18 ♘e4 b5!.

18 ♔f1 ♘e5?!

After this move, Black's troubles grow in thickets and now he gets tied down with some strategic jujitsu on White's part. I think this move hurt more than helped, since it stabilized the centre and handed White control over e4. I would go into confusion/disruption mode with something like 18...♗f6 19 ♗f4 (Black complicates after 19 ♘e4 b5!?). White should still hang on to a clear advantage after a line like 19...♗d4 20 ♕d2 gxf5 21 ♗xd6 fxg4 22 ♕h6 f5 23 ♗xf8 ♕xf8 24 ♘xd4 cxd4 25 ♘b5 ♘e5 26 ♖d1. I still prefer White, but this looks better than what Black got in the game.

19 ♘xe5 dxe5 20 ♔g2 ♔h8

The frustrated king weaves his fingers into the wire mesh of the fence which imprisons him, but after 20...♗g5 21 ♖g1 ♗xc1 22 ♖axc1 ♕h4 23 ♔h1 ♘e8 24 ♖cf1 White is doing all the attacking.

21 ♖f1

Manual castling complete. Black's defensive leeway continues to constrict. Notice the purposelessness of the h4-bishop, which actually gets in the way.

21...b6 22 ♔h1 ♗d7 23 ♕g2

I like 23 ♕d2! which seizes control over g5 and also contemplates ♕h6.

23...gxf5

Black, in the wake of punishing strategic losses, feels he has no choice but to push forward, mounting a desperado assault. He tentatively intuits that such a drastic measure is a necessary step for continued survival. So he takes a gamble, however improbable, and prays his position, 90% submerged, still retains a 10% survival leeway by mobilizing the open g-file against White. An attempted resurgence – even a delusional one – is always born of hope. In this instance, his position lacks sufficient energy to marshal even a final stand, but 23...♗g5 24 ♗xg5 ♕xg5 25 ♘e4 ♕h4 26 ♖f3!, intending ♖h3, looks like curtains for Black.

24 gxf5 ♘h5

24...♖g8 25 ♕e2! ♘e8 (Black's only chance) 26 ♗d2 ♕e7 27 ♕h5 ♘g7 28 ♕h6 ♕f6 29 ♕xf6 ♗xf6 30 ♘e4 ♗h4 31 ♘d6 ♖af8 32 ♗h6 looks hopeless as well.

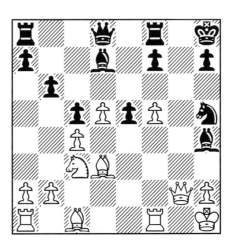

Exercise (combination alert): Black's last move,
24...♘h5, allows White a tactic. What is it?

Answer: Double attack.

25 ♕e2! ♘f6 26 ♕xe5 ♖g8

26...♖e8 27 ♕f4 ♘g8 28 ♘e4 is crushing as well.

27 ♘e4

White threatens ♗d2 and ♗c3.

27...h5

If 27...♖e8 28 ♕c3.

28 ♗d2 ♔h7

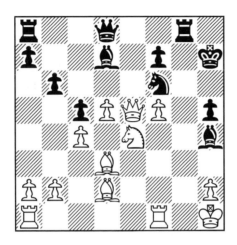

Exercise (combination alert): Black's king, who isn't so
thrilled in his new job as crash-test dummy, escaped the pin
only to land into even more trouble. How did White respond?

Answer: Double attack on h6 and h4.

29 ♕f4! 1-0

The ground before Black's feet parts, only to display the terrifying face of the abyss.
29...♘g4 would be a futile exercise, reminding us of Charles Manson's repeated applications for parole. The move is met with the simple 30 h3.

Summary: In the position after 10...♗e7, White achieves a nagging space advantage, akin but superior to what White gets in the Exchange Alekhine.

Game 4
V.Laznicka-A.Zubarev
Vitoria 2006

1 d4 ♘f6 2 ♗g5 ♘e4 3 ♗f4 c5 4 f3 ♕a5+ 5 c3 ♘f6 6 d5 ♕b6 7 ♗c1 e6 8 e4 exd5 9 exd5

♗e7?!

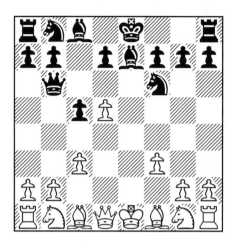

> **Question:** Is there any difference between this move order and 9...d6?

Answer: The only difference is Black loses the fianchetto option, but if he intends to play the bishop to e7, then there is no difference and we soon transpose to 9...d6 positions.
10 c4 0-0 11 ♗d3 ♖e8 12 ♘e2 d6

There; no difference now between a 9...♗e7 and a 9...d6 move order.
13 ♘bc3 ♘bd7 14 b3!

A new move in the position, and a good one. White avoids the rote 14 0-0?! ♘e5 15 b3 ♘xd3 16 ♕xd3 which allows Black to pick off the bishop-pair, reduce the danger to his king and partially free himself from his previously cramped lodgings, J.Garcia Gil-T.Learte Pastor, correspondence 2005.

> **Question:** Last game White played an early f4 idea. Does that work here as well?

Answer: Yes, the move is equally effective here. The weakening of e3 isn't an issue since White has use of tactical tricks to deal with it: for example, 14 f4 ♘g4 15 0-0 ♗f8 (White has no fear of invasion on e3) 16 ♘g3 ♘e3? 17 ♗xh7+! ♔xh7 18 ♕d3+ g6 19 ♗xe3 and now Black tried to regain the lost pawn with 19...♕xb2? 20 ♖ab1 ♕a3 21 ♗c1! ♕a5 22 ♘ce4 ♕d8 23 ♗b2 which gave White a crushing attack, V.Yemelin-D.Kovachev, Kallithea 2008.
14...♗f8 15 0-0

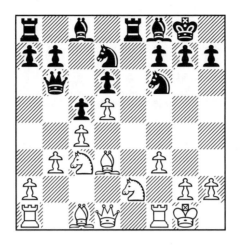

15...g6

Question: Didn't you say earlier: "Black loses the fianchetto option?"

Answer: Black's move comes under the better-late-than-never category, despite the obvious loss of time with ...♗e7, ...♗f8, ...g6 and ...♗g7. If this is the case, then perhaps the entire development scheme of an early ...♗e7, even though often played, comes into question and the early fianchetto plan may be Black's best option.

I don't much care for Black's position if he keeps his kingside pawns intact: for example, 15...♘e5 16 ♗c2 ♗d7 17 ♘g3 a6 18 h3 ♕d8 19 f4 ♘g6 20 a4 b5 (or 20...♖b8 21 a5 with a space advantage on both wings) 21 axb5 axb5 22 ♖xa8 ♕xa8 23 cxb5 ♕b7 24 ♗d3 hangs on to the extra pawn since d5 is taboo. If 24...♘xd5?? 25 ♕f3 ♘ge7 26 ♗c4 ♗e6 27 f5 wins.

16 h3

Question: Why did White weaken the dark squares?

Answer: He intends f4, without allowing ...♘g4 counterplay.

16...♗g7 17 ♗d2!

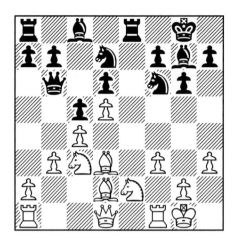

> **Question:** If White played b3, then isn't the logical course to fianchetto?

Answer: Not here. White's strategically most vulnerable square is e3 and he nurtures the square by retaining the bishop on the c1-h6 diagonal.

17...♕d8

Once again, Black's queen finds no solace on b6 and returns home, at the cost of time.

18 f4

As always in this chapter, the implementation of f4 divests all black e5-pretenders of a good chunk of their authority.

> **Question:** Are there any rules of thumb of when to play f4?

Answer:

1. Play f4 after playing h3, to insure against ...♘g4 and ...♘e3 nuisances.

2. Play f4 only if you are certain that you will not lose control over the e4-square later on.

18...a6 19 a4

Black lacks counterplay on either wing. Prié writes: "White has obtained the optimal set-up. Black has no squares for his pieces and is condemned to the role of defender against the forthcoming kingside attack."

19...♘f8

It's a bad sign to develop a knight to f8, with no real prospects from the square. Black sees the coming kingside assault and digs in for a tough defence.

20 ♖f3 b6 21 ♕c2 h6

Slightly weakening his kingside, but it's hard to wait. Perhaps Black should avoid this move and play 21...♖a7, intending to swing over to e7.

22 ♖af1 ♖a7 23 g4!

Here he comes. Force is the universal language all creatures understand. The not-so-vague contours of White's plan emerge: load up on the kingside and play for mate. What White's plan lacks in sophistication, it more than makes up for with raw power.

23...♖ae7 24 ♘g3

Unbelievably *Houdini*, whose assessment rating in some positions is equivalent to a below average intelligence oyster's ability, rates the position at virtually even. We humans know better. White is poised for a massive kingside assault. So much so that Black lashes out in quasi-desperation on his next move.

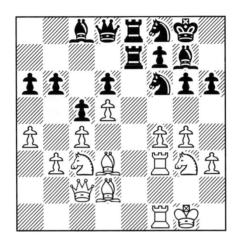

24...♘xg4!?

Well, why not? Who among us doesn't resent coercion? Black, by now a bit unglued by the unwanted scrutiny of White's gathering attackers, tries a quasi-sound pre-emptive strike before White's kingside attack even begins. And his fears are not without ample cause. He feels that incremental changes won't do the job, and his position requires a fundamental overhaul to confront the crisis facing his king. Still, this counterattack, much like prodding a particularly stubborn mule up a steep incline, goes nowhere.

> *Question:* If you say that Black's counter comes across as a poorly wrapped gift, then how about a plan of doing nothing? When caught in the grips of an overwhelming power, with no way to wiggle out, sometimes the best defensive bet is to ride the wind and hope for the best. How does White make progress if Black dithers about, marking time?

Answer: There are probably many attacking plans for White. A couple of samples where I played White versus *Houdini* after 24...♕c7.

Plan A, play for a g5 break: 25 ♔g2 ♕d8 26 g5 hxg5 27 fxg5 ♘6d7 28 ♘ce4 ♘e5 29 ♖f6! (threats continue to flow into Black's position in a steady current; the rook experiences de-

lightful emotions, similar to a dog who inadvertently strays into a cat-infested backyard)
29...♖d7 30 h4 ♘h7 31 h5! b5 (Black can't survive 31...♗xf6 32 ♘xf6+ ♘xf6 33 gxf6) 32 axb5
axb5 33 ♖6f2 bxc4 34 bxc4 ♖a7 35 hxg6 fxg6 36 ♘f6+. I bring the jury's attention to Exhibit
A: Black's king. White's attack is decisive.

Plan B, play for f5: 25 f5 g5 26 ♘ce4 ♘8d7 27 ♔g2 ♘xe4 28 ♘xe4 ♘f6 29 ♘g3 ♕d8 30
♗c3 ♖e3 31 ♖xe3 ♖xe3 32 ♕d2 ♕e8 33 ♔f2 ♖e7 34 ♕b2 ♕d8 35 ♔f3 ♖e8 36 ♖g1! ♗d7 37
h4! b5 (37...gxh4?? 38 ♘h5! is crushing) 38 ♘e4 ♘xe4 39 ♗xg7 ♕e7 40 ♗xh6 f6 41 axb5
axb5 42 hxg5 bxc4 43 bxc4 ♘xg5+ 44 ♗xg5 fxg5 45 ♕d2. White remains up a pawn and
threatens ♖h1 and ♖h5. Black's exposed king is easily recognized and his disguise is as
lame as Superman's when he puts on a pair of glasses, thinking he has everyone fooled,
'disguised' as Clark Kent.

25 hxg4 ♗xg4

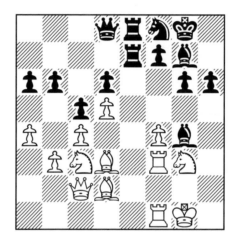

26 f5!

Clearly a 'provoke-me-and-I-will-destroy-you' reply. Initiative is paramount and all other
considerations are swept under the couch. 26 ♖3f2? loses the initiative to 26...♗d4 27 ♔g2
(or 27 f5? ♖e3! when, suddenly, it is White's king who finds himself in grave danger)
27...♗xf2 28 ♖xf2 f5 when Black looks fine.

26...♗d4+ 27 ♔g2 ♗xf3+ 28 ♖xf3 ♔h7

Black's king slides over to h7 with the air of a martyr attempting to get as comfortable
as possible before the inquisitors toast him at the stake. Note how Black's absolute control
over the e-file doesn't help him even a bit. 28...g5 29 f6 ♖e5 30 ♖f1 ♘d7 31 ♘f5 ♘xf6 32
♘xh6+ ♔f8 33 ♘f5 ♘h5 34 ♖h1 is hopeless for Black.

29 ♘ce4 ♗e5

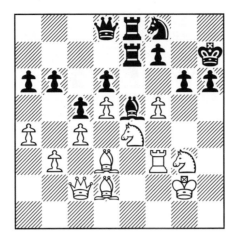

Exercise (planning): Black's king remains in
desperate trouble. Which square should White target?

Answer: The h6-square, after which Black's resistance reserves are depleted to the point of
empty.

30 ♕c1! 1-0

The queen's face grows crimson with hate, fuelled by lethal intention. Now all hope for
Black lies in shards. 30...h5 31 ♗g5 is hopeless for him.

Summary: GM Eric Prié actually punishes Black's bishop development to e7 with a full
question mark, claiming the fianchetto plan (which we looked at in the first game of the
chapter) is Black's only playable plan against our set-up. Looking at this game, I'm beginning to think his claim may be correct.

Game 5
I.Ivanisevic-D.Solak
Vrnjacka Banja 2005

1 d4 ♘f6 2 ♗g5 ♘e4 3 ♗f4 c5 4 f3 ♕a5+ 5 c3 ♘f6 6 d5 ♕b6 7 ♗c1 e6 8 e4 exd5 9 exd5 ♗d6

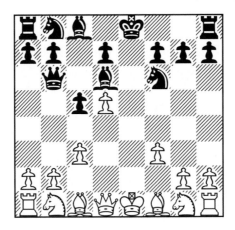

Question: What is Black's idea behind this artificial-looking move?

Answer: Two-fold:

1. Black, not liking either fianchetto or ...♗e7 developing schemes, decides to try an aggressive counterattack instead. He usually plays ...♛c7 soon, loading up on h2.

2. In some cases Black has options of ...♗e5 and ...♗xc3+, followed by ...d6, ridding him or herself of a problem piece.

10 ♘a3!

The main idea in the position. The knight, seeking to exploit Black's last move, eyes both the b5- and c4-squares, taking aim at the queen and bishop-pair. Next game we look at the more familiar set-up, 10 c4.

10...0-0 11 ♗d3!

More accurate than 11 ♘c4 ♖e8+ 12 ♔f2 ♛c7, B.Predojevic-S.Dyachkov, Moscow 2008.

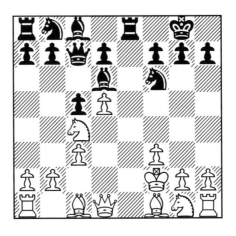

Now White can go for 13 ♗g5, but after 13...b5 14 ♘xd6 ♕xd6 15 ♗xb5 h6 16 ♗xf6 ♕xf6 17 ♘e2 ♘a6 Black's development lead and the coming ...♖b8 provide full compensation for the pawn.

Answer: 13 ♘xd6?! ♕xd6 14 c4 ♘c6! 15 ♘e2 b5! leaves White dangerously behind in development.

11...a6?

Black wastes a precious tempo, while leading in development. Prié explains: "In addition to a6 being an important square for either his queen or his queen's knight, Black does not need this move as, in fact, White will soon be forced to play ♘c4 to blockade the c4-square from the discovered check if he intends to castle kingside."

Correct is 11...♖e8+ 12 ♘e2 ♗f8 13 ♘c4 ♕d8 14 ♘e3 d6 15 0-0 g6!? (once again we see the belaboured fianchetto from Black's side) 16 a4 ♗h6 17 ♘c4 ♗xc1 18 ♖xc1 b6 19 ♘g3 ♗b7 20 ♘e4 ♘xe4 21 fxe4, but even here, Black struggles in a sour looking Benoni set-up. White's open f-file ensures an enduring edge, I.Ivanisevic-V.Kotronias, Kavala 2007.

Instead, 11...♘xd5?? hangs a piece to 12 ♘c4 ♕c6 13 ♘xd6 ♕xd6 14 ♗e4 ♖e8 15 ♘e2.

12 ♘c4 ♕c7 13 a4 b6 14 ♗g5

Black is in full retreat.

14...♘h5

14...♘e8 doesn't look terribly appealing either.

15 ♘e2

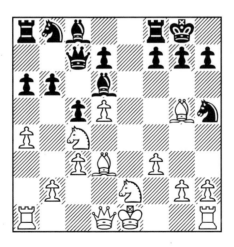

15...h6

Answer: There is gambling and there is suicide. Taking h2 is firmly in the latter category after 15...♗xh2?? 16 d6! when Black loses a piece (and probably gets mated soon). Remember this tactical theme when an opponent is tempted into taking h2.

16 ♗e3 ♖e8 17 ♔f2

The safest spot for White's king, who also adds support to e3.

17...♗b7

Now that d5 looks somewhat insecure, White deems it the proper time to swap on d6.

18 ♘xd6 ♕xd6 19 c4

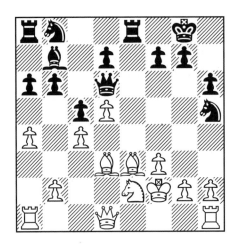

Black's counterplayless wasteland isn't a pretty sight:

1. White has an unassailable central space advantage.

2. g4 is coming, increasing White's space and adding a kingside attack to the equation.

3. White owns bishop-pair and control over the dark squares.

4. Black's constipated queenside reminds us of the uncomfortable 'before' scene in a laxative commercial.

Conclusion: Black is strategically busted.

19...♕f6

Not very tempting is 19...b5 20 b3 bxc4 21 bxc4 ♕e7 22 ♕d2 d6 23 g4! ♘f6 24 ♘g3, which looks like the Benoni from hell from Black's perspective.

20 g4! ♕h4+ 21 ♘g3

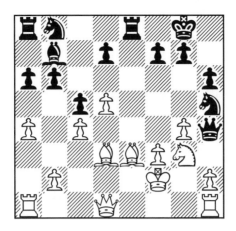

21...♘f6

> **Question:** Should Black consider giving up an exchange on e3 to attack?

Answer: The exchange sacrifice drives White's king into the middle, but there is a big catch: Black lacks attackers, so the sacrifice fails after 21...♖xe3 22 ♔xe3 ♘xg3 23 hxg3 ♕xg3 24 ♕e1 ♕e5+ 25 ♔f2 ♕xb2+ 26 ♔g3. White's king is safe and Black, completely undeveloped, is the one about to do the defending.

22 ♕d2 d6 23 ♔g2

Threat: ♘f5.

23...♗c8

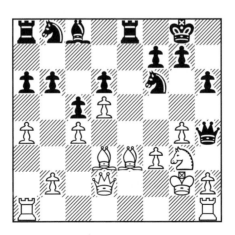

> **Exercise (planning):** White either picks off material or forces Black into a downward spiral of passivity. What would you play here?

Answer: Target Black's weakest link, d6.

24 ♗f4! ♘xg4

Desperation. If 24...♖d8 25 ♖ae1 a5 (25...b5 is strongly met with 26 ♕a5!) 26 ♗f5! ♗a6 27 b3 ♖a7 28 ♕e3 ♖a8 29 ♗xd6! and Black is crushed.

25 fxg4 ♗xg4 26 h3

White easily rebuffs the attack, covering Black's single entry point on h3.

26...♗h5

26...♗c8 27 ♗xd6 is resignable as well.

27 ♘f5 ♕f6 28 ♘xd6 ♖e5 29 ♗xe5 ♕xe5

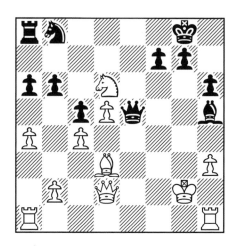

Exercise (combination alert): Black refuses to resign. How did White force it?

Answer: Targeting the weak back rank again.

30 ♖ae1! ♕xd6 31 ♖e8+ 1-0

Summary: I like the 10 ♘a3 plan against the ...♗d6 set-up. White's knight has access to both c4 and b5, and I don't believe Black equalizes here either.

Game 6
V.Moskalenko-D.Alsina Leal
Barcelona 2011

1 d4 ♘f6 2 ♗g5 ♘e4 3 ♗f4 c5 4 f3 ♕a5+ 5 c3 ♘f6 6 d5 ♕b6 7 ♗c1 e6 8 e4 exd5 9 exd5 ♗d6 10 c4

Play this move if you feel structurally more comfortable here, than in the unfamiliar waters of 10 ♘a3!, which we looked at last game.

10...0-0 11 ♗d3 ♖e8+ 12 ♘e2 ♕c7 13 ♘bc3

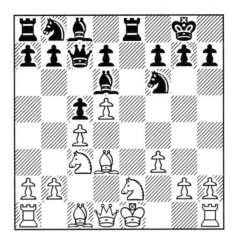

13...a6

Question: Is h2 still poison for Black?

Answer: It sure is: 13...♗xh2? 14 ♘b5 ♕e5 15 ♔f1! (threat: f4!, disconnecting the queen from the h2-bishop) 15...♘h5 16 f4! ♘xf4 17 ♘xf4 ♗xf4 18 ♗xh7+ ♔f8 19 ♗xf4 ♕xf4+ 20 ♕f3 ♕xf3+ 21 gxf3 (queens may be off the board, but this does little to help Black, who remains hopelessly behind in development) 21...♘a6 22 ♗g6! leaves Black in huge trouble:

a) 22...fxg6?? 23 ♖h8+ ♔f7 24 ♘d6+ wins.

b) 22...♔g8 23 ♘d6 ♖e7 24 ♗h7+ ♔f8 25 ♗e4 ♔g8 26 ♔f2! and Black is curiously helpless against the simple idea of doubling rooks on the open h-file.

14 ♕c2 ♗e5

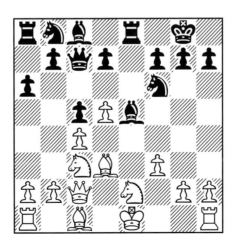

15 ♗g5!?

A risky plan, conceding the dark squares for the initiative, yet, as it turns out, quite dangerous for Black.

> **Question:** What would you suggest instead?

Answer: Something like 15 a4 clamping down on ...b5 breaks: 15...h6 16 ♗d2 d6 (*Houdini* suggests the greedy 16...♗xh2, but I don't like Black's chances after 17 0-0-0) 17 0-0. Now castling is safe, once the heat from h2 disappeared. White prepares a kingside attack, pretty much the same way as we have seen all chapter.

15...h6 16 ♗xf6!?

> **Question:** Didn't White just hand over control of a
> good chunk of dark-square control to his opponent?

Answer: I wouldn't have played this and it was, indeed a risky, decision. White's plan looks untenable on strategic grounds alone. However, hidden tactics are the x-factor which perhaps lifts Moskalenko's plan into the realm of playability.

16...♗xf6 17 ♘e4 ♗e7

Otherwise:

a) 17...♗e5 18 0-0! ♗xh2+ (otherwise White plays f4 next, attacking for free) 19 ♔h1 (threat: f4, trapping the bishop) 19...♗d6 20 ♘xd6 ♕xd6 21 ♖ae1 and suddenly White accrued a scary development lead. Just look at Black's dormant queenside. It feels like he plays without three quarters of his army.

b) 17...♗h4+! 18 g3 ♗e7 19 0-0 d6 20 ♔g2 ♘d7 21 f4. Now Black should unravel his queenside as quickly as possible with 21...b5! 22 b3 (22 cxb5?! ♘b6 23 ♘4c3 ♗f6 24 a4 ♗b7 offers Black considerable Benko Gambit-like pressure) 22...♘f6 23 ♘2c3 b4 24 ♘xf6+ ♗xf6 25 ♖ae1 ♗d7 26 ♘e4 ♗d4 27 f5. *Houdini* says even, while I slightly prefer White's space and monster light-square control over Black's dominance over the dark squares.

18 0-0 d6 19 ♘2g3 ♘d7 20 ♖ae1

White's space and attacking chances easily compensate for his deficiency on the dark squares.

20...b5?

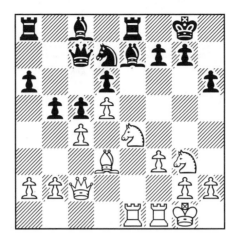

21 b3?

White misses it as well.

Answer: Pin! The shot 21 ♘xd6!! isn't so deep. It's just very hard for a human to see, because the illusion of coverage is so complete over d6. And yet it falls: 21...♛xd6 22 ♘f5 ♛f6 23 d6 and White regains the piece with a dominating position.

21...bxc4 22 bxc4 ♘e5 23 ♗e2

White can give up both bishops for knights in pursuit of attack after 23 f4!? ♘xd3 24 ♛xd3 ♗d7 25 f5! Opposing forces stalk one another: White's knights and kingside potential, versus Black's bishops. In this case I believe the scales should tip slightly toward White's side: 25...♗f8 26 f6 g6 27 h4 ♖e5 28 h5 gxh5! (28...g5?! 29 ♖b1 looks good for White, mainly due to the entombed f8-bishop) 29 ♘d2! and I still prefer White's attacking chances.

23...f5?

White takes over the initiative after this gorgonzolaesque move, which stinks up Black's kingside. The impulsive lashing out runs counter to the principles by which the defence is governed and violates the creed: secure your own base before launching offensive action. Black keeps disadvantage to a minimum with 23...♗h4 24 f4 ♘g6 25 ♗d3 ♛d8 26 ♛e2! (threat: ♘f6+) 26...♗d7 27 f5! ♘e5 28 ♘xd6 ♘xd3 29 ♛xd3 ♖xe1 30 ♖xe1 ♛c7 31 ♘de4 ♗xf5 32 d6, although even here, White's chances look clearly superior.

24 f4! ♘f7

Alternatives are grim as well:

a) 24...♘g6 25 ♗h5! ♖f8 (25...♔h7?? 26 ♘g5+! hxg5 27 ♘xf5 is crushing) 26 ♗xg6 fxe4 27 ♘xe4 leaves White up a clean pawn.

b) 24...fxe4? 25 fxe5 dxe5 26 ♕xe4 intending ♗d3 is decisive.

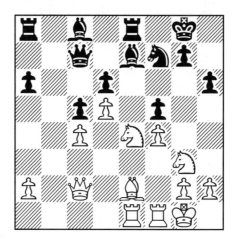

> **Exercise (combination alert):** After 24...♘f7 White sits on the threshold of
> discovery of a brilliant attacking idea, which is very difficult to spot. What is it?

25 ♘c3?!

Black is the blessed recipient of a heaven-sent semi-reprieve.

Answer: Luck's fickle glance (some would call it a tactical geometrical anomaly) sheds its
light on the position, by bestowing upon White a startling, hidden sequence – but only if
he can find it. White can play the shocking 25 ♘h5!! which is decisive. The immediate
threat is 26 ♕c3. Now if Black chops with 25...fxe4 (25...♗h4 26 ♕b2 ♘h8 27 ♘xd6! wins),
there follows 26 ♕xe4 (threat: ♗d3) 26...♘h8 27 ♘xg7!! (the knight brushes by Black's king,
silent yet noticed) 27...♔xg7 28 ♗d3 ♔f8 29 ♕h7, which leaves Black completely helpless:
29...♘f7 30 ♗g6 ♗f6 31 ♖xe8+ ♔xe8 32 ♕g8+ mates.

25...g6 26 ♗d3 ♗d7?

Black's only chance lies in 26...♕d8!, and if 27 ♘xf5!? gxf5 28 ♗xf5 ♗h4 29 ♖xe8+ ♕xe8
30 ♗e6! ♔g7 31 f5 with chances for both sides.

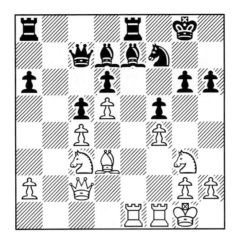

Exercise (planning): It appears as if the defence bows before the raging storm yet doesn't break, but this just isn't the case. The inherent weakness of e6 and f5 has left indelible scars on Black's defensive landscape and Moskalenko found a way to fan White's attack. What did he see?

Answer: An interference/strategic exchange sacrifice. Take control over the light squares by infiltrating e6. A GM would probably play such a move intuitively, not worrying about the details until they arrive.

27 ♖e6!

"Noblesse oblige," sighs the rook, whose honour requires that he give the attack a helping hand. White's rook openly defies the d7-bishop's authority, without fear of reprisal. What was once considered a minor glitch (the weakness of e6 and f5), morphs into a life-threatening strategic impediment, from which Black's position teeters on the edge of collapse.

27...♘h8

27...♗xe6 28 dxe6 ♘h8 29 ♘d5 ♕a7 (29...♕b7 30 ♗xf5! gxf5 31 ♘xf5 is crushing) 30 ♗xf5! (the recurring theme: load up on f5 and sacrifice) 30...gxf5 31 ♘xf5 ♗d8 32 ♘xh6+ ♔f8 33 ♕f5+ ♔g7 34 ♖f3! forces mate.

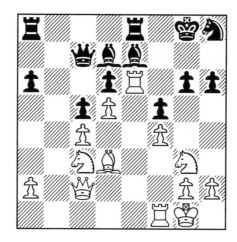

Exercise (combination alert): Black's last move, 27...♘h8, brings only marginal relief and his core strategic troubles remain. The key moment is close at hand. Continue White's attack.

Answer: After the sacrifice on f5, Black's hopes are thrust into oblivion.

28 ♗xf5!

Both White's bishop and g3-knight audition for the lead role of f5-sac'er and both understand there is only room for one. This is the logical follow-up. White's ♖e6 weakened Black's control of f5, which for so long severely constrained White's attacking ambitions. The key factor to White's interference sacrifice on e6 is that it weakened Black's grip on f5 into a level ripe for further sacrifices.

28...gxf5 29 ♘xf5 ♗f8 30 ♘xh6+ ♗xh6 31 ♖xh6

In the sacrifice's aftermath, Black's chances evoke nothing but gloom. His extra piece is no match for White's attack and three extra pawns.

31...♖e7 32 ♘e4

32 f5 is also deadly.

32...♔g7

Neither can Black survive 32...♖f8 33 f5! ♗xf5 34 ♕c3! ♖g7 35 ♘xd6.

33 ♖h5 ♘f7 34 ♕c3+ ♔g8 35 ♘f6+ ♔f8 36 ♕g3

Threatening mate on the move.

36...♖e2 37 ♖h7

The annoying rook continues to tread on everyone's toes.

37...♔e7 38 ♕h4 ♖f8

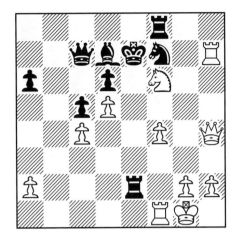

Exercise (combination alert): White to play and force mate.

Answer: Death looms over g7.

39 ♘h5+! 1-0

Summary: 10 c4 keeps us in more familiar territory. However, I still encourage you to go for 10 ♘a3!, which we looked at last game, as it is White's objectively best shot at an advantage against the ...♗d6 set-up.

Game 7
V.Moskalenko-M.Llaneza Vega
Barcelona 2008

1 d4 ♘f6 2 ♗g5 ♘e4 3 ♗f4 c5 4 f3 ♕a5+ 5 c3 ♘f6 6 d5 ♕b6 7 ♗c1 e6 8 e4 exd5 9 exd5 ♗d6 10 c4

As we saw last game, Moskalenko prefers the normal c4 set-up over 10 ♘a3!.

10...♕c7

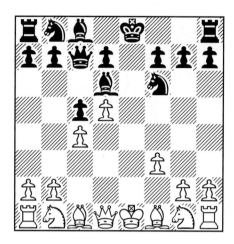

Question: Is there any real difference between
this move and castling, as we saw last game?

Answer: By putting castling on hold, Black immediately targets h2, which isn't such a tempting target once Black castles, since the open h-file takes direct aim at his king in that scenario. But in reality, the 'threat' to h2 turns out to be a bluff, since White soon offers it and Black declines.

11 ♗d3!

White happily offers h2, Black having castled or not.

11...b5

Question: What is wrong with grabbing h2 now?

Answer: It still looks exceedingly dangerous for Black: for example, 11...♗xh2?! (*Houdini*-approved but no human, at least in my database, has grabbed the pawn) 12 ♘e2 ♗d6 13 ♘bc3 a6 14 g4 when g5 is coming and Black's position looks awful, with the extra pawn offering very little in the area of consolation.

Instead, 11...0-0 12 ♘c3 a6 13 ♘ge2 b5 14 ♗g5 ♘h5 15 ♘e4 ♘f4 16 ♘xd6 ♘xd3+ 17 ♕xd3 ♕xd6 was Z.Rahman-P.Konguvel, Kolkata 2008. Now White can try 18 ♗f4 ♕b6 19 0-0 bxc4 20 ♕c3 a5 21 ♘g3 when Black has yet to develop a single piece besides his queen. White's attacking and strategic compensation easily outstrips Black's rather forlorn extra pawns.

12 ♘c3

White ignores it.

12...bxc4 13 ♗xc4

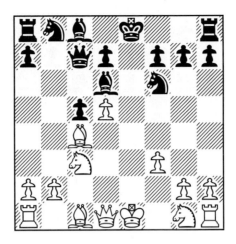

13...0-0

> *Question:* I keep looking at h2 with longing. Can't Black take the pawn now?

Answer: As always, White gets more than enough after 13...♗xh2 14 ♕d3! (preventing both
...♗a6 and ...♘a6) 14...♗e5 (the check on g3 only helps White move his king to f1, the
square he wants for his king) 15 ♘ge2 d6 16 g4 when Black lags dangerously behind in development and has no safe spot on the board for his king.

14 ♘b5 ♕b6 15 ♘e2 ♗a6?!

This innocent-looking, natural move leads to a complete tangle of his queenside.

> *Question:* Shouldn't Black strive to hang on to his dark-squared bishop?

Answer: White obtains a bind after 15...♗e7 16 d6! ♗d8 17 0-0. Now if 17...a6 18 ♘c7! ♗xc7
19 dxc7 ♕xc7 20 ♗f4 ♕b6 21 ♗d6 ♖e8 22 ♘c3!, intending ♘e4!, or if 22...♕xb2? 23 ♖c1
♘c6 24 ♖f2 ♕a3 25 ♘e4! when Black's two extra pawns are not going to save him from
White's ferocious attack.

16 a4!

The position has the look and feel of a Benko Gambit Declined, gone wrong for Black.
Black has huge problems in developing his queenside rook and knight.

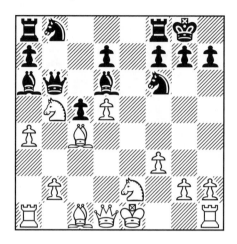

16...♗xb5 17 axb5 a6!?

Perhaps Black exaggerates the sacrifice's effectiveness and underestimates its negative implications. As it turns out, there remains the deepest of gulfs between Black's ambitions and their actual effectiveness. However, 17...♖e8 18 0-0 a6 19 ♗g5 doesn't give Black much cause for encouragement either.

18 ♕d3 ♖e8 19 bxa6

The a-pawn's air is that of a criminal who pulled off the heist with success. White is up a pawn, with no ill-effects.

19...♗e5

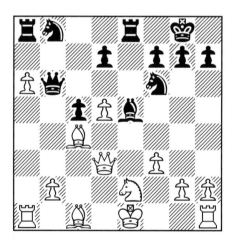

20 ♔d1?!

An overreaction. Moskalenko behaves contrary to expectations and such labyrinthine musings aren't necessary, since White's king isn't as safe on the queenside.

> **Question:** White's king dives for cover like a hunted hare.
> But why? I don't understand why White simply didn't castle.

Answer: He avoided a trap: 20 0-0? walks into 20...♘xa6! when White can't recapture, due to the ...c4+ threat. Saying this, I add: a plan can't be founded on traps alone.

I think White is better off playing 20 g4! followed by manual castling with ♔f1 and ♔g2. Then White just continues attacking on the kingside.

20...d6 21 f4

I'm not so sure about this move either.

21...♗d4?!

After this move, the once impassioned onslaught flounders without purpose. Sometimes an impulsive move, when examined more closely, is merely the logical tail justification of a previous series of inaccurate moves. In essence, such moves are the natural expression of compiled frustration. Black should play 21...♘g4! 22 ♔c2! (Black obtains full compensation for the piece after 22 ♕f3 ♗xb2! 23 ♖b1 ♕b4! 24 ♕xg4 ♕xc4 25 ♗xb2 ♕d3+ 26 ♔c1 g6 27 ♘c3 ♘xa6) 22...♘f2 23 ♕b3 ♕xb3+ 24 ♔xb3 ♗xb2 25 ♗xb2 ♘xh1 26 ♖xh1 ♘xa6 when he should hold the game, since White's position remains loose and he struggles to cover several entry points.

22 ♘xd4 cxd4 23 ♖e1 ♘bd7 24 ♖xe8+ ♖xe8 25 ♕b3

White has a winning position. His extra pawn, bishop-pair and deeply passed a-pawn outweigh any attacking chances Black may have hoped for.

25...♕a7?!

White has the game under control in the line 25...♕c7 26 ♕b5 ♘e4 27 ♕c6 ♕a7 28 ♖a5!. Still this was better than the game's continuation.

26 ♕b7

Destroying the a7 blockade.

26...♕c5

Black can't survive a queen swap.

27 ♗d3

Threat: a7 and a8♕.

27...♘b6 28 a7

White feels the a-pawns soothing influence, like a fountain's spray on a hot summer's breeze.

28...♘a8

This knight is destined to ferment in pained silence on a8 and the black hole of strategic woes feels bottomless. It is in the nature of great understatement when I declare that Black's pieces are jarringly out of tune. He hopes for the impossible: launch an attack when half his army is tied up trying to halt the passed a-pawn.

29 ♕c6 ♕b4

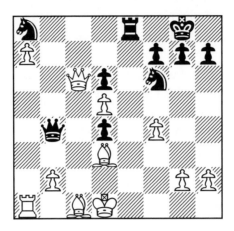

Exercise (planning): Time to banish the superfluous and embrace the essential elements. How did White press home his advantage in the most efficient manner?

Answer: The reformation process begins: complete development by offering the b-pawn.

30 ♗d2! ♕xb2

Suicide, but the ending is hopeless after 30...♕b3+ 31 ♗c2 ♕xd5 32 ♕xd5 ♘xd5 33 ♗a4.

31 ♖b1 ♕a3 32 ♖b8!

Ignoring the hanging d3-bishop and playing on Black's weak back rank.

32...♔f8 33 ♗b5

Simplest was 33 ♖xa8 ♖xa8 34 ♕xa8+ ♘e8 35 ♔e2.

33...♕b3+

"Order! Order!" cries Black's queen, banging a mallet in a futile attempt to restore calm in her realm of turmoil. Black does his best to resist, but some positions are so hopeless that salvation is beyond anyone's best.

34 ♕c2 ♕xd5 35 ♗xe8 ♘xe8 36 ♕c8 ♕e4 37 ♖xa8 1-0

White converts with languid grace after 37...♕b1+ 38 ♔e2 ♕e4+ (the purple-faced frustration painted on the queen's complexion is a far cry from her normally attractive pink bloom) 39 ♔f2 and there is no perpetual.

Summary: Be prepared to sacrifice h2, whether Black has castled kingside or not. White always gets more than enough compensation.

Game 8
H.Nakamura-K.Lie
Gjovik (rapid) 2009

1 d4 ♘f6 2 ♗g5

Compare the position we get with the following Sämisch Benoni line 2 c4 g6 3 ♘c3 ♗g7 4 e4 d6 5 f3 0-0 6 ♗g5 c5 7 d5 e6 8 ♕d2 exd5 9 cxd5.

2...♘e4 3 ♗f4 c5 4 f3 ♕a5+ 5 c3 ♘f6 6 d5 ♕b6 7 ♗c1 g6

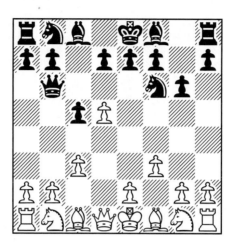

Question: How do the positions here differ from the 7...e6 lines?

Answer: With 7...g6 Black doesn't want early confrontation and completes development with ...♗g7 and ...0-0 before playing ...e6. Now the difference in this line is that White has time for the traditional Benoni c4 and cxd5 recapture, bringing the positions much closer to a real Benoni structure.

Question: So do we get a direct transposition to a Benoni?

Answer: Not quite. The difference is that Black gets the extra move ...♕b6. Now this may sound like we are in a Benoni a move down, but this just isn't the case, since a strong argument can be made that ...♕b6 may actually harm Black, since it blocks the natural ...a6 and ...b5 plan.

8 e4 d6 9 c4

Next game we examine 9 a4.

9...e6 10 ♘e2!

More accurate than 10 ♘c3 as we shall soon see.

10...exd5

Sometimes Black keeps White guessing if and when about the d5-swap. Indeed, sometimes it is never played: for example: 10...♗g7 11 ♘ec3! 0-0 12 ♗e2 e5!? (now we enter a convoluted Sämisch King's Indian) 13 g4! (this is why it may be better for White to delay castling) 13...a6 14 ♕c2 ♕a5 15 ♗e3 ♘bd7 16 ♘a3! (now the ...b5 break/pawn sacrifice won't be very tempting for Black since White may seize control over c4, along with the ex-

tra pawn) 16...♘e8 17 0-0-0 h6 18 h4 and I prefer White, who clamped down on both the
...b5 and ...f5 breaks, G.Cuadrado Wentwort Hyde-P.Cutillas Ripoll, correspondence 2004.
11 cxd5 ♗g7 12 ♘ec3!

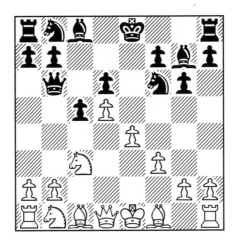

White's most harmonious knight posting.

> **Question:** What is the point of this move? It feels as if
> both white knights are willing to share a single square on c3.

Answer: In the normal KID Sämisch Benoni set-up, White's most cumbersome, problem
piece is the g1-knight, which searches for a home on g3, or c1 via e2, or plays to f2 via h3. In
all cases, the posts are sub-optimal. In the Trompowsky version, White transfers his 'bad'
g1-knight to c3 – a good square – and preserves the other for a3, where it eyes c4 and also
Black's ...b5 break.

12...0-0 13 ♗e2 a6 14 a4

A new move, but perfectly logical. Nakamura's move may be slightly more accurate
than castling, since it keeps g4, h4 and h5 attacking options on the table a bit longer, keeping Black guessing to our intent.

14...♘bd7 15 ♘a3

Clamping down on both ...b5 and ...c4 ideas. I feel this position is more favourable for
White than one reached via the KID Sämisch Benoni.

15...♕d8

As nearly always in this line, Black's queen retreats to its square of origin. 15...♕c7 is the
alternative. Lie probably felt it was better to return to d8, where the queen might be trans-
ferred to the kingside. Also, he keeps c7 open for a knight, in order to fight for a ...b5 break.

16 0-0 ♖b8

Black experiences great difficulties implementing either a ...b5 or ...c4 push, with
White's knights so perfectly placed to frustrate.

17 ♗e3

White can also try 17 ♗g5 with a kingside attacking plan based on an eventual f4.

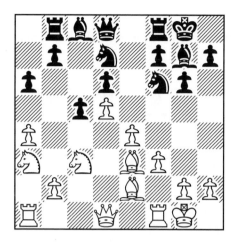

17...♘e8

Question: Why did Black retreat voluntarily?

Answer: By retreating, Black keeps ...f5 options on the table and also considers ...♘c7, in preparation for an eventual ...b5 break.

18 ♕d2 ♘c7

18...f5 hopes to generate activity at the cost of slight weakening. I still prefer White's game after 19 exf5 ♖xf5 20 ♖fe1, although I think Black would have been better off going in this direction than the path he took in the game.

19 ♖ab1!

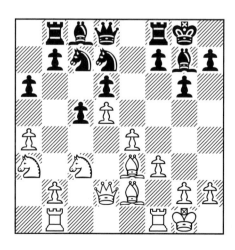

Nakamura reveals his intent: a queenside attack, with b4 to follow.

19...♕e7 20 b4

White rapidly gains a stranglehold over the queenside.

20...♖e8 21 ♗f2

A precaution, removing a vulnerable piece off the e-file, in case Black contemplates ...f5.

21...b6 22 ♘c4

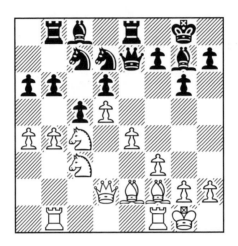

22...b5?

An agitated wave of unrest shudders through the position. Once in a while, we all make moves antithetical to our own survival. This misguided attempt to seize the initiative violates the principle: don't challenge the opponent on your weak wing.

Black should stifle the urge to retaliate and continue with a milder version with 22...cxb4 23 ♖xb4. Black keeps his disadvantage to a minimum after 23...a5 24 ♖b3 ♗a6 25 ♖fb1 f5 (this move has to be played, sooner or later, if Black is to muster any counterplay) 26 ♗d4 ♗xc4 27 ♗xc4 ♗xd4+ 28 ♕xd4 when his dishevelled structure may be a bit of an eyesore, but he bases hopes on some compensating piece activity and dark-square control.

23 axb5

Houdini prefers retaining the pawn tension with 23 ♘a5 ♕f6 24 ♖fc1.

23...axb5 24 ♘a5

The knight hovers, poised to strike in waspish irritation on c6.

24...♕f6 25 ♖fc1

Black's peril remains at its most acute level.

25...♖a8

The rook sneaks away, as if from a creditor. Black's last move drops material and *Houdini* considers it a mistake. I'm not so sure, having played through its suggested sequence 25...c4 26 ♘c6 ♖a8 27 ♗e3! (threatening ♗g5) 27....♗f8 28 ♘a7 ♖b8 29 ♖a1 ♘e5 30 h3 ♖b7 31 f4 ♘d7 32 ♗f3 Now what? Black can barely move. If 32...♗g7 33 e5! dxe5 34 ♘xc8 exf4 35 ♗xf4 ♖xc8 36 d6, which is crushing, since b7 and c7 hang simultaneously.

26 ♘xb5 ♞xb5 27 ♗xb5 cxb4 28 ♕xb4

Naka denudes the queenside with resounding success. He picked off a pawn and now has eyes for d6.

28...♖d8

28...♖f8 29 ♘c4 drops a second pawn on d6.

29 ♘c6 ♖f8

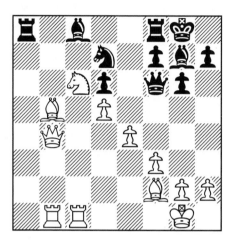

> *Exercise (Combination alert):* White refuses to be placated with merely a single pawn. How did Naka win a second pawn by uprooting a defender from its natural groove?

Answer: White drives the only defender of d6 away from its protective embrace.

30 ♗d4!

The impolite bishop harrows the black queen's delicate psyche beyond the limits of her tolerance.

30...♕g5

The d6-pawn, emitting a sad groan, looks on in dismay at the rapidly receding form of his last defender, who apologetically disclaims all previous defensive commitments.

31 ♗xg7 ♚xg7 32 ♕xd6

Black is down two pawns for nothing.

32...♖a2

Threatening mate on the move.

33 ♕g3

White's queen barely suppresses a yawn when musing upon her tiresome sister's un-sensational labours to undermine her authority. Although White bulges with prosperity, he still must deal with a final issue: consolidation.

33...♕e3+

Black's queen quickly slides away from her sister, the way a seal exits an ice flow and enters the frigid water upon spotting an approaching, dog-paddling polar bear.

34 ♔h1 ♘f6 35 ♖e1 ♕d2?

35...♕c5 prolongs the game, but doesn't save it for Black.

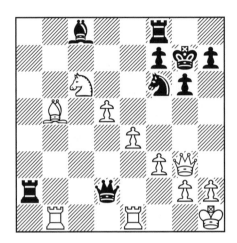

> **Exercise (combination alert):** Black's queen arrives on the scene with
> the suggestion of fresh peril for White's king, but this simply isn't the
> reality. Black's non-attack lost its force (which it lacked to begin with),
> and has nothing left to offer. Black's calculations sprung a leak and he
> just blundered in a hopeless position. How did Nakamura exploit it?

Answer: X-ray attack. Black has no good way to cover the now loose a- rook, and sac'ing the queen isn't going to cut it either.

36 ♖e2 1-0

Summary: After 9 c4 we end up in a strange Sämisch Benoni, where Black's 'extra' ...♕b6 move may actually harm more than help him. Also, keep in mind the strange ♘e2, ♘ec3, a4 and ♘a3 idea, which maximizes White's knight's potential in this variation.

> *Game 9*
> **A.Kinsman-J.Littlewood**
> British League 1998

1 d4 ♘f6 2 ♗g5 ♘e4 3 ♗f4 c5 4 f3 ♕a5+ 5 c3 ♘f6 6 d5 ♕b6 7 ♗c1 g6 8 e4 d6 9 a4

This is for players who may not feel comfortable in the Sämisch/Benoni structure of the last game.

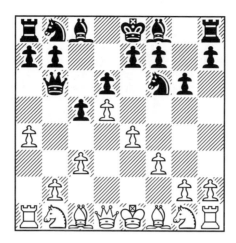

Question: What is White's idea of holding back on c4?

Answer: White holds back on c4 in the hope of occupying the square with a knight. He tosses in 9 a4 to secure c4 from ...b5 ideas.

9...♗g7 10 ♘a3 0-0 11 ♘c4 ♕c7

This isn't really a tempo loss, since Black normally moves the queen back from b6 even when unprovoked, as we have seen throughout the chapter.

12 ♘e2

Question: Where is this knight going?

Answer: As I mentioned last game, White's problem piece in the Sämisch/Benoni (and this is still a hybrid of one) is the g1-knight, which in this case plans to roost on g3. Admittedly not the ideal square, but we make do with what we have before us.

12...♘bd7

Note one benefit to our ♘c4 set-up: Black has a much tougher time engineering ...e6, since White directs heat at d6.

After 12...b6 13 g4!? (ambitious; 13 ♘g3 is the safer alternative) 13...♗a6 14 ♘g3 ♖d8, as in A.Almonti-P.Peto, correspondence 2000, I like the look of White's attacking chances after 15 g5 ♘e8 16 f4 e6 17 ♘e3.

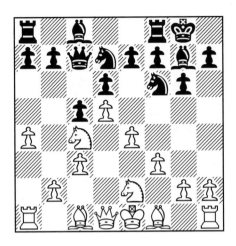

13 ♘g3

> **Question:** What about posting a knight on f4?

Answer: I don't like f4, because it loses White's central pawn push options: 13 ♘f4 b6 14 ♗e2 a6 15 0-0 ♖b8 16 ♘a3 (to halt ...b5) 16...♘e5 and now White had nothing better than moving the misplaced knight again with 17 ♘d3 ♘xd3 18 ♕xd3 ♗d7 19 ♕xa6 ♖a8 20 ♕d3 ♖xa4, M.Lostuzzi-D.Sermek, Pula 2001.

13...♘b6

Challenging White's most annoying piece, at a cost of time for Black. The position must favour White, who continues to enjoy a healthy space advantage. Also, Black lost all three games from this position in the database – not an auspicious omen for the anti-Tromp forces.

After 13...♘e5!? 14 ♗g5 h5 15 ♘xe5 dxe5 16 c4 ♔h7 17 ♕d2 ♘g8 18 ♗d3 ♗h6 (eliminating Black's worst piece) 19 0-0 a5 (Black feared an eventual b4 and allows a hole on b5) 20 ♘e2 ♖a6 21 ♘c3 ♗d7 22 g3! White looks slightly better, with extra space and f4 coming, N.Kabanov-M.Ismailov, Pavlodar 2012.

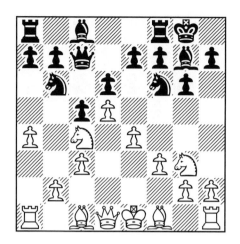

14 ♗e3

A theoretical novelty. Previously White had preferred:

a) 14 ♘a3.

> ***Question:*** Why would White retreat a well-placed piece?

Answer: Principle: the side with extra space should strive to retain pieces on the board. 14...♗d7 was Duong The Anh-N.Vakhidov, Bandar Seri Begawan 2010, and here White can continue 15 a5 ♘c8 (15...♘a4? should lose to 16 ♘b5 ♕xa5 17 ♖xa4 ♕b6 18 ♘a3 ♗xa4 19 ♕xa4) 16 ♘b5 ♕d8 17 c4. I still like White, who looks like he entered a slightly favourable King's Indian.

b) 14 ♗f4 (striving to halt ...e6 by applying pressure on d6) 14...h5 (a commonly played move in such positions, yet I am always happy to see it as White in such KID/Benoni structures, since any pawn push by Black on the kingside tends to weaken his king) was J.Maldonado Pacheco-J.Alvarez Sabor, correspondence 2009. Play may go 15 a5 ♘xc4 16 ♗xc4 h4 17 ♘e2 which looks dynamically balanced. Black's advanced h-pawn could be a curse or a blessing.

14...h5

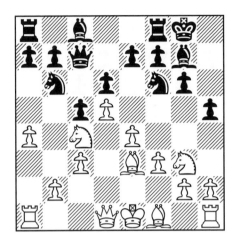

Answer: As I mentioned in the above notes, this is a common occurrence in Sämisch KID/Benoni structures. Black hopes to disrupt and gain tempi with ...h4 and sometimes ...h3. On the downside, the pawn can become a weakness later in the game, and Black's king safety also becomes a shade looser.

15 ♗e2 ♘e8 16 0-0 e6

At long last, Black achieves the ...e6 break.

17 ♕d2

Which White simply ignores.

17...h4!?

The less cautious your opponent, the more likely his or her defeat – and yours as well. This move is consistent and bold, yet such semi-indiscriminate decisions have a nasty way of haunting us later in the game if matters don't fall perfectly according to our plans.

18 ♘h1

Not as bad as it looks, since h1 is just a temporary residence for the knight.

18...exd5 19 exd5 ♗d7?!

Possibly inaccurate. Black probably gets a better version of the game continuation with 19...♘f6! 20 ♘xb6 axb6 21 ♘f2 h3 22 g4!? (maybe the more restrained 22 g3 can be tried as well) 22...♖e8 23 ♗b5 (or 23 ♗c4 ♘d7 24 ♖fe1 ♘e5 25 ♗e2 f5 26 g5 when I like White due to his space and potential to pick off h3, but *Houdini* thinks Black gets full compensation and assesses at even; Black can speculate with 26...f4!? 27 ♗xf4 ♕f7 28 ♘e4 ♖f8 29 ♗g3 ♕xf3! 30 ♗d1 which looks completely unclear) 23...♗d7 24 ♗g5 ♗xb5 25 axb5 c4 26 ♗xf6 ♗xf6 27 ♖xa8 ♖xa8 28 ♘e4 ♗g7 29 ♔f2 ♕e7 30 ♔g3 ♖a5 31 ♖e1 ♖xb5 32 f4 ♖a5 33 ♔xh3 and it's anybody's game.

20 ♘xb6 axb6 21 b3!

Freezing Black's queenside pawns. White has earned an enduring edge.

21...♘f6 22 ♘f2 ♖ae8 23 ♗c4 ♖e5?

Black should play 23...♘h7 to prevent ♗g5.

24 ♗g5!

Targeting h4.

24...h3

Inciting a violent schism in White's structure, yet not enough to actually inflict any real harm.

25 g4!

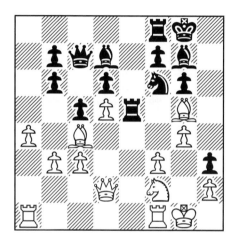

The most ambitious move. White cuts off the f5-square from Black's pieces and also severs the connection to h3.

25...♘h7 26 ♗f4 ♖e7 27 ♘xh3

Simple assassination of a target requires much less energy than abduction.

> **Question:** Did Black acquire compensatory play, since White also weakened his kingside to grab the pawn?

Answer: I don't believe enough, despite White's rather loose-looking kingside. Just watch how Kinsman consolidated in the game.

27...f5?

This strategic blunder is merely a symptom of the overall dysfunction in Black's ability to coordinate forces in offensive harmony. After this move, any attacking chances Black may have grow cold. He passes the threshold of effective resistance and his position grows utterly counterplayless, as his aimless pieces float like dying suns, breathing out their last. From this point, Black's pieces await, poised motionless for an attack which never comes to pass. Black had to try something like 27...♗e5 when he remains in bad shape, but better off than in the game continuation.

28 g5

Of course. White clogs attacking lines. With loss of territory also comes restricted free-dom of assembly for Black, who abruptly runs empty of counterplay-producing ideas.

28...♗e8

I don't believe Black has any useful attacking plan at this stage.

29 ♖ae1 ♗f7 30 ♖xe7

Every swap helps White.

30...♕xe7 31 ♖e1 ♕d8

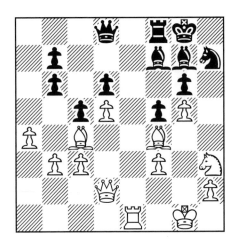

Exercise (planning/combination alert): How does White earn a crushing bind?

---

32 ♗b5

Answer: The e6-square is the fountain of Black's trouble. The strategic exchange sacrifice idea, which we saw earlier in Moskalenko-Alsina, applies here as well: 32 ♖e6!. The familiar exchange sacrifice begins with the weakened d6-square as its catalyst, as well as the light squares and a deadly passer if Black accepts with 32...♗xe6. The diagnosis corresponds with the ailment: e6 must be surgically removed, or the patient (Black) will die. If Black re-fuses the gift, then d6 falls and his position remains hopeless there as well. After 33 dxe6 d5 34 ♕xd5 ♕xd5 35 ♗xd5 ♔h8 36 e7 ♖e8 37 ♗d6 Black has no good way to halt ♗f7.

32...♔h8 33 ♘f2 ♗e5

Desperation. Black is almost out of moves, other than random shuffles.

34 h4

34 ♗xe5+ dxe5 35 c4 ♘xg5 36 ♕c3 is also decisive.

34...♗xd5

Life moved on and left Black's hibernating, wished-for attack in Rip Van Winkle fashion. So now warmer emotions prevail and Black decides upon a futile set of sacrifices, bunging in a pair of pieces for the honours. Black crossed a line he previously dared not cross, based on the philosophy: a desperate person ceases to fear repercussions, since he or she faces another equally distasteful set of repercussions upon failure to act. Neither can Black survive 34...♗xf4 35 ♕xf4 ♗xd5 36 ♖d1 ♗xb3 37 ♖xd6.

35 ♗xe5+ dxe5

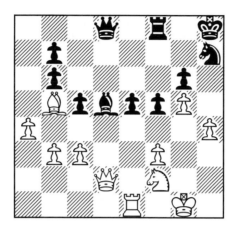

Exercise (combination alert): Here is the easiest combination alert in the entire book. White to play and force the win of material.

Answer: Pin. So easy that the move isn't really even worthy of an exclam or a combination alert.

36 ♖d1

"But, but, but you promised to spare me if I surrendered!" Black's bishop sputters to White's queen. She responds: "At the moment, memory fails me in regard to the exact agreement of our pleasant conversation."

36...♕e7 37 ♕xd5 ♘xg5

Such a move betrays half-hidden resentments. Well, why not? Littlewood obviously felt cheated out of his natural inheritance: an attack. So a previously unauthorized action is now authorized, since desperation has its own set of rules. The offending g5-pawn has been the cause of great inconvenience to Black, who resolves to deal with the matter in the harshest of methods.

38 hxg5 ♕xg5+ 39 ♔f1 ♕g3

It is in the nature of grave understatement when I tell you that Black's non-attack and massive material deficit casts a gloomy shadow upon the proceedings. Black's queen feels a leaden sense of inferiority in comparison to her radiant sister.

40 ♕d6 1-0

Black's decrepit king, too feeble to run, remains where he is, awaiting the inevitable.

Summary: This line is for those of us who don't feel comfortable in a pure Sämisch/Benoni structure, so we leave open c4 for occupation by our knight.

Chapter Two
2...♘e4 3 ♗f4 d5

1 d4 ♘f6 2 ♗g5 ♘e4 3 ♗f4 d5

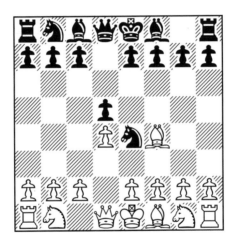

In this chapter Black avoids the Benoni-like positions of Chapter One and decides to stake out a fair share of the centre with ...d5. Now we have a choice of crazy or calm.

After 4 f3 ♘f6 5 e4 it isn't so difficult to guess the sequel. We earmark e4 as personal property and resent Black's assertion to rights of any kind over the disputed square. We decide upon disciplinary action, with just a shade of rebuke added for good measure by entering a Blackmar-Diemer Gambit a full move up. Our ♗f4 is free since our bishop took two moves to reach the square while Black's knight required three to reach f6. I'm not a big believer in the BDG, but sign me up if I get it a full move ahead of schedule.

If the gambit – even a move up – doesn't appeal to you, then we can also take the safer route with a London-like position with 4 e3.

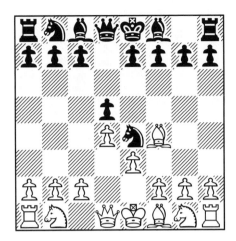

Now this may look good for Black (reality always trails a few steps behind illusion), but in my opinion this just isn't the case and White seems to arrive in a slightly favourable version of a London System.

Question: Why slightly favourable?

Answer: Black's e4-posting for his knight may be a hindrance more than the infliction of any injury to our side, since it allows us tricky undermining efforts with ♗d3 and ♗xe4, or c4. We also retain f3 possibilities.

Game 10
G.Kasparov-M.Carneiro
Sao Paulo (simul) 2004

1 d4 ♘f6 2 ♗g5 ♘e4 3 ♗f4 d5 4 f3

We look at 4 e3 in the final three games of the chapter.

4...♘f6

Later in the chapter we look at 4...♘d6.

5 e4

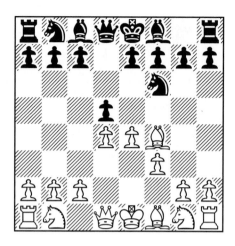

Answer: We enter the version you may want to play, since we are up a full move (♗f4) over the normal BDG.

Answer: You can always play the quieter 4 e3 line, which we look at later in the chapter. Still, I encourage you to give this line a fair try. In such favourable versions, the matter of one's style is perhaps irrelevant. Sometimes one should lay aside personal stylistic likes and dislikes, and simply go with what may be the most favourable line. But saying this, I sometimes chicken out and play 4 e3, even though I think 4 f3 is superior, if the tournament situation requires caution.

5...dxe4

We look at the declined 5...e6 line later in the chapter.

Instead, 5...c5 6 ♘c3 dxe4 7 d5 exf3 8 ♘xf3 g6 9 ♘b5! ♘a6 was G.Hertneck-V.Gavrikov, German League 1993 (9...♘xd5?? hangs to 10 ♕xd5!). At this point *Houdini* gives White a clear plus after 10 d6!.

6 ♘c3

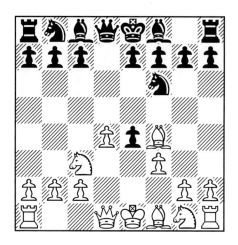

6...exf3!?

In the days of the great Romantics, the chivalric code dictated that the defender was honour-bound to accept all sacs. Black opts for the bravest or most foolhardy option. Black, clearly an optimist, thinks: "I will grab a pawn against one of the greatest attacking players of all time, at the cost of development. What could possibly go wrong?"

Question: Doesn't Black nullify White's development lead by declining with 6...e3?

Answer: It is certainly a safer route and I think possibly Black's best. White loses his extra tempo if he captures e3 with his bishop: 7 ♗xe3 (7 ♕d3!? is an attempt to remain up a tempo: 7...e6 8 ♕xe3 ♗e7 9 0-0-0 0-0 10 ♔b1 and White is ready for g4 and h4 in this sharp, opposite wing attacks position, J.Benjamin-A.Yermolinsky, Modesto 1995) 7...e6 8 ♘ge2 ♘bd7 9 ♘g3 ♗e7 10 ♕d3!? 0-0 11 0-0-0 a6 12 ♘ge4 ♘d5 13 h4 was V.Milov-B.Gelfand, Biel 1995. The position resembles the Burn Variation of the French Defence. I still like White's chances and if a GM is willing to try this line on Gelfand, it is a powerful testimonial to its inherent soundness.

Black can also try:

a) 6...♗f5 7 fxe4 ♘xe4 (or 7...♗xe4 8 ♘xe4 ♘xe4 9 ♕f3!?, which is the nuclear option, offering a second pawn; after 9...♕xd4 10 ♖d1 ♕a4 11 ♗d3 ♘c5 12 ♘e2!? – Hodgson isn't interested in c7 and continues to increase development lead – 12...♘bd7 13 0-0 ♘xd3 14 ♖xd3 White's massive development lead easily compensates for two pawns, J.Hodgson-A.Kalka, German League 1994) 8 ♕f3 ♘xc3 9 bxc3 ♕c8 10 ♗c4 e6 was P.Cech-E.Pinter, Czech League 2009. White gets ample attacking chances for the pawn after 11 ♘e2 ♘d7 12 0-0.

b) 6...♘d5 (Black returns the pawn in this line) 7 ♘xd5 ♕xd5 8 ♗xc7 ♘c6 9 c3 ♗f5 10 ♗e2 e5 11 ♗xe5 ♘xe5 12 dxe5 ♕xe5 13 ♕a4+ ♗d7 14 ♕xe4 ♕xe4 15 fxe4 when Black's bishop-pair and control over the dark squares may compensate for the pawn. Still, queens are off the board and a pawn is a pawn, R.Djurhuus-F.Elsness, Gausdal 1995.

7 ♘xf3

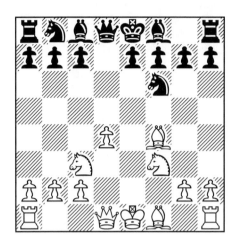

Here we are: the BDG, a full move up for White.

7...♗g4

Alternatively:

a) 7...e6 8 ♗c4 c6 9 ♕e2 ♘bd7 10 0-0-0 ♘b6 (ensuring that White will never be allowed the thematic d5 break) 11 d5! (hey, I said "ensuring that White will never..."; oh, never mind) 11...♘bxd5 12 ♗xd5 ♘xd5 13 ♖xd5! cxd5 14 ♘b5 and Black found himself in deep trouble in V.Jansa-G.Sosonko, Amsterdam 1975.

b) 7...c6 8 ♗c4 ♗f5 (transposes to variation 'a') 9 0-0 e6 10 ♘e5 (the set-up 10 ♕e2 ♘bd7 11 ♖ad1 is also possible) 10...♗e7? (Black should try 10...♘bd7 11 ♗d3 ♘xe5 12 ♗xe5 ♗g6 13 ♕f3) 11 ♘xf7! ♔xf7 12 ♗xb8 ♗xc2 (12...♖xb8 13 ♖xf5 is also terrible for Black) 13 ♕e2! ♖xb8 14 ♗xe6+ ♔f8 15 ♕xc2 and Black is obviously busted, with his king trapped in the centre, A.Almeida Saenz-S.Colli Lopez, Aguascalientes 2008.

c) 7...♗f5 8 ♗c4 e6 9 ♕e2 ♗b4 10 0-0-0! ♗xc3 11 bxc3 0-0 12 ♘e5 ♘d5 13 ♗d2 ♘d7 14 g4 ♘xe5 15 dxe5 ♗g6 16 h4 and White's attack looks exceedingly dangerous, C.Coco-H.Krueger, correspondence 1996.

d) Next game we look at 7...g6.

8 h3 ♗xf3

8...♗h5?! allows White free attacking pawn pushes: 9 g4 ♗g6 10 ♘e5 ♘d5 (as in V.Milov-S.Battesti, Bastia 2004; Black also looks like he is in deep trouble after 10...c6 11 h4 e6 12 h5 ♗e4 13 ♘xe4 ♘xe4 14 ♕f3) 11 ♗g2! c6 (11...e6 12 ♘xd5 exd5 13 ♕e2 ♗e7 14 0-0-0 0-0 15 ♕b5 looks awful too for Black), and now White should respond with 12 ♘xg6 hxg6 13 ♘xd5 cxd5 14 c4. Black is in deep trouble, chronically behind in development.

9 ♕xf3 c6 10 0-0-0 e6 11 ♗c4 ♘bd7?

11...♗e7 12 ♔b1 0-0 (even on the seemingly impregnable kingside, Black's king will find life full of incident and stress) 13 h4 ♘d5 14 ♘e4 b5 15 ♗d3 ♘d7 16 ♘g5 ♘7f6 17 ♗e5 a5 18 ♖df1 a4? (Black looks clearly slower even after the superior 18...h6 19 g4) 19 ♗xh7+!

♘xh7 20 ♕h5 and 1-0 was a terrifying example of what can happen to Black in this line, S.B.Hansen-H.Olafsson, Reykjavik 1995.

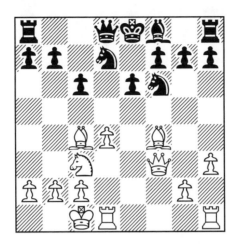

Exercise (combination alert/planning): With 11...♘bd7 Black
committed the original sin, dating back to Morphy's time:
don't fall behind in development (especially against a world champion).
How did Kasparov destroy Black's illusion of solidity in this position?

Answer: Principles: open the position and create confrontation when (massively) leading in development. An avalanche of white attackers pours forth.

12 d5!

Opposing forces dove-tail into one another, with d5 as ground zero.

12...cxd5 13 ♘xd5 ♘xd5?

13...exd5! was Black's best hope: 14 ♖he1+ ♗e7 15 ♗d6 (that extra tempo sure comes in handy in the BDG) 15...dxc4! (after 15...0-0 16 ♗xe7 ♕c7 17 ♗xd5! is even stronger than taking on f8; 17...♘e5 18 ♖xe5! ♕xe5 19 ♗xb7 ♕xe7 20 ♗xa8 leaves White up a clean pawn) 16 ♗xe7 ♕xe7 17 ♕xb7 with clear advantage to White, but Black still hangs in there, unlike in the game continuation.

14 ♗xd5 a5?

Black's pieces begin to scatter in all directions, like an audience emerging from a movie theatre. 14...exd5 15 ♖he1+ ♗e7 16 ♗d6 ♘e5 17 ♗xe5 0-0 18 ♖xd5 ♗g5+ 19 ♔b1 ♕b6 20 ♗xg7 is obviously hopeless for Black, but still infinitely superior to the game's continuation.

15 ♗xb7 ♖a7

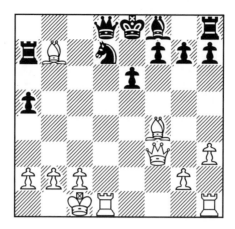

Exercise (combination alert): Long queues of agitated attackers form around Black's king, each anxious to take his shot. Sprawlingly dysfunctional would-be black defenders do little more than exist, like unfortunate starfish washed up on the beach. Continue White's attack in the most efficient manner.

Answer: Pin/mating net.

16 ♖xd7! ♕f6

Desertions can be a growing issue for a general leading an army in a losing campaign. 16...♔xd7 17 ♕c6+ ♔e7 18 ♕c5+ ♔e8 (18...♔f6 19 ♕g5 Mate!) 19 ♕xa7 doesn't look so healthy for Black, while 16...♕xd7 17 ♗c6 wins on the spot.

17 ♖hd1 ♗e7 18 ♖xe7+! ♕xe7

Or 18...♔xe7 19 ♗d6+ ♔d8 20 ♗c5+ ♔c7 21 ♕c6+ ♔b8 22 ♗d6 mate.

19 ♕c6+ ♔f8

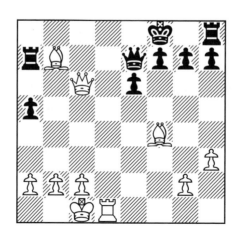

20 ♗d6

Oops, this forces mate in eight. Kasparov, burdened with multiple simul games, misses:

Answer: 20 ♕c8+! ♕e8 21 ♗d6+ ♔g8 22 ♕xe8 is mate.

20...g6 21 ♗xe7+ ♔xe7

"My dear friend, justice should be tempered with mercy and gentle tolerance," bleats the black king to White's queen.

22 ♕c5+ ♔f6

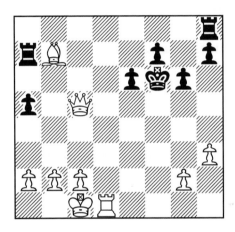

23 ♕xa7

The simul move: take whatever is hanging and move on to the next board.

Answer: White forces a quick mate with 23 ♖f1+! ♔g7 24 ♕e5+ (the stoic queen receives the enraged black king's outpouring harangue in the manner of a nurse absorbing a dementia patient's angry outflow of complaint each day) 24...♔g8 25 ♖d1.

23...♖f8

Black interprets the position with a mind unclouded by orthodoxy's doctrine and refuses to resign, clinging to survival with leach-like persistence. Endless, unfruitful defence is a spirit-clogging experience (I mean for the winning side), which all of us endured. In this instance, Black takes it to entirely new levels.

Back in the mid 1990's I taught a student named Alina, rated at about 1650, who was also in her mid 90's (she lived to the age of 103, which is GM-strength longevity genetics). I was paired with her in the first round of a local weekend tournament and didn't want to consume a lot of energy. So, I went for a quick kill with 1 e4 e5 2 f4!, King's Gambiting her. After 15 moves she was down a rook with queens off the board, but she wouldn't resign and ate up all her time.

We reached move 40 (at this point she was down something like -35.00 according to *Fritz*), and then got an extra hour on her clock, which she also used up. Alina's bottomless will to play on was monotony, taking physical form before my bewildered, swimming eyes. After the game, with agitation sprouting like wild mushrooms, I demanded an answer from her in my most righteously indignant tone: "Alina, why in God's name didn't you resign when you lost a full rook to a player who outrates you by almost 1,000 rating points?" She answered: "I paid good money for my entry fee and wanted to get my money's worth. See you on Thursday for our next lesson."

24 ♕d4+ e5 25 ♕d6+ ♔g7 26 ♕xe5+ ♔g8 27 ♕f6 h5 28 ♗d5 ♔h7 29 ♗xf7 1-0

Three 'yeas' and two 'nays' in favour of carrying out the black king's pending execution: The motion is carried. Meeting adjourned. Well, at least he didn't play on until mate, the way Alina did.

Summary: Don't be afraid of the BDG if our side gets an extra move.

Game 11
J.Hodgson-A.Panchenko
Bern 1994

1 d4 ♘f6 2 ♗g5 ♘e4 3 ♗f4 d5 4 f3 ♘f6 5 e4 dxe4 6 ♘c3 exf3

Criminals tend to feel remorse, not for the commission of the crime itself, but in the bungling of its perpetration. Once again Black attempts a dangerous smash and grab, entering the BDG a move down.

7 ♘xf3 g6

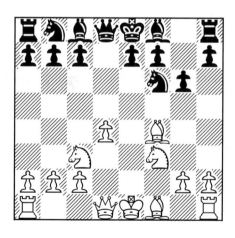

The ...g6 line is considered to be one of Black's best options versus the normal Blackmar-Diemer Gambit. In this case Black's position faces a much sterner test, a full move down over normal BDG lines.

Question: Why is the ...g6 line considered one of Black's optimal lines versus BDG?

Answer: A couple of reasons:

1. Lines taking aim at h7 don't work out as well for White since a bishop posted on d3 hits a wall on g6.

2. Black's bishop tends to provide greater coverage for Black's king than on e7.

8 ♗c4

The f7-square is the logical target for White, who can pile up on it with ♗c4, ♘e5 or ♘g5, and with major pieces loaded up on the open f-file.

8...♗g7 9 ♕e2

Hodgson prefers to keep watch over e5, rather than go 9 ♕d2, which challenges the fianchettoed bishop from h6: 9...0-0 10 0-0-0 ♗g4 11 ♖hf1 ♘bd7 12 ♗h6 ♘b6 13 ♗b3 c6 14 ♖de1 ♘bd5 (I would reduce attackers by chopping on f3) 15 ♘e5 ♘xc3 16 bxc3! (16 ♗xg7 ♘xa2+ picks off a second pawn) 16...♗c8 17 g4 (going after the tender f7-square) 17...♘d5 18 ♖f3 f6?! (*Houdini* suggests the defence 18...♗xe5 19 ♖xe5 ♗xg4 20 ♖g3 ♕d7 21 ♗xf8, rating the position at dead even) 19 ♖h3 g5? (Black's last chance to remain in the game was with 19...♗h8 20 ♗xf8 ♕xf8 21 c4 ♘c7 22 ♘d3 ♗xg4 23 ♖g3, although even here, White stands well, with attacking chances) 20 ♕d3! f5 21 ♗xg5 and White had a winning attack, P.Zielinski-S.Macak, Presov 2004.

9...0-0 10 0-0-0 c6

Also after 10...♗g4 11 h3 ♗xf3 12 ♕xf3 ♘c6 13 d5 ♘a5 14 ♗e2 (threat: b4) 14...b6 15 g4 ♘b7 16 h4 ♘d6 17 h5 White is the one doing all the attacking, G.Benedetto-B.Belokopyt, correspondence 1996.

11 d5!

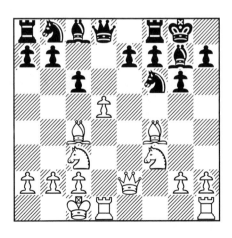

The same principle as in our last game: open the position and cultivate confrontation when leading in development.

11...cxd5

After this move Black's queen get harassed, but 11...♕e8!? 12 ♖he1 isn't very tempting for Black either.

12 ♘xd5 ♘xd5 13 ♖xd5 ♕b6

With hindsight, Black has a better shot with the counterintuitive self-pinning 13...♘d7! 14 ♖hd1 e6 15 ♖d6 ♕f6 16 ♖6d4 (White threatens ♗g5, followed by ♖xd7) 16...♕f5 17 g4! ♕xg4 18 ♗e5 ♘xe5 (forced- 19 ♖xg4 ♘xg4 when he obtains rook, bishop and two pawns for the queen – a fair trade. His king looks safe enough, but he still experiences difficulty developing his queenside. *Houdini* rates it at even.

14 ♖b5!

Hodgson violates the principle: don't bring your rook out in a crowded middlegame. This is an exception since Black's queen finds herself uncomfortable, even on an open board.

14...♕c6

14...♕f6? walks into 15 ♗g5, winning e7.

15 ♘e5 ♕e8

Black's queen, a Rembrandt forced to paint houses for a living, feels overworked and underused. I don't think Black can afford to hand over his dark-squared bishop for the e5-knight.

16 h4!

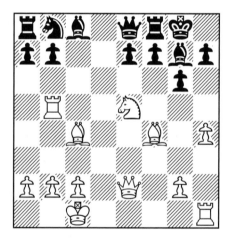

It becomes obvious that White's massive development lead and upcoming kingside attacking chances easily outweigh Black's extra pawn.

16...♘c6

Otherwise:

a) 16...a6 17 ♖b3 ♘c6 18 h5! ♘d4 19 ♕e3 ♘xb3+ 20 ♗xb3 leaves White with a winning attack, despite Black's extra exchange and pawn.

b) 16...h5?? walks into 17 ♘xg6. Such a tactic is by now so common and so hackneyed, that it really doesn't warrant an exclam.

17 h5 g5?

Sometimes we just can't say no to an ill-advised, impractical idea if it catches our fancy. Black, clearly in acute discomfort, hopes this idea contains the germ of something, anything, which permits renewal of counterplay. So he places groundless aspiration on a scheme with which his king derives not an iota of assistance. Imagination boggles with an open mouth at the monumental defensive difficulties which lie ahead for Black.

This move feels too desperate and is perhaps an overreaction. I have observed a subtle life principle, perhaps an offshoot of Murphy's law, which states: You only get things exactly when you don't need them. Case in point: when I don't need a cab, at least three or four pass me by per minute. Conversely, if I am desperately late to the airport to catch a flight, the cab supply mysteriously shrivels to zero per minute. In just the same way, Panchenko desperately needs a viable defensive plan, when none exists.

Black probably felt that the repair of his position was not a matter he should leave to time, which was most certainly not on his side, with a prosaic line like 17...e6 18 ♕e3 b6 19 ♔b1 ♘xe5 20 ♗xe5 ♗xe5 21 ♖xe5. I hate Black's position even here, but his chances to save the game are much better than in the game continuation.

18 ♘xc6 ♕xc6

18...♗f6 19 ♘e5 gxf4 20 ♕e4 threatening ♗d3 is also crushing.

19 ♖xg5 ♕f6

"We have been granted the great blessing of divine infallibility," declares Black's queen who double attacks both f4 and b2. She soon begins to harbour doubts about her theory, however, after White's next move.

20 ♕e5!

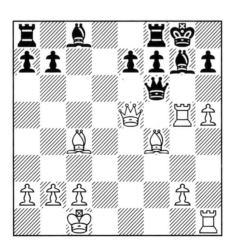

Interference. The quality and strain of the queen's dark silences convey sinister meaning to those around her. Hodgson makes good use of the pinned g7-bishop, and Black's pseudo-initiative unravels and diffuses in a single move.

20...h6

Question: Doesn't 20...♔h8 short circuit White's plan?

Answer: No. White responds with the countershot 21 h6! ♕xe5 22 hxg7+ (a zwischenzug) 22...♕xg7 23 ♖xg7 ♔xg7 24 ♗h6+ ♔g8 25 ♖h5! (threatening a monster check on g5) 25...♖d8 26 ♖g5+ ♔h8 27 ♗xf7 when there is no defence to the coming mate on g7.

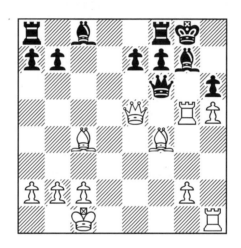

Exercise (combination alert): After 20...h6 White can simply trade queens, with a superior ending. However, Hodgson found something much stronger. What did he see?

Answer: Pin. An old grievance makes its tiresome return, as the pushy rook continues to butt into everyone's business.

21 ♖g6! ♕xg6

21...♕xe5?? 22 ♗xe5 is an instant game-ender.

22 hxg6 ♗xe5

Matters get rather awkward when opposing queens perish in the battle and they inadvertently bump into one another in paradise.

23 ♗xe5

Black, up a full exchange in the ending, is completely busted since White's attack rages on.

23...♗e6 24 ♖xh6

Threatening mate on the move. Black's next move is forced.

24...f6 25 ♗xe6+ ♔g7

Double attack on h6 and e5.

26 ♗f4

Double defence. White covers everything and Black's rook is no match for White's bishops.

26...♖h8 27 ♖xh8 ♖xh8

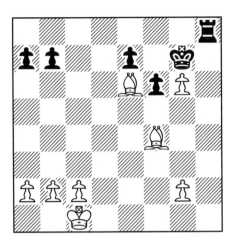

> **Exercise (planning):** Come up with a clear conversion plan for White.

Answer: Step 1: Let g6 go and utilize the queenside pawn majority.

28 c4!

Hodgson, oozing with philanthropic thoughts, wisely adds a pawn to his charitable contributions. Much weaker is the line 28 ♗f5? ♖h1+ 29 ♔d2 ♖f1 30 g3 e5 31 ♔e2 ♖b1 32 ♗e3 ♖xb2 33 ♗xa7 ♖xa2 when Black is still kicking.

28...♔xg6

Step 2: Freeze Black's kingside pawn majority, rendering it worthless.

29 g4!

Hodgson's conversion technique runs so smoothly that one gets the impression that he conducts it an a blasé manner, almost as an afterthought. His last move renders Black's passed e-pawn, never much of a sprinter, into the column of also-rans, well behind White's surging queenside majority. Also, White's bishops continue to toil, side by side, to prevent Black king entry.

29...♖h3 30 ♔d2 a5 31 c5 a4 32 b4

The queenside majority slowly sifts and winds its way up the board.

32...axb3 33 axb3 1-0

Summary: The BDG ...g6 lines don't fare as well when down a full move against our souped-up Tromp, extra tempo version. This game is a model example of how to attack in BDG style.

Game 12
C.Lakdawala-I.Ivanov
Los Angeles (rapid) 2000

Question: Are you regifting this game, which appeared in your London book?

Answer: Well, yes. Having grown ever so much wiser over the last four years, I decided to re-annotate the game from a Tromp perspective.
1 d4 ♘f6

Question: How does the game position arrive from a London move order?

Answer: Like this: 1...d5 2 ♗f4 c5 3 e4!? ♘f6 4 e5 ♘fd7 5 c3 ♕b6 6 ♕d2 e6 7 ♗e3 and we soon transpose to the game. Compare too the position we get in the game to the French Tarrasch line 1...e6 2 e4 d5 3 ♘d2 ♘f6 4 e5 ♘fd7 5 f4 c5 6 ♘df3 ♘c6 7 c3 ♕b6.
2 ♗g5 ♘e4 3 ♗f4 d5 4 f3 ♘f6 5 e4 e6

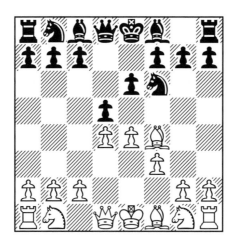

Black, not liking the look of a move-down Blackmar-Diemer Gambit, declines and swerves the position in an odd, French-like situation.
6 e5
White scores a robust 63.5% from this position, according to my database.

Question: Can White retain the central tension?

Answer: White can, but then loses the central-supporting c3 option. White tends to score better with 6 e5, as played in the game.

After 6 ♘c3 ♗b4 (now we get Winawer-like positions) 7 e5 ♘fd7 8 a3 ♗xc3+ 9 bxc3 c5 10 ♗e3 ♕a5 11 ♗d2 ♕a4 12 ♕b1 ♘c6 13 ♗b5 ♕a5 14 ♘e2 a6 15 ♗xc6 bxc6 we have a tale of two colours. Black is weak on the dark, and White weak on the light squares. *Houdini* rates at even. My French intuition warns me that Black got the better of the bargain in P.Ponkratov-N.Matinian, Uljanovsk 2012.

6...♘fd7

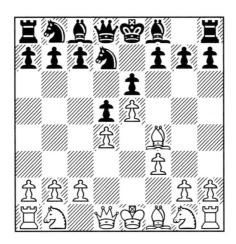

Question: Isn't this a French from hell for White? Black's position looks like a normal Classical French, but White's looks silly, with a redundant f3 and a misaligned f4-bishop.

Answer: It does, indeed, appear that way, but games by top GMs taking on White have convinced me otherwise and I'm not even convinced Black can equalize. I actually argue that White gets a favourable French here. The x-factor: White hasn't played ♘c3, which always allows Black the undermining ...c5 and ...cxd4 in Classical French lines. In the case of our Trompowsky version, we get to play c3, backing up our gargantuan centre. Also, since White is up a tempo, our ♗e3 doesn't constitute a loss of time. Take a close look at this game and the next, and see if you still like Black after about 15 moves into the game.

7 ♗e3 c5 8 c3 ♕b6

I also faced 8...♘c6 9 f4 cxd4 10 cxd4 ♕a5+ 11 ♘d2 ♗b4?! (a bad idea; Black either wastes time after a future a3, or else hands White his good bishop and control over the dark squares; however, 11...♕b4 12 ♖b1 ♘xd4 is met with 13 a3 ♕b6 14 ♔f2! f6 15 exf6 gxf6 16 ♕h5+ ♔d8 17 ♘gf3 e5 18 g3! ♗e7 19 ♗xd4 exd4 20 ♕xd5 when Black is down a pawn and busted) 12 ♘gf3 0-0 13 ♗d3 f5 14 ♖g1 (no need to castle; White plans to attack with g4 next) 14...♗xd2+?! 15 ♗xd2 ♕b6 16 ♗c3 with a clear advantage to White who owns extra space, the bishop-pair, dark-square control and has the potential to attack down the g-file, C.Lakdawala-R.Aeria, San Diego 2004.

9 ♕d2 f6

More normal is 9...♘c6 10 f4 a5, Black's best scoring move in the position (next game we look at 10...♗e7). However, after 11 ♘f3 a4 12 ♗e2 cxd4 13 cxd4 ♗b4 14 ♘c3 a3 15 b3 (the pin looks scary, but it is really just an empty threat, as Kasparov too demonstrates in the next game) 15...0-0 16 ♖c1 ♖e8 17 0-0 ♘f8 18 ♗d3 ♗d7 19 ♕f2 ♖ac8 20 ♘a4 ♕a5 21 ♘c5 ♗xc5 22 ♖xc5 Black was strategically busted with weak dark squares, a massive kingside space disadvantage and a looming white kingside attack, C.Lakdawala-A.Pixton, Internet (blitz) 2000.

10 f4 g5!?

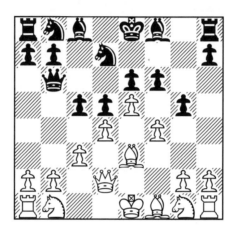

One is reminded of the Geto Boys rap from the movie *Office Space*: "Damn it feels good to be a gangsta!" Such high-stakes risk is rarely rewarded without negative consequences towing along. I add though, any form of attack – even one born of unprincipled abandon – must be treated with respect by the defender. We arrive in one of those positions of unease, for reasons we have trouble defining.

My decades long friend, the late GM Igor Ivanov considered your writer a bit of a donkey in dynamic positions (possibly correctly so), so he follows his complicate-against-the-tactically-blind-man philosophy and unleashes chaos. I'm not sure who is undermining whom here. This is exceedingly dangerous for Black, since he has the potential to fall behind in development from his cramped position.

I expected a quieter line like 10...♘c6 11 ♘f3 ♗e7 12 ♗e2 0-0 13 0-0 a6 14 ♘a3 where I felt White still retained an edge.

11 ♘f3

When in doubt, develop, but this is not White's best option:

a) 11 fxg5?! fxe5 12 dxe5 ♘xe5 when Black already stands better, having wiped out my proud centre.

b) I strongly considered 11 exf6 gxf4 12 f7+ (this zwischenzug disrupts and ensures that Black's king can't castle away to the queenside) 12...♔xf7 13 ♗xf4 ♘c6 14 ♘f3. White looks better since he plans the simple ♗e2 and 0-0, with the safer king.

Answer: I was obsessed with maintaining a huge centre. With hindsight I like this path better for White.

11...g4!?

Igor is intent on mucking the game up. I like Black's position after the simple 11...gxf4!
12 ♗xf4 fxe5 13 ♘xe5 ♗g7 14 ♗e2 0-0 when Black achieved his aim of dismantling White's
central dominance.

12 ♘h4

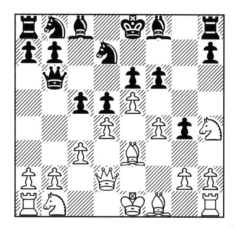

Answer: Well, yes, but I had to stomach it. I just didn't like the look of 12 ♘g1 and would
rather take the knight on the rim than undevelop.

12...♘c6 13 ♗e2 fxe5!?

Black may be overplaying his hand, assuming too much that opening the position favours his side. He should consider locking it up a bit with 13...f5!? 14 h3 h5 15 ♘g6 cxd4!
(15...♖g8? 16 ♘xf8 ♖xf8 17 hxg4 hxg4 18 dxc5 gives White a winning position) 16 cxd4
♗b4 17 ♘c3 ♖g8 18 hxg4! hxg4 (18...♖xg6?! 19 gxf5 looks terrible for Black) 19 ♖h6 ♔f7 20
♘h4 when I feel that White still retains a strategic edge.

14 fxe5 cxd4 15 cxd4

I felt I stood clearly better here.

15...♘dxe5!?

A new crime must be committed to suppress the old. It's a trying experience to face an
opponent who constantly jolts your psyche with endless unpredictability. I overlooked this
tactical idea, but Black's new-found freedom has been won at great cost and the position
still favours White, no matter how I play it.

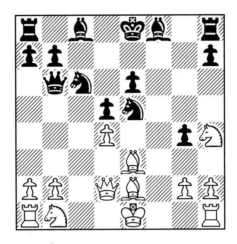

16 0-0!

Simply increasing development lead. Igor expected 16 dxe5 d4 17 ♗f2 ♗b4 18 ♘c3 ♕c5 19 0-0 ♕xe5 20 ♗xg4 0-0 21 ♖ac1 dxc3 22 bxc3 ♗d6 with immense complications.

16...♘g6!

Black is hopelessly behind in development and busted after 16...♘c4? 17 ♗xc4 dxc4 18 ♕f2! ♕c7 19 ♘c3.

17 ♘xg6 hxg6 18 ♘c3 ♗d6 19 g3

I didn't fear his attack down the h-file, due to the principle: the development-down side shouldn't launch an attack.

19...♗d7 20 ♘b5

I didn't want him to castle away after 20 ♗xg4 0-0-0, although *Houdini* still likes White here.

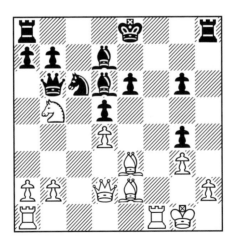

20...♗b8?

I don't understand Igor's abstract desire to go after White's king (well, yes, I do, since Igor gauged extravagant value on a pure attack since he saw that I was his opponent), when his own house is in such disarray. When clocks begin to run low, abstract impressions and half-baked schemes crowd out our bewildered consciousness' ability to properly assimilate the data. Black mistakenly continues to play for mate and pays a heavy price. Retribution directed against the wrong target never fails to create headaches. Two examples:

1. When I was eight years old, I bunged a snowball at the inviting target of my neighbour Francois' fat head, inadvertently clobbering his mother, who lurked just behind him.

2. George W. Bush invaded Iraq as payback for the 911 attack.

Black can't afford to contort like this. Now he never gets the chance to castle long. He had to try 20...♗b4. At times, the only logical avenue open is a dignified reappraisal of intent. I still, though, like White's odds after 21 ♕d3 0-0-0 22 a3 ♗f8 23 b4.

21 a4!

The push of the a-pawn heavily disrupts Black's plans of eventually castling long.

21...a6

21...a5 22 ♗xg4 and Black's king is hopelessly stranded in the middle.

22 a5! ♕d8

22...♘xa5?? hangs a piece to 23 ♖xa5 when b5 doesn't fall.

23 ♗g5 ♘e7

23...♕c8 24 ♗d3 ♘e7 25 ♗xe7 is also hopeless.

24 ♘c3 ♗d6 25 ♗f6 ♖h7 26 ♕g5

Targeting g6.

26...♖h5

26...♕c7 27 ♗xe7 ♖xe7 28 ♕xg6+ ♔d8 29 ♖f8+ ♗e8 30 ♗xg4 ♗xg3 31 hxg3 ♕xg3+ 32 ♔f1 ♔c7 33 ♕f6 ♖h7 34 ♘xd5+! forces mate.

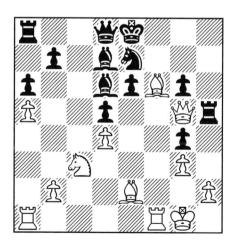

27 ♕xg4?!

Even the hero of a story may have her off days. This wins, but much stronger was:

Answer: The queen sacrifice 27 ♗g7! when Black has no reasonable defence to the f8-threat. Why is it that we are so wise after the fact and so utterly dumbfounded before the event? Such is the nature of our mistakes in life and also over the chessboard.

27...e5

Black can avoid the coming combination with 27...♖f5, but is still busted after 28 ♗d3.

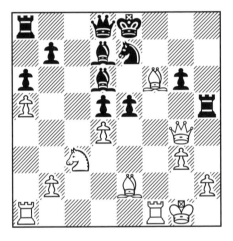

Answer: 28 ♕xh5!

Hooray! Shower the board with gold coins! This move is clear proof of the theory that if you place a monkey at a keyboard and allow him to peck away an infinite number of words, he eventually types in the complete works of Jane Austin.

To witness his half-wit sister bestowed with honours and praise exasperates Black's king beyond his measure of tolerance. For a technical endings player like me, who normally only wins 98-move games by a single tempo, such a sacrifice looks so achingly beautiful that I weep as I write these words. White's queen glances in admiration at her latest acquisition: Black's unfortunate king.

28...gxh5 29 ♗xh5+

White's queen can't do the job by herself, so she sends the bishop to murder Black's king by proxy.

29...♔f8 30 ♗xe7+! ♔xe7

30...♔g8 (not all captains decide to go down with their sinking ship; Black's king decides to join the others in an already overcrowded lifeboat) 31 ♗xd8 ♖xd8 isn't much of a save, since it leaves Black down a rook.

31 ♘xd5+ 1-0

Igor smiled, pointed to the f7-square and offered his hand in resignation. 31...♔e6 32 ♗f7 is mate. The old priest likes to give his blessings with a crowbar. "I realize that you are in great pain," he lectures the king, adding: "but please understand that your suffering is merely a reflection of your own past sins."

Summary: Don't be afraid to enter the French-like 6...e6 7 e5 line, after which it isn't so easy for Black to deal with his or her massive space deficit.

Game 13
G.Kasparov-L.Ribeiro
Lisbon (simul) 1999

1 d4 ♘f6 2 ♗g5

Apparently the Tromp is a major simul weapon for Kasparov.

2...♘e4 3 ♗f4 e6

Be aware that we can transpose to last game's position from this move order as well. Our normal order is 3...d5 4 f3 ♘f6 5 e4 e6 6 e5.

4 f3 ♘f6

We covered 4...♗d6 in the notes to the first game of Chapter One.

5 e4

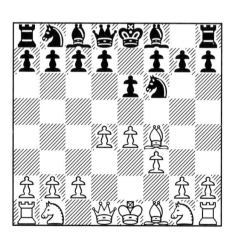

5...d5

Question: Can Black transpose to a Chapter One-type position with 5...c5 6 d5 exd5 7 exd5 ♛b6?

Answer: There is no reason for us to play the retro ♗c1 this time. We can offer the b-pawn with 8 ♘a3!, which is even more powerful than development to c3, which also favours White. We menace both ♘b5 and ♘c4. Now if Black goes for it with 8...♛xb2 White takes over a powerful initiative, starting with 9 ♘b5 ♘a6 (9...♘xd5 10 ♛xd5! ♛xa1+ 11 ♔f2 ♘a6 12 ♗c4 ♛f6 13 ♘h3 ♗e7 14 ♘d6+ ♔f8 15 ♗xa6 wins) 10 ♛e2+! ♔d8 11 ♗e5 ♛b4+ 12 c3 ♛h4+ 13 g3 ♛h5 14 d6 ♘e8 15 0-0-0. Although Black is up a pawn, his entire army looks paralyzed in perpetual stasis.

6 e5 ♘fd7 7 ♗e3

We transpose back to the last game's position.

7...c5 8 c3 ♘c6 9 f4 ♛b6 10 ♛d2 ♗e7

Black sensibly develops.

11 ♘f3 0-0

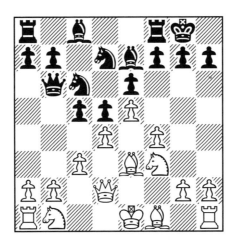

12 ♗e2

Question: Why not develop the bishop to the more aggressive posting on d3?

Answer: That is the move I would play. Perhaps Kasparov was concerned about a ...cxd4 and ...♘b4 counter. 12 ♗d3 cxd4 13 cxd4 ♛a5 (13...♘b4 doesn't seem so scary for White, who can simply back off with 14 ♗e2) 14 ♘c3 b6 (preparing to swap away the bad French bishop via a6) 15 ♖c1 ♗a6 16 0-0 ♗xd3 17 ♛xd3 ♖ac8 (17...f5 18 exf6 ♖xf6 19 a3 looks favourable for White as well) 18 f5 ♘b4 19 ♛b1 ♛a6 (White quickly builds up a winning attack after 19...exf5 20 ♛xf5 ♘b8 21 e6 f6 22 a3 ♘4c6 23 ♘h4 ♖cd8 24 ♛g4 ♔h8 25 ♘f5 g6

26 ♗h6 ♖fe8 27 ♞xe7 ♖xe7 28 ♖xf6 and Black is crushed) 20 ♖cd1 ♞c6 was V.Milo-
L.Sandler, Suncoast 1999. Now 21 f6! looks like a promising pawn sac: 21...gxf6 22 exf6
♗xf6 23 ♗h6 and Black's king is in grave danger.

12...cxd4

> *Question:* Shouldn't Black be tossing in 12...f6?

Answer: I still like White's chances after 13 0-0 ♕a5 14 a3 fxe5 15 fxe5 cxd4 16 cxd4 ♕xd2
17 ♞bxd2. Black may have removed the queens from the board, but hasn't quite reached
the level of full equality, due to White's nagging space advantage.

13 cxd4 ♞a5

Provoking White's next move, which weakens him on the dark squares.

14 b3!

> *Question:* Isn't White concerned about ...♗b4?

Answer: If you go back to the last game and take a look at my game in the notes against
Pixton, we see that Black can't make tangible gains with the pin.

14...♞b8?!

A move suffused with idealism, rather than practicality. Black contorts in the hopes of
unravelling his queenside, wandering the periphery of the real issue: his king's safety or
lack of it. Alternatives were:

a) 14...♗b4 15 ♞c3 and then what? Black has no good way to exploit the pin. Meanwhile, White continues to build for a kingside attack.

b) I would toss in 14...f5! which makes Black's king a lot safer.

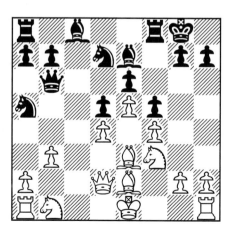

> *Question:* How would White continue in that case?

Answer: Something like this: 15 ♘c3 ♘b8 16 ♘a4 ♕d8 17 ♕b2! (seizing control over a3 and thereby preventing ...♗a3 shenanigans) 17...b6 18 ♗d2 ♗a6 (Black feels the squeeze after 18...♘ac6 19 b4!) 19 ♗xa5 bxa5 20 ♗xa6 ♘xa6 21 0-0 ♖c8 22 ♖ac1 when White retains a slight edge due to his extra space.

15 ♘c3 ♗d7

15...f5 isn't so effective if a black knight is unable to recapture on f6: 16 exf6 ♖xf6 17 0-0. Black suffers strategically, due to the e5 hole and the backward e6-pawn.

16 0-0 ♘a6 17 f5! ♖ac8?

Black had to try 17...♗b4 18 f6 ♖fc8 (the correct rook: f8 must be kept clear for the dark-squared bishop) 19 ♖ac1 g6 with at least some hope of surviving White's coming kingside onslaught.

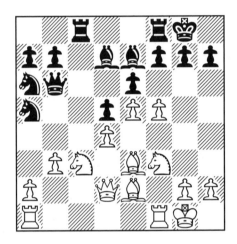

> **Exercise (planning):** If you are going to start an argument, then choose your time wisely. Black's attempt at queenside confrontation couldn't have come at a more mistimed moment, and reminds us of the officer who requested Napoleon for a raise in pay during the retreat from Moscow. Black's last move gave Kasparov an opportunity to launch a devastating attack. What would you play here?

Answer: Demolition of the king's position. Offer a pawn to pry open the kingside. In such situations confrontation becomes the much needed drug for the attacker's side.

18 f6! ♗b4

Black bleeds time and money on maintenance of his queenside concern, which should be dissolved as painlessly as possible to see to the needs of his king. This looks scary, but soon the volume of Black's queenside threats gradually diminish, until they reach zero. However, if 18...gxf6 19 exf6 ♗xf6 (19...♗b4?? 20 ♗h6 forces mate) 20 ♘e5! (both f6 and d7 hang; Black's next move is forced) 20...♗xe5 21 dxe5 ♕b4 22 ♗h6 when Black's king has no chance of survival.

19 ♖ac1?

Kasparov misses a quick crush with 19 fxg7! ♖fd8 (19...♗xc3 20 gxf8♕+ ♔xf8 21 ♗h6+ ♔e8 22 ♕g5 is slaughter) 20 ♘g5! ♖xc3 21 ♗h5! ♗e8 22 ♕f2 ♕c7 23 ♕h4! h6 24 ♗xf7+ forcing mate. We must remember that this is a simul game and White, in a sense is merely a facsimile Kasparov, who frantically divides his brain-power to 25 or so other boards.

19...♕c7?

If 19...g6 20 ♗f2 ♖fd8 21 ♘g5 (intending ♕e3 and ♕h3) 21...♗f8 22 ♕e3.

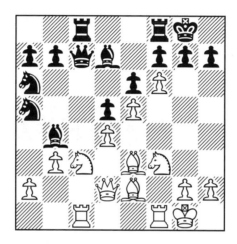

> **Exercise (combination alert):** The hanging
> c3-knight is irrelevant. White to play and force the win.

20 ♗f2

White touches upon the chord, but misses the combination's full pattern. Black's structure is clearly susceptible to further degradation on the dark squares. White's bishop removes the camouflage, revealing true intent: ♕g5, which if allowed, forces mate. There is a fine distinction between making a threat and actually taking action. Much stronger was:
Answer: 20 ♗h6! (after the general plan is formulated, the ironing out of details is never inconsequential) 20...g6 21 ♗xf8 ♗xf8 (this unfortunate unpin is forced, since Black must cover against ♕h6) 22 ♘xd5 ♕d8 23 ♘e7+ ♗xe7 24 fxe7 ♕b6 25 ♖xc8+ ♗xc8 26 ♕h6 mates.

20...h6 21 ♕f4!

The queen approaches with sinister calm. So far her contribution to the overall discussion hasn't been much, but now her reticence is about to change. For the first time in the game, Black's king is reminded of the queen's existence, and she has the feeling he won't soon forget her. Also crushing is 21 fxg7 ♔xg7 22 ♗h4.

21...♕d8

If you spitefully toss a person into a body of water and then, thinking better of it, rescue the person from drowning, this doesn't make you a hero. This is exactly what happened in this game to Black's king. Black's future appears as endless grey, devoid of joy of any kind. Black philosophizes: it's a tough juggle to turn tail and run, and at the same time, keep one's dignity intact. But if there is a trade-off between loss of dignity and survival, we should take survival every time. In this case, however, it's too late for Black's king, who is beyond all saving.

Instead, 21...♗xc3 22 fxg7 ♔xg7 23 ♗e3 ♖h8 24 ♕f6+ ♔g8 25 ♘g5 ♗c6 26 ♗h5! mates.

22 ♕g3 g6 23 ♕f4

Black's king just can't seem to rid himself of the hospitable queen's tiresome society.

23...♖e8

23...♔h7 24 ♗e3 forces mate.

24 ♕xh6 ♗f8 25 ♕h4

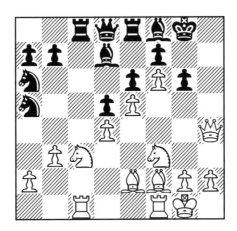

The embarrassed black king stammers incoherently at the queen's monstrous imputation: he will soon be mated. "Can we not let bygones be bygones?" he asks the queen. Unfortunately, from her hateful expression, he surmises her answer: "No!". The threat is ♘g5, to which there is no defence. Black's king reacts to the queen's advances in much the same way I did at age six, after being kissed repeatedly by a giant, great aunt. My cheeks twitch involuntarily to this very day, in recollection of those wet, puffy lips.

25...♗g7 26 ♘g5 1-0

Summary: White's space advantage in this French-like declined line can easily morph into a deadly kingside assault.

Game 14
S.Drazic-A.Papastavropoulos
Corinth 2000

1 d4 ♘f6 2 ♗g5 ♘e4 3 ♗f4 d5 4 f3 ♘d6

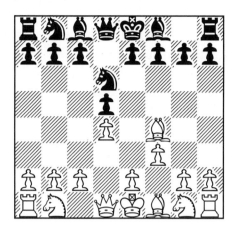

Question: Why would Black choose d6 over the more natural f6 retreat?

Answer: Black, as in the last two games of the chapter, plans to decline the tempo-down Blackmar-Diemer Gambit. Which means we enter another hybrid, French-like position. When White engineers e4 and e5, Black's knight heads for f5, rather than d7, which we saw in the last two games. I'm not sure if this line is better or worse than the f6 alternative and I think it just may be a matter of taste.

5 ♘c3 c6

5...e6 6 e4 c6 transposes to our next game.

6 e4 dxe4?!

Black, seeking some freedom, agrees to a high cost by allowing White central dominance. Next game we look at the superior line 6...e6.

7 fxe4 ♕b6

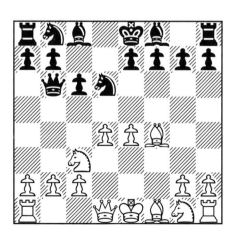

Black banked on this disruptive move to justify his abandonment of central control.

8 b3

A new move, and more logical than 8 ♖b1, as in R.Wilczek-U.Reinartz, Leverkusen 1998, since with b3, White can later try and build with c4.

> *Question:* Can White offer a pawn with 8 ♕d2?

Answer: No one has ever been brave enough to try it, but it looks logical to me. White gets tons of compensation after 8...♕xb2 9 ♖b1 ♕a3 10 ♘f3 with a massive development lead. Look, if your normally chicken-hearted writer is willing to sacrifice the pawn, then everyone should as well.

8...♕a5 9 ♕d2 e6

> *Question:* Since White weakened the dark squares with b3,
> should Black fianchetto to take aim at the d4- and c3-squares?

Answer: It's not very effective after 9...g6 10 ♘f3 ♗g7 11 e5! ♘b5 (11...♘f5 drops a piece to 12 g4) 12 ♘xb5 ♕xd2+ 13 ♔xd2 cxb5 14 ♗xb5+ with a clean extra pawn in the ending, along with the superior position as well.

10 ♗d3 ♘a6

Houdini suggests the odd unravelling scheme 10...f6 intending ...♘f7, which looks awfully slow to me.

11 ♘ge2 ♘b4

He gets the bishop-pair at the cost of falling even further behind in development.

12 0-0 ♘xd3 13 ♕xd3

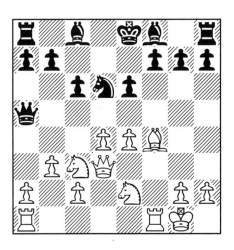

13...♘b5

Answer: The trouble is your suggestion is met with 14 ♛g3! with a deadly double attack on
d6 and g7.

Answer: White responds with 14 e5 ♞f5 (14...♞b5 15 ♞e4, intending c4, is even worse for
Black) 15 g4!, and if 15...♞h4 16 ♝g5 ♞g6 17 ♞e4. Now if Black tries to castle queenside,
starting with 17...h6, White crosses up the intention with 18 ♛f3!. White's queen flashes a
smile in the black king's direction with calculated insincerity. Sometimes good, old-
fashioned conniving beats hard work on the chessboard. After 18...hxg5 19 ♛xf7+ ♚d8 20
♛xg6 Black can resign.

14 ♞xb5 ♛xb5

14...cxb5 15 ♝d2 ♛b6 16 ♛f3 also looks rough for Black, who is grossly behind in development.

15 c4 ♛h5 16 ♝e3

Even stronger is the entrenchment plan 16 c5! f6 17 ♝d6.

16...f6

More non-development. This move substantiates Black's misgivings about his early decision to fall so far behind in development. Black probably feared 16...♝e7 17 ♞f4.

17 ♞f4 ♛f7 18 e5

Principle: create confrontation when leading in development.

18...♝e7 19 d5!

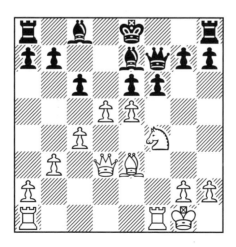

Same principle applied.

19...0-0

Question: Isn't Black playing curiously without ambition?
Shouldn't he try something more active like 19...exd5?

Answer: Black is unlikely to survive 20 cxd5 fxe5 21 ♘e6 ("Her ladyship will be most displeased," laments the c8-bishop at the knight's intrusion into the queen's chambers) 21...♗f6 22 ♕c4 ♗xe6 23 dxe6 ♕c7 24 ♖ad1 (threat: ♖d7) 24...♖d8 25 ♗xa7.

20 d6

Clogging Black's bishops and erecting a deeply entrenched passed d-pawn, which soon induce Black's forces into a near-cataleptic state. The last few moves have proven to be strategically profitable for White.

20...♗d8

The long suffering bishop's great curse is that his profession doesn't allow scope for malicious slander, which he would so dearly like to do this moment in the direction of the d6-intruder.

21 g4!?

After winning a war, the victorious general must soothe the simmering anger of the conquered populace, who may be easily incited into insurgency. Such a move feels antithetical to White's goal of consolidation. I don't see the necessity for this potentially weakening move. Why not just the weakness-free 21 ♗d4 with a crushing bind?

21...♗d7

Black decides to humour the outburst and ignore it. Black can't develop or survive after 21...fxe5 22 ♘d5 exd5 (or 22...♕e8 23 ♖xf8+ ♕xf8 24 ♖f1 ♕e8 25 ♘c7 ♗xc7 26 dxc7) 23 ♖xf7 ♖xf7 24 cxd5 ♗xg4 25 dxc6 bxc6 26 ♖f1. The d6-pawn is too cramping and White's queen has access to multiple pawn targets.

22 h3 b6

22...fxe5? 23 ♘xe6! ♕xe6 24 ♖xf8+ ♔xf8 25 ♕xh7 gives White a winning attack.

23 c5 bxc5 24 ♗xc5 f5

Equally depressing is 24...fxe5 25 ♘g2 ♕e8 26 ♖xf8+ ♕xf8 27 ♖f1 ♕e8 28 ♘e3 ♗f6 29 ♘c4 a5 30 ♕e4.

25 gxf5 ♕xf5

Black labours strenuously to keep White's ambitious forces at bay, and the defence manages to pull itself together – just barely – through a painfully laborious process. Black agrees to enter a wretched ending, since even worse is 25...exf5 26 ♖ae1 ♗e6 27 d7 ♗e7 28 ♘xe6 ♕xe6 29 ♗xe7 ♕xe7 30 e6.

26 ♕xf5 ♖xf5 27 ♘d3 ♖g5+ 28 ♔h2 ♗b6 29 ♖f4 ♖d8 30 ♖e1 ♖f8 31 ♖ef1 ♖gf5 32 ♖xf5 exf5

The trouble is now White gets a stranglehold with his two deep passers.

33 h4!

An alert move, preventing Black from easily rolling his majority with ...g5.

33...♖e8 34 ♖f4 ♗e6

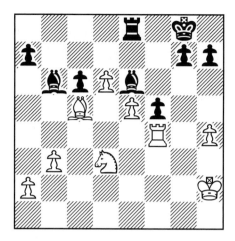

Exercise (planning): A casual glance at White's passers tell us he is winning. Come up with a clear consolidation plan.

Answer: Apply heat to b6, after which the defence collapses. The b6-defender clearly overstayed his welcome.

35 ♖b4!

Nothing passes by with the white rook's knowledge. In his terrible realm, he is the all-seeing creature with 100 eyes. Until now, the opposing bishops were resolved and their opinions coincided, both thinking: "b6 is mine!".

35...♗d8

The shamed bishop, by his abandonment of b6, leaves his brother in charge by default. White responds to 35...♖b8 with 36 a4.

36 ♖b8 ♔f7 37 ♖b7+ ♔g6

Now Black's king comes under fire as well, but 37...♔g8 38 d7 is curtains.

38 ♘f4+

The knight waves a fluttery adieu to Black's king, who is too busy running to notice.

38...♔h6

Black's king, now all alone, attempts to make himself as small as possible. It does him no good, since white attackers know the location of his hiding place.

39 ♗e3

With a deadly discovery threat. "I find your answers to my questions...unsatisfactory," White's bishop tells Black's king, with a terrifyingly long pause.

39...g5 40 ♘xe6 ♖xe6 41 ♗xg5+ 1-0

Removing the final defender to promotion of his d6-pawn.

Summary: If Black is going to enter the 4...♘d6 line, he should avoid 6...dxe4?! which hands White central dominance.

Game 15
J.Hall-E.Jensson
Hafnarfjordur 1997

1 d4 ♘f6 2 ♗g5 ♘e4 3 ♗f4 d5 4 f3 ♘d6 5 ♘c3 e6

Question: Does it make any difference if Black plays 5...c6 first?

Answer: No. After 6 e4 e6 we transpose. Instead, 6...dxe4?! 7 fxe4 ♕b6 transposes to the last game.

6 e4 c6

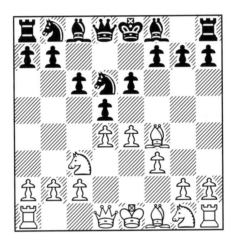

Black erects a Caro-Kann-like wall and dares White to attain something tangible with his space advantage.

7 ♕d2

Question: Is there any difference between this move and 7 ♗d3?

Answer: The latter move allows Black to go pawn hunting with 7...♕b6 8 ♘ge2 ♕xb2 9 ♖b1 ♕a3 10 0-0, E.Bricard-L.Bergez, Paris 1998. There have only been two tests of this position (White lost both!), but it feels to me like White gets loads of compensation for the pawn. Obviously, more tests are needed – maybe one of your games?

7...♘d7

The trouble with this move is Black condemns himself to a bad c8-bishop. One other reason to play ♕d2 before ♗d3 is that if Black plays 7...b6! intending ...♗a6, we can take on a6 in one tempo, rather than two. I think this is still Black's best plan in the position. M.Granados Gomez-E.Camps Tarres, Sant Cebria 1998, continued 8 0-0-0! (logical, since a future ...b5 now comes with tempo loss for Black) 8...♗e7 9 g4 ♗a6 10 ♗xd6 ♕xd6 11 ♔b1 (I would consider taking on a6, which may slightly displace Black's knight) 11...♗xf1 12 ♖xf1 b5 13 e5 ♕d7 14 ♘ge2 c5 15 dxc5 ♗xc5 16 ♘d4 b4 17 ♘ce2 0-0 18 f4 with a Classical French-like position which looks difficult to assess – perhaps dynamically equal. Such a position requires Stone Age logic: I will kill you before you kill me.

8 ♗d3 ♗e7 9 ♘ge2 b5!

A new move, and a good one, with dual purpose:

1. Black pretty much puts an end to speculations about White castling queenside.

2. Black seizes valuable queenside space.

Instead, after the 9...♘c4 10 ♗xc4 dxc4 of I.Argandona Riveiro-J.Diaz Rodriguez, Burgos 2003, perhaps White can try 11 e5!? intending to occupy e4 with a knight.

10 0-0

White can also toss in the immediate 10 b3.

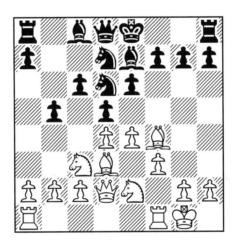

10...♘b6

Question: What happens if Black enters c4?

Answer: It looks to me like White maintains a tiny edge after 10...♘c4 11 ♕c1!? b4 12 ♘d1 ♕b6 13 ♗xc4 dxc4 14 ♘e3 ♗a6 15 c3.

11 b3 0-0 12 e5

Battle lines are drawn and White prepares a kingside attack.

12...♘f5 13 g4

The logical follow-up. With the expansion, the slow trend of the game is about to alter sharply, as White begins to express designs on his neighbours to the South.

13...♘h4 14 ♗g3 a5

Black intends to keep expanding on the queenside.

15 f4 g6?!

Civility is a much overvalued commodity in the midst of raging war. Suddenly, this is getting scary for Black, since malevolent, amorphous shapes twist and blur, just outside the black king's range of vision. Still, this move feels wrong and Black should have held back. Not only does Black's last move create kingside pawn weakness (to suppress f5), but he also leaves his knight dangling on h4, without a retreat square. Now Black's robust counterattack unexpectedly contracts a serious illness.

I think he was better off leaving the kingside pawns alone and pressing on with a central counter with 15...b4 16 ♘d1 c5 17 f5 exf5 18 gxf5 (threat: f6) 18...♗g5 19 ♗f4 ♗e7 (Black threatens both ...c4 and ...♘xf5) 20 ♘e3 cxd4 21 ♘xd4 ♗c5 22 c3 ♖e8 with a completely unclear situation, which *Houdini* rates as even. It's 50-50 if White's pawns are over-extended or a potent attacking force.

16 ♔h1

Just in case he needs ♖g1 later on.

16...♔g7

If 16...b4 17 ♘d1 ♗b7 18 f5 ♗g5 19 ♘f4 c5 20 f6 ♘d7 21 ♗xh4 ♗xh4 22 ♘g2!.

17 ♕e3 h6 18 ♖g1 ♘c4?

This move only helps White. Black remains in the game after 18...b4 19 ♘d1 a4 20 ♖b1.

19 bxc4 bxc4

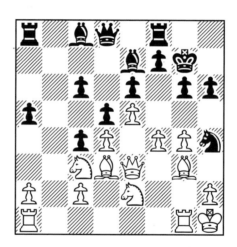

> *Exercise (planning/combination alert):* If you find the correct idea,
> Black's plans are thrown violently off track into a losing position.
> So far, White's pieces assumed the easy attitude of one lying in wait
> for a target's approach. Now it's time to push White's game from
> the angry rhetoric stage to open violence. What would you play here?

Answer: 20 ♗xh4!

Step 1: Lure Black's bishop to h4.

20...♗xh4

Now comes Step 2: Entomb the h4-bishop, who is doomed to live out his days in isolation.

21 g5!

Black's incongruous bishop, much like the uncle who shows up at your wedding wearing a Hawaiian shirt, looks totally out of his element on h4.

21...cxd3 22 cxd3 ♖h8 23 ♖g4!

Forcing Black to open the f-file.

23...hxg5 24 fxg5

There is no good defence to ♕f4.

24...♖h5

24...♗a6 25 ♕f4 ♗xg5 26 ♖xg5 ♗xd3 was also hopeless for Black.

25 ♘f4! ♖h7

25...♖xg5 26 ♖xh4 picks off the bishop.

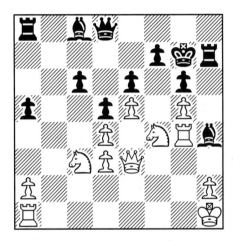

> **Exercise (combination alert):** White to play and win the h4-bishop.

Answer: Simply attack it more than it can be defended.

26 ♘g2

The trapped bishop lies still as a carcass, hanging in a meat freezer in the back of the butcher's shop. Black, with a lump in his throat, can do nothing but mutely watch White's open thievery.

26...♕h8

Black's queen rapidly loses all authority in her shrinking realm.

27 ♕f4

"It is your prerogative: die quickly or die slowly. It depends on your answer to my question," White's queen informs the bishop.

27...♗f2

Black's bishop, with little hope of engineering a reconciliation with his team-mates, decides to plot one final (and not so hard-to-see) cheapo.

28 ♖f1 1-0

The speechless bishop is hard pressed to fit an adjective to the white army's rudeness. Certainly not 28 ♕xf2?? (it was Zoloft-seeking King Lear who lamented: "O, that way madness lies!") 28...♖xh2+ 29 ♔g1 ♖h1 mate. Such fairy tale endings happen so very rarely in real life – especially against a GM.

Summary: The 4...♘d6, ...e6, ...c6 formation is in my opinion one of Black's best choices verses the BDG line. The positions are French-like and, I believe, a better version for Black than the ...♘f6 BDG declined lines.

Game 16
C.Lakdawala-R.Bruno
San Diego (rapid) 2007

1 d4 ♘f6 2 ♗g5 ♘e4 3 ♗f4 d5 4 e3

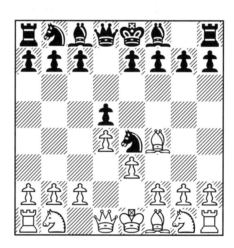

"Clearly the best choice for White," writes Tromp expert IM Richard Pert. White seeks a quieter game and refuses the f3 tempo gain.

> *Question:* Have we transposed to a London System?

Answer: Not quite. If Black's knight were on f6, then we would be in a London.

> *Question:* Does Black's knight on e4 constitute a plus or a minus for our side?

Answer: I think a plus, since we can play to undermine Black's knight, or later gain a tempo with f3, or create imbalance with a timely ♗d3 and ♗xe4, depending on circumstances.

4...c5

In this chapter we concentrate on this, Black's main move. Alternatives:

a) 4...e6 5 ♗d3 (5 ♘d2 may be too milquetoast to offer White an edge, although after 5...b6?! 6 ♘xe4 dxe4 7 ♗b5+ c6 8 ♗a4 White leads in development and has the superior structure, C.Lakdawala-D.Arutyunov 2010; however, I doubt that White can make anything of his slight development lead after the simple 5...♘xd2 6 ♕xd2 ♗d6 7 ♗d3) 5...♗d6 and now:

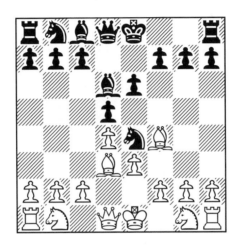

a1) 6 ♘e2 was given an exclam by GM Peter Wells, and is also Pert's choice. However, I think White's best shot is with the move I played, chopping on e4. I may be wrong, but the e2 posting in a London-like position looks too sedate to produce an much of an edge for White.

a2) 6 ♗xe4!? (the most combative; White creates a quick imbalance) 6...♗xf4 7 exf4 dxe4 8 ♘c3 ♘c6 (8...f5 9 f3 ♘c6 10 fxe4 ♕xd4 11 ♕xd4 ♘xd4 12 0-0-0 – White enjoys a huge development lead in the ending – 12...c5 13 exf5 exf5 was C.Lakdawala-S.Ramanujam, San Diego (rapid) 2013, and now after 14 ♘f3! ♘xf3 15 gxf3 0-0 16 ♖he1 Black has a devil of a time completing development) 9 ♘ge2 f5 10 ♕d2 b6 11 0-0-0 ♗a6 12 d5! (opening the position when leading in development) 12...exd5 13 ♘xd5 ♗c4. In this position Mamed took a big gamble with 14 ♕c3!? (the simple 14 ♘ec3! 0-0 15 ♕e3 ♕c8 16 f3 exf3 17 ♕xf3 looks quite favourable for White, who once again leads massively in development) 14...♗xd5 15 ♕xg7 ♖g8 16 ♕xh7 ♕d6 17 ♕xf5 with a completely unclear position, S.Mamedyarov-Wei Ye, Tromso 2013.

b) 4...♗f5 5 f3 (this move, far from weakening, can be a useful extra tempo in this line as well) 5...♘f6 6 c4 e6 7 ♘c3 (now ♕b3 is in the air) 7...♗b4 8 ♕b3 ♘c6 9 a3 ♗xc3+ 10 ♕xc3 0-0 (10...♘h5 11 ♗g3 dares Black to open the h-file) 11 ♘e2 ♗g6 12 h4!? (12 ♗g3 would be the strategic route) 12...♖e8 was M.Carlsen-J.Polgar, Rishon Le Zion (blitz) 2006, where Polgar played for a central ...e5 disruptive thrust. Carlsen should probably have gone for 13 ♖d1 and followed with g4, with an ultra-sharp battle ahead.

c) We examine 4...c6 in the final game of the chapter.

d) 4...g6 5 ♗d3 ♗g7 6 ♗xe4 dxe4 7 ♘c3 c5 8 ♘ge2 ♗g4 9 ♘xe4 cxd4 10 exd4 was G.Hernandez Guerrero-A.Martinez, San Luis 2013. Now if Black wants his pawn back he must enter 10...♗xe2 11 ♕xe2 ♕xd4 12 c3 ♕a4 13 ♘d6+ ♔f8 14 ♘e4 with a clear developmental lead for White.

e) 4...♘d7 (Black keeps both ...g6 and ...e6 possibilities open) 5 ♗d3 and then:

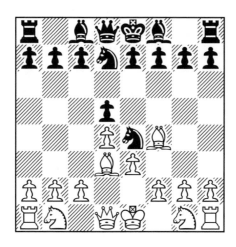

e1) 5...♘df6?! (Black's main move and in my opinion inferior to 'e2') 6 f3 ♘d6 7 ♘c3 e6 (Black may have been better off with 7...g6 8 e4 ♘h5 9 ♗e3 c6 10 ♘ge2, although I still like White due to his extra central influence) 8 e4 ♘h5 9 ♗e3 ♗e7 10 g4! (Black's game just gets worse and worse) 10...dxe4 11 fxe4 ♗h4+ 12 ♔f1 f5 (12...♘f6 13 e5 doesn't look encouraging either for Black) 13 e5 fxg4 14 ♕xg4 0-0+ 15 ♔e2 ♘f5 16 ♘f3 and Black has precious little compensation for the piece he is about to lose, J.Hodgson-D.Paunovic, Cacak 1996.

e2) After 5...g6 6 ♗xe4 dxe4 7 ♘c3 ♘f6 8 ♗e5 ♗h6 9 ♘ge2 0-0 10 ♗xf6 exf6 11 ♘xe4 Black's bishop-pair may offer some compensation for the pawn, I.Schneider-L.Gutman, Schwaebisch Gmuend 2010. If given a choice I still take White, though, as his position looks solid enough and a pawn is a pawn,

f) 4...♘c6 (the Tromp Chigorin?) 5 ♗d3 f5!? 6 ♘c3!? e6 7 ♗xe4 dxe4 8 ♘b5 ♗d6 9 ♕h5+ g6 10 ♕h6 ♕e7 11 ♘xd6+ cxd6 12 ♘e2 and White's dark-square bind gave him the better chances, C.Bauer-J.Le Roux, Belfort 2003.

Returning to Black's main choice, 4...c5:

5 ♗d3

Our tabiya position for this line.

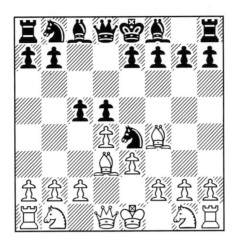

5...♘f6

The players assess and arrive at different conclusions. This is Black's main move in the position, which leads to a London System a full move down for Black, since he took three moves for his knight to reach f6, while it took us only two to get our bishop to f4.

> **Question:** Is it a big deal to enter a London a move down?
> Can White exploit an extra move in such a quiet opening?

Answer: I admit this isn't exactly scintillating stuff, but I play the London as White, so for me at least, it feels like Christmas day when I get a normal position a full move up. I'm not so confident in Black's alleged equality here. In the coming games we look at 5...cxd4.

Instead, after 5...♘c6 6 ♗xe4 dxe4 7 d5 Black's knight loses time. The position has the look and feel of an Albin Countergambit in reverse.

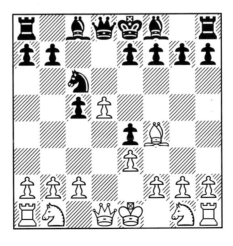

Answer: In the Albin, Black sacrifices a pawn for a development lead. In the Tromp version, White remains materially even while retaining the developmental benefits. We have:

a) 7...♘b4 8 ♘c3 e6 (not much of a freeing move, but after the 8...♗f5 9 a3 ♘a6 10 ♘ge2 g6 of H.Nakamura-S.Mamedyarov, Moscow (blitz) 2010, *Houdini* rates the position as substantially better for White after 11 ♘g3 ♗g7 12 0-0 ♕d7 13 ♘gxe4 ♗xe4 14 ♘xe4 ♖d8 15 c4 ♗xb2 16 ♖b1 when d6 looms over Black, who is desperately behind in development) 9 d6 (this move puts a damper on Black's development plans; White scores over 80% from this position) 9...♘c6 10 ♘ge2 sees White leading in development.

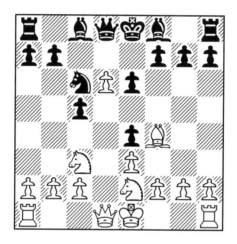

10...f5 is multipurpose:

1. Black hangs on to his e4-pawn.

2. Black offers his king luft on f7, which becomes exceedingly important after White's next move.

Answer: Because White has no intention of moving his bishop and giving up d6. White would play 11 ♘b5! exf4 12 ♘c7+ ♔d7 13 ♕d5! ♘b4 (or 13...♖b8?? 14 ♕xf7+ ♘e7 15 0-0-0 and Black could resign) 14 ♕xf7+ ♔c6 15 0-0-0 ♗xd6 16 ♘xa8. *Houdini* rates the game at even, but we humans all understand that in real life White has good practical chances to win since Black's defensive task isn't easy.

After 10...f5 11 ♘b5 ♔f7 12 ♘c7 ♖b8 13 g4! Black's king faced a fierce kingside assault in V.Ivanchuk-B.Jobava, Havana 2005.

b) Also possible is the counterattacking 7...e5 8 ♗g3 ♘e7 9 ♘c3 f6 (as in H.Nakamura-J.Polgar, London (rapid) 2013; I also like White's development lead after 9...h5 10 f3 h4 11

♗f2 exf3 12 ♘xf3). At this point *Houdini* offers the line 10 ♕h5+ g6 11 ♕e2 with advantage to White, who will castle queenside. Also ♕b5+ is in the air.

> **Question:** What if Black goes pawn hunting with 5...♕b6 6 ♗xe4 ♕xb2?

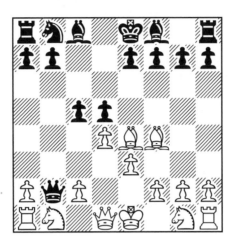

Answer: I would be overjoyed if Black went pawn hunting like this. White gets loads of compensation after 7 ♘d2 dxe4 8 ♘e2 cxd4 9 ♘xd4 f5 10 ♖b1 ♕xa2 11 ♘b5 ♘a6 12 c4, E.Vegh-S.Torok, Hungarian League 2008; ♗e5 comes next, when Black can barely move. Black will be hard pressed to survive the next 20 moves.

We now return to the much more solid 5...♘f6:

6 c3 ♘c6 7 ♘d2 e6

Instead, 7...♗g4 8 ♘gf3 e6 9 0-0 (9 ♕a4!? in Queen's Gambit Declined, Cambridge Springs style is interesting) 9...♗d6 10 ♕b3! ♕e7 (10...♖b8 11 dxc5! wins a pawn) 11 ♗xd6 ♕xd6 was B.Bogosavljevic-D.Boskovic, Kragujevac 2013. Black fails to obtain compensation for the pawn after 12 ♕xb7 ♖b8 13 dxc5 ♕xc5 14 ♕a6 0-0 (14...♖xb2?? drops a rook to 15 ♕c8+) 15 b4!.

8 ♘gf3 ♗d6 9 ♗g3

Daring Black to open the h-file. Meanwhile, White plans a Stonewall style attack with ♘e5 and f4. Remember, I am used to this position a full move down for White, so this feels like a crushing position from my perspective!.

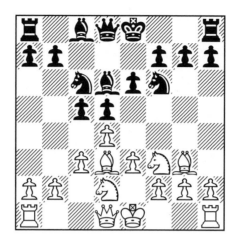

9...cxd4?!

A new move. This d4 capture is commonly played in London, Colle and Torre Attack positions, but not-so-great for Black in all three.

> *Question:* How does this move help White's side?

Answer: It opens the e-file for White, which means Black's thematic ...e5 break becomes very difficult to achieve. Also, White's control over e5 means it will be easier for our side to play ♘e5, building up for a kingside attack. Black should try something like 9...♗xg3 10 hxg3 ♕d6 11 ♕e2, but not then 11...e5?!. Believe it or not, Black's thematic last move was premature, M.Rodshtein-A.Huzman, Beer Sheva 2013. In this position White had 12 dxe5 ♘xe5 13 e4!. Suddenly Black finds himself in danger: 13...♘xd3+ 14 ♕xd3 ♕e7 15 e5 h6 16 0-0 ♘g4 17 ♕xd5 ♗e6 18 ♕e4 0-0 and Black doesn't have enough compensation for the pawn.

10 exd4 ♗xg3!?

It isn't all that easy for White to make use of the open h-file. Black can also consider 10...0-0.

11 hxg3 h6 12 ♕e2 ♕c7 13 0-0!?

The sharper 13 0-0-0!? may be better, but doesn't suit my style.

13...0-0 14 ♖fe1 b6 15 ♖ad1 ♗b7 16 ♗b1 ♖fe8

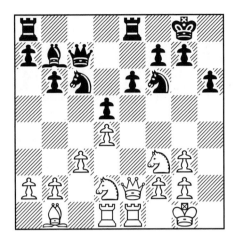

17 ♕d3!?

> *Question:* Why did you allow your opponent to free his game
> with ...e5, when you could clamp down on it with 17 ♘e5?

Answer: It's a stylistic decision. I preferred to play a favourable isolani position rather than build for an attack with your suggested move.

17...e5!?

When I was in college, I was fascinated with the stars and toyed with the idea of an astronomy minor. Then I took Astronomy 101, which was full of maths, physics and other distasteful subjects, none of which had to do with the important matters of stars, aliens or spaceships. Moral: just because you are attracted to something, doesn't mean you will like it when you get it. Often our default reaction to strategic misfortune is to lash out at an uncaring universe. Black's freeing break is logical, yet I don't believe fully equalizes. If he doesn't play it, though, White begins to build for a kingside attack, based on occupation of e5, along with kingside pawn pushes.

18 dxe5 ♘xe5 19 ♘xe5 ♖xe5 20 ♖xe5 ♕xe5 21 ♘f3 ♕h5

Black persists in his preoccupation of kingside activity. This 'attack' feels too straightforward, too easy to refute – a two dimensional entity in a 3D world. I would have played 21...♕c7 to keep queens on the board.

22 ♕f5

An endgame favours White because of Black's isolani and bad bishop. The counterattack is met with a counter, counterattack. Black faces strategic retribution for the presumption of initiative, when he never really owned it in the first place.

22...♕xf5

The hoped-for attack evaporates.

23 ♗xf5 ♖e8

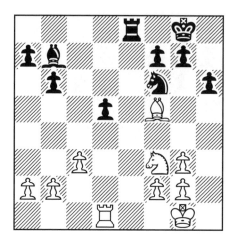

Answer: 24 ♘d4

White's plan: f3, ♔f2, ♗c2, ♗b3, ♘c2, ♘e3 and ♖d4, exerting maximum pressure on Black's already creaking position.

24...g6 25 ♗c2 a6 26 f3 h5 27 ♔f2 ♔g7 28 ♗b3 ♖e5!?

Lateral defence by a rook tends to be awkward. The trouble is d8 is vulnerable to an eventual c4, playing on the pin.

29 ♘c2 ♔f8 30 ♘e3 g5!?

Sometimes when our best policy is to simply wait, our tendency is to play an 'interesting' move, even if it further erodes our defensive barrier. He accepts a weakness at f5 in exchange for the more abstract notion of staying 'active'. I would have left this pawn alone.

31 ♖d4

Mission accomplished. This is the position I had in mind. Black, badly tied down, faces a futureless future of eternal stasis. Also, contamination of the weakened dark squares slowly leaks into every aspect of his troubles.

31...♔e7 32 ♗c2

Eyeing f5. Also possible is the immediate 32 f4 gxf4 33 gxf4 ♖e4 34 ♗c2.

32...♗c8?

32...♖e6 was necessary.

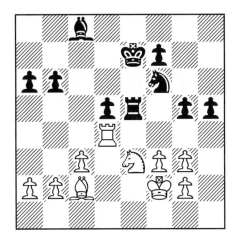

Exercise (combination alert): Time pressure, mixed with frustration, is a movie played too fast, with disconnected images and half-remembered recollections of surreal perspectives which veer from the truth. Black blundered on his last move. Now he doesn't quite own d5; he only holds it in trust. How did White exploit it?

Answer: Removal of a defender.

33 f4

It's that simple: White wins a pawn. If we lacked the ability to forget our blunders, the asylums of the world would be overcrowded with chess players.

33...gxf4 34 gxf4 ♖e6 35 ♘xd5+ ♘xd5 36 ♖xd5

Black is oppressed with the enormity of his difficulties. Not only is he down a pawn, but he also must deal with a weak h-pawn. We all blunder. The trick though is to be quick to recover from the bombardment of complex emotions which assail us immediately after we recognize our error. Sometimes one can survive a double question mark move, just as long as it doesn't produce a secondary error, which Black now commits.

36...♖d6?

Black has no chance in the bishop ending. As psychologically difficult as it is, Black should defend passively with 36...♖h6.

37 ♖xd6 ♔xd6

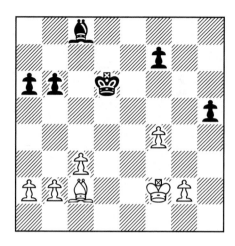

> ***Exercise (planning):*** Come up with a multi-step winning plan for White.

Answer: 38 g3!

Step 1: Fix h5 as a permanent weakness. Now precious little buffer stands between the h5 straggler and harsh reality.

38...♗g4 39 ♗d3!

Step 2: Swing the bishop over to challenge g4.

39...a5 40 ♗e2

Ensuring the win of a second pawn or entering a pawn-up king and pawn ending.

40...♗e6

40...f5 41 ♗xg4 fxg4 42 ♔e3 ♔d5 43 a4 ♔d6 44 ♔e4 ♔e6 45 b4 ♔f6 46 bxa5 bxa5 47 c4 is hopeless for Black, since White doesn't need his king to promote.

41 a3 ♔d5 42 ♔e3 ♗g4

To a zealot, the desire to die for a cause overrides the will to live for it. Black arrives at one of those: on the one hand/on the other hand, impasses. Rather than enter a bishop ending two pawns down, he takes his chances within the primal fear: a dreaded king and pawn endgame a pawn down. He strives to circumvent White's route to victory with a (temporary) superior king position, but it just isn't enough.

42...f6 43 ♗xh5 ♔c4 44 ♔d2 ♔b3 (in the background, we hear the droning of Black's king issuing commands and threats, which get him nowhere) 45 ♔c1 f5 46 ♗d1+ ♔c4 (or 46...♔a2 47 ♗a4 ♔c8 48 c4 ♗e6 49 ♔c2! ♗c8 50 ♗c6 ♗e6 51 ♗d5 and Black must resign, since 51...♗c8 is met with 52 c5+) 47 ♔d2 ♗d7 48 b3+ ♔d5 49 ♗f3+ ♔c5 50 ♔d3 ♗b5+ 51 c4 ♗d7 52 ♔c3 ♗e6 53 b4+ axb4+ 54 axb4+ ♔d6 55 ♔d4 ♗d7 56 c5+ bxc5+ 57 bxc5+ ♔e6 58 ♗d5+ ♔f6 59 c6 is hopeless too for Black.

43 ♗xg4 hxg4 44 ♔d3

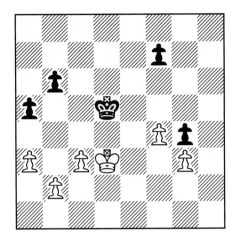

44...b5

Black still has some cheapo draw potential with 44...a4 45 c4+ ♔c6 46 ♔c3 ♔c5 47 f5 f6 48 b3 axb3 49 ♔xb3 ♔d4 50 a4! (Black should hold a draw after 50 ♔b4?? ♔e4 51 ♔b5 ♔f3 52 ♔xb6 ♔xg3 53 c5 ♔f4 54 c6 g3 55 c7 g2 56 c8♕ g1♕+) 50...♔e4 51 c5! bxc5 52 ♔c4 ♔f3 53 a5 ♔xg3 54 a6 ♔f2 55 a7 g3 56 a8♕ g2 57 ♕c6! g1♕ 58 ♕xc5+ ♔f1 59 ♕xg1+ ♔xg1 60 ♔d5 and White wins.

45 b3 a4 46 bxa4 bxa4 47 c4+ ♔c5 48 ♔c3 f5 49 ♔d3 ♔c6 50 ♔d4 ♔d6 51 c5+ ♔c6 52 ♔c4 ♔c7 53 ♔b5 1-0

"East? West? South? North? Which direction shall I conquer first?" asks White's power-mad king to himself.

Summary: I don't believe in Black's full equality after 5...♘f6, which accepts a London System position a full move down.

Game 17
J.Hodgson-P.Wells
Oxford 1998

1 d4 ♘f6

Compare 1...c6 2 e4 d5 3 exd5 cxd5 4 ♗d3 ♘f6 5 c3 ♘c6 6 ♗f4 from the Exchange Variation of the Caro-Kann to the one White reached in the game.

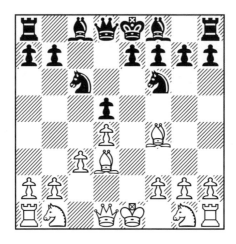

Question: What is the main difference?

Answer: The difference is in the Trompowsky version, Black's knight is allowed to go to e4, without loss of tempo. But the key question is does this represent a benefit or a liability for Black? In the Tromp version, White is offered ♗xe4 unbalancing options.

2 ♗g5

There is nothing more disconcerting than to have an opponent employ your own speciality against you. In this case, Tromp authority Hodgson plays the Trompowsky against Tromp authority Wells.

2...♘e4 3 ♗f4 d5 4 e3 c5 5 ♗d3 cxd4

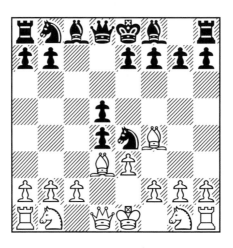

Unlike the last game, Black refuses to relinquish the e4-posting for his knight and exchanges in the centre, in Caro-Kann, Exchange Variation fashion.

6 ♗xe4

> *Question:* Does White have to play this unbalancing option?

Answer: I think avoiding the e4 swap is too tame and allows Black equality after 6 exd4 ♘c6 7 c3 ♗f5 8 ♘e2 e6 9 f3 ♘d6 10 ♗xd6 ♗xd6 11 ♗xf5 exf5 12 f4 0-0 13 0-0 ♖e8 14 ♘d2 ♕c7 15 g3 ♘a5. White's knights look awkward and Black controls the e-file, with a slight edge, N.Vitiugov-S.Karjakin, Moscow 2010.

6...dxe4 7 exd4

> *Question:* Can White extract an edge in the ending after 7 ♕xd4 ♕xd4 8 exd4?

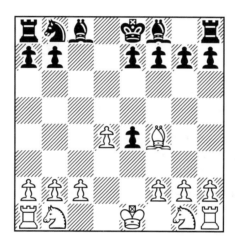

Answer: Houdini says no; I say yes. Take your pick. After 8...♘c6 9 c3 b6 10 ♘d2 ♗b7 11 ♘e2 0-0-0 12 ♘g3 h6 13 h4 (I slightly prefer White at the end of the variation 13 ♘dxe4! g5 14 ♗e3 f5! 15 ♘xf5 ♘b4 16 f3! ♘c2+ 17 ♔e2 ♘xa1 18 ♖xa1; White got two healthy pawns for the exchange, perhaps good enough for an edge) 13...g6 14 ♘dxe4 ♗g7 15 0-0-0 f5 16 ♘d2 e5 17 dxe5 ♘xe5 18 ♗xe5 ♗xe5 19 ♘f3 ♗f6 Black's bishops should provide enough compensation for the pawn, S.Lputian-M.Rytshagov, Istanbul Olympiad 2000.

7...♘c6 8 ♘e2

I believe this is White's best move in the position:

a) 8 d5 e5! 9 ♗e3! (9 ♗g3 is met with 9...♕a5+ 10 c3 ♘e7 11 ♗xe5 ♘xd5 when I prefer Black, who will soon lead in development) 9...♘e7 10 ♘c3 ♘f5 11 ♕d2 ♗b4 12 ♘ge2 ♘d6 and I'm not crazy about White's position ...♘c4 is in the air, as well as ...f5.

b) 8 c3 e5! (we must be aware of this temporary pawn sac, a recurring idea in this variation) 9 dxe5 ♕xd1+ 10 ♔xd1 was T.Hoang-J.Douwes, Budapest 2003. Black leads in development and there is a high likelihood that he will regain the lost pawn with advantage after 10...♗f5 11 ♘e2 g5!. Now if White bites with 12 ♗xg5 then comes 12...♖g8 13 ♗f4

♖xg2, and if 14 ♗g3? 0-0-0+ 15 ♔e1 e3! with a winning initiative.

8...♗g4

8...e5 isn't as strong when White refrains from c3: 9 dxe5 ♕xd1+ 10 ♔xd1 ♗g4 11 ♘bc3 0-0-0+ 12 ♔c1 h6 13 ♖e1 g5 14 ♗d2 ♗g7 15 ♘xe4 ♘xe5 16 ♗c3 ♖he8 17 ♘2g3. I don't believe in Black's full compensation for the pawn and Wells went on to win from here in P.Wells-Y.Visser, London Crowthorne 2006.

9 ♘bc3

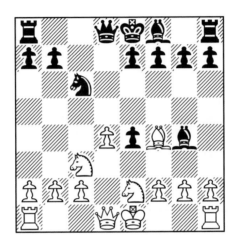

9...e6

A theoretical novelty at the time. Practice has seen too:

a) 9...♕b6 10 0-0 0-0-0 11 ♗e3 e5 12 d5 ♕a6 13 ♕d2 (White intends ♘g3 next) 13...♗xe2 14 ♘xe2 f5 15 ♖fd1! Now if 15...f4? 16 ♘xf4 exf4 17 ♗xf4 leaves Black's king in serious danger. If he wants to retain the extra piece, he has to go for 17...♗b4 18 c3 ♗e7 19 ♕c2 ♘b8 20 ♖d4 ♗d6 21 ♕xe4, but White gets three healthy pawns for the piece and stands at least equal.

b) 9...♕a5 10 h3 ♗h5 11 0-0 0-0-0 was J.Gallagher-M.Rytshagov, Elista Olympiad 1998. I like the look of White's attacking chances after 12 ♕e1 ♘xd4 13 ♘xd4 ♖xd4 14 ♗e3 ♖d8 15 b4!.

10 h3 ♗h5

After 10...♗f5 11 0-0 ♗g6 12 ♕d2 ♘b4 13 ♘g3 ♘d5 14 ♘cxe4 White wins a pawn. If 14...♘xf4?! 15 ♕xf4 ♕xd4?? 16 ♘f6+! ♕xf6 17 ♕a4+ ♔d8 (or 17...♔e7 18 ♕b4+) 18 ♖ad1+ White wins.

11 ♘xe4 ♗xe2

Black must give up the bishop-pair to regain the lost pawn.

12 ♕xe2 ♘xd4 13 ♕d3 ♘c6 14 0-0-0 ♕xd3 15 ♖xd3

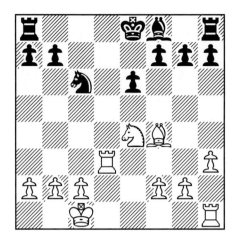

Answer: We have opposite wing pawn majorities. The factor which may still offer White an edge is his slight yet nagging development lead.

15...♘b4 16 ♖b3 ♘d5 17 ♗g3 b6 18 ♖d1 ♖c8 19 ♔b1 ♖c6

Black runs into delays and more interminable delays in the implementation of defensive wishes. Wells is worried about d6 and takes a precious tempo to cover the square. I suspect that White stands a microbe better in the line 19...♗e7 20 ♖d4! 0-0 21 c4 ♘f6 22 ♘d6 ♖c5 23 ♘b5 e5 24 ♖d1 ♘e4 25 ♘xa7 ♘xg3 26 ♖xg3 ♖xc4 27 ♖e3 f6 28 a3 ♗c5 29 ♖e2 ♖f4 30 f3 ♖a4 31 ♘b5.

20 ♖d4!

A fragile ceasefire isn't the same as lasting peace. Black is just short of the equilibrium he so desperately seeks. Those nasty white rooks prove to be exacting bosses, difficult to please. Hodgson proves he still retains the edge. Idea: c4. Principle: create confrontation when leading in development. The agent provocateur on d4 does his best to sow anarchy and turmoil in Black's camp.

20...♗e7 21 c4 ♘f6 22 ♘d6+

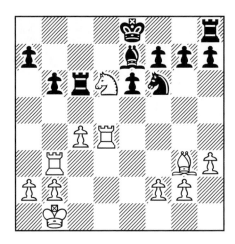

The knight continues to impose, violating the etiquette of social hierarchy by usurping d6.

22...♗xd6

No choice. Now White's bishop remains firmly anchored, with no way to dislodge the intruder, but 22...♔f8? 23 ♘b5 a6 24 ♘a7! wins.

23 ♗xd6 ♘d7

Black swaddles his king with defenders, yet in the end they are not enough. Instead, if 23...♘e4 24 ♗f4! ♘c5 (24...♘xf2?? 25 ♖f3 traps the knight) 25 ♖a3 a5 26 b4! (same principle: White creates confrontation when leading in development – even in an ending) 26...♘b7 27 bxa5 ♘xa5 28 ♗d2 e5 29 ♖e4 f6 30 ♗xa5 bxa5 31 ♖xa5 when White wins a pawn and has all the winning chances.

24 ♖g3

Before attempting a strike, White requires preliminary work, softening Black's defensive barrier.

24...g6

If 24...♖g8 (intending ...f6) 25 ♖a3 a5 26 ♖ad3 and if 26...f6 27 ♗g3 ♘c5 28 ♖d6! ♖c8 29 ♖a3 and Black loses a pawn.

25 ♖gd3

Even stronger was 25 b4! e5 26 b5 ♖c8 27 ♖d5 f6 (27...♖xc4 28 ♖a3! is winning) 28 ♖a3 ♖a8 29 ♗b4, which leaves Black in a bad way.

25...f6?

Black's only chance to resist was with 25...e5 26 ♖e3 f6 27 f4 ♔f7 28 fxe5 ♖e8 29 b3 fxe5 30 ♖d2.

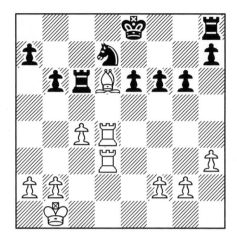

Answer: Clearance/attraction.

26 ♗e7! ♘e5

26...♖c7 is met with 27 ♗xf6! ♖f8 28 ♗h4 when White wins a pawn while retaining his bind.

27 ♖a3!

White's rooks, gibbons competing to attract a mate, swing from tree to tree. Double attack: a7 and f6 remaining hanging, and White's bishop is untouchable.

27...♘xc4

After 27...♔xe7 Black's king feels a nameless unease; he is alone yet not alone. He reasons: "If I am in a terrible mess, then why not commit an outrage? After all, my life can't get any worse." Unfortunately, it does get worse: 28 ♖xa7+ ♔e8 (28...♔f8 29 ♖d8 mate isn't much of an improvement!) 29 ♖a8+ pops the rook in the corner.

28 ♖xa7 e5 29 ♖d8+ ♔f7

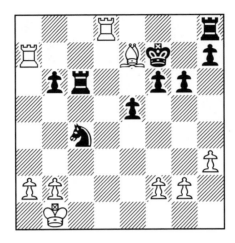

Exercise (combination alert): Black's king attempts to earn
the kidnapper's trust, hoping a lowered guard may assist
in his escape attempt. What should White play here?

Answer: Zwischenzug/defensive move. This was a test of your alertness.

30 ♗b4+! 1-0

The bishop compounds the treachery and now Black's h8-rook really does hang. "Did
you really believe I would lack the resources to hunt you down?" White's bishop asks
Black's startled king. I hope everyone avoided the greedy 30 ♖xh8?? ♘d2+. White's secret
embarrassment: he gets back ranked after 31 ♔a1 ♖c1.

Summary: White retains a tiny yet enduring development lead after either 7 exd4 or 7
♕xd4. It feels like Black falls just a touch short of equality in both lines.

Game 18
C.Lakdawala-D.Kishnevsky
San Diego (rapid) 2004

1 d4 ♘f6 2 ♗g5 ♘e4 3 ♗f4 d5 4 e3 c6

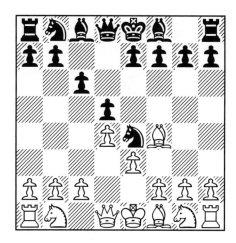

Question: What is Black's idea behind his last move?

Question: What is Black's idea behind his last move?

Answer: Black sees ...c5 as overly confrontational, so he takes a more moderate Slav-like path, fortifying d5 and preparing to hit White in the soft spot of b2.

5 ♗d3 ♘d6

Question: Why did Black retreat?

Answer: His dual purpose idea:

1. Black eliminates all ♗xe4 tricks.
2. Black hopes to inhibit c4.
3. Black makes ...♗f5 possible, with the intention of swapping off his bad bishop.

Saying this, I suspect Black's last artificial move isn't the best. Safer is 5...♕b6 6 ♕c1 (White can also speculate with 6 ♗xe4!? ♕xb2 7 ♘d2 dxe4 8 ♘e2 f5 when he probably extracted full developmental compensation for the pawn, M.Lopez-M.Do Prado, correspondence 2000) 6...♕a5+ 7 c3 ♗f5, M.Adams-P.Leko, Groningen 1995. Here White can try 8 ♘d2 ♘d6 (after 8...♘xf2 9 ♗xf5 ♘xh1 10 ♘gf3 g6 11 ♗h3 White eventually gets around to winning the stranded h1-knight, with the superior position) 9 ♗xf5 ♘xf5 10 ♘gf3 e6 11 e4 ♘d6 12 0-0 with only a tiny development edge.

6 ♘d2

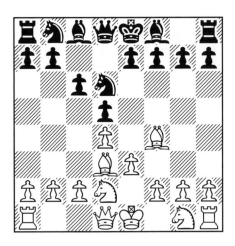

6...♕b6?!

A new move and not such a good one.

> **Question:** It looks fine to me. Doesn't Black's last move produce
> a concession of either ♕c1 or a b3 weakening from White?

Answer: Not with a knight on d6. Indeed, b3 actually helps White, who threatens an eventual c4 and c5, forking queen and knight. So in essence, the move loses time for Black. Alternatives are:

a) 6...♘d7 was E.Prie-A.Istratescu, Nantes 2003. White stands a shade better after 7 ♘gf3 g6 8 0-0 ♗g7 9 c4.

b) 6...g6 7 h4!? (this plan makes sense since Black is missing a knight on f6) 7...♗g7 (after 7...h5 8 ♘gf3 ♗g7 White may even attempt queenside castling and go after Black's king on the other side) 8 h5 ♘d7 9 ♘gf3 ♘f6 10 h6 ♗f8 11 ♘e5 ♗e6 12 c3 ♘d7 13 ♕c2 ♗f5 14 ♗xf5 ♘xf5 15 0-0-0 and White is ready to open the game with e4 while Black lags behind in development, M.Richter-G.Lueders, Berlin 2003.

7 b3

Black can't easily exploit the temporary weakening of the queenside dark squares. Meanwhile, c4-c5 is in the air.

7...♕a5

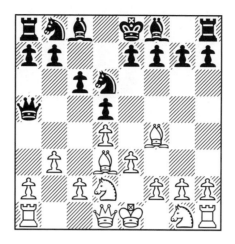

8 ♘e2?!

In order to keep an eye on c3. I fuss over an issue of little or no importance, posting my knight on an inferior square in doing so.

Question: Why criticize the move?

Answer: The trouble is it weakens White's grip on e5. I should have gone for 8 ♘gf3!. I feared 8...♕c3?, but the lone queen, a commander without an army to command, is a dysfunctional attacker when going it alone. *Houdini* dismisses this move after 9 0-0 e6 (or 9...♗g4 10 h3 ♗h5 11 ♗xd6 exd6 12 e4! when Black is in trouble; if 12...dxe4? 13 ♘xe4 ♗xf3 14 ♕xf3 ♕xd4 15 ♗c4! d5 16 ♖fe1! ♔d8 17 ♕xf7 with a winning attack for White) 10 a3! (threat: b4! followed by ♖a2 and ♘b1, trapping Black's queen) 10...♕a5 ("My friend! I rescind my previous threats and now wish you all the very best!" Black's queen tells White's king, with a rather feeble Charlie Brown smile) 11 c4 and Black's c3-infiltration adventure is a failure, since he is worse off here than in the game.

8...♘d7 9 c4?

9 0-0 was correct.

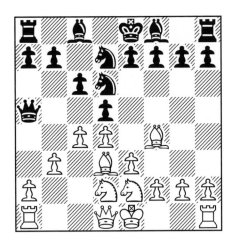

9...♘f6?

From time to time, I get the disquieting feeling that the vast majority of my wins tend to arise from making fewer errors than my opponents, and not from any form of brilliant play from my side. Now White gets the position he was after. Black missed an opportunity here.

Answer: 9...dxc4! 10 bxc4 e5! 11 dxe5 (11 ♗g3? e4 12 ♗c2 ♘xc4 wins a pawn, and worse, Black threatens ...♗b4) 11...♘xe5 when Black achieved an excellent position.

10 0-0 ♗g4

After 10...♗f5 (it makes sense to try and swap light-squared bishops, since White owns the good bishop) 11 ♕c2 ♗xd3 12 ♕xd3 ♕a6 13 ♘g3 e6 14 ♕c2 ♗e7 15 c5 ♘c8 16 ♘f3 White is in control of the position, threatening a build up with a4, b4, ♖fb1 and b5.

11 ♕c2 ♗xe2

He rids himself of his bad bishop.

12 ♗xe2 e6 13 ♗d3 ♗e7 14 b4! ♕d8

Of course, it is suicide to take b4 and allow White's pieces infiltration into b7:

14...♕xb4?? 15 ♖fb1 ♕a5 (15...♕a3 16 c5 ♘b5 17 ♖b3 ♕a5 18 a4 ♘c7 19 ♖xb7 ♘a6 20 ♘b3 wins) 16 c5 ♘c8 17 ♖xb7 ♕d8.

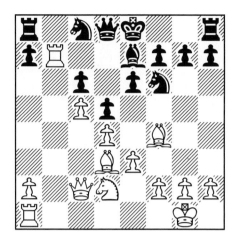

Exercise (combination alert): White to play and win.

Answer: Attraction/queen trap. 18 ♗b5!! is not so easy to find over the board. 18...cxb5 19 ♗c7 ♕d7 20 c6 traps the queen.

Question: Ah, but the question arises: would you have seen 18 ♗b5!!?

Answer: To be honest: probably not. Of course, *Houdini*'s analysis is a non-human construct, not very practical or useful to us flawed humans, who rarely spot lines this anomalous over the board.

15 c5 ♘c8

The surreal begins to supplant the commonplace; c8 is a God-awful square for the knight. *Houdini* hates this move, but there are no good choices here:

a) 15...♘b5 16 a4 ♘c7 17 b5 leaves Black strategically busted.

b) 15...♘de4 16 ♘xe4 dxe4 17 ♗xe4 ♘xe4 18 ♕xe4 ♕d5 19 ♕c2 when Black is down a clean pawn for nothing.

16 b5!

This is stronger than taking time out to preserve the f4-bishop with 16 h3.

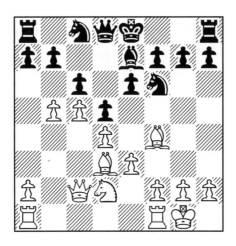

16...a5

> ***Question:*** So why can't Black pick off your f4-bishop with 16...♘h5?

Answer: Black's last move follows a universal truth: I have what I don't want and you have what I want. The tactics fail for Black after 17 bxc6 bxc6 18 ♗e5, and if 18...f6? 19 ♘f3!!. Now if 19...fxe5 20 ♘xe5 ♗f6 21 ♗g6+ ♚f8 22 ♘f7 ♕e8 (or 22...♕e7 23 ♘xh8! and the g6-bishop is taboo due to a knight fork) 23 ♘xh8 hxg6 24 ♘xg6+ ♚g8 25 g4! e5 26 gxh5 exd4 27 exd4 ♗xd4 28 ♖ae1 with a winning attack for White.

17 bxc6 bxc6 18 ♕a4 ♘a7 19 h3!

It's important to hang on to the powerful f4-bishop, who controls both the e5- and b8-squares.

19...0-0 20 ♖ab1

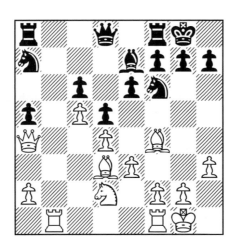

Even a cursory examination of the position reveals an obvious truth, that Black is strategically busted:

1. White owns the only open file, which Black is unable to challenge due to White's control over b8.

2. Infiltration on b7 is a huge concern for Black.

3. White owns the bishop-pair against unimpressive black knights.

4. Both a5 and c6 pawns are targets.

20...♘d7

Black desperately hopes to achieve ...e5, with some kind of central distraction.

21 ♘f3

Of course, White isn't about to allow it so easily.

21...f6

Once again, angling for ...e5.

22 ♕c2 h6

22...f5 23 ♗a6 is also hopeless, since ♗b7 is next.

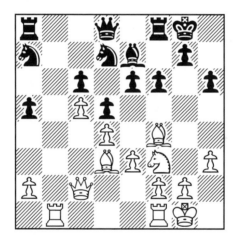

23 ♖b7

If I'm winning, I tend to play it safe, sometimes even if I see the combination. I don't remember if I saw the line 23 ♗xh6! gxh6 24 ♗h7+ ♔h8 25 ♕g6 ♕e8 26 ♕xh6 ♖f7 27 ♗f5+ ♔g8 28 ♕g6+ ♔f8 29 ♗xe6, winning. But even if I saw this, I would probably still opt for the move I played in the game.

> **Question:** Why on earth wouldn't you have played this line, even when you saw it?

Answer: Our irresistible stylistic compulsions (let's admit it – we all have them) make us simultaneously dangerous and vulnerable. My philosophy is: in rapid games you maximize your score by avoiding unnecessary risk. The move I played over the board, 23 ♖b7, wins without risk of miscalculation.

23...e5

Black's e-pawn, believing himself to be the saviour of the world, refuses to be deflected from his intention and decides to intervene in places where he shouldn't. Dimitry tosses in this natural move which compromises his king's safety and slices the light squares into sashimi. It's hard to criticize Black for his last move, since passive play is simply slow death after 23...f5 24 ♖fb1 ♖f7 25 ♖c7, intending to double rooks on the seventh rank.

24 ♗h7+

White offered Black the ...e5 bait. Now it's time to draw blood.

24...♔h8 25 ♗f5

Attacking d7. Black's light squares leak like a colander.

25...♘xc5 26 dxc5 exf4

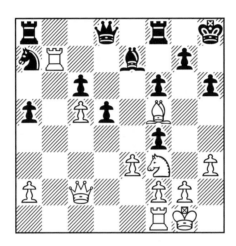

> **Exercise (planning):** This one isn't so difficult. Always strike when your opponent is off balance, since you never get a better opportunity. How did White continue his light-square attack?

Answer: Infiltrate g6 with the knight.

27 ♘h4

Too obvious to deserve an exclam. The knight manipulates public opinion against Black's king.

27...♖f7 28 ♗e6 1-0

Attackers race by as if at the Indy 500. 28...♕e8 ("No bickering!" demands Black's queen to her king's disorganized, inept defenders) 29 ♘g6+ ♔g8 (or 29...♔h7 30 ♘f8+ ♔g8 31 ♕h7+ when the queen plays her trump card: herself; 31...♔xf8 32 ♕h8 is mate) 30 ♖xe7 is all over.

Summary: 4...c6 leads to Slav-like positions which slightly favour White, since Black's e4-knight tends to remain a liability.

Chapter Three
2...e6 3 e4 h6 4 ♗xf6 ♕xf6

1 d4 ♘f6 2 ♗g5 e6 3 e4 h6 4 ♗xf6 ♕xf6

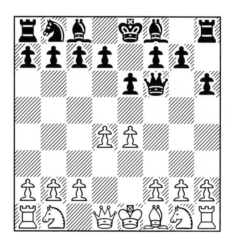

This chapter is a battle of imbalances. Our Trompowsky side hands Black the bishop-pair – a required subsidy to feed our war effort – as early as the third move. As compensation we seize central control and also a development lead, made even more potent with Black's exposed queen's position. We have a choice of plans:

a) In the sharper Yusupov rapid development plan, our vast ambition is exposed: White plays ♘f3, ♘c3, ♕d2 and castles long, usually leading to violent opposite wing attacks. The coming assault is designed on a scale to stagger and overwhelm the Black's defenders, and often concludes with nail-biting, hair-trigger finishes. Now if after examining the games from this variation we develop a case of cold feet, then we can go for the safer Pert line, examined at the end of the chapter.

b) Walls are erected to safeguard the population and keep the enemy out. We do just that with the solid Pert Variation: White sets up with: c3, ♘d2, ♗d3, ♘e2, 0-0 and f4, with a pseudo Modern Defence, Austrian Attack(ish!) position.

Game 19
A.Yusupov-K.Bischoff
Munich 1990

1 d4 ♘f6 2 ♘f3 e6 3 ♗g5

Question: Isn't this a Torre Attack?

Answer: The Torre Attack and Trompowsky are linked opening systems and in many cases one transposes to the other. Our Trompowsky move order runs 2 ♗g5 e6 3 e4 h6 4 ♗xf6 ♕xf6 5 ♘f3 directly transposing to our game.

3...h6 4 ♗xf6

In this chapter we hand over the bishop-pair to seize the centre, and more importantly, lure Black's queen to f6, from which she becomes a target, resulting in future loss of time.

4...♕xf6 5 e4

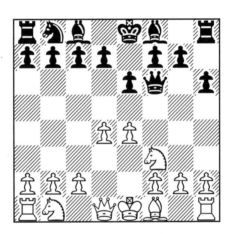

Our starting position in this chapter.

Question: Didn't we hinder our options with
an early ♘f3, blocking out f4 ideas later on?

Answer: This is one flaw with the early ♘f3 lines.

Question: Then why not study the early ♘c3, lines, keeping open the f4 possibilities?

Answer: I don't think the early 5 ♘c3 is so wonderful for White, since the ...♗b4 pin becomes quite annoying. Later in the chapter, we look at an early 5 c3, replacing ♘f3. This allows us f4 options.

5...d6

This flexible response is Black's main choice in the position. Other options:

a) After 5...b6 6 ♗d3 ♗b7 7 ♘bd2 d6 8 ♕e2 a6 9 0-0-0 ♘d7 10 ♔b1 e5 11 c3 ♗e7 12 ♘c4 0-0 13 ♗c2 ♖fe8 14 d5 c5?! (Black should hold off on this move, retaining ...c6 options; the semi-closing of the queenside only helps White) 15 ♘e3 ♗f8 16 g4! Black's queen became an inviting target for h4 and g5. Korchnoi went on to crush his future World Champion opponent in V.Korchnoi-A.Karpov, Hastings 1971/72. This game is annotated in the forthcoming *Korchnoi: Move by Move*.

b) 5...d5 6 ♘bd2 (White does best to retain the central tension since Black is unable to play ...♗e7) 6...g6 7 c3 ♗g7 8 ♗d3 0-0 was B.Macieja-V.Anand, Calvia Olympiad 2004. In the game White castled with an approximately even position. He might consider the sharper, untested idea 9 e5 ♕e7 10 h4!? with h5 to follow. Here 10 b4!? hindering ...c5 is also an unplayed, interesting idea.

c) I'm convinced 5...c5?! is inaccurate. Black rashly challenges in the centre, not fearing a potential opening of the game with White leading in development: 6 e5 ♕d8 (6...♕g6 7 ♘c3, with ideas of ♘b5, d5, and even ♗d3!?, looks too dangerous for Black) 7 d5! d6 (or 7...♕b6 8 ♘c3 ♕xb2 9 ♘b5 ♔d8 10 ♖b1 ♕xa2 11 c4 a6 12 ♘c3 ♕a5 13 ♕c1 when I would take White here any day of the week: Black can barely move and two extra pawns aren't of much comfort if you get mated) 8 ♗b5+ ♗d7 was B.Malich-H.Gruenberg, Leipzig 1973. At this point, Black lags dangerously behind in development after 9 ♘c3.

6 ♘c3

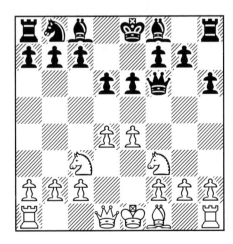

Our rule of thumb: we play ♘c3 only when Black is denied access to ...♗b4.

6...♘d7

Black's most flexible move and the main line:

a) 6...g5!? is a radical option. Black Reverse Grobs us, deciding that if he refuses confrontation, the cost of silence is too high. Black hopes to intimidate with ...g4 ideas later on and also inhibits White's kingside ambitions, at the cost of potential weakening. 7 e5 (principle: create confrontation when leading in development) 7...♕e7 8 ♗b5+ ♗d7 9 0-0 d5 was J.Timman-A.Karpov, 9th matchgame, Holland 1993. At this point I would play 10 ♕e2 ♘c6 11 ♗xc6 ♗xc6 12 ♘d2. I like White's space advantage and the knights, which more than hold their own versus Black's unimpressive bishop-pair.

b) 6...g6 can easily transpose to our main line, but note too 7 ♕d2 ♕e7 8 0-0-0 a6 9 h4 ♗g7 10 g3 b5 11 ♗h3 b4 12 ♘d5 exd5 13 ♗xc8 0-0 14 ♗b7 ♖a7 15 ♗xd5 c6 16 ♗b3 ♕xe4 17 ♕d3 ♕xd3 18 ♖xd3 with a molecule of an edge for White. Once again, Korchnoi managed to defeat Karpov, this time with supernatural endgame play in V.Korchnoi-A.Karpov, 19th matchgame, Moscow 1974. One wonders if he would have been World Champion if he had taken up the Torre/Trompowsky more often in his legendary career. This game is also annotated in *Korchnoi: Move by Move*.

7 ♕d2

White prepares to castle queenside. Since queenside castling is not easy (or even desirable) for Black to achieve, many of these Tromp/Torre positions result in ultra-sharp, opposite-wing attacks.

7...a6

Dual purpose. Black covers against ♘b5 tricks and also thinks about future ...b5 ideas, in case of opposite wing attacks. Next game we examine 7...♕d8.

8 0-0-0

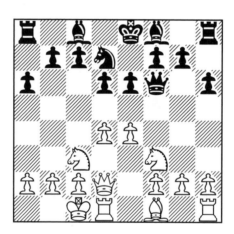

At this point Black realizes that longing for peace is wasted hope when facing an enemy intent upon destruction. White decides he has had enough of tweaking here and pulling strings there, and unveils an openly hostile intent. The time for subtlety has ceased and the will for total obliteration arises. In castling long, we cross a dangerous marker, leaving ourselves with no fallback position should our kingside attack fail.

8...♕e7

> ***Question:*** Why did Black block in the dark-squared bishop?

Answer: Black plans to fianchetto, but this costs him more time and allows White an obvi-ous h4-h5 prying mechanism. 8...♕d8 is more commonly played: 9 h4 b5 10 g4 is Finegold-Benjamin, which we look at later in the chapter. *Houdini* claims the game is even. I don't know about you, but I prefer White here. Surely the massive development lead must take precedence over Black's theoretical advantage of the bishop-pair, if not objectively, then perhaps with a position easier to navigate, since we are the ones in command of the initia-tive.

9 ♗d3 g6

Black wisely configures his structure to avoid confrontation of any kind.

10 ♖he1 ♗g7 11 h4 0-0 12 e5

Yusupov (FIDE really needs to hold a conference and decide once and for all: is it 'Yusu-pov' or 'Jussupow?', and the same goes for 'Trompowsky' and 'Trompovsky') seizes space and finally confronts Black.

12...d5

Following principle by closing the game when behind in development. Otherwise:

a) 12...b5 was J.Sutherland-M.Barlow, Auckland 1997. After 13 h5 g5 14 ♘e4 ♗b7 15 ♔b1!? chances look about even in this sharp position. *Houdini* analysis runs: 15...dxe5 16 ♘xe5 ♘xe5 (16...♗xe5 17 dxe5 ♘xe5 18 ♕c3 offers White enough initiative for the pawn) 17 dxe5 ♗xe5 18 ♘xg5 ♗xb2 19 ♘xe6 (or 19 ♘xf7 ♗g7 20 ♘xh6+ ♗xh6 21 ♕xh6 ♕b4+ 22 ♔c1 ♕a3+ 23 ♔b1 ♕b4+ with perpetual check) 19...♗h8 20 ♘xf8 ♕a3 21 ♗h7+ ♔xf8 22 c3 ♗xc3 23 ♕xh6+ ♗g7 24 ♕d2 (threat: ♕d8+, mating) 24...♗c3 with a draw by repetition of moves.

b) 12...c5 13 ♘e4 cxd4 14 ♘xd6 ♘xe5 15 ♘xe5 ♕xd6 16 f4 b5 17 h5 with clear attacking compensation for the pawn, K.Chernyshov-A.Volokitin, Sochi 2005.

13 ♘e2

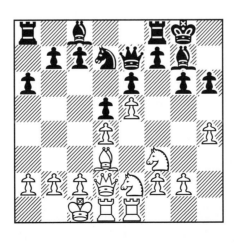

Dual purpose: White transfers another attacker over to the kingside and also prepares to meet ...c5 with c3.

13...c5 14 c3 cxd4 15 ♘exd4

Natural, but it gives Black c5 for his knight. I would consider the unplayed 15 cxd4!, which may be an improvement. I couldn't find a way for Black to equalize. Play might continue: 15...b5 16 h5 g5 17 ♘h2 f6 18 f4 fxe5 19 fxe5 ♘b6 20 ♗c2! ♘c4 21 ♕d3 (threatening mate in two moves) 21...♖f5 (after 21...♕b4 22 ♕h7+ ♔f7 23 ♗b3 ♖a7 24 ♘g4 ♔e8 25 ♘xh6 ♖c7 26 ♔b1 ♔d8 27 ♕g6 *Houdini* gives a clear advantage to White) 22 ♘g3 ♕b4 23 ♕b3! ♕xb3 24 axb3 ♖f2 25 bxc4 ♖xg2 26 ♘hf1 bxc4 27 ♖e2 ♖xe2 28 ♘xe2 and White's extra knight is clearly superior to Black's two extra pawns in this ending.

15...♘c5 16 ♗b1

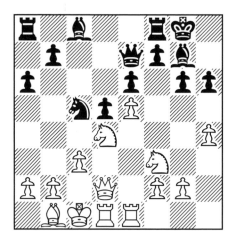

This is likely better than the 16 ♗c2 ♗d7 17 h5 g5 18 ♘h2 of A.Weindl-K.Bischoff, Lenk 1993.

Question: What is the difference between b1 and c2?

Answer: I like Yusupov's choice of b1 for the bishop, since it keeps ♕c2 options open, going after Black via h7. That said, a bishop on c2 covers a4 and allows White's king to slip away to b1, off the open c-file if necessary. It's hard to decide which of the two bishop postings is best. For the record, *Houdini* favours 16 ♗b1.

16...♗d7 17 h5

Utilizing the h5-prying mechanism.

17...g5 18 ♖e3

The rook may have designs upon the g3-square.

18...♖fc8 19 ♘h2 b5?

This natural move may actually be inaccurate. Isn't it strange how sometimes your opponent possesses full comprehension of your intent and still your plan works. This happened in Capablanca's games all the time. GM George Thomas complained: he always knew how Capa would beat him, but there was nothing he could do about it. The reason this happens is the defender overlooks some subtlety or detail, which seems unimportant at the time, but as the game progresses, becomes critical to his or her defence. This happened to Bischoff in this game when he missed a subtlety.

Black should toss in 19...♗a4! to gum up White's ♕c2 intention. Black may not yet have committed to a sacrifice, but with his last move he certainly signs a promissory note. The position remains sharp after 20 ♖de1 (after 20 b3 ♗e8 White weakened c3 and Black gets a much better version than in the game's continuation) 20...b5! (self-trapping the bishop; Black agrees to part with a thing of great value in exchange for a chance to go after an item he considers of even greater value: White's king) 21 b3 b4 22 bxa4 bxc3 23 ♕c2 ♘e4 24 ♘g4 ♖c4 25 ♘b3. I have a feeling Black receives full compensation for the piece. *Houdini* rates at 0.00 and agrees.

20 ♕c2

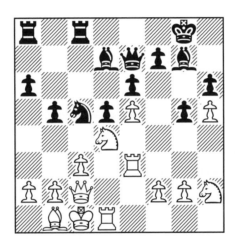

> ***Exercise (critical decision):*** If, if, if – the position is permeated with
> so many ifs. Black, already in trouble, must find the correct
> continuation. The candidate moves are 20...b4, 20...♘e4 and 20...g4. Only
> one of these moves keeps him in the game. Which one would you play?

20...g4?

This attempt to circumnavigate the issue fails. Finding the correct defence here isn't so easy. Black's last move fails to take necessary precautions against White's coming attack.

The natural 20...b4?? gets crushed by 21 ♕h7+ ♔f8 22 ♘g4 bxc3 (or 22...♕d8 23 ♖f3 ♗e8 24 ♘f6 bxc3 25 b4! and White wins since there is no defence to ♕g8+) 23 ♘xh6 cxb2+ 24 ♔xb2 is hopeless for Black.

Answer: He had to try 20...♘e4!, which is the best practical chance. Sometimes a problem, no matter how dire, must be dealt with head on. After 21 f3 b4 22 fxe4 bxc3 23 bxc3 ♖ab8 24 ♔d2 ♕a3 25 ♘b3 d4! 26 ♖f3 ♗a4 27 c4 ♕b4+ 28 ♔e2 ♗xe5 29 ♘g4 ♖xc4 30 ♕d2 ♗g7 31 ♕xb4 ♖bxb4 White stands clearly better with a piece for two pawns, but Black remains in the game.

21 ♘xg4

The immediate queen check to h7 is the most accurate continuation of the attack, after which White mounts a crushing offensive: 21 ♕h7+! ♔f8 22 ♘xg4 ♕g5 23 ♘f6 ♗xf6 24 ♘f3! (a powerful zwischenzug) 24...♕g7 25 exf6 ♕xf6 (25...♕xh7 26 ♗xh7 leaves Black dealing with the threat of ♘e5, followed by ♖g3 and ♖g8 mate) 26 ♘e5 ♔e7 27 ♖xd5! with a winning attack.

21...♕g5

White also forces a win after 21...♘e4 22 f3 ♘g5 23 f4 ♘e4 24 ♖xe4! dxe4 25 ♕xe4 ♔f8 26 g3, and if 26...♔e8 (or 26...b4 27 ♕h7! bxc3 28 ♘xh6 cxb2+ 29 ♔xb2 ♕b4+ 30 ♘b3 ♕c3+ 31 ♔a3 ♗xh6 32 ♕xh6+ ♔e8 33 ♕h8+ ♔e7 34 ♕f6+ ♔e8 35 ♗g6! fxg6 36 ♕h8+ ♔e7 37 ♕g7+ ♔e8 38 ♖xd7, forcing mate) 27 ♕h7 ♕f8 28 ♘f6+ ♗xf6 29 exf6 b4 30 ♗c2! bxc3 31 ♘xe6!!. Deception is second nature to the pure tactician. White wins.

22 ♘f6+ ♗xf6 23 ♘f3!

White can also play 23 ♕h7+! ♔f8 24 ♘f3! ♕g7 25 exf6, which favourably transposes to the note to his 21st move.

23...♕g7

Black can prolong the game after 23...♕f5 24 ♕xf5 exf5 25 exf6, but can't save it.

24 exf6 ♕xf6 25 ♘e5 ♔f8

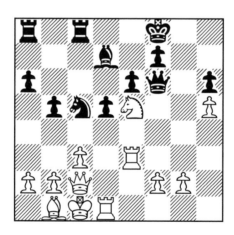

Exercise (combination alert): How did Yusupov demolish Black's king safety?

Answer: Pin. Black king and queen's bewilderment is finally put to rest. Sometimes it's more comforting to know for certain you are lost, rather than speculating upon the fear of being lost.

26 ♘xf7!

This shot marks the end of so many hopes. The knight is immune from either recapture and Black's king too exposed to survive. *Houdini* prefers the alternative solution: 26 ♕h7! (threat: ♘g6+!) 26...♔e7 27 ♖xd5! when Black can't effectively deal with the coming ♘g6+.

26...♔e7 27 ♘e5 ♔d6 28 ♕d2 b4 29 ♘c4+!? ♔c7 30 cxb4 ♘a4 31 ♗c2 ♔d8 32 ♘e5 ♘b6

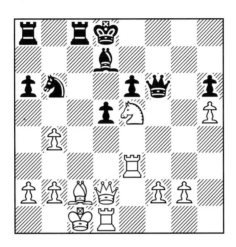

Exercise (combination alert): How did White force the win of material?

Answer: Double attack/discovered attack. White threatens b6, as well as ♘c6+, winning Black's queen.

33 ♕d4! 1-0

Pretentions and false claims of power wither and die in the queen's presence. The psychotic, megalomaniac queen thinks to herself: "One method of ruling the world is to eliminate everyone in it but me."

Summary: The position we reach after White's fifth move can arise from the Torre, as well as the Trompowsky. Our development lead, coupled with Black's shaky queen position on f6, easily compensates for departing with the bishop-pair. Expect an ultra-sharp, opposite-wing attack situation. Also, think about the unplayed idea 15 cxd4!, which may be an improved version for White.

Game 20
A.Yusupov-A.Vyzmanavin
Moscow (rapid) 1995

1 d4 ♘f6 2 ♘f3 e6 3 ♗g5 h6 4 ♗xf6 ♕xf6 5 e4 d6 6 ♘c3 ♘d7 7 ♕d2 ♕d8

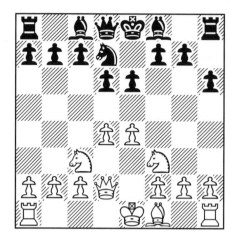

Question: Why would Black back the queen
off when White hadn't even attacked it yet?

Answer: The problem is at some stage Black's queen gets hit with something. Perhaps e5, or maybe h4, g4 and g5. So Black decides to move it now, so he doesn't have to worry about it on each move. Saying this, I feel that d8 is perhaps an inaccurate retreat square. I would actually have played the queen back to e7 instead.

Question: But on e7, you plug up the f8-bishop's development, don't you?

Answer: Just as Black did last game, the bishop can be fianchettoed.

8 h4

Informing Black as to just what is coming on the kingside should he decide to castle on that side. The idea also may be to suppress ...g5.

8...g6 9 0-0-0 ♝g7 10 e5!

Black can't pick off the e5-pawn due to the pin on the d-file. This is perhaps another reason why e7 was a superior retreat square for Black over d8. To my mind Yusupov's choice of 10 e5 (similar to the way he played last game) is more logical than going for a light-squared strategy with 10 d5!?, since this activates Black's unopposed dark-squared bishop: 10...0-0 11 ♞d4 was J.Bellon Lopez-D.Garcia Ilundain, Madrid 1992. Now Black can play 11...exd5 12 exd5 ♜e8 13 h5 g5 14 ♞f5 ♝xc3! 15 ♛xc3 ♛f6 when he stands at least equal.

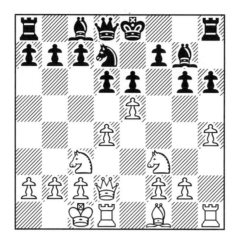

10...a6 11 ♗d3

Offering e5.

11...♛e7

A clear admission that 7...♛d8 was inaccurate.

Question: Can Black get away with taking e5?

Answer: Yes and no. He can take the pawn if he is willing to hand White a long-term attacking initiative after 11...dxe5 12 dxe5 ♘xe5 13 ♘xe5 ♗xe5 14 ♗b5+ ♔e7 15 ♛e3 ♗d6 16 ♗c4 ♔f8 17 ♘e4. *Houdini* assesses at dead even. I wouldn't feel comfortable taking on Black here, whose dangerous lag in development looks difficult to navigate for just one pawn.

12 ♖he1

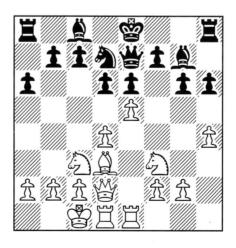

12...d5

Like last game, Black deems it wisest to keep the centre closed when he lags so far behind in development.

> *Question:* What happens if Black just castles and retains the tension?

Answer: Let's look: 12...0-0 13 h5 g5 14 ♕e3 dxe5 (14...b5?? is met with the killing double attack 15 ♕e4) 15 dxe5 and ♕e4 is in the air, although maybe Black is okay here as well. *Houdini* rates the chances at even.

13 ♘e2

To meet the coming ...c5 with c3.

13...c5

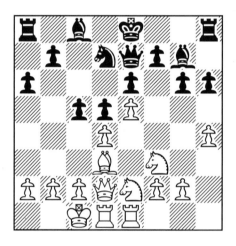

14 c3

> *Question:* Since White remains ahead in development is 14 dxc5!? logical?

Answer: Your idea looks playable since it clears d4 for a white piece: 14...♘xc5 15 ♔b1 b5 16 h5 g5 17 ♘fd4 ♕c7 18 f4 gxf4 19 ♘f3 ♗d7 (Black's king gets caught in the middle after the greedy 19...♗xe5?? 20 ♘xe5 ♕xe5 21 ♘xf4 ♕g7 22 ♕b4) 20 ♘ed4 0-0-0 21 ♕xf4 ♖hf8 22 ♘b3 with a sharp, French-like position where I prefer White's chances.

14...b5

Black wisely refrains from castling kingside this game.

15 ♘f4

Eyeing g6 sacs.

15...♗b7?

The contradictory forces disrupting Black's position must be resolved and harmonized if he is to survive. Black retains even chances with 15...cxd4! 16 cxd4 ♘b6 17 ♔b1 (17 ♗xg6??

fails to 17...fxg6 18 ♘xg6 ♕c7+) 17...♘c4 18 ♕e2 0-0 19 g4 and it's anybody's game. Here the g6 sacrifice doesn't look so great anymore for White: 19 ♗xg6 fxg6 20 ♘xg6 ♕f7 21 ♘xf8 ♕xf8 and I prefer Black, whose minor pieces look at least the equal of White's rook and two pawns.

16 ♗xg6!

Now White gets a good version of the g6-sacrifice. Moreover, it really doesn't qualify as a sacrifice if you attain a material surplus after the fact.

16...fxg6 17 ♘xg6 ♕f7 18 ♘xh8 ♗xh8 19 ♕xh6

This is the difference. White picks off a third pawn, and his rook and pawns outweigh Black's two bishops, who don't function well in the still rigid structure.

19...0-0-0?

19...♗g7 was necessary.

20 ♘g5!

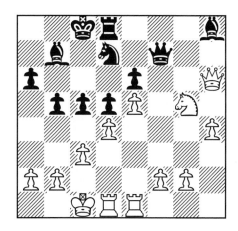

Now e6 falls.

20...♕f4+

20...♕xf2 21 ♘xe6 ♖g8 22 ♖f1! ♕g3 (or 22...♕xg2 23 ♖g1 ♕xg1 24 ♖xg1 ♖xg1+ 25 ♔d2 and the h8-bishop is trapped) 23 ♘xc5 ♘xc5 24 dxc5 ♗xe5 25 c6 ♗a8 26 ♖f3! ♕g6 27 ♕xg6 ♖xg6 28 ♖f8+ wins.

21 ♖d2 cxd4 22 cxd4 ♔b8 23 ♕xe6 ♖c8+ 24 ♔d1

White's king remains safe and Black's minor pieces are unable to participate.

24...♕xh4 25 ♘f7 ♘f8 26 ♕h3

More accurate is 26 ♕h6! ♕g4+ 27 f3 ♕e6 28 ♕xe6 ♘xe6, which is winning for White, whose kingside passers decide the game.

26...♕e7!?

Hopeless, but Black felt he just couldn't save the ending after a queen swap.

27 ♘xh8

Needless to say, Black doesn't have sufficient compensation for an exchange and three pawns.

27...♘e6 28 ♘g6 ♕f7 29 ♘h4 ♕h5+ 30 f3 ♖c6 31 ♘f5 ♕g6 32 ♕g4 ♕h7 33 ♘d6 ♗c8 34 ♘xc8

The more pieces off the board, the better for White.

34...♔xc8 35 ♔e2 ♔b7 36 ♔f2 ♕h6 37 ♖ed1

White's king is safe.

37...♘f4 38 ♔g1 ♖c7 39 e6?!

Mistakenly played with the thought: in war if you are unable to seize control over a resource, then the next step is to destroy it, denying the enemy control over it. From this stage, Yusupov begins to tire, mishandles the position and sees ghosts (unfortunately, fatigue doesn't absolve us from fulfilling our tasks at the board). What is worse, this single incident becomes the beginning of a negative pattern. There was no need to hand Black a pawn. He missed 39 g3!, and if 39...♖g7 the simplifying 40 ♖h2! wins on the spot.

39...♘xe6 40 ♖e2 ♘f4 41 ♖e8 ♕f6 42 ♕g8!

Going after Black's king via b8.

42...♔b6

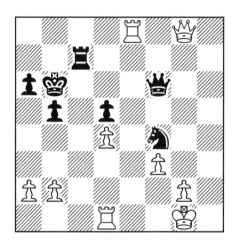

> *Exercise (planning):* White is up a huge amount of material. He may
> have conquered, yet it isn't so easy to rule due to a rising Black
> kingside insurgency. How can White shut down Black's counterplay?

43 ♖f8?!

Answer: 43 b4! ends the game since Black's king is denied an a5-escape route: 43...♔b7 44 ♖b8 squelches Black's attack and threatens the simplifying ♕d8+.

43...♕h4

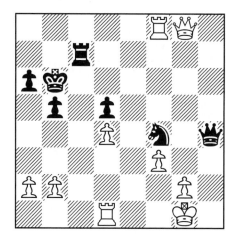

> ***Exercise (critical decision):*** Should White go on the attack with 44 ♖b8+, or
> should he hand back more material with 44 ♖xf4 to kill Black's initiative?
> Be careful. One of the decisions should win, while the other leads to a draw.

44 ♖b8+?

Violating the principle: when attacking, don't chase the enemy king to safety. White should hand back more material to regain the initiative.

Answer: 44 ♖xf4! ♕xf4 45 ♕e6+ ♖c6 46 ♕e5 ♕h4 47 b4! (threatening mate on the move; White should co-opt the b-pawn as the leader of the uprising) 47...♔b7 48 ♖e1 threatens ♕e7+, which is decisive.

44...♔a5 45 ♕d8 ♘e2+!

As all programmers understand: firewalls can be pierced and the information behind them hacked into. Also sufficient is 45...♘h3+! 46 ♔h2 ♘g5+ 47 ♔g1 ♘h3+ 48 gxh3 ♕g3+ with an instant draw.

46 ♔f1 ♘g3+ 47 ♔g1 ♘e2+ 48 ♔f1 ♘g3+ 49 ♔g1

49 ♔f2 ♘e4+ 50 ♔g1 ♕f2+ 51 ♔h1 ♔a4!! (threatening ...♖h7+) 52 b3+ ♔a3 53 ♕xc7 ♕h4+ 54 ♔g1 ♕f2+ is perpetual check.

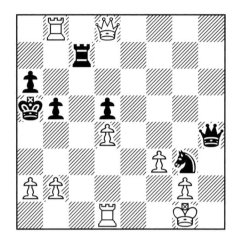

> *Exercise (critical decision):* If a formally intractable enemy suddenly proclaims
> friendship and peace, should we accept the offer, or regard it with suspicion?
> Nagging suppositions of the effectiveness or ineffectiveness of Black's attack
> swirl in his mind. Fear and ambition tug at Black in turns. Should Black bow to
> his cautions side and take a draw, or should he listen to the raging inner voices
> of ambition and go for the full point with 49...♕f4? What would you do?

49...♕f4??

Answer: Abandon hope for perpetuals or mates, all ye who enter here! In the other direction, Black received his life; in this one a life sentence. GMs seem to possess an inbred sense
of self-confidence, which we non-GMs seem to lack. The worst mistake in poker is to display signs of tremendous self-confidence if you hold a barely playable hand. Double ex-
clams and double question marks tend to arise, not from cold calculation and logic, but
from impulsive, creative flashes. Vyzmanavin, without a fig leaf of a reason, grossly overes-
timates his chances and plays for the loss. A seducer (that awful thought: "Maybe I can
win!") holds tremendous sway over the seduced (our ambition). He should have been satisfied with perpetual check.

50 ♖c8

Of course. There is no mate and Black drops material for nothing, and even worse, lacks
the perpetual check resource he had just a moment ago.

50...♔a4 51 ♕xc7 ♕e3+ 52 ♔h2

The chastened king escapes from the danger zone.

52...♘e2

52...♘f1+ 53 ♖xf1 ♕h6+ 54 ♔g1 ♕e3+ 55 ♖f2 ♕e1+ 56 ♔h2! ♕xf2 57 ♕c3! simultaneously cuts off the perpetual attempt, while forcing mate.

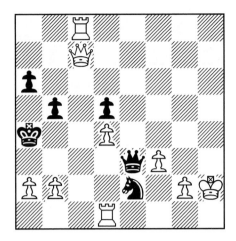

Exercise (combination alert): Black threatens mate
on h6, but White beats him to it by mating first. How?

Answer: 53 ♕c2+ 1-0

"That's right. Let it all out. I'm here to take care of you," comforts White's queen, with a
wicked smile for Black's weeping king. After 53...♔a5 54 b4+! ♔xb4 55 ♖b1+ ♔a5 56 ♖xb5+!
axb5 57 ♕c7+ ♔b4 58 ♕c5+ White's queen is obviously devastated by the black king's sudden and unexpected death: "Oh well, it won't do to dwell on such unhappy matters," she
declares, adding, "Musicians! Play us a merry tune!" 58...♔a4 59 ♖a8 is mate.

Summary: I suspect that chances are approximately even in this line when Black and White
castle on opposite wings. The trick is to understand the dynamics of attack and defence
better than your opponent.

Game 21
B.Finegold-J.Benjamin
US Championship, Saint Louis 2010

1 d4 ♘f6 2 ♗g5

Finally, we get our position through a true Trompowsky move order.

2...e6 3 e4

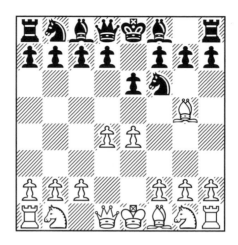

3...h6

Besides this move, the main line, Black has a couple of options:

a) 3...♗e7 (Black isn't afraid of e5 and allows it) 4 ♘d2 (after 4 e5 ♘d5 5 ♗xe7 ♕xe7 6 c4 ♕b4+ 7 ♘d2 ♘e7 the comps don't think much of White's space advantage, but when it comes to us humans, Black doesn't score well from this point), and then:

a1) 4...d5 5 e5 ♘fd7 6 ♗xe7 ♕xe7 7 f4!? (a pawn sacrifice; I would toss in 7 c3 first) 7...c5 (perhaps Black should risk the pawn grab 7...♕b4!? 8 ♘gf3 ♕xb2 and make White prove his compensation) 8 ♘gf3 ♘c6 9 ♗d3 ♘b4 10 ♗e2 f6 11 c3 ♘c6 12 0-0 0-0 13 a3 ♖b8 14 b4 b6 15 ♗d3 saw White reach a favourable Classical French-like position, with space, a good bishop, and kingside attacking possibilities, G.Kasparov-Centea, Deurne (simul) 2000.

a2) 4...b6 5 ♘gf3 ♗b7 6 ♗d3 c5 7 c3 ♘c6 8 a3! (an alert move, preventing ...cxd4 followed by ...♘b4) 8...0-0 9 0-0 ♖c8 10 ♖e1 cxd4 11 cxd4 d5 12 e5 ♘e8?! (Black should try 12...♘e4!? 13 ♗xe7 ♘xe7 14 ♘xe4 dxe4 15 ♗xe4 ♗xe4 16 ♖xe4 with some compensation for the pawn due to control over d5) 13 ♗f4 (principle: avoid swaps when you have a spatial advantage) 13...♘a5 14 ♘f1 ♘c4 15 ♕e2 ♖c7 16 ♘g3 ♕c8 17 h4 (Black's queenside counterplay is too slow and Kasparov builds a model kingside attack) 17...h6 18 ♖ad1 ♖c6 19 ♗c1 ♘c7 20 ♘h5 a6? (20...♘e8 21 ♘h2 f5 was forced) 21 ♗b1! ♖e8 22 ♕d3 g6 23 ♘f4 1-0, G.Kasparov-A.Baptista, Lisbon (simul) 1999. Black is defenceless to the coming ♘xg6.

b) 3...c5 4 d5 (Pert's choice, and I think White's best; I have tried 4 e5 h6 5 ♗h4 g5 6 ♗g3 ♘e4 in blitz and felt overextended here) 4...d6 (4...♕b6 5 ♘c3 ♕xb2 6 ♗d2 transposes to a favourable version for White of the Vaganian Gambit, which we look at later in the book) 5 ♘c3 ♗e7 6 ♗b5+ ♗d7 (6...♘bd7 7 ♗xf6!, and if 7...♗xf6 8 dxe6 fxe6 9 ♕xd6 ♗xc3+ 10 bxc3 ♕e7 when I don't think Black gets enough compensation for the pawn) 7 dxe6 fxe6 8 e5! dxe5 9 ♗xf6 ♗xf6 (it's a stretch to believe Black can survive White's withering attack after 9...gxf6!? 10 ♕h5+ ♔f8 11 0-0-0 ♕e8 12 ♕h6+ ♔f7 13 ♗c4 ♕g8 14 ♕h3) 10 ♗xd7+ ♕xd7 11 ♘e4 when White's domination of e4 and powerful knight offers more than enough for the pawn, A.Moiseenko-Y.Kruppa, Alushta 2004.

4 ♗xf6 ♕xf6 5 ♘f3 d6 6 ♘c3 ♘d7 7 ♕d2 a6 8 0-0-0 ♕d8

As I mentioned last game, my preference would be to develop the queen to e7 and then fianchetto the dark-squared bishop.

9 h4

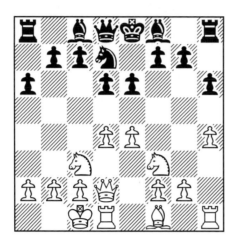

9...b5!?

Black aggressively seizes queenside space, even while lagging in development.

> **Question:** Can he be punished for this?

Answer: Only if White manages to open the position, which isn't so easy to do here. On 9...♗e7, I suggest 10 g4! with a position similar to our game, Z.Klaric-M.Schlosser, Cannes 1990.

10 g4

White engages in a comprehensive set of radical alterations, without gradations, and Black feels the constriction of tight boundaries.

> **Question:** Isn't this move rash if White
> doesn't know yet where Black's king will end up?

Answer: I don't think so. Black's position is so passive that White can easily get away with this Sicilian, Keres Attack-style kingside expansion. Instead, 10 e5 follows our familiar strategy: 10...d5 11 ♖h3 c5 12 dxc5 (White can't allow ...c4, which would give Black a strong attack) 12...♗xc5 13 ♖g3 ♕b6 14 ♖xg7 ♔f8 15 ♖g4 ♗xf2 (threatening a cheapo on e3) 16 ♔b1 h5 17 ♖g5! (Black gets the better ending after 17 ♖b4?! ♕e3) 17...♗e3 (17...♕e3? fails to 18 ♘xd5! ♕xd2 19 ♖xd2 ♗c5 20 ♘f6) 18 ♕e1 was H.Wunderlich-F.Velilla Velasco, correspondence 2009. White gets full compensation for the exchange in the form of a dark-square attack. *Houdini*'s analysis continues: 18...♗xg5 19 ♘xg5 ♕c7 20 ♕f2 ♘xe5 21 ♕f4

♔g7 22 ♘xf7! ♕xf7 23 ♕xe5+ ♕f6 24 ♕c7+ ♕f7 25 ♕g3+ ♕g6 26 ♕e5+ with perpetual check.

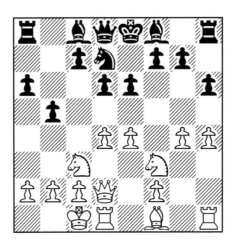

10...c5!?

Benjamin decides to edit the queenside to his liking. Different players, facing an identical crisis, rarely make the same decisions. Benjamin's philosophy: when you face an opponent who refuses to negotiate, sometimes the solution is a pre-emptive strike of overwhelming force. Black, refusing to go on the defensive, crosses a red line, after which war is inevitable. Logical in that Black immediately commences a queenside attack against White's king. Yet the trustworthiness of this plan remains in question, since the move violates the principle: avoid confrontation when lagging in development. Black must balance the ends with the means. Just because we are capable of an action, doesn't mean we would be wise in initiating it.

> **Question:** If not this move then what would you suggest?

Answer: Black can also try to lock the centre first, with 10...♗b7 11 d5 e5 12 g5 (the untried 12 ♗h3! looks more logical to me: 12...♕f6 13 ♕e2 b4 14 ♘b1 ♘c5 15 g5 ♕f4+ 16 ♘bd2 a5 17 ♖dg1 ♗a6 18 ♕e1 h5 19 ♗f1 and I prefer White's position; his control over the light squares looks more important than Black's domination on dark) 12...g6 13 ♗h3 h5 14 ♘e1 ♗g7 15 ♘d3 0-0 16 ♘e2. This maybe contemplates a sacrifice on h5. The position looks rather unclear to me, but I prefer White's side, S.Rocha-A.Vitor, Lisbon 2008.

11 ♗h3

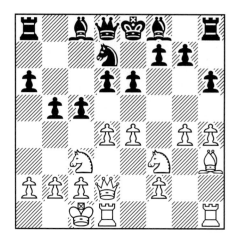

11...♕a5

> **Question:** Can Black play the position like a pure
> Open Sicilian with the bishop-pair, with 11...cxd4?

Answer: *Houdini* says chances are even here. To my mind the position looks like a very favourable Najdorf for White. Black's bishop-pair is small change when contrasted with White's nasty development lead. Indeed, after 12 ♘xd4 b4 (or 12...♗b7 13 g5! b4 14 g6!! bxc3 15 gxf7+ with a winning attack for White; I played out several scenarios and clobbered *Houdini* who played Black) 13 ♘ce2 ♗b7 14 g5 ♗xe4 15 f3 ♗d5 16 ♘f4 ♕a5 17 g6 Black is crushed.

12 ♔b1 ♗b7 13 d5 ♘b6!?

After this natural move it feels like Black launches a rather inoffensive offensive. He can also try his luck in the line 13...b4 14 ♘e2! (after 14 dxe6 bxc3 15 exd7+ ♔d8 16 ♕f4 ♕b4 17 b3 ♕a3 18 ♕c1 ♕xc1+ 19 ♔xc1 ♗xe4 20 ♗g2 ♗e7 21 ♖he1 ♗c6 22 ♖e3 ♖b8 23 ♖xc3 Black looks okay in the ending) 14...c4 15 a3 c3 16 axb4 cxd2 17 bxa5 exd5 18 ♘xd2 dxe4 19 ♘c3 d5 20 ♘b3 0-0-0 21 ♘xd5 ♘e5 22 ♘b6+ ♔c7 23 ♖xd8 ♔xd8 24 ♗g2 when White's dangerous development lead still outweighs Black's bishop-pair.

14 g5

Perhaps more accurate is to toss in the exchange on e6 first: 14 dxe6! fxe6 15 g5 ♘c4 16 ♕d3 ♕b4 17 b3 ♘a3+ 18 ♔b2 ♘c4+ 19 ♔a1 ♘a3 20 ♗xe6 c4 21 ♕d2 g6 22 ♔b2 ♗g7 23 gxh6 ♖xh6 24 ♘d4 with enormous complications, which *Houdini* claims favours White.

14...e5

After 14...b4 15 ♘e2 ♘xd5! 16 g6! f5 17 exd5 ♗xd5 18 ♘c1 ♗xf3 19 ♕e3! ♗xh1 20 ♕xe6+ ♔d8 21 ♖xh1 ♕a4 22 ♕xf5 I don't think Black survives those chronically weak light squares, despite the extra exchange. White has attacking ideas like ♘d3 and ♘f4, adding to the black king's insecurity.

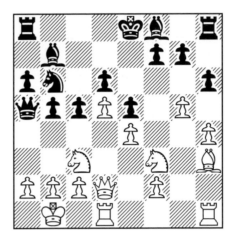

Exercise (planning): With 14...e5 Benjamin logically attempts to close the game. The players may share similar goals, yet White's means are significantly more potent in achieving them. Come up with a clear attacking plan for White.

Answer: Temporarily sacrifice a pawn, weakening g6, f7 and e6. White's attack is the faster.

15 g6! fxg6

15...f6 closes lines, but the era of freedom is over for the f8-bishop. Black looks borderline strategically lost after 16 ♗e6 ♘c4 17 ♕c1 ♔d8 18 ♘d2.

16 ♖hg1 ♗e7 17 ♖xg6 ♖f8?

Black has to try 17...♗f6 18 ♖dg1, which *Houdini* assesses as favourable for White, but Black still gets to attack on the other side.

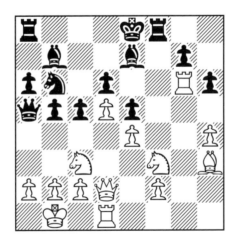

Exercise (combination alert): There are times in a chess game where whatever plans we concoct don't play out exactly as we envisioned. Up to this point, Black's king operated in an environment of impunity. This is about to change. After his last move, a blunder, Black's hopes skid into a muddy ditch. Proceed with White's attack.

Answer: Offer the f3-knight in exchange for infiltration.

18 ♖xg7!

At this point Benjamin must have contemplated the wreckage of his position, now too painful to describe with words.

18...♗c8

Black grudgingly refuses the f3-offer in an attempt to appease the unappeasable. So, undeterred, he rubs ointment into the gash and continues as if nothing happened. Benjamin saw he wouldn't survive 18...♖xf3 when the knight turns out to be an indigestible lump in the rook's stomach: 19 ♛xh6 (threatening both ♛e6 and ♛h5+) 19...♗c8 (if 19...♖xh3 20 ♛e6 ♘c8 21 ♖g8 mate) 20 ♛h5+ ♚d8 (the flustered king walks away quickly from the white queen's indecent proposal) 21 ♛xf3 is completely hopeless for Black.

19 ♗xc8 ♖xc8 20 ♛xh6 ♖f6 21 ♛h5+ ♚d7

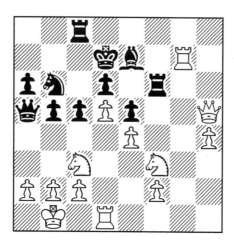

Exercise (combination alert): Find White's knockout blow.

Answer: Pin(s)/double attack.

22 ♘xe5+!

The knight's entry into the attacking equation brings with it a sense of finality of the end result.

22...dxe5 23 ♛xe5

"Everything will turn out fine. You'll see," lies White's queen in her most soothing tone to Black's worried king. White simultaneously threatens e7 and f6.

23...♖e8 24 ♕xf6 1-0

Summary: Keep in mind that White can also go for a g4 plan, rather than the e4-e5 strategy we have seen so far in this chapter.

Game 22
C.Lakdawala-J.Banawa
Southern California State Championship 2010

1 d4 ♘f6 2 ♘f3 e6 3 ♗g5

In the 2010 Southern California State Championship (the U.S. Chess Federation splits California into two states, since the Golden State is larger than many countries), I temporarily emerged from retirement from long-time control tournaments, but my accursed, Tony Miles-like bad back forced me once again into the semi-retirement zone of one-day rapid events. So this was my final long-control tournament. I posted a mediocre first weekend and my opponent, IM Joel Banawa, surged a full point and a half ahead of the field, going into the second weekend. To have any chance of first place, I had to take down the leader in this game.

Question: If this is the case, then why on earth would you play the rather sedate Torre Attack?

Answer: Your cruel words inflict excruciating mental anguish. The Torre isn't as boring as everyone thinks (as we have seen from the games in this chapter). My choice of opening may strike you as the tell-tale sign of the petty bureaucrat's refusal to make an exception to the rule – even when logic dictates it. But I argue: when you are desperate for a win, isn't your best bet to avoid an artificial opening choice and just go with the positions you feel most comfortable? Sometimes on the chess board, obstinate predictability represents a beneficial virtue, and flexibility a flaw. My opening choice strikes me as the former.

3...h6 4 ♗xf6 ♕xf6 5 e4 d6 6 ♘c3 ♘d7 7 ♕d2 c6

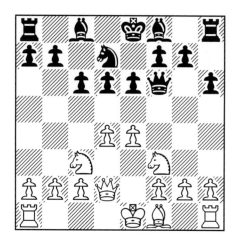

Answer: Black replaces the traditional ...a6 with ...c6, which covers both d5 and b5.

Answer: Ah, but not for long. Black plans to challenge White's central space advantage with ...e5 at the appropriate moment.

8 0-0-0 e5

It's possible this natural and most often played move may be mistimed. However, I'm not so sure it helps Black to wait before allowing an opening of the position:

a) 8...♗e7 9 e5!? (a promising pawn sacrifice; safer is 9 ♔b1 e5 10 h4, J.Hodgson-B.Carlier, Stavanger 1989) 9...dxe5 10 dxe5 ♘xe5 11 ♘e4 ♕f5 12 ♘d6+ ♗xd6 13 ♕xd6 ♘d7 14 ♗d3 ♕c5 15 ♕f4 0-0 16 ♖de1 a5 17 h4 a4 18 a3 ♕xf2 19 ♖hf1 ♕a7 20 g4 and White got a ferocious attack for the two-pawn investment in K.Chernyshov-S.Mishra, Chennai 2011.

b) 8...♕d8 9 ♔b1 ♗e7 10 h4 a6 11 e5 d5 12 ♖h3 b6 13 ♖g3 ♗f8 14 h5 a5 15 ♘e1 ♕h4 16 ♖h3 ♕e7 17 f4 ♗b7 18 g4 0-0-0 when Black's unimpressive bishop-pair doesn't compensate for White's monster space advantage, I.Rogers-D.Pikula, Baden-Baden 1999.

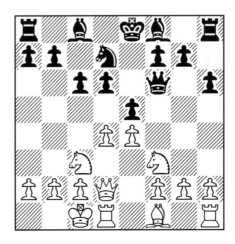

9 dxe5

Principle: open the position when leading in development.

> ***Question:*** But what about Black's bishop-pair?

Answer: Principle: a development lead normally takes precedence over the bishop-pair.
9...dxe5?

Black had to try 9...♘xe5 10 ♘d4 (intending f4; also possible is 10 ♘xe5 ♕xe5 – no choice, since 10...dxe5?? 11 ♘b5! ♕e7 12 ♕a5! b6 13 ♕c3 is game over – 11 f4 ♕a5 12 ♗c4, which Houdini claims is even, but I don't trust Black's position when so far behind in development, J.Plaskett-C.Ward, Hastings 1989/90) 10...g5 when his position looks loose, but still playable, J.Anguix Garrido-L.Comas Fabrego, Spanish Championship 1993.

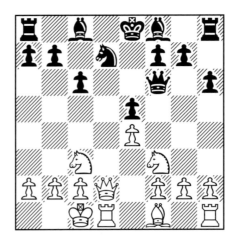

Exercise (combination alert): After 9...dxe5 if Black is allowed ...♗b4,
he stands better. Opportunity is fast evaporating. White must act and
act now. Believe it or not, Black's last move loses, since marching an army
in formation against a shadowy, hidden enemy can be suicidal. Find
one powerful idea and White's attack grows to winning proportions.

Answer: Pin. The knight inflicts havoc since Black can't afford the high cost of its capture.
10 ♘b5!

Now Black walks perilously near to Morphy versus Count and Duke territory. The knight acts as an intermediary between White's attack and its possible success or failure. Undesired problems well up in profusion for Black. After the game I basked in the god-like afterglow of my tactical abilities (at least to my deluded perspective), until I actually looked up this position. To date this position has occurred 16 times in my database (this game included), which downgraded a would-be masterpiece (somehow the title 'masterpiece' is disqualified if 15 other people played the same way you did) to merely a book trap.

10...♔d8!

Banawa finds the path of greatest resistance after a massive 40-minute think. He hopes to damper White's celebratory attitude down a notch with a calm defensive move. His king, far from being a one-man chain gang, languishing on d8, basically taunts White with the words: "Here I am. Come and get me if you can!" Alternatives are:

a) 10...cxb5? 11 ♗xb5 ♛e6 12 ♘xe5! and Black can resign, since 12...♛xe5?? is met with 13 ♗xd7+ ♔e7 14 ♗xc8 ♖xc8 15 ♛d7+, popping the c8-rook.

b) 10...♖b8 11 ♘xa7 (threatening to undermine the defender of d7) 11...♛f4 (11...♛e6 12 ♗c4! ♛xc4 13 ♘xc8 ♛e6 14 ♘xe5! is crushing as well) 12 g3 ♛xd2+ 13 ♖xd2 ♘c5 14 ♘xc8 ♖xc8 15 ♘xe5 and Black, unable to take e4, found himself down two pawns for no compensation, I.Rogers-I.Glek, Linz 1997.

11 ♛a5+!

A spasmed twitching at the corners of her mouth is as close to smiling as the queen comes, as the black king's proposal for peace is met with a mirthless laugh from her. The combination fails without this indispensable adjunct. White must replenish his initiative or watch it sag. After a lax move like 11 ♗c4? ♗c5 Black remains alive and well.

11...b6

Once again the best response. If 11...♔e7? 12 ♘d6 ♘b6 13 ♘xc8+ ♖xc8 (13...♘xc8 14 ♛c7+ mates next move) 14 ♛xa7 and Black collapses.

12 ♛c3

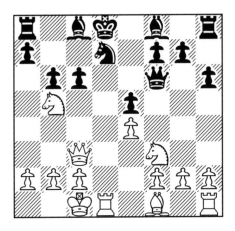

Targeting the two softest spots in Black's position: c6 and e5.

12...a6

12...cxb5? is still out of the question, since 13 ♗xb5 threatens ♘xe5, which leaves Black defenceless: for example, 13...a6 (13...♗d6 14 ♕c6 is an instant game-ender) 14 ♗xd7 ♗xd7 15 ♘xe5 ♖a7 (15...♗d6?? is met with the crushing 16 ♖xd6) 16 ♖d5! (White must avoid 16 ♘c6+ ♔c7 17 ♘xa7+?? ♕xc3 18 bxc3 ♗a3+ 19 ♔b1 ♖a8 and Black stands clearly better) 16...♖c7 17 ♕d4 ♕e6 18 ♖d1 and game over.

Instead, 12...♗c5 was tried in E.Rozentalis-V.Nithander, Gothenburg 2012. Now White's strongest follow up is 13 ♕xe5! cxb5 14 ♗xb5 when Black has no good way to prevent the threatened ♕d5!, and if 14...a6 15 ♗xd7 ♗xd7 16 ♕d5 ♖a7 17 ♘e5 is curtains.

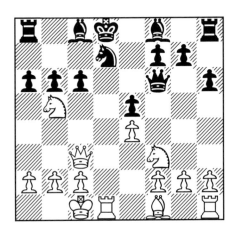

Exercise (combination alert): Black's last move, 12...a6, attempts to eject the unwanted b5-houseguest from the premises. Find the shot which shatters Black's earlier defensive handiwork to bits.

Answer: Interference/double attack.

13 ♘d6! ♗xd6

Otherwise:

a) 13...♔c7?? isn't much of a consideration due to 14 ♘e8+ and Black's queen loses consciousness, as she gets whacked behind the ear with a blackjack (do criminals still use blackjacks?).

b) 13...c5 14 ♘xc8! ♔xc8 15 g3! (threat: ♗h3; Black can't bear the logistical strain of a two-front war) 15...♔c7 (15...♕e6 16 h4! changes nothing, since Black can't afford to take on a2) 16 ♗h3 ♖d8 17 ♖xd7+ ♖xd7 18 ♗xd7 ♔xd7 19 ♖d1+ ♗d6 20 ♘xe5+, and if 20...♔c7 21 ♖xd6! ♔xd6 (21...♕xd6 22 ♘xf7 ♕f8 23 ♘xh8 ♕xh8 24 ♕e5+ is an easy win for White) 22 ♕d2+ ♔e7 23 ♕d7+ ♔f8 24 ♕c8+ ♔e7 25 ♕c7+ ♔e8 ("Woman, you forget yourself! Know your place!" Black's king lectures White's queen; she responds: "My place is on your throne") 26 ♘c6! When Black's king is tried in absentia and found guilty. Black must hand over his queen to avoid mate.

14 ♕xc6

Double attack on a8 and d6.

14...♔e7

Defiance, when coming from a prisoner, represents the final remnant of freedom. Black offers an exchange in desperation to unravel. After 14...♗b7 15 ♕xb7 ♔e7 16 ♗c4 ♖hd8 17 ♗d5 when White dominates.

15 ♕xa8 ♘c5 16 ♕a7+

A theoretical novelty. 16 ♗c4 b5 17 ♕a7+ ♗b7 was S.Drazic-B.Damljanovic, Podgorica 1996, and now the strongest is 18 b4!.

16...♗d7 17 ♗xa6 ♖b8

17...♗b8 is met with 18 ♖xd7+ ♘xd7 19 ♕b7.

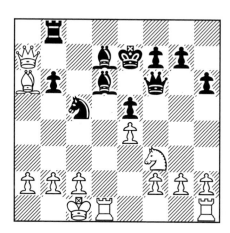

Exercise (combination alert): White can win even more material. How?

Answer: Removal of a key defender/deflection.

18 ♖xd6! ♕xd6 19 ♖d1 1-0

Summary: The ...c6 and later ...e5 plan may be playable for Black, but even when it is played correctly, I still like White's attacking chances. Handing Black the bishop-pair feels like a small price to pay for our development lead and central control.

Game 23
V.Fedoseev-A.Zubov
Voronezh 2012

1 d4 ♘f6 2 ♗g5 e6 3 e4 h6 4 ♗xf6 ♕xf6 5 c3

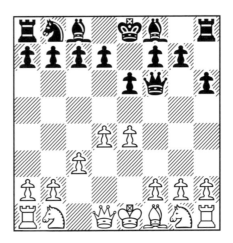

The Pert Variation. This line is a speciality of IM Richard Pert, who has to be the world's leading authority in this position, since his games encompass around 17% of the entire database in this line.

> **Question:** I realize that White avoided an early ♘c3 because he wanted to avoid the ...♗b4 pin, but the question is why avoid ♘f3?

Answer: Unlike the earlier games of this chapter, White hopes to engineer f4, or at least keep it on the table. So 5 c3 is in a way a compromise move between the poles of 5 ♘c3 ♗b4 and the 5 ♘f3 lines, which eliminate f4 ideas. One of the appealing things about this line is that White's plan is very simple: we play ♘d2, ♗d3, ♘e2, 0-0 and f4, virtually every time. As a bonus, Black's queen is completely misplaced on f6 and later loses time retreating.

5...d6

By far the most popular response. Black sensibly plays for ...e5, challenging White's dominance in the centre.

Question: Are there other formations for Black besides a direct ...e5?

Answer: Black can also play for a French Defence formation with 5...d5 6 ♘d2 (the capture on e4 costs Black time with his queen) 6...c5!? (in open positions where the imbalance is development lead over bishop-pair, I always put my money on the development lead) 7 ♘gf3 cxd4 8 ♘xd4 ♗c5 was I.Ivanisevic-M.Pavlovic, Zlatibor 2007. Now I would play 9 ♘2b3 ♗b6 10 ♗b5+ ♗d7 11 ♗xd7+ ♘xd7 12 exd5 ♕e5+ 13 ♕e2 ♕xd5 14 0-0 0-0 15 ♖fd1. White still has a touch of a development lead in this c3-Sicilian-like, opposite-wing majorities position. Objectively it may be even, but I prefer White.

Possible too are:

a) 5...c5 6 ♘f3 ♕e7!? (or 6...♘c6 7 d5 ♘e5 8 ♗e2 ♘xf3+ 9 ♗xf3 exd5 10 ♕xd5 ♕e6 11 ♕d3 ♗e7 12 0-0 0-0 13 ♘d2 b5! 14 ♖fe1 ♖b8 15 e5 c4?! 16 ♕d4 ♕b6 17 ♕xb6 ♖xb6 18 a4 a6 19 axb5 axb5 20 ♖a7 when White established a small but nagging edge, M.Hebden-M.Adams, Kilkenny 2006, but the comp trick 15...d5! equalizes) 7 ♗d3 g6 8 0-0 ♗g7 9 ♘bd2 0-0 10 e5 cxd4 11 cxd4 d6 12 ♕e2 ♗d7 13 ♖ac1 dxe5 14 dxe5 ♗c6 15 a3 ♖d8 16 ♗e4 ♗xe4 17 ♕xe4 ♘c6 18 ♘c4 with dynamically even chances, P.Harikrishna-S.Karjakin, Lugo 2006.

b) 5...b6 6 e5 ♕g6!? (6...♕d8 is safer) 7 ♕f3! ♘c6 (Black can also try 7...♕c2!? 8 ♘d2 ♘c6 9 ♖b1 ♕a4, but his queen looks oddly placed on a4 and I still prefer White) 8 ♗d3 f5 (Black loses more time after 8...♕g5 9 ♘d2 ♗b7 10 ♘e4) 9 exf6 ♕xf6 10 ♕h5+ ♔d8 11 ♘d2 with a pleasant edge for White, due to Black's disjointed king's situation, J.Klinger-K.Bjerring, Liechtenstein 1988.

6 ♗d3 e5

Black demands a fair share of the centre. Next game we look at 6...♘d7.

7 ♘e2

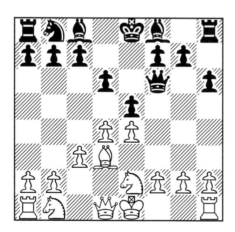

Remember, e2 over f3 development for this knight. In doing so, White stays away from possible ...♗g4 pins. The main reason is White's plan: castle and follow with f4, made all the more effective with Black's queen stationed on f6.

7...g6

Black's main move. Instead, 7...♞c6 (hoping to induce d5, which places all of White's pawns on the wrong colour for his remaining bishop) 8 0-0 g5!? (a radical way of halting the coming of f4; as beginners we all once fell for the tactical idea 8...exd4?! 9 cxd4 ♞xd4?? 10 ♞xd4 ♛xd4?? 11 ♗b5+) 9 ♗b5 ♗d7 10 ♛a4 ♛d8 was V.Milov-S.Tatai, Bratto 2003. Now White can continue 11 ♞d2 ♗g7 12 d5 ♞e7 13 ♞c4! a6 14 ♗xd7+ ♛xd7 15 ♛b4 0-0-0 16 a4 ♚b8 17 ♞g3. Both the attacking ♞a5 and the strategic ♞e3 are in the air, with a clear advantage for White.

8 0-0 ♗g7 9 f4

The implementation of White's main set-up in this variation, where he hopes to redraw the map to his territorial advantage. Previously, the kingside represented ungoverned land, until now when White makes his claim.

9...♛e7 10 ♞d2 0-0 11 ♞f3

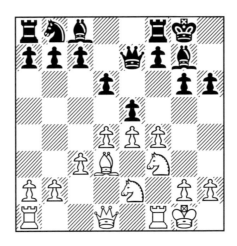

11...♗g4!?

Black decides to hand back the bishop-pair, turning the game into an opposite-coloured bishop fight.

> **Question:** Why would Black give away his
> main asset in the position, the bishop-pair?

Answer: I assume to reduce White's kingside attackers. I knew a guy 30 years ago who drove a piece-of-junk jalopy of a car – if you could call it that. He installed an elaborate alarm system to guard his precious treasure. Moral: an object of little or no value to one person can be a treasure to another, to be loved and cherished. We all have our prejudices concerning bishops over knights. Most players – at least to my mind – tend to over-value the bishop-pair. We Tromp players, on the other hand, tend to fall into the category of knight lovers, since early on in the game we willingly play ♗g5 and ♗xf6 so often. The problem with Black's plan is that it violates the principle: opposite-coloured bishops favour the attacker – in this case clearly White.

> ***Question:*** I don't see a good plan for Black. What would you suggest?

Answer: I would go for a plan based on ...exd4 and ...c5 for two reasons:

1. By doing so, Black increases the influence of his unopposed dark-squared bishop.

2. Black follows the principle: counter in the centre when attacked on the wing.

Play may continue: 11...♘d7 12 ♕d2 c6 13 ♖ae1 exd4! and now perhaps White can try a more radical approach with 14 ♘exd4 (the natural move allows Black counterplay after 14 cxd4 c5 15 ♘c3 ♘b6 16 f5 cxd4 17 ♘d5 ♕d8 18 f6 ♗xf6 19 ♘xf6+ ♕xf6 20 ♕xh6 ♗g4 21 ♘g5 ♕g7 22 ♕h4 ♗e6 23 b3 ♘d7; Black looks like he defends here) 14...a6 15 h4!? ♘f6 16 f5, which is obviously dangerous for Black, but perhaps still better than the game continuation.

12 ♕b3

Hitting b7, but more importantly, also f7, the point which represents the origination of Black's coming troubles.

12...b6?!

I'm not crazy about this move, which further degrades Black's light squares. Once again Black should think about 12...exd4!, following the principle cited above. After 13 ♕xb7 ♘d7 14 cxd4 c5 15 ♖ab1 ♖fe8 it feels to me like Black gets full compensation for the pawn.

13 h3 ♗xf3 14 ♖xf3 ♘d7 15 ♖af1

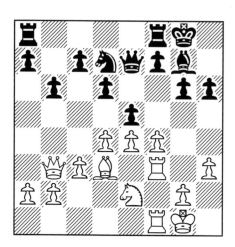

White continues to build force against f7.

15...♘f6

When a person deliberately shuts you out by ignoring you and not speaking to you, isn't it in a strange way, focusing absolute attention on you alone? Black, worried about the building pressure on the f-file, clings to f7, as if the square was his only friend in the world.

His barely-holding defence appears constructed more for ornament than for efficiency. This time 15...exd4 comes too late, since 16 ♘xd4 ♘c5 (maybe Black can try the more radical 16...♗xd4+!? 17 cxd4 c5) 17 ♘c6 ♕d7 18 ♕d5 gives White a light-squared bind.

16 ♕b5?!

Intending to add pressure to e5, but in doing so, White allows his intent to decant for too long. After this inaccuracy the lustre of White's initiative threatens to fade somewhat. He should pursue the pressuring of f6/f7 strategy with 16 fxe5! dxe5 17 ♗c4 ♖ae8 18 ♕a3! exd4 (18...♕xa3 19 bxa3 exd4 20 ♖xf6 ♗xf6 21 ♖xf6 ♔g7 22 ♖c6 ♖xe4 23 ♘xd4 also favours White) 19 ♕xe7 ♖xe7 20 ♖xf6 ♗xf6 21 ♖xf6 (threat: ♖xg6+) 21...♔g7 22 ♖c6 dxc3 23 ♘xc3 with advantage in the ending.

16...exd4?!

The much demanded central counter is mistimed. This move hinders, but doesn't yet behead Black's overall defensive plan. 16...c5! cuts off the white queen's access to e5: 17 fxe5 (17 dxe5 dxe5 18 f5 ♖ad8 also looks fine for Black) 17...dxe5 18 d5 ♘e8, intending ...♘d6, and Black looks fine.

17 e5! dxe5?

This move fails to meet Black's kingside defensive obligations and cedes White carte blanche to raid and pillage at will. Black had to take his chances in the line 17...♘h7 18 ♘xd4 (18 cxd4 c5 19 ♗c4 cxd4 20 ♘xd4 dxe5 21 ♘c6 ♕e8 22 fxe5 ♘g5 23 ♖d3 ♖c8 24 ♖d6 ♘e4 25 ♖xg6 ♔h8 26 ♖xg7 ♔xg7 27 ♗d5 also doesn't look very healthy for Black, who finds himself under light-square fire all across the board, with king safety issues added, but this is still better than the game's continuation) 18...dxe5 19 ♘c6 ♕d7 20 ♕c4! exf4 21 ♗xg6 ♘g5 22 ♖d3 ♕e6 23 ♕xe6 ♘xe6 24 ♗h5 when Black continues to struggle against the light-squared bind.

18 fxe5 ♘h7

18...♘d7 19 cxd4 leads to crushing pressure on f7. Black essentially can't do much about the coming ♗c4 and ♕b3, or ♕d5.

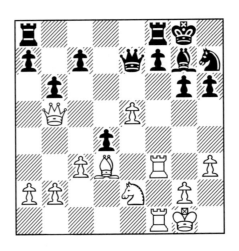

Answer: Double attack/pin: f7 isn't as secure as Black imagined.

19 ♖xf7!

An overwhelming force has no need to lie in wait.

19...♖xf7 20 ♖xf7 ♛c5

Desperation:

a) 20...♚xf7 is met with 21 ♗c4+ ♚f8 22 ♛d5 with a deadly double attack on g8 and a8.

b) 20...♛xf7 meets with the killing pin 21 ♗c4.

21 ♛d7!

Not fearing Black's discovered check. White's queen smoothly projects herself into the argument.

21...dxc3+ 22 ♚h1 ♗xe5

If 22...♛xe5 and now the simplest is 23 ♖xg7+ ♛xg7 24 ♛d5+. White puts his fiscal house in order, picking up the a8-rook with check.

23 ♖xh7

Threatening mate on the move.

23...♖f8

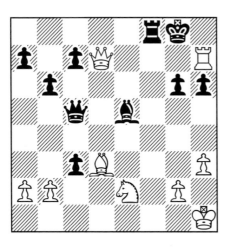

Answer: 24 ♕e6+! 1-0

"I'm afraid you don't get a vote in matter of your living or dying," White's queen informs Black's king. 24...♔xh7 25 ♕xg6+ ♔h8 "You! You are the monster who brought me down," rages Black's king, as he points a trembling, accusatory finger at White's queen. She responds with a malicious smile: "How can I bring down someone who was never up?" 26 ♕h7 is mate. An aerosol of the king's blood spray-paints the wall, after the queen slices open his jugular.

Summary: With 5 c3, White hopes to avoid both 5 ♘c3 ♗b4, and also 5 ♘f3, which blocks f4 ideas. Our set-up is easy to remember after 5 c3: ♘d2, ♗d3, ♘e2, 0-0 and f4.

Game 24
V.Laznicka-A.Moiseenko
San Sebastian 2012

1 d4 ♘f6 2 ♗g5 e6 3 e4 h6 4 ♗xf6 ♕xf6 5 c3 d6 6 ♗d3 ♘d7 7 ♘e2 g6

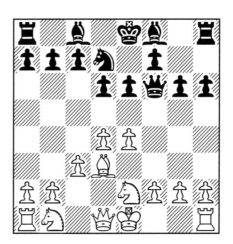

Question: What is the difference between
Black's plan in this game and the last game?

Answer: This game Black decides not to stake out a central claim with ...e5, playing the position in Modern Defence (1...g6) style.

Question: How can avoidance of ...e5 benefit Black in any way?

Answer: Going ...e5 provokes confrontation, especially in this line after White plays f4, which favours the better developed side – in this case White. So in a way Black actually follows principle by avoidance of ...e5.

8 0-0 ♗g7 9 f4

The position resembles a funky kind of Modern Defence, Austrian Attack, with a pawn on c3, rather than a knight. White gave up the bishop-pair. As compensation, he obtains both a development lead and a daunting space advantage.

9...0-0 10 ♘d2 ♕e7

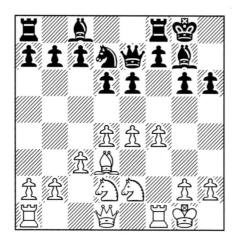

11 e5

Cramping Black further. Now e5 proves to be a secure base, around which White may build and launch a kingside attack. He can also swing the queen to g3 first with 11 ♕e1, Tromp guru Hodgson's favourite plan in the position: 11...b6 12 ♕g3 ♗b7 13 e5 ♖ad8 (opening the f-file only benefits White: 13...dxe5?! 14 fxe5 ♕g5 15 ♕xg5 hxg5 16 ♗e4 ♗xe4 17 ♘xe4 ♗h6 18 g4! c5 19 ♖f2 cxd4 20 cxd4 ♖ac8 21 ♘2c3 a6 22 ♖af1 ♖c7 23 ♘d6 ♘b8 24 ♘ce4 ♖e7 25 ♖c2 when White dominates across the board, J.Hodgson-P.Saint Amand, Philadelphia 2000) 14 ♘e4 b5! (Rowson does his best to dismantle White's imposing central dominance; I don't like Black's chances if he switches to French Defence mode and closes the centre with 14...d5?! 15 ♘f2 c5 16 ♘g4 cxd4 17 cxd4 ♕b4 18 ♖ab1 h5 19 ♘e3 when an f5 sacrificial breakthrough is in the air) 15 ♖ae1 b4! 16 h4! bxc3 17 bxc3 ♔h8 18 h5 gxh5 19 ♕h3 h4 20 exd6!? cxd6 21 f5 d5 22 f6!? (I prefer White after 22 ♘f2 e5 23 ♗b5 ♘f6 24 ♕xh4) 22...♘xf6 23 ♘xf6 ♗xf6 24 ♘f4 ♖d6 25 ♗c2 (White gets full attacking compensation for the two pawns) 25...♖g8 26 ♘h5 ♗g5 27 ♕d3 f6 28 ♘xf6!

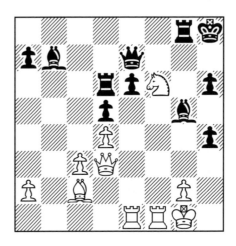

28...♗xf6?? (it's anybody's game after 28...♖g7! 29 ♘h5 ♗a6 30 ♕d1 ♗xf1 31 ♘xg7 ♕xg7 32 ♖xf1) 29 ♖xf6 ♕g7 30 ♕f3! (there is no good defence to ♖f7) 30...♖c6 (30...♖d7 doesn't help either: 31 ♖exe6 and White wins) 31 ♖f7 ♖xc3 32 ♖xg7 ♖xf3 33 ♖h7 1-0 J.Hodgson-J.Rowson, Oxford 1998.

11...b6 12 ♗e4

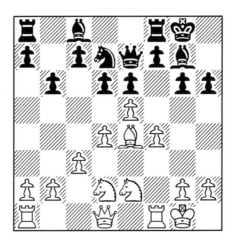

> *Question:* What is the sense in such a move if
> Black can simply play ...d5, gaining a tempo?

Answer: The problem is 12...d5 violates the principle: don't close the centre when attacked on the wing. By closing, Black reduces his central counterplay and allows White's kingside attack leisure time to build after 13 ♗f3 (or 13 ♗d3 c5 14 ♘f3 and White can follow with the Hodgson plan of ♕e1, ♕g3 and h4, when Black's queenside and central play arrives slower) 13...♗b7 14 c4 c6 15 ♖c1 when Black's sorry-looking bishop-pair is clearly inferior to White's space.

12...♖b8 13 ♕a4

White gains a tempo on a7 to swing the a1-rook into the fight.

13...a6

Superior to 13...a5 which weakens the queenside light squares: 14 ♗c6 and it's not so easy to shake White's queenside light square grip, R.Panjwani-N.De Firmian, Calgary 2010.

14 ♖ae1 b5 15 ♕c2 c5 16 ♔h1

A new move. White's king gets off the g1-a7-diagonal as a precautionary measure. Instead, after 16 ♗f3 cxd4 17 cxd4 ♘b6 18 ♘e4 dxe5 19 fxe5 ♘c4 20 ♘2g3 White's knight dangerously eyes the c5-, d6- and f6-squares, J.Saada-C.Rihouay, French League 2009.

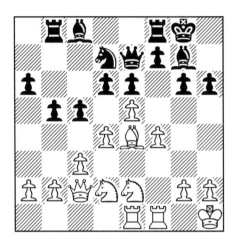

16...d5?!

Violating the principle we discussed earlier. This may be the inception point of Black's future difficulties and acts as a barrier to his wishes. It's hard to resist a tempo when it is there for the taking. Perhaps, though, Black should consider 16...♗b7! 17 ♗xb7 ♖xb7 18 ♘e4 d5! (this is the correct timing) 19 ♘d6 ♖b6 20 ♕d2 ♖fb8 21 ♕e3 c4 22 b4 ♖xd6! 23 exd6 ♕xd6. I think Black is okay here with a pawn for the exchange and active pieces.

17 ♗f3

The bishop and d5-pawn part amicably for now.

17...b4

Black labours intensely on the queenside without making much of a difference. His queenside attack turns out to be a fiction. 17...c4 18 g4 ♕h4 19 ♘g3 intending f5, isn't so tempting for Black, but is perhaps a better chance than what he got in the game.

18 c4! ♗b7?

This plan looks like a bad business model: too much work, with too little reward. Black collapses on the kingside after this. It's understandable that he didn't want to enter 18...dxc4 19 ♘xc4 ♗b7 20 ♗xb7 ♖xb7 21 ♘d6 ♖c7 22 ♖c1 which leaves Black in deep trouble strategically, yet less so than the game's continuation.

19 cxd5 ♗xd5

19...exd5 20 f5 gxf5 21 ♘g3 f4 22 ♘f5 ♕g5 23 ♗d1!, intending ♘f3, gives White a winning position.

20 ♗xd5 exd5

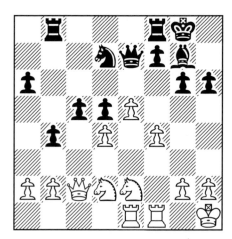

Black's objective will not come cheaply. White's kingside attack is far more dangerous than anything Black can muster on the other side, and we sense a dissipated defensive force, slowly drained of function.

21 f5

Black's shady strategic past rises to the surface, as Laznicka marshals his thoughts into singular intent: strip Black's king of protectors. Disruption at f5 is White's ticket to Black's king and White's kingside majority proves to be far more potent than Black's worthless model on the other side.

21...gxf5 22 ♘g3

Clearly there will be tough times ahead for Black's king.

22...cxd4 23 ♘xf5 ♕g5 24 ♘f3 ♕d8 25 ♘3xd4 ♖b6

One can't forestall that which is inevitable. Black's position lies in ruins:

1. White's knights hover menacingly over Black's king.

2. Black nurses three isolanis and a loose structure.

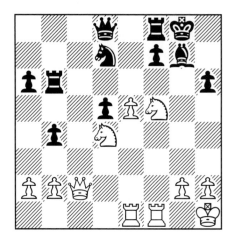

Answer: Black can't afford e7 and must fork over a full exchange.

26 e6!

This move keeps Black off balance.

26...fxe6

26...♗xd4? 27 ♘xh6+ ♔h8 28 ♘xf7+ ♖xf7 29 ♖xf7 ♘f6 30 ♕d3 forces mate.

27 ♘xe6 ♖xe6

Black burns through defensive resources at a much faster rate than he can replenish. At the current rate, munitions deplete to near zero in just a few moves.

28 ♖xe6 ♔h8 29 ♖fe1 ♗f6

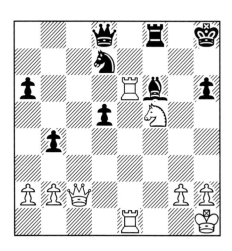

> *Exercise (combination alert):* Black's remaining defenders are ineffective, mismatched remnants of a once powerful king's guard. *Houdini* announces mate after this move. How would you conduct White's attack?

30 ♘h4

Clever, but stronger is:

Answer: 30 ♕d2!, and if 30...♗g5 31 ♖xh6+! ♔g8 32 ♕xd5+ ♖f7 33 ♖g6+ ♔f8 34 ♖xg5! (deflection/weak back rank) 34...♕xg5 (34...♕b6 35 ♖e7! is also a pretty finish) 35 ♕a8+ with mate in two moves.

30...♖g8 31 ♘g6+ ♔g7 32 ♘e7

Threatening a queen infiltration via g6.

32...♘f8

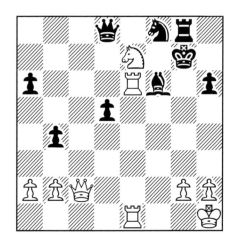

> *Exercise (combination alert):* There are two ways for White to finish Black off. Find one of them.

Answer: Removal of a defender/pin.

33 ♘f5+!

Even more effective is the obliteration of the king's position with 33 ♖xf6! (a terrible presence appears on the scene, in the wrathful form of White's rook) 33...♔xf6 ("Well, at least this is a character building experience," muses Black's long suffering king) 34 ♕f5+ ("You will reform, if not by persuasion, then perhaps by the whip," declares White's queen to Black's king) 34...♔g7 35 ♕g4+ ♔f7 (Black's king bellows futile orders to defend him, which go unheeded) 36 ♕xg8+. The queen firmly believes that her enemies should be executed thoroughly and often.

33...♔h8 34 ♖d6! 1-0

The rook arrives at the negotiating table with great leverage and bargaining power. 34...♘d7 35 ♕d2 ♖g6 36 ♖xd5 wins the knight.

Summary: When Black plays in Modern Defence style with 7...g6, he or she hopes to avoid an early central clash while behind in development. If this is the case, then let's bring the confrontation to Black on the kingside, based on our gigantic central space advantage.

Chapter Four
2...d5 3 ♗xf6

1 d4 ♘f6 2 ♗g5 d5 3 ♗xf6 exf6

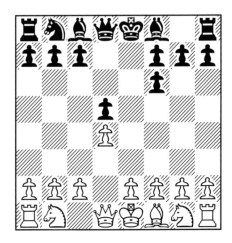

The diagrammed position may be the most important one for us in the entire book. We deliberately disarrange Black's once immaculate structure at the cost of offending against the strategic aesthetic: we hand over the bishop-pair, all in the name of generating an early imbalance.

At club level, most of our opponents hold merely glancing knowledge of the Trompowsky and will strive mightily to avoid an ultra-sharp theoretical fight. Black's secret is exposed by implication when they play 2...d5, hoping to steer the game into a normal Queen's Gambit or Slav direction. We deny them their wish by chopping on f6 and Black can either recapture away from the centre, agreeing to a slightly degraded structure in compensation for freedom of movement, or capture toward the centre. In the book you have the option of psycho or strategic plans. Here is a glimpse of what can happen if we decide to go Hodgson on our opponents, with a bombs-away, shock and awe campaign:

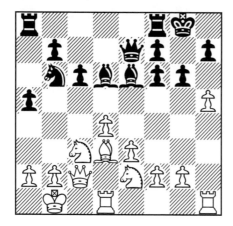

This is Hodgson-Gokhale, where one side or the other is sure to get mated.

Aggressive-minded opponents may try 3...gxf6, after which we may end up in equally sharp positions like the following:

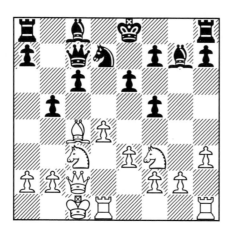

This is Hodgson-Martin, where once again, both kings appear to be in grave danger. In either case, we the Tromp side give free-reign to our imaginative impulses and force Black into a fight on our turf.

> ## Game 25
> ## J.Hodgson-J.Gokhale
> British Championship, Dundee 1993

1 d4 ♘f6 2 ♗g5 d5

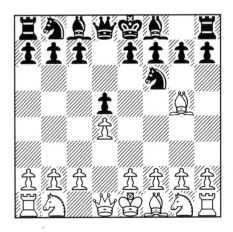

3 ♗xf6

> **Question:** Oh, no! Not another variation where we hand Black the bishop-pair?

Answer: As far as the Trompowsky is concerned, bishop lovers need not apply. In this book we cover the 3 ♗xf6 lines, but White isn't obliged to take. We can also play:

a) 3 ♘c3 transposing to the Veresov.

b) 3 ♘f3 transposes to Torre Attack, and can even morph into Queen's Gambit and Slav lines, depending on how both sides play it.

c) With 3 e3 White keeps all options open:

c1) 3...e6 4 c4 c6 5 ♘c3 ♗e7 transposing to an old school QGD, or 5...♘bd7 6 ♘f3 (6 cxd5 exd5 7 ♗d3 is the QGD, Exchange Variation) 6...♕a5, which is the Cambridge Springs.

c2) 3...♘e4 4 ♗f4 transposes to Chapter Two.

c3) 3...♘bd7 with a further choice:

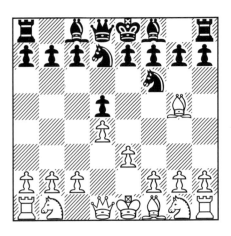

c31) 4 ♘f3 h6 (4...g6 5 c4 ♗g7 6 ♘c3 c6 7 cxd5 cxd5 8 ♕b3 is a strange Exchange Slav-like position where Black's kingside fianchetto bites into a wall on d4, C.Lakdawala-N.Arutyunov, San Diego (rapid) 2013; instead, here 5...dxc4?! 6 ♗xc4 ♗g7 7 ♘c3 0-0 8 ♖c1 c5 9 0-0 cxd4 10 exd4 is advantage White, since we reach a classical isolani position where White reached a QGD Tarrasch, a full two moves up from Black's version, C.Lakdawala-R.Bruno, San Diego (rapid) 2013) 5 ♗h4 g6 6 c4 c6 7 ♘c3 ♗g7 8 ♖c1 ♕a5 9 cxd5 ♘xd5 10 ♗c4 with a Grünfeld-like position, C.Lakdawala-B.Baker, San Diego (rapid) 2013

c32) 4 ♘d2 h6 (4...e5 5 dxe5 ♘xe5 6 ♘gf3 is a kind of reversed Caro-Kann-like position, a move up for White, which is probably still equal) 5 ♗f4!? (now it's a kind of London where Black gets the free move ...h6, which White can use as grist for a future ♖g1, g4, h4-style attack) 5...e6 6 ♗d3 ♗d6 7 ♘gf3 ♗xf4 (Black is probably better off avoiding this swap, which gives White a grip over e5 and opens the e-file for his rooks) 8 exf4 c5 9 dxc5! ♘xc5 10 0-0 ♘xd3 11 cxd3 0-0 12 ♘b3 ♗d7 13 ♘bd4 ♕b6 14 ♕d2 ♖ac8 15 ♖fc1. Advantage White, whose knights roost along the central dark squares, C.Lakdawala-B.Baker, San Diego (rapid 2007.

d) 3 ♘d2 has pretty much the same idea as 3 e3, except White discourages ...♘e4 in this version. Here 3...♘bd7 4 ♘gf3 e6 5 e3 ♗e7 6 ♗d3 h6 7 ♗f4 0-0?! (Black shouldn't commit to castling this early) 8 g4! was a new move at the time and an improvement over 8 h3.

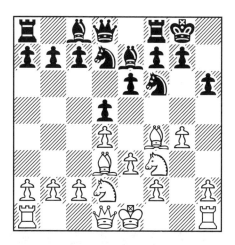

White, who may castle queenside, plans g5, opening kingside lines: 8...g5!? (8...♘xg4?! 9 ♖g1 gives White a ferocious attack) 9 ♗g3 ♔g7 (9...♘xg4 10 h4 gives White more than enough for the pawn) 10 h4 ♖h8 11 ♘e5 c5 12 c3 cxd4 13 exd4 when White castled queenside and generated a winning attack, C.Lakdawala-K.Arnold, San Diego (rapid) 2004.

3...exf6

GM Aaron Summerscale writes: "A fairly reliable method of defending against the Trompowsky is to grab a share of central space with 2...d5. As after 3 ♗xf6 and c4, Black is forced to give up his central foothold, but in compensation gains the bishop-pair."

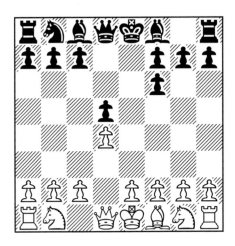

Answer: The recapture away from the centre does indeed lessen Black's central influence, yet greatly enhances freedom of development and opens the e-file – not such a bad deal for Black. Think about the Exchange Ruy Lopez: 1 e4 e5 2 ♘f3 ♘c6 3 ♗b5 a6 4 ♗xc6 and now Black nearly always plays 4...dxc6, recapturing away from the centre. Black's Trompowsky version applies the same logic. We examine 3...gxf6 later in the chapter.

4 e3

White's most logical move, switching the pawn structure to the opposite colour of our remaining bishop.

4...♗e7?!

Inaccurate. This move is redundant to the mission, since Black normally posts this bishop on the more active d6-square. Alternatives:

a) We examine Black's most natural posting, 4...♗d6, in the next few games. Here is a 5-3 blitz game I played against a GM, which followed Hodgson's attacking plan: 5 c4 dxc4 6 ♗xc4 0-0 7 ♘c3 f5 8 ♘ge2 ♘d7 9 ♕c2 ♘f6 10 ♗d3 g6 11 h3 c6 12 0-0-0 (yes, your writer was a braver man when he was still young, thin and devilishly handsome) 12...♕e7 13 ♔b1 ♗d7 14 g4!? (in opposite-wing attacks, hesitancy is synonymous with failure; like it or not, White must sacrifice material to open lines) 14...fxg4 15 hxg4 ♘xg4 16 e4!? (clearly, Caligula would approve of White's crazy excess; 16 ♘e4 ♗f5 17 ♘2c3 is a safer way to play the position) 16...♘xf2 17 e5 ♗b4 18 ♘e4 ♘xe4 (Shipov wisely plays it safe, avoiding the terrors of 18...♘xh1 19 ♖xh1 ♔g7 20 a3 ♗a5 21 ♕c1 h5 22 ♘f6 ♖h8 23 ♕g5 ♖ag8 24 ♘f4 with a scary strong attack) 19 ♗xe4 ♗g4 20 ♖dg1 ♗xe2? (Black strives to reduce material to weaken White's attack, but accomplishes the opposite; according to *Houdini* Black had to try 20...♕g5! 21 ♗f3 ♗xf3 22 ♖xg5 ♗xh1 23 ♘f4 ♖ad8 24 ♖g1 ♗d5 25 ♘h5 ♗e7 26 ♕d2) 21 ♕xe2 f5 22 ♗c2 ♖ad8 23 ♗b3+ ♔h8 24 ♖xg6?! (stronger is to first insert 24 a3! ♗a5 25

♖xg6) 24...♖xd4 25 ♖gh6 ♖g4 26 e6 ♖g7 27 ♕e5 ♔g8 28 ♗c2 ♗d6 29 ♕d4 c5 30 ♕d5 ♗f4 31 ♖6h5 ♗g5 32 ♗xf5 h6 33 ♗c2 ♖d8 34 ♕e4 b5 35 a3 c4 36 ♖xh6! ♗xh6 37 ♖xh6 ♖g1+ 38 ♔a2 b4 39 ♕xc4 bxa3 40 ♖h7? (40 ♕c3! forced mate) 40...♖g7 41 ♖xg7+ ♔xg7 42 ♕g4+ ♔f8 43 ♕f5+ ♔g8 44 ♕g6+ ♔f8 (44...♔g7?? loses instantly to 45 e7) 45 ♕h6+ ♔g8.

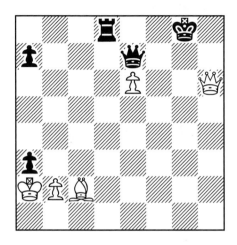

Exercise (combination alert): White to play and win material:.

Answer: Deflection/double attack: 46 ♗h7+! ♕xh7 (46...♔h8?? 47 ♗g6+ ♔g8 48 ♗f7+ wins the queen) 47 ♕g5+ ♕g7 48 ♕xd8+ ♔h7 49 ♕d3+? (49 ♕d7! ♔h6 50 ♔xa3 wins) 49...♔g8 50 ♕xa3. This may be a win for White but Shipov managed to hold the draw on move 102, C.Lakdawala-S.Shipov, Internet (blitz) 2001.

b) With 4...c6 Black plays in Slav formation and leaves options open for his dark-squared bishop: 5 c4 (White can also avoid c4 and play 5 ♗d3 which we examine in Mamedyarov's game later in the chapter) 5...♗b4+ (the rapid development strategy means Black will probably later hand back the bishop-pair) 6 ♘c3 0-0 7 cxd5 cxd5!? (I expected 7...♕xd5 8 ♘ge2 followed by a3) 8 ♘ge2 ♘c6 9 a3 ♗xc3+ 10 ♘xc3 (the d5-isolani gives White an edge, despite Black's development lead) 10...♖e8 11 ♗e2 f5 (toying with ...f4 undermining ideas) 12 0-0 ♗e6 13 ♖c1!? (I could also discourage Black's next move with 13 g3) 13...f4!? 14 exf4 ♕f6 15 ♘b5 (threatening a fork on c7) 15...♕xf4 16 g3 ♕b8 17 ♗f3 ♖d8 18 ♖c5 (the pressure on d5 mounts) 18...a6 19 ♘c3 ♕d6?! (Black decides to sacrifice d5 to generate piece play; more prudent was 19...♘e7 20 ♘e2 with only a tiny edge for White) 20 ♗xd5 ♗xd5 21 ♖xd5 ♕xd5!? (I expected 21...♕f6 22 ♖xd8+ ♖xd8 23 d5 ♘d4 24 ♕d3 when White had good chances of converting with a clean, extra d-pawn) 22 ♘xd5 ♖xd5 23 ♕b3 ♖b5 24 ♕c3 ♖d8 25 ♖e1 h6 26 ♖e4 ♖bd5 27 ♔g2 ♖xd4 28 ♖xd4 ♖xd4 and I managed to convert in the technical ending which followed, C.Lakdawala-D.Kishnevsky, San Diego (rapid) 2013.

c) With 4...♗e6 Black suppresses c4. Then 5 ♗d3 (5 g3 is also possible) 5...♗d6 6 ♘d2 c6 7 ♕f3 is a set-up we examine later in the chapter.

5 c4 dxc4 6 ♗xc4 0-0 7 ♘c3

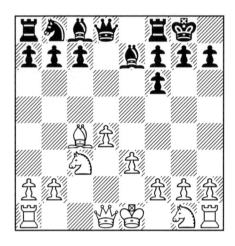

7...c6

Black's most common structural set-up.

> ***Question:*** Can Black try and open for the bishop-pair with 7...c5?

Answer: This isn't played often, but it looks reasonable. White can continue 8 ♘ge2 ♘c6 9 0-0 cxd4 10 ♘xd4 ♘xd4 11 exd4 ♗f5 12 ♖e1 ♖c8 13 ♗b3 when I like his position. The d4-pawn may be an isolani, but in essence it's extra, since Black's extra pawn on the kingside gives him a crippled majority. Black's bishop-pair in the open position should compensate.
8 ♘ge2

> ***Question:*** Why e2 rather than f3?

Answer: Here f3 isn't such a great square since Black controls e5. White's knight greatly increases its options from e2, because it can later play to g3, f4, or even a vacated c3-square.
8...♘d7

White can also play it safer and castle kingside. An example: 8...f5 9 ♕c2 g6 10 0-0 ♘d7 11 ♖fd1 ♗d6 12 g3 ♘f6 13 a3 ♕e7 14 b4 with dynamically balanced chances, M.Adams-P.Thipsay, London 1992.
9 ♕c2 ♗d6 10 ♗d3

More accurate than the immediate 10 0-0-0 f5! when 11 ♕xf5?? ♘e5 wins material.
10...g6

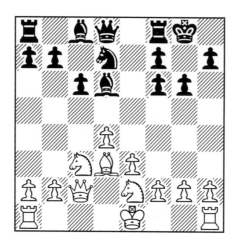

11 h3!

In order to meet ...f5 with the g4 prying mechanism.

Question: Why not the immediate 11 h4?

Answer: That is also possible, even though Black can deal with the opening of the h-file: for example, 11...f5 12 h5 ♘f6 13 hxg6 hxg6 14 0-0-0 ♔g7 (leaving open ...♖h8 options) 15 f3 ♗e6 16 ♕d2 ♖h8 17 e4 fxe4 18 fxe4 ♘g4 19 e5 ♗e7 20 ♖xh8 ♕xh8 21 ♘f4 ♗d7 22 ♔b1 ♕h6 23 ♖f1. I prefer White due to superior attacking chances, while *Houdini* rates it as dead even.

11...♕e7

11...f5 is met with 12 g4.

12 0-0-0

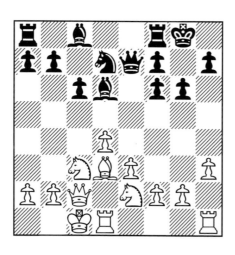

If one venomous snake swallows another live snake, equally venomous, then who digests whom? To play such a move we must first push open a psychological gate. Now the margin between abundant riches and bankruptcy is razor thin. If you are familiar with such a position as White, this constitutes a huge advantage over an opponent who is new to town.

> **Question:** It appears to me like White's king is exposed to greater danger. Isn't Hodgson's construct more of a risky abstraction, rather than a truly sound attack?

Answer: Never, never take our patron Saint Julian's name in vain, my child, for it is a sin. If you play through the positions with a comp turned on, you see that chances are approximately even under *Houdini*'s objective gaze.

12...a5 13 ♔b1 ♘b6

Understandable, since Black is anxious to avoid 13...f5 14 g4!.

14 h4!

This move is made all the more potent if Black lacks the ...♘f6 defensive option. The menace which first merely appeared as attacking vapours, now forms into concrete, very real threats. If Black can't find a method to stem the flow of the game, it will be the onset of certain ruin.

14...♗e6

Otherwise:

a) 14...f5?! 15 h5 ♗e6 16 g4! transposes to the game.

b) Black had to risk the weakening of g6 with 14...h5!, his best bet against White's coming attack: 15 e4 (15 ♗xg6? is too early and unsound: 15...fxg6 16 ♕xg6+ ♕g7 and White's attacking chances are not worth the piece he gave up) 15...a4 16 f3 ♖d8 17 g4 hxg4 18 f4 c5 19 e5 c4 20 ♗e4. I still like White's chances, but this is better than what Black got in the game.

15 h5 f5?

Black had to risk 15...♖fe8 16 e4 g5 17 g3 ♗b4 18 f4.

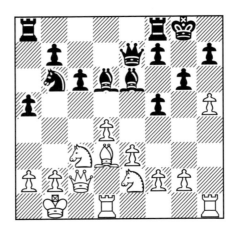

Answer: Target the soft underbelly: g6.

16 g4!

Hodgson, long past regrets, conducts the attack in the most forceful manner. The poison has been ingested, which soon leaves Black's king wheezing and rasping, from a rapidly constricting throat.

16...♘d5!

Intending ...♘b4. Black finds the only path to stay alive. After 16...fxg4? 17 hxg6 fxg6 18 ♗xg6 kick-off is scheduled from g6 (18...hxg6?? 19 ♕xg6+ picks up two pieces).

17 gxf5

Also quite promising is 17 ♘xd5 ♗xd5 18 hxg6 ♗xh1 19 ♖xh1 hxg6 20 gxf5 with a winning attack, since 20...g5? loses to 21 ♖h6 f6 22 ♕d1 b5 23 ♕h1 when Black drops his queen.

17...♘b4 18 ♕d2 ♘xd3 19 ♕xd3 gxf5!?

It's hard to believe Black survives 19...♗xf5 (threats without military power to back them up are no more than bluster) 20 e4 ♗e6 21 ♖dg1, when all of White's pieces take aim at his king. Moreover, f4, f5, central pawn disruptions are in the air.

20 d5!

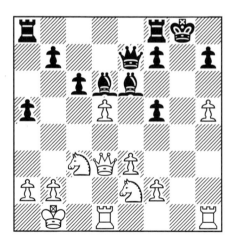

Clearing d4 for his pieces and the a1-h8 diagonal for his queen. Now Black's king will never feel secure on h8.

20...cxd5 21 ♘xd5

Most accurate is 21 ♕d4! f6 22 ♘xd5 ♕d8 (or 22...♕f7 23 ♖dg1+ ♔h8 24 ♘df4 ♗xf4 25 ♘xf4 with a winning attack, since ♘g6+ is coming) 23 ♖hg1+ ♔h8 24 ♘b6! ♗e5 25 ♕c5 ♕c7 26 ♕xc7 ♗xc7 27 ♘xa8, which is hopeless for Black.

21...♕d8

21...♗xd5 22 ♕xd5 ♗e5 23 f4 ♗f6 24 ♕xf5 looks pretty bad for Black as well.

22 ♖dg1+ ♔h8 23 ♕c3+

Loosening Black's defensive line further. The queen's eyebrows rise in arrogant arches at the sight of her almost-defeated enemy on h8.

23...f6 24 ♘df4 ♕d7

What to do? Confronting White leads to disaster; avoiding confrontation leads to disaster. Black's array of unsatisfactory alternatives:

a) 24...♗g8?? is met with 25 ♘g6+! hxg6 26 hxg6+ ♔g7 27 ♘d4 ♕d7 28 ♕d3 ♖fd8 29 ♘xf5+ ♔f8 30 g7+ ♔f7 31 ♕d5+ ♕e6 32 ♘xd6+ ♖xd6 33 ♕xb7+, which finishes Black off.

b) 24...♗xf4 25 ♘xf4 ♕d6 26 ♖d1 ♕e7 27 ♖d4 and now 27...♖fd8 is met with 28 ♘g6+! hxg6 29 hxg6+ ♔g8 30 ♖dh4 with a winning attack.

c) 24...♖c8?? 25 ♘xe6 ♖xc3 26 ♘xd8 drops a piece.

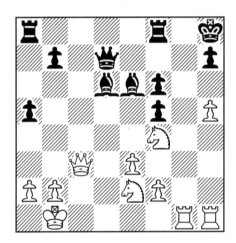

> ***Exercise combination alert:*** Black's last move
> loses on the spot. How did Hodgson continue?

Answer: Obliteration of the black king's cover/fork.

25 ♘g6+!

"Listen carefully to my coming threats, for they are nothing less than your deepest, secret fears," the knight instructs Black's king.

25...hxg6 26 hxg6+ ♔g8

"Sharper than a serpent's tooth..." thinks Black's king of the ingrates around, who refuse to protect him.

27 g7 ♖fc8

Otherwise, 27...♖f7 28 ♖h8 is mate, and 27...♕xg7 is obviously futile for Black, since getting mated or losing a queen is a distinction without much difference.

28 ♕xf6

There is no defence to ♖h8.

28...♗xa2+ 29 ♔a1 1-0

Summary: Hodgson's queenside castling attacking plan leads to psychotic mutual attacks. Specialize in this plan and you will likely turn to chutney your unfamiliar opponents at the club level.

> ### Game 26
> ### J.Hodgson-K.Arkell
> London 1991

1 d4 ♘f6 2 ♗g5 d5 3 ♗xf6 exf6 4 e3 ♗d6

Clearly the better square for the bishop, over e7, as we saw last game.

5 c4

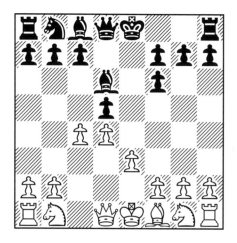

5...dxc4

> *Question:* It feels to me like this helps White develop. Why not play a Slav formation with 5...c6?

Answer: Opponents try this formation on me from time to time, and to the best of my recollection, I picked off d5 in every single encounter. Black gets tied down to the defence of d5 after something like 6 cxd5 cxd5 7 ♘c3 ♗e6 8 g3 (White's simple plan: load up on d5 with everything you have) 8...♘c6 9 ♗g2 0-0 10 ♘ge2 (there is no rush to grab d5; if 10 ♗xd5 then 10...♗a3 offers Black counterplay) 10...♘e7 11 ♕b3 ♕d7 12 0-0 (most certainly not 12 ♘xd5?? ♘xd5 13 ♗xd5 ♗xd5 14 ♕xd5 ♗b4+) 12...♖b8, as in P.Nidl-J.Vavra, Czech League 2005. Play might continue 13 ♘c1 b6 14 ♘d3 ♗c7 15 ♘b4 ♖fd8 16 ♖fc1. This isn't lost by any means for Black, but it certainly is an unpleasant position, since his only plan is to just keep defending d5, while White probes for weakness.

6 &xc4 0-0 7 &c3

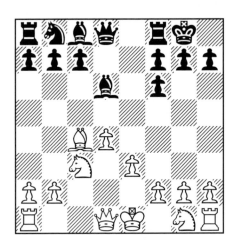

7...a6

Black seeks to expand with ...b5, ...&b7, ...&d7 and ...c5.

> ***Question:*** Why can't Black play the immediate 7...c5?

Answer: A trap! White wins material after 8 dxc5 &xc5 9 &xf7+! &xf7 10 ♕h5+, regaining the piece with an extra pawn.

Alternatives:

a) 7...c6 leads to the set-up we examined last game.

b) 7...f5 8 &ge2 &d7 9 ♕c2 is once again similar to what we looked at last game, N.Vitiugov-Ding Liren, Sochi 2009.

c) 7...&d7 8 &d3 c5 9 &ge2 cxd4 10 &xd4 (White's knight gets a stable outpost on d4; 10 exd4 is also completely playable) 10...&e5 11 0-0 &d7 (I must be a bishop-snubbing Trompowsky player to the core, since I still like White better after 11...&xd3 12 ♕xd3; his knights control key central squares, and he also enjoys the superior structure and a slight development lead) 12 &e4 &c6!? (I would play 12...&c8) 13 &xc6 &xc6 14 &xc6 bxc6 15 &a4 ♕a5 16 &c1 &ac8 17 &c4 ♕e5 18 g3 &c7 19 ♕f3 sees White work a clear target on c6 and the knight looks better than Black's remaining bishop. Later in the game White can play for b3, &b2 and &c4, with a grip on the light squares, I.Miladinovic-D.Ivanovic, Mataruska Banja 2007.

8 a4

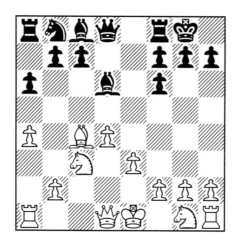

Answer: It does both. We must be flexible. White still controls a good chunk of the centre and maintains the superior structure.

Answer: White can try messing up Black's plans with 8 ♕f3. White avoids weakening b4, and at the same time prevents ...b5. After 8...c5 9 ♘ge2 cxd4 10 ♘xd4 ♘d7 intending ...♘e5. 11 ♕e2 ♘e5 12 ♗b3 *Houdini* says even, but I still like White a little more due to that influential d4-knight, J.Wegerle-K.Spraggett, Arinsal 2009.

8...♘d7

A new move:

a) 8...c5? 9 dxc5 ♗xc5 and we apply the same trap we looked at in the above note, with 10 ♗xf7+!.

b) 8...♗e6 challenges White's most powerful piece. I would continue with 9 ♕b3.

c) 8...♘c6 was I.Drogovoz-M.Putin, Khanty-Mansiysk 2011. I would play this way as Black, who seizes control over the b4-hole. Chances look approximately even after 9 ♘ge2 ♘b4 10 0-0 f5 11 g3 ♕e7 12 ♘d5 ♘xd5 13 ♗xd5 c6 14 ♗g2 ♗e6 15 ♘c1, intending ♘d3.

9 ♘ge2

Hodgson once again shows he prefers e2 development to f3 in this line.

9...c5

The break is fine now since our trap no longer works.

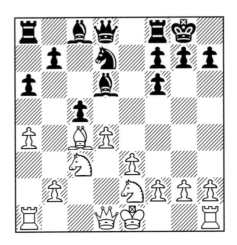

10 dxc5

I'm not crazy about this move, which violates the principle: don't be the one to release the central pawn tension without a sound strategic or tactical reason behind it. He should let Black do the trading and simply castle here.

> *Question:* Should White consider a bypass with 10 d5?

Answer: Your suggestion is untried. I wouldn't play it since it violates the principle: don't fix your pawns on the same colour as your remaining bishop. The move greatly reduces White's influence on the dark squares and also hands Black e5.

10...♗xc5

Arkell probably wanted to retain control over b4, and so recaptured with the bishop.

11 0-0 ♘e5 12 ♗d5

Seizing absolute control over d5.

12...♕b6

Not really attacking b2, as much as clearing d8 for a black rook. However, b6 isn't a stable square for the queen and perhaps should be substituted with 12...♕e7.

13 a5! ♕c7

The queen backs off with foot-dragging resentment, realizing her intended b2-project requires a heavy lift: 13...♕xb2 14 ♘a4! (White can also take an immediate draw with 14 ♖a2 ♕b4 15 ♖a4 ♕b2 16 ♖a2) 14...♕b4 15 ♕c2 ♗a7 16 ♖fb1 ♕e7 17 ♘b6 ♗xb6 18 ♖xb6 leaves Black tied down. White gets more than enough compensation for the pawn.

14 ♘f4

Dual purpose:

1. The knight supports and enhances domination of d5.
2. White makes it harder for Black to play ...♗e6.

14...♗d7 15 ♕b3

Zoning in on f7 and b7, Black's weakest points. The queen also clears the path for either rook to d1.

15...♘c6

A schism appears on the queenside over ownership of White's extended a-pawn. Target: a5, which Black regards as a blot on White's otherwise pristine landscape. Arkell hopes to prove that White's 13th move overextended past structural tolerance.

16 ♘e4!

After an East to West survey, we see Black's troubles mounting. Hodgson realizes a5 represents a sentimental memento, of no practical value, other than to his heart.

16...♘xa5?

A blunder. Black's pieces, drunk with a feeling of successful acquisition, overreach by taking a bite from the forbidden fruit. He can't afford the time and resources for this rather optimistic grab. He had to play 16...♗e7 17 ♖fc1 when White continues to hold an edge.

17 ♕c3! ♗b6

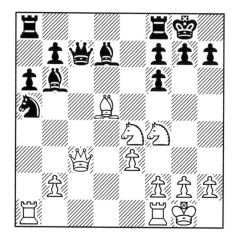

> ***Exercise (combination alert):*** Black's forces feel out of synch. Their mutual interests touch here and there, yet fail to coincide in harmony. Hodgson found a crushing shot on his next move. Do you see it?

Answer: Demolition of the king's position/double attack/knight fork. The knight clips f6, as if a snipped-off thread off an old sweater. Now the fury of White's initiative refuses to ebb.

18 ♘xf6+! ♔h8

Arkell projects his king into the background, seeing he won't survive the acceptance with 18...gxf6 19 ♕xf6. White's queen regards her brother's failings with an indulgent smile. She instructs him: "Before you are paper, ink and pen. I advise you to craft your confession carefully." The threat is ♘h5, and mate on g7. Black's defender-free kingside sways like a newly planted aspen and it becomes clear that all is not well. Black's current state of enfeeblement is directly attributable to a pair of causes:

1. A lack of defenders around his king.
2. The weakened dark squares around his king.

After 19...♖ae8 (or 19...♕d8 when the simplest is 20 ♘h5! winning) 20 ♖fc1 ♕d8 (20...♗c6 is met with 21 ♘g6! hxg6 22 ♕xg6+ ♔h8 23 ♕h6+ ♔g8 24 ♖xa5! ♗xa5 25 ♖c4 forcing mate) 21 ♘h5! ♕xf6 22 ♘xf6+ ♔g7 (Black is forced to shower wealth on his opponent) 23 ♘xd7 the final double attack is fatal.

19 ♕xc7

Too many Black pieces hang.

19...♗xc7 20 ♘xd7 ♖fd8

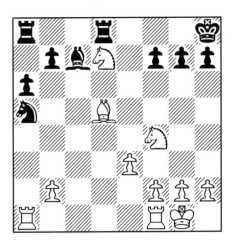

> *Exercise (combination alert):* Many white pieces are loose and it feels as if Black should regain his material. In this instance one of life's banana peels finds its way underfoot for Black. How can White escape with all his extra material intact?

Answer: White's knight returns from the dead and about now, Black must have experienced similar emotions as Hamlet when his father's disembodied spirit popped up, bobbing along on the currents of the draughty castle.

21 ♘c5! 1-0

The position conspires against Black, who suffers heavy material loss, no matter how he continues: 21...g5 (or 21...♗xf4 22 exf4 ♖xd5 23 ♖xa5 b6 24 ♖xa6! when White remains up a piece), and now the pretty shot 22 ♘ce6! wins.

Summary: Unlike last game, where all thought of restraint was tossed into the wind, in this game White played more prudently. We don't have to castle queenside and go crazy every game in this line. If Black tosses in an early ...a6, then we should switch to positional play and castle kingside, the way Hodgson did in the game.

Game 27
S.Mamedyarov-A.Bagheri
Abu Dhabi 2003

1 d4 ♘f6 2 ♗g5 d5 3 ♗xf6 exf6 4 e3 c6

Black opens with a Slav formation, keeping his options open.

5 ♗d3

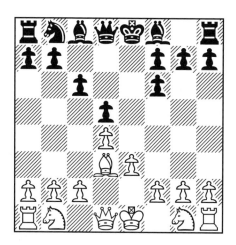

In this case White decides against an early c4.

> **Question:** Why would White want to avoid c4?

Answer: By avoiding c4, White conforms to the principle: if your opponent has the bishop-pair, don't open the position. After 5 c4 ♗b4+ 6 ♘c3 0-0 7 cxd5 cxd5!? (we continue the discussion from the last game; in my opinion Black shouldn't take on this inferior isolani and I expected 7...♕xd5 8 ♘ge2 ♖e8 9 a3 ♗xc3+ 10 ♘xc3 ♕d6) 8 ♘ge2 ♘c6 9 a3 ♗xc3+ 10 ♘xc3 ♖e8 11 ♗e2 (to transfer the bishop to f3, later on if necessary) 11...f5 12 0-0 ♗e6 13 ♖c1!? (13 g3 would discourage Black's next move) 13...f4 14 exf4 ♕f6 15 ♘b5 (threatening a fork on c7) 15...♕xf4 16 g3 ♕b8 17 ♗f3 ♖d8 18 ♖c5 a6 19 ♘c3 ♕d6?! (this pawn sacrifice looks unsound; White is only slightly better after the correct 19...♘e7 20 ♘e2 ♕d6 21 ♘f4) 20 ♗xd5 ♗xd5 21 ♖xd5 ♕xd5! (probably a better practical try than 21...♕f6 22 ♖xd8+ ♖xd8 23 d5 ♘d4 24 ♕d3; White is up a clean pawn and should convert) 22 ♘xd5 ♖xd5 23 ♕b3 ♖b5 24 ♕c3 ♖d8 25 ♖e1 h6 26 ♖e4 ♖bd5 27 ♔g2 ♖xd4 28 ♖xd4 ♖xd4 it wasn't easy to break down Black's attempted fortress, but I eventually won the technical ending, C.Lakdawala-D.Kishnevsky, San Diego (rapid) 2013.

5...♗d6

By far the most commonly played move, but in my opinion, perhaps not Black's best. I think Black's most accurate move order is 5...f5! which essentially forces White back into c4 channels after 6 ♘d2 ♗d6 7 ♘e2.

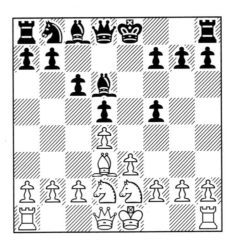

Answer: It's playable, but White gets an inferior version to the Mamedyarov game after 7...g6 8 ♘e2 h5! 9 h3 ♘d7 (now White, seeing his g4 plan isn't working this time, decided to toss in c4 anyway) 10 c4 ♘f6 11 ♘c3 ♗e6 when White's queen looks misplaced on f3, N.Legky-V.Lazarev, Cannes 1992.

After 7 ♘e2 g6 8 c4 dxc4 9 ♘xc4 ♗c7 (on 9...♗b4+!? I would play 10 ♔f1 and castle by hand) 10 0-0 0-0 11 ♖b1 Black's bishop-pair compensates for White's superior central and queenside influence, A.Grigoryan-I.Kurnosov, Moscow 2011.

6 ♘d2 0-0

Once again, 6...f5! is Black's most accurate move order.

7 ♕f3!

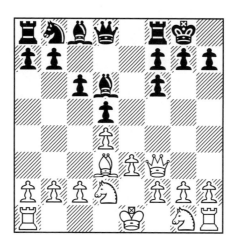

The correct timing. White suppresses ...f5 and increases his grip on the kingside light squares.

Answer: Yes. Play ♕f3 only if Black hasn't played ...f5 and you can prevent the move with g4 later on.

7...♘a6

V.Georgiev-M.Mikavica, Bern 2004, saw 7...♖e8 8 ♘e2 ♘d7 9 g4!. This is the kind of attacking position we are after. White gets a fast, automatic attack after h4, castling queenside and ♖dg1.

8 c3

8 a3 ♘c7 9 ♘e2 ♘e6 10 c4 ♘g5 11 ♕h5 g6 12 ♕h4 ♖e8 13 cxd5 cxd5 14 ♘c3 ♗e7 15 f4 f5 was J.Hodgson-M.Taimanov, Yerevan 1986. I still prefer White after 16 ♕f2 ♘e4 17 ♘dxe4 dxe4 18 ♗b5 due to the passed d4-pawn. Also, White's bishop and knight hold their own versus Black's bishop-pair in the still rigid structure.

Answer: That is also possible, but it's risky to hand Black both of our bishops for knights. I would actually consider playing this way, since we inflict serious damage to Black's structure. An example: 8...bxa6 9 ♘e2 a5 10 0-0 (White shouldn't castle queenside after opening the b-file for Black) 10...♗a6 11 ♖fb1 a4 12 b4! ♖b8 13 a3 ♕c7 14 ♘g3 ♖fe8 15 ♖c1 ♗b7 16 c4 ♕d8 (Black loses material after 16...dxc4 17 ♖xc4 c5 18 ♕g4 ♗c8 19 ♕d1 ♗e6 20 ♖c3 c4 21 ♕xa4) 17 ♕d1 when Black is about to drop a pawn on the queenside and I don't believe the bishops fully compensate, A.Moskalenko-R.Skomorokhin, Izhevsk 2013.

8...♘c7 9 ♘e2

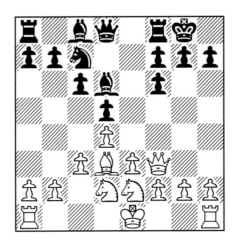

9...g6

9...♞e6 10 h4! (preventing ...♞g5 ideas) 10...♖e8 11 0-0-0 a5 12 g4 and maybe I'm bi-ased, but White's attack looks faster than Black's, A.Delchev-V.Spasov, Bulgarian Championship 1995.

Question: Can Black force his way to ...f5 with 9...♕d7?

Answer: Wow, your suggestion never occurred to me. As ...f5 really can't be prevented, maybe White can try 10 h3. This has the benefit of halting ...♕g4. After 10...f5 11 ♖g1 (per-haps White should just switch to positional play with 11 0-0, intending c4 next move) 11...g6 12 g4 fxg4 13 hxg4 *Houdini* rates the chances at even.

10 g4!

What was once a scuffle, now gravitates into a life and death struggle for supremacy of the kingside. A critical adjunct to our set-up: don't allow Black ...f5. White inserts this sup-pressing move at a moment calculated to confuse and disrupt the smooth flow of Black's defence.

10...c5!?

The fragility of Black's position grows more marked after his last move, since he hands White the d4-square. Perhaps Black should try 10...b5 11 h4 ♕d7 12 ♖g1 when at least he lures White's rook off the h-file.

11 dxc5!

White can play this move since Black's knight lacks easy access to e5. Not only did White weaken and isolate d5, but he also opened d4 for his knight.

11...♝xc5 12 h4

Intending to deliver checkmate down the h-file. *Houdini* grossly misassesses this posi-tion as equal. In reality Black is borderline busted, if not already there. I see no source of counterplay, while White's attack plays itself.

12...b5 13 h5

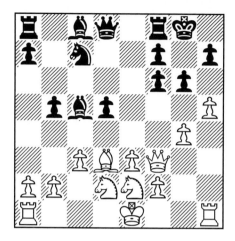

13...♘e6

> **Question:** Shouldn't Black try and shut down attacking
> lanes and reupholster his broken kingside with 13...g5?

Answer: After your suggestion, Black's king may be marginally safer, but you created a huge gash on f5. Also, if White manages a queen and bishop battery along the b1-h7 diagonal, I'm not sure how Black can defend: for example, 14 ♘b3 ♗d6 15 ♘bd4 (threat: ♘c6! followed by ♕xf6) 15...♗e5 16 ♘f5 ♗e6 17 ♘ed4 ♕d7 18 0-0 ♖fb8 19 ♖ac1 intending ♖fd1, ♗b1, ♕e2 and ♕d3, with a powerful attack. Black's attempted queenside counterplay just doesn't cut it here.

14 ♘f4!

Targeting d5 and inducing a knight swap, which eliminates one of Black's best defenders.

14...♘xf4

Alternatively, 14...♘g5 (the knight remains near his king, hoping to be the poultice which relieves) 15 ♕xd5 ♕b6 16 ♘e4! ♗xe3 17 hxg6! ♗b7 18 ♘xg5!! (Black can't seem to move without stubbing his toe on one of the nettlesome white knights) 18...♗xf2+ 19 ♔f1 ♗xd5 20 ♘xd5 ♕d8 21 gxf7+ ♖xf7 22 ♗xh7+ ♖xh7 23 ♘xh7 ♔g7 24 ♘hxf6 ♗c5 25 ♖h7+ ♔g6 (Black's mortally wounded king attempts to gather his spewing entrails and stuff them back into the gaping hole, which was once his belly) 26 ♔g2 (White threatens to swing the a1-rook into the attack, with deadly efficiency; note how remarkably safe his seemingly exposed king is) 26...♗f8 (26...♕xd5+ 27 ♘xd5 ♔xh7 28 a4 is also hopeless for Black, down two clean pawns in the ending) 27 ♖d7 ♕c8 28 ♖c7 ♕d8 29 ♖f1 ♗g7 30 ♖f5 (threatening mate in two, starting with ♘f4+) 30...♕d6 31 ♘e4 ♕a6 32 ♖g5+ ♔h7 33 ♘ef6+ ♔h6 34 ♖cxg7 forces mate.

15 ♕xf4 b4?

This is not the way to remedy the gaping defect on h6. Black's paralytic aversion to ...g5 continues. He can still put up a fight with the lane-blocking 15...g5! 16 ♕f3 b4 17 c4 dxc4! 18 ♗xc4 ♗e6 19 ♘e4 f5 20 ♘xc5 ♗xc4 21 ♕xf5 ♕d5 22 ♘e4 ♕xf5 23 gxf5 f6 when Black still has reasonable chances to hold the game.

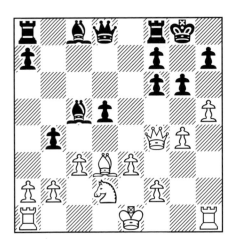

> **Exercise (planning):** This side issue is immaterial to Black's
> overall defensive goals and now his tolerance for abuse reaches
> a saturation point. How would you conduct White's attack?

Answer: Infiltration. The h-file is the funnel through which Black's position leaks.

16 ♕h6

"Unfortunately, there are limits to our friendship," White's queen tells Black's king.

16...♕c7?

16...♕d7 attempts to clean up the mangled fragments of his position, prevents the coming combination, but fails to save the game after 17 ♖d1! ♕b7 (or 17...bxc3 18 ♘e4!!, and if 18...dxe4 19 hxg6 fxg6 20 ♗c4+ forces mate) 18 c4! ♗xg4 19 hxg6 fxg6 20 ♗xg6 ♕g7 21 ♗xh7+ ♔f7 22 ♕xg7+ ♔xg7 23 ♖g1 ♔xh7 24 ♖xg4 (threat: ♔e2 and ♖h1 mate) 24...f5 25 ♖h4+ ♔g7 26 cxd5 with two extra pawns and an easy win.

17 hxg6 fxg6

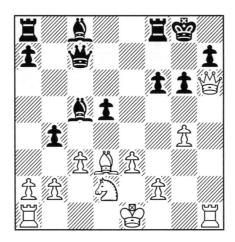

Exercise (combination alert): Black's foundations begin to quiver and crack, and his abysmal position grows yet more abysmal. How did White finish?

Answer: Demolition of the black king's position. The bishop gazes pontifically at the heavens, as if seeking a sign and then martyrs himself with a look of holy ecstasy on his face.

18 ♗xg6! 1-0

If 18...hxg6 19 ♕h8+ (at this stage Black's queen dubiously chews her lower lip, in anticipation of her sister's treachery) 19...♔f7 20 ♕h7+ ♔e6 21 ♕xc7 and after executing her sister, White's queen nods in triumphant vindication, telling herself: "I always knew I was the rightful heir."

Summary: Give the non-c4 kingside attack plan a try, but only play it if you achieve ♗d3, ♕f3 and g4! before Black plays ...f5.

Game 28
K.Georgiev-A.Horvath
European Club Cup, Fuegen 2006

1 d4 ♘f6 2 ♗g5 d5 3 ♗xf6 exf6 4 e3

4 g3 is another move order for White. After 4...c6 5 ♘d2?! (a dubious move order; 5 e3 is correct) 5...♗d6 (Black equalizes with 5...♕b6! 6 ♘b3 a5 7 a4 ♕xb3! 8 cxb3 ♗b4+, regaining the queen with a nice position) 6 ♗g2 0-0 7 e3 ♖e8 (7...♗f5 8 ♘e2 ♘a6 9 a3 ♕d7 10 0-0 ♗h3 was C.Lakdawala-R.Richard, San Diego 2004, where I prefer White after 11 c4) 8 ♘e2 ♘d7 9 0-0 f5 10 c4 dxc4 11 ♘xc4 ♗c7 12 ♖c1 ♘f6 objectively the position may be even. White can look forward to queenside gains later on, while Black concentrates on control over the central light squares, C.Lakdawala-B.Baker, San Diego (rapid) 2013.

4...c6 5 g3

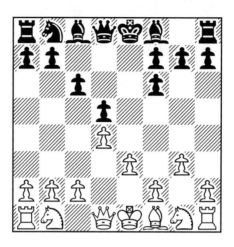

Question: This set-up is radically different
from the e3 lines we have seen so far, correct?

Answer: Correct. This simulacrum falls short of our attacking glory from the earlier games in the chapter. When White plays an early g3, we play in pseudo-Catalan style, concentrating exclusively on the queenside in most cases.

5...♗d6 6 ♗g2 0-0

Alternatives:

a) 6...♗e6 (Black logically plays to suppress White's c4-break) 7 ♘d2 ♘d7 8 ♘e2 f5 9 0-0 ♘f6 (9...b5!? has never been tried here; White should slowly build for a c4 break, preceded with c3 and b3) 10 c4! dxc4 11 ♕c2 0-0 12 ♘xc4 ♗c7 13 ♖ac1 g6 14 b4 ♗d5 when Black's central light-square play compensates for White's queenside space, M.Turov-Ju Wenjun, St Petersburg 2009.

b) 6...f5 7 ♘d2 ♘d7 8 ♘e2 ♘f6 9 0-0 0-0 10 c4 dxc4 11 ♘xc4 ♗c7 when the nature of the position is virtually superimposeable with 'a', J.Hodgson-P.Leko, Moscow Olympiad 1994.

c) However, natural doesn't always equate with good, as we can see with 6...♕b6?! . I have always felt that an early ...♕b6 versus the fianchetto line harms more than helps Black.

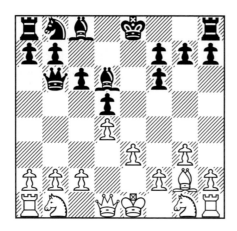

Answer: For the simple reason that b3 supports an eventual c4 and is desirable for White. When White achieves c4, then Black's queen tends to lose a tempo when White achieves c5, or ♘xc4, or bxc4 and ♖b1. After 7 b3 0-0 8 ♘e2 ♗g4 9 0-0 ♖e8 10 ♖e1 ♘d7 11 a3! (alert; White seizes control over b4 before playing c4) 11...♕a6 12 ♘d2 ♘b6?! 13 ♗f1! (giving notice to Black that he can't stall c4 for all eternity) 13...♘d7 14 c4 dxc4 15 ♘xc4 ♗f8 16 ♕c2 (Black's queen is clearly misplaced when compared to normal lines) 16...b5 17 ♘d2 ♕b6 18 ♗g2 ♖ac8 19 b4 a5 20 ♕c3 axb4 21 axb4 White had a queenside bind and went on to squeeze Black in R.Pert-N.Povah, British League 2011.

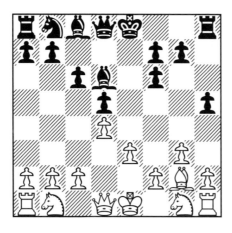

Answer: Your suggestion is rarely played, but scores well for Black. I wouldn't allow ...h4, and would continue 7 h4 and stall kingside castling, possibly considering f1 as a home for White's king: for example, 7...♗g4 8 ♘e2 ♕b6 9 b3 a5 10 a3 a4 11 b4 ♕a6, which was Duong Thanh Nha-S.Gravel, Montreal 2005. Here I would continue with 12 ♕d3 0-0 13 ♕xa6 ♘xa6 14 ♘d2 b5 15 ♗f3 which looks even, although I still like White due to the knights in the blocked position.

7 ♘e2 ♗e6

Black goes for the c4-suppression plan, which as we have seen from the notes, is just a temporary fix, since White nearly always manages to engineer the move later on.

8 0-0 ♘d7 9 ♕d3!

More accurate than the immediate 9 ♘d2. White's queen keeps an eye out for both c4 and even possibly e4 pawn breaks in the future.

9...f5 10 b3

I really like this idea and have never cared much for White's position when c4 is played without b3-backup. This is a reason Black shouldn't play an early ...♕b6?!. In this case Georgiev plays b3 without provocation, to retain bxc4 options in case Black trades on c4. White can also forego b3 and go for 10 ♘d2 ♘f6 11 c4, D.Andreikin-E.Tomashevsky, Khan-ty-Mansiysk 2011.

10...♘f6 11 c4 ♕d7

Black decides not to take on c4, not liking the fact that White gets greater control over the centre and an open b-file after 11...dxc4 12 bxc4.

11...♕a5?! makes very little sense to me, since Black's queen simply hands White a tempo when he plays b4: 12 c5 ♗e7 13 a3 b5 14 b4 ♕c7 15 a4 was N.Sedlak-M.Vukic, Subotica 2008. Now if 15...a6 16 ♘d2 ♘e4 17 ♖a2 when White can double or even triple on the a-file, with a clear edge.

12 ♘bc3

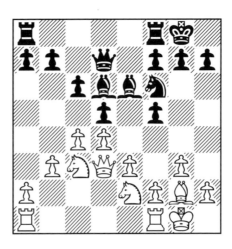

GM Eric Prié writes: "This is the ideal set-up for White, and having bypassed the concern

...d5xc4, he now has the pleasant choice of fixing the opposing structure with an isolated pawn on d5 or continuing to expand on the queenside."

12...♖ac8 13 c5

The queenside expansion plan looks even more promising than the isolani plan.

13...♗c7 14 b4

White plans to double rooks and break through on b5.

14...h5

Black hopes to generate compensating kingside counterplay.

15 h4!

White easily suppresses the attempted uprising with the quiet strength of one who possesses abundant resources. As it turns out, Black's kingside threats are ephemera, morning dew on the rose petal.

15...♖fe8 16 ♘f4 ♗xf4!?

Black compromises with a half-measure and one is reminded of the saying: you can't have it both ways. He eliminates White's powerful knight at a steep cost.

17 exf4

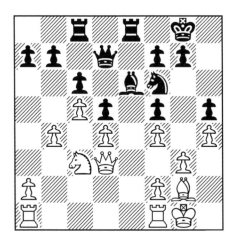

Question: Isn't the position even here?

Answer: *Houdini* rates at 0.00, which I believe is a misassessment. It appears as if Black enjoys the trappings of a solid position. When examined deeper, though, we also discover troubling issues. I rate it as an undisputed advantage for White, for the following reasons:

1. White owns a huge queenside space advantage and can leisurely build for a b5 pawn break.

2. Black has a bad bishop.

3. Black, although quite solid, still lacks an active plan and must simply await White's intentions.

17...♘e4 18 ♘e2

Principle: the side with space should avoid swaps. White plans to eject the e4-intruder with f3 next.

18...b5

This eliminates White's b5-break, but doesn't absolve Black from his queenside troubles, since White simply goes for an a4-break.

19 a4 a6 20 f3

Back into your cage, buddy.

20...♘f6 21 ♖a3

White plans to take full control over the a-file.

┃21...♕b7 22 ♕d2 ♖a8 23 ♖fa1 ♖eb8 24 ♗f1 ♘e8 25 ♘c1

The knight has the pleasant choice between the d3 and b3 posts.

25...♘c7 26 ♘d3 f6 27 ♗e2 ♕c8 28 ♘c1 ♗d7 29 ♗d3

White probes for weaknesses.

29...♕f8 30 ♘e2 ♕e8 31 ♔f2 g6 32 ♘c3 ♔g7 33 ♘d1

Heading for e3.

33...♗e6 34 ♘e3! ♕d7 35 ♕c2!

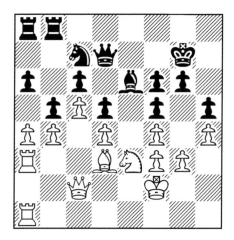

A move which Black fails to properly appreciate. White unexpectedly improves his position with this single, furtive motion and Black's position, almost imperceptibly streams in a downward trajectory. White eyes f5 sacrifices and g4 breaks, working his way into the g6-underbelly.

35...♖h8 36 axb5 axb5 37 ♖a7 ♖xa7 38 ♖xa7 ♖a8?

38...♗f7 39 ♕a2 is unpleasant but necessary, when Black has a chance of fortressing.

39 ♖xa8 ♘xa8

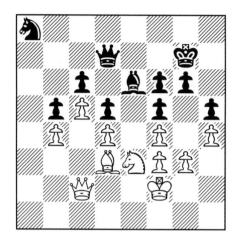

Answer: Pawn breakthrough/undermining. White's g-pawn rams the kingside amidships, knocking the wind out of her captain on g7.

40 g4!

A fist sometimes persuades easier than rational argument. The salient part of White's idea emerges. This well-timed break offers to open negotiations for the rights to g6.

40...hxg4

Alternatively, 40...fxg4 41 &xg6 gxf3 42 &xh5 &f7 43 &xf7 ♕xf7 44 ♕f5 ♘c7 45 ♕c8 &h7 46 ♘f5 &g6 47 ♘d6 ♕g7 48 h5+ &h7 (48...&xh5 49 ♕h3+ &g6 50 f5+ &g5 51 &g3! forces mate) 49 &xf3 when White completely dominates.

41 fxg4 ♕c7

If 41...fxg4 42 &xg6 ♘c7 43 f5 &g8 44 ♘xg4 with an extra pawn and winning position for White.

42 ♘g2

The human move. *Houdini* prefers White in the complications after 42 &g3!? g5, which no human would ever allow.

42...fxg4 43 &xg6

Black is busted: f5 artificially isolates the g4-straggler and his position seeps copiously along the light squares.

43...♕a7

Almost in unison, Black's defenders begin to withdraw their support for their king.

44 f5

Joyful tidings flow from f5. This move dooms Black's g4-pawn.

44...&f7 45 ♕e2! &xg6 46 ♕xg4

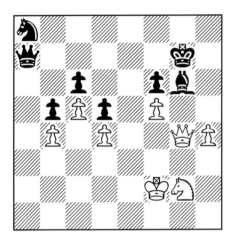

Black's king offers his hand, yet White's queen makes no motion to shake it. "I consider your very existence an impertinence," she informs her brother. "Hold your tongue, Madame!" demands Black's king. She, however, has a lot more to say on the matter. Black's king loses his source of protection and power, and walks about with a Macbeth-like taint.

46...♕a2+

The queen, late for her appointment with counterplay, finally arrives, her face a glowing pink with exertion. Hurtful words tumble forth from her pouty lips, with ill-concealed malice at White's cocky king. 46...♕f7 47 ♘f4 is completely hopeless as well.

47 ♔g3 1-0

The insurgency's goal is to quick-strike, and then recede into the darkness and anonymity of the masses. White's smirking king murmurs hasty apologies and hides on h2.

Summary: This is a much safer line for White than the ones we looked at previously in the chapter. I like Georgiev's idea of playing b3 first, before c4, in the fianchetto line. This means that Black's standard ...dxc4 can be met with the strategically desirable bxc4.

Game 29
N.Povah-D.Ledger
British League 2001

1 d4 ♘f6 2 ♗g5 d5 3 ♗xf6 gxf6

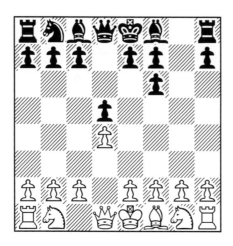

4 c4

A challenging continuation for Black.

Answer: The position often transposes into a Veresov after 4 e3 c5 5 ♘c3 e6 6 ♗b5+ (it's an ordeal to get old; I forgot my own suggestion from *A Ferocious Opening Repertoire* of 6 ♕h5!) 6...♗d7 7 ♗xd7+ ♕xd7 8 ♘ge2 (sigh...; 8 ♕h5! was still correct) 8...♘c6 9 0-0 cxd4 10 exd4 ♗e7 11 f4 f5 12 ♘c1 b6 13 ♘3e2 ♗f6 14 c3 h5 15 ♘d3 h4 16 ♔h1 ♘a5 17 b3 ♘b7 18 ♘e5 ♕c7 19 ♖c1 by when the game was dynamically balanced, C.Lakdawala-P.Graves, San Diego (rapid) 2013.

4...dxc4

In the next two games we examine 4...c5 and 4...c6. With 4...e5!? Black blasts open in the other direction. This move isn't played very often, yet looks quite playable: 5 ♘c3 ♗b4 6 e3 exd4 7 ♕xd4 ♗e6 8 cxd5 c5 was V.Kotronias-I.Stathopoulos, Vrachati 2013. At this point White can play 9 dxc6 (9 ♕f4 ♕xd5 10 ♕xf6 ♖g8 11 ♘ge2 ♘d7 12 ♕h4 ♕f5 13 ♖c1 ♖g4 14 ♕h6 ♘e5 15 ♘f4 ♗xc3+ 16 bxc3 0-0-0 is evaluated at even by the comps, but looks quite dangerous for White, who lags dangerously behind in development) 9...♕xd4 10 exd4 ♘xc6 11 ♘ge2 0-0-0 12 0-0-0 ♘e7 13 ♘f4 ♗xc3 14 bxc3 ♗xa2 when he obtains more than enough compensation for the pawn and *Houdini* prefers our side.

5 e3

Hodgson experimented with the ultra-sharp 5 e4!? ♘c6! 6 d5 ♘e5 7 f4 ♘d3+ 8 ♗xd3 cxd3 9 ♕xd3 ♕d6 10 ♘e2 f5 11 e5 ♕b6 12 ♘d2 e6 13 ♘c3 ♗b4 14 ♘c4 ♕a6 in J.Hodgson-H.Sonntag, Benidorm 1989. I don't trust Black's development lag, despite his bishops, and prefer White's chances after 15 0-0-0.

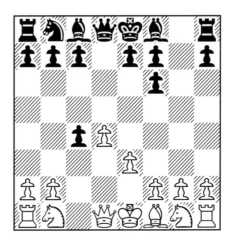

5...c5

> *Question:* Can Black try 5...b5, hoping to hang on to c4?

Answer: Not a good idea. White plays 6 a4 and Black is already in deep trouble, since 6...c6? 7 axb5 cxb5?? 8 ♕f3 wins on the spot.

6 ♗xc4 cxd4 7 exd4

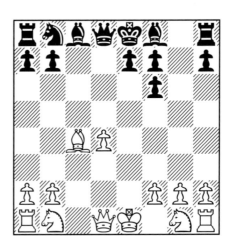

Welcome to the Trompowsky version of the Queen's Gambit Accepted.

> *Question:* Isn't White exceeding the speed limit here? This looks to me like a nice anti-isolani position for Black, since he also has the bishop-pair?

Answer: Just what exactly is it that makes White's position so terrible? If we examine the

constituents individually, we discover that his game isn't as bad as it first appears. I actually favour White for the following reasons:

1. Unlike a normal QGA-style isolani position, in this version, blockade of d5 looks very
difficult for Black to achieve.

2. I think Black's king is less safe than in a normal QGA isolani position, since ...gxf6 airs
out the kingside.

3. White continues to lead slightly in development, which is more dangerous than it
looks since we are in an open position.

Pert suggests an interesting unplayed idea: 7 ♘c3!? ♘c6 (most certainly not 7...dxc3?? 8
♗xf7+) 8 ♕h5 e6 9 0-0-0 ♕a5 10 ♕xa5 ♘xa5 11 ♗b5+ ♔e7! (my suggestion over Pert's
11...♘c6) 12 ♖xd4 ♗g7 and Black looks okay to me, with the bishop-pair.

7...♗g7 8 ♘c3 ♘c6 9 ♘ge2 f5

After 9...0-0 10 0-0 f5 11 d5! ♘e5 12 ♗b3 a6 13 ♕d2 ♕d6 14 ♕f4 ♔h8 15 ♖fe1 ♕f6 16
♖ad1 ♖g8 17 ♘d4 ♘g6 18 ♕c7 ♕h4? (18...♕d6 19 ♕xd6 exd6 looks okay for Black, whose
dark-square control compensates for White's space and superior structure) 19 ♘f3 ♕g4 20
h3! (luring Black's queen to an unfavourable square) 20...♕f4 (20...♕h5 21 d6! is also awful
for Black) 21 ♖xe7! White was up a pawn with a winning position, R.Palliser-K.McPhillips,
Millfield 2004.

10 d5!

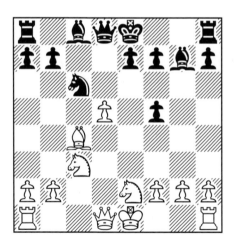

> *Question:* In earlier games in the chapter, you said d5 handed Black
> the dark squares. Here you praise the same move. What changed?

Answer: In both cases, d5 cramps Black at the cost of losing more control over the dark
squares. The difference here is Black's e7-pawn will be eternally weak along the open e-file.

10...♘e5 11 ♗b3

11 ♗b5+ should be met with 11...♔f8!.

11...♗d7

I'm not crazy about this move. Black needs his light-squared bishop to keep control over f5.

Answer: It leaves Black vulnerable to ♗a4!, forcing the bishops off the board. 11...♕d6 seizing more control over the dark squares looks logical.

12 0-0 ♕b6

I prefer the immediate castling over this coming adventure.

13 ♖c1

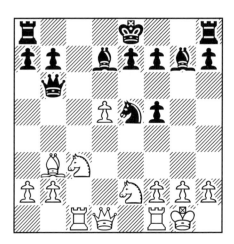

13...♕h6?!

Once again, castling looks better. Black's plan for now appears somewhat incoherent, so he fishes about for substance and meaning on the kingside.

Answer: I think it's a little of both. Black may have ...♖g8 ambitions and so swings the queen to h6, which also keeps his king better defended in case he decides to castle in that zone.

14 ♗a4!

Dual purpose:

1. White finds a clever method of severing Black's diplomatic relationships with f5, by eliminating the pawn's key defender.

2. White follows the principle: when your opponent owns the bishop-pair, swap one of them off if possible.

I like White's move better than 14 d6!? ♕xd6 15 ♕xd6 exd6 16 ♖fd1 ♖c8 17 ♖xd6 ♘c4 18 ♗xc4 ♖xc4 19 ♖cd1 ♗c6 20 ♘d4 0-0 21 ♘xf5 ♗xc3 22 bxc3 ♖xc3 23 f3, although here I like White's structure and that powerful knight. Still, it looks like Black should hold the game.

14...0-0

After 14...♖d8 15 ♘d4 ♘g4 16 h3 ♕f4 (if 16...♘e3? 17 ♗xd7+ ♖xd7 18 ♕a4! ♕g5 (18...♘xf1? 19 ♘ce2! ♔d8 20 ♘xf5, and if 20...♕g6 21 ♕xa7 mates)) 17 ♗xd7+ ♖xd7 18 hxg4 ♕xd4 19 gxf5 White wins a pawn.

15 ♗xd7 ♘xd7 16 ♘g3

Targeting f5, both the pawn and the square.

16...♗e5 17 ♕f3 ♗f4

Black clearly begins to contort, in order to hang on to his material. The trouble with 17...e6 is that it hangs a pawn to 18 dxe6 fxe6 19 ♕xb7.

18 ♖ce1 ♘e5

18...♖fe8 19 ♕d3 picks off f5.

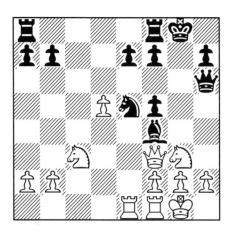

> **Exercise (combination alert):** Black's clumsy pieces trip over
> each other. Find one accurate move and Black drops a pawn.

Answer: Overload.

19 ♕h5!

Now we see White's underlying premise: f5 can't be defended.

19...♕f6?!

Allowing White to retain queens on the board looks wrong and now Black's king has the look of an office worker who slept in the suit he wears now.

After 19...♕xh5? 20 ♘xh5 ♘g6 21 ♘xf4 ♘xf4 22 ♖xe7 Black's game is a wreck. Relatively best was 19...♕g6 20 ♕xf5 ♗xg3 21 ♕xg6+ ♘xg6 22 hxg3 when Black can fight on a pawn down.

20 ♞xf5

White is winning, up a clean pawn, with an attack.

20...♞g6

Houdini hates this move. But its suggestions didn't seem to help Black's cause either.

21 g3

Even stronger is 21 ♞e4! ♛xb2 22 ♜e2 ♛h8 23 ♞g5 ♜ae8 24 ♜fe1.

21...♝g5

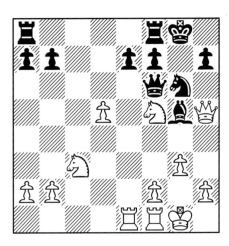

> *Exercise (combination alert):* One may still feel that with
> luck, Black may yet survive. But luck doesn't seem to be
> trending Black's way these days. How should White continue?

Answer: Double attack. Black's kingside collapses when White's knight reaches g5.

22 ♞e4!

The Trojan horse enters the compound.

22...♛xf5 23 ♞xg5 ♜fd8

23...♞h8 24 ♜xe7 is also resignable.

24 ♛xh7+

The queen mastered the art of hiding her feelings – mainly due to the fact that she has no feelings to hide.

24...♚f8

Black's king, knowing what is good for him, edges away to the safety of the shadowed nook on f8. "An evasive zig here and a conniving zag there, and my escape is complete," thinks the optimistic king to himself.

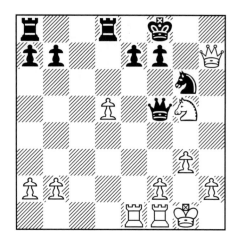

Exercise (combination alert): Black's king plays to a capacity
audience of white attackers. White has access to a shot
which visibly discomposes the black defenders. Do you see it?

Answer: Overload/deflection.

25 ♖e5!!

The rook flies down the board, as if on a bobsleigh run, and Black's queen and knight
are left to ponder his audacity with marvelling shakes of their heads.

25...♕f6 26 ♘e6+! 1-0

White plays a second combination for an encore. This deflection shot purees Black's
kingside. Black resigned here, since repeated pain has a marvellous way of dulling even the
most powerful of our survival instincts. After 26...fxe6 (or 26...♔e8 27 ♖f5! when the rook's
overwhelming presence engulfs the room, like a gas explosion) 27 ♖xe6 ♕g7 28 ♕xg6
♕xg6 29 ♖xg6 ♖xd5 White consolidates with 30 ♖e1 ♖d2 31 ♖e4! (threat: ♖f4+, followed
by ♖g8+, winning the a8-rook) 31...♔f7 32 ♖ge6 ♖e8 33 ♖e2.

Summary: I like White's isolani position in the 3...gxf6 line for two reasons:

1. Black's king is less safe than in normal isolani lines.
2. Black has trouble blockading d5, unlike normal isolani lines.

1 d4 ♘f6 2 ♗g5 d5 3 ♗xf6 gxf6 4 c4 c5!?

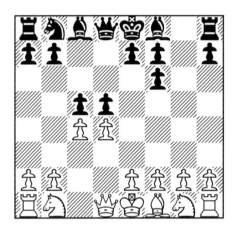

> **Question:** Are we going to arrive in the same
> position we did last game with this move?

Answer: We can, but not necessarily.

5 cxd5!?

This move gives the game an independent flavour. Instead, 5 e3 cxd4 (5...dxc4 6 ♗xc4 cxd4 7 exd4 transposes to the position we looked at last game) 6 exd4 ♘c6 (we enter a funky sort of Panov-Botvinnik Attack) 7 ♘c3 dxc4 8 d5 ♘e5 9 ♗xc4 ♘xc4 10 ♕a4+ ♗d7 11 ♕xc4 ♖g8 was P.Anisimov-A.Aleksandrov, Aix-les-Bains 2011. The position is a battle between Black's bishop-pair and White's superior attacking chances, since Black's king lacks a safe haven. Play might go 12 g3 ♕b6 13 ♘ge2 f5 14 0-0 ♖c8 15 ♕d3.

5...♕xd5 6 ♘f3 cxd4 7 ♘c3!

White gains a tempo with this move and it becomes a battle between his development lead and Black's bishop-pair.

7...♕d8

Black decides to return home to keep his queen out of harm's way. Instead, after 7...♕a5 8 ♘xd4 ♗d7 9 ♕b3 ♘a6 10 e3 ♘c5 11 ♕c4 ♘e6?! (perhaps Black should try 11...e5 12 ♘b3 ♘xb3 13 ♕xb3 ♗b4 14 ♗c4 ♗a4 15 ♗xf7+ ♔f8 16 ♕c4 ♗b5! 17 ♕b3 ♗a4 with a draw) 12 ♘xe6 fxe6!? (Black should consider the inferior ending after 12...♗xe6 13 ♕b5+ ♕xb5 14 ♗xb5+ ♔d8) 13 ♖d1 ♗g7 14 ♗e2 ♖d8 15 0-0 Black found himself in deep trouble and blundered on his next move: 15...♔f7? 16 ♘d5!, V.Georgiev-A.Beliavsky, Gothenburg 2005.

8 ♘xd4 e6

A new move. After 8...a6 9 g3 (I like this Catalan-style posting for the light-squared bishop, who soon exerts pressure down the h1-h8 diagonal) 9...e6 10 ♗g2 ♗g7 11 0-0 0-0 Black has yet to solve his queenside development issues, N.Eliet-C.Marzolo, Mulhouse 2004. I would go for 12 e3 intending ♕e2, ♖fd1 and ♖ac1, with irritating strategic pressure along Catalan lines.

9 e3

I would opt for 9 g3 a6 transposing to the above note.

9...a6 10 ♕h5!?

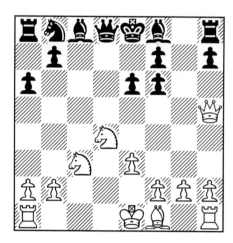

A Hodgsonian move which opens Pandora's box and leads to consequences neither side could possibly have foreseen.

Question: What is White's idea?

Answer: Possibly three-fold:

1. White sets up ♗c4 and ♘xe6 tricks.
2. White clears d1 for a rook, possibly even allowing for queenside castling.
3. White discourages ...♖g8, since h7 would then hang.

10 ♗e2 is the quieter, more strategic course.

10...♗b4 11 ♖c1 ♕a5

Black threatens ...♕xa2, as well as a welcome queen swap.

12 ♕f3!?

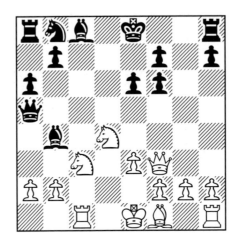

Hodgson is having none of it and offers two pawns.

12...♘d7

Black adopts a submissive posture to placate a powerful enemy. After this move Black suffers without even a pawn as payment for his troubles.

> **Question:** Can Black get away with 12...♕xa2?

Answer: He can and I think he should have grabbed the pawn, since White holds the initiative anyway when a2 is declined. From my experience, the best chance for an underdog to upend a powerful opponent is to understand his or her motivations and desires. In Hodgson's case, it is an almost worshipful reverence for the initiative. When I face similar-minded GMs, I take what they offer, knowing their generosity doesn't always equate with success. Still, Black must endure a long initiative after 13 ♗d3 ♘d7 14 0-0 ♕a5 (Black is too far behind in development to survive 14...♕xb2? 15 ♖c2 ♕a3 16 ♖fc1 ♗a5 17 ♕h5 ♘e5 18 ♗e4 ♔e7 19 ♘f5+! exf5 20 ♘d5+ ♔d6 21 ♗xf5 when the coming ♖d1 will be decisive) 15 ♗e4 ♖b8 16 ♖fd1 ♗e7 17 ♕h3. It isn't so simple to interpret the conflicting data. My guess is that White still retains full compensation since Black's king will know no peace, with no safe haven and undeveloped forces.

13 ♗e2!?

Hodgson is a bold guy. I would have played 13 a3 and heaved a sigh of relief.

13...♕g5!?

I still think Black's best chance was 13...♕xa2 and make White prove the compensation.

14 0-0 f5 15 ♕h3

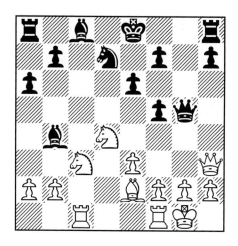

Answer: Hodgson wants to toss in f4, to take back some of the centre and seize control over e5. This way he can play ♗f3, without worry of ...♘e5.

15...♘b6 16 ♖fd1 ♗d7 17 f4!

There we go.

17...♕e7

17...♕g7 was also a thought, perhaps enabling kingside castling in the future.

18 ♗f3 ♖b8 19 ♔h1!

White is ready for e4!.

19...♗xc3?!

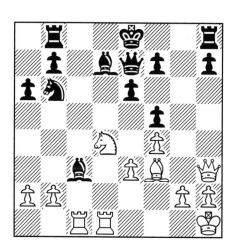

Past strategic sins create new ones for the present. Black hands over his only advantage in the position to reduce the attacking force. Yet by doing so, he creates fresh weaknesses on the dark squares, a colour he formally ruled with this bishop.

20 ♖xc3 ♞a4 21 ♖c7!?

More aggressive than 21 ♖c2 0-0 22 e4 fxe4 23 ♗xe4 f5 24 ♗f3, which also looks quite pleasant for White, who can go after e6.

21...♞xb2 22 ♖b1 ♞d3

Threatening a fork on f2.

23 ♕h6 ♖c8 24 ♖cxb7 ♕a3

Hoping for back-rank tricks and also ...♞f2+ followed by ...♕xe3. Hodgson gives little credence to Black's counterattack and pushes on as if nothing happened.

25 h3

Removing Black's threats.

25...♞f2+ 26 ♔h2 ♕xe3

Black does his best to hamper and obstruct, yet White's position steadily continues to improve.

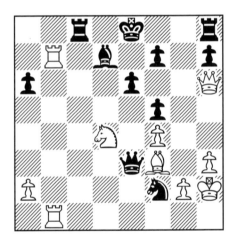

Exercise (combination alert(s)): White's swarming attackers begin to encompass the defensive barrier which once protected Black's king, like superimposed holographic images, configured over a blank screen. The markers for combinational geometry lay all around and White has no less than three ways to win. But we can't beat an opponent x 3, so all you need to do is to find one of them:

Answer: Demolition of the king's position.

27 ♞xf5!

Also good were:

a) The same theme: 27 ♕g7! ♖f8 28 ♖xd7! ♔xd7 29 ♖b7+ ♖c7 30 ♗c6+ and mates.

b) 27 ♖xd7! ♔xd7 28 ♕f6 with monster threats on f7 and b7. The black king's anguish grows with each passing move. If 28...♖hf8 29 ♖b7+ ♗c7 30 ♖xc7+ ♔xc7 31 ♕e7+ ♔b6 32 ♕d6+ ♔a5 33 ♕c5+ ♔a4 (such life situations tend to give rise to Hobbesian – please note the clear difference between Hodgsonian and Hobbesian – fears about life being "nasty, brutish and short") 34 ♗c6 mate. The coroner draws the chalk outline around a4.

27...exf5

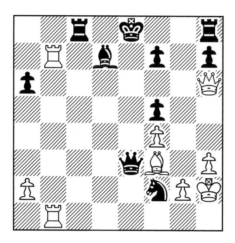

28 ♕d6?!

A soldier must obey a commanding officer's order, even if it's unwise. The solution lies just outside the periphery of Hodgson's analytical focus. In my games I find it prudent to budget for one or two lapses in concentration. This move is just such an example. We sense a loosening of the grip which was once around the black king's throat. White wins instantly with:

Answer: 28 ♖xd7! ♔xd7 29 ♖b7+ ♔e8 30 ♗c6+ ♖xc6 31 ♕xc6+ ♔f8 32 ♕c4! ♕e8 33 ♕c5+ ♔g7 34 ♕d4+ ♔g8 35 ♕xf2 h5 36 ♕b2 ♔h7 37 ♕f6 ends it.

28...♕e6 29 ♕d4!? 1-0

We Trompers must brace ourselves since my words may wound some of us: Hodgson, our king, isn't infallible and remains human. This move only clouds the issue further and Hodgson continues to miss his morning bus by seconds. How odd that the 'winning' move is actually perhaps not his best choice. Our most vulnerable moment in a chess game is the one where we are engulfed in an overconfidence of triumphant inevitability. Fortunately for Hodgson, Lukacs believed him and resigned. 29 ♖xd7! still works and is a clearer path to the win.

Answer: I believe so. The position may actually be lost for Black, but I certainly would play on and make White prove it. He may have been discouraged by White's endless threats. After 29...0-0 Black's king escapes with merely a flesh wound and still clings to his life: 30 ♕xf2 ♗b5 31 ♖b3! (threat: ♕b2 and ♗d5!, a clearance shot, followed by ♖g3+) 31...♕f6 32 ♗d5 ♔h8 33 ♖g3 ♖cd8 34 ♗xf7! and overloads. White wins. But Black should probably play on to this point, since these moves are not so obvious for White with a clock ticking away.

Summary: After 4 c4 c5!? I believe White's development lead means more than Black's bishop-pair. Also, think about a g3, Catalan set-up as an alternative to Hodgson's ultra-aggressive e3/♕h5 idea.

> ## Game 31
> ## J.Hodgson-A.Martin
> British Championship, Plymouth 1992

1 d4 ♘f6 2 ♗g5 d5 3 ♗xf6 gxf6 4 c4 c6

A sensible approach. Black refuses to fall behind in development – a clear danger, as we have seen from the last two games – and decides to adopt a Slav formation with the bishop-pair.

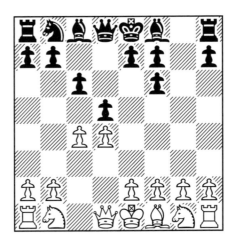

Question: How does this compare with a real Slav position?

Answer: It's a Slav, with one huge difference: ♗g5 and ♗xf6 has been tossed in which means Black gets the bishop-pair at a cost of structural damage and king safety – perhaps a fair deal for both sides.

5 e3 e6!?

Playing in Semi-Slav style.

> **Question:** Why would Black voluntarily block in
> his light-squared bishop when 5...♗f5 is possible?

Answer: I think the main reason is Black wants to preserve his bishop-pair. By playing to f5, he allows White options of future ♘h4 and ♗d3 ideas, swapping away Black's bishop: for example, 6 ♘c3 ♕b6 7 ♕d2 e6 8 ♘f3 ♘d7 9 ♘h4 and there it is. White can pick off the bishop, although Black looks okay to me here, K.Georgiev-D.Castillo Sanjuan, Zaragoza 2011.

6 ♘c3

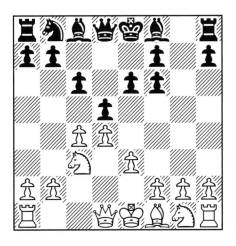

6...f5

Now it's a funky sort of Stonewall Dutch.

> **Question:** How do we proceed if Black avoids the Stonewall set-up?

Answer: If Black avoids the Stonewall, then White's most logical plan is to play on our development lead and work in an e4-break: for example, 6...♘d7 7 cxd5 cxd5 8 ♗d3 a6 9 ♘ge2 b5 10 0-0 (10 e4 at this point looks safer) 10...♗b7 11 e4!? (a piece sac) 11...♘b6 (Black declines; after 11...b4!? 12 exd5! bxc3 13 dxe6 fxe6 14 ♘f4 White gets a dangerous attack for the investment) 12 ♘f4! ♗d6 (White offers it once more, in the form of 12...b4 13 exd5!) 13 ♘h5! b4 14 ♘a4 when *Houdini* likes White's chances, and so do I, K.Rusev-A.Dragojlovic, Bar 2008.

7 ♘f3 ♗g7 8 ♕c2 ♘d7

A new move, deviating from:

a) 8...a6 9 h3! (taking up Hodgson's prying mechanism idea) 9...h5 10 b4 ♘d7 11 a4 ♘f6 12 c5 when White can eventually play for the b5 break, S.Kartsev-C.Regert, Dortmund 2001.

b) 8...0-0 9 h3! (also following Hodgson's lead) 9...dxc4 10 ♗xc4 was L.Konrad-

M.Stockmann, German League 2009. If 10...c5 11 0-0 (I have a feeling Hodgson would play 11 0-0-0!? followed by g4) 11...cxd4 12 exd4 I like White's isolani position because Black, once again, experiences difficulty fighting for d5.

9 h3!

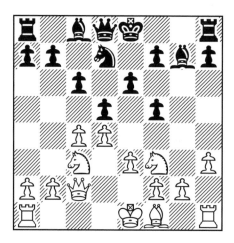

Question: What is the idea behind the move?

Answer: White plans to castle long and then smash open the kingside with g4. This plan essentially leaves Black worried about where to place his king for the remainder of the game.

9...dxc4!?

Not even waiting for ♗e2, or ♗d3. I also prefer White after 9...♘f6 10 0-0-0 h5 (10...♘e4 11 ♔b1 ♕a5 12 g4 ♘xc3+ 13 bxc3 fxg4 14 hxg4 Black's bishop-pair looks rather unimpressive here) 11 ♔b1 ♘e4 12 ♘e5.

10 ♗xc4 ♕c7 11 0-0-0!?

Forcibly altering the plot and opting for a policy of full disclosure, laying forth his aggressive intent for all to see. Clearly, suppressed inhibitions are not an issue for Hodgson, who isn't a castle-kingside kind of player. White invites opposite-wing castling, realizing he is fast with the g4 break.

11...b5 12 ♗b3?!

Threat: ♘xb5. This placement turns out to be of a dubious construct, since the bishop is vulnerable to future ...c5 and ...c4 ideas. White's attack looks clearly the more dangerous one after 12 ♗d3! a6 13 g4 fxg4 14 hxg4 c5 15 ♗e4 ♖b8 16 d5!.

12...♗a6?!

This form of a queenside campaign turns out to be ineffective. The bishop's attitude reminds us of when the general orders his chief officer to sound the attack and is told: "Sorry, I'm not in the mood." Black should play 12...a6! 13 e4 c5 (threat: ...c4; faint signs of life begin to appear in Black's once drab position), when perhaps Hodgson had planned for the sacrifice 14 exf5!? (14 dxc5 ♘xc5 15 exf5 ♘xb3+ 16 axb3 0-0 offers Black dangerous compensation for the pawn) 14...c4 15 fxe6 fxe6 16 ♕e4 cxb3! 17 ♕xe6+ ♔f8 18 ♕xb3, but I prefer Black in this admittedly unclear situation.

13 g4

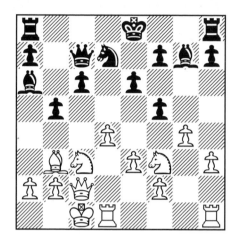

The thematic break arrives, shaking up the illusion of solidity in Black's centre.

13...f4?!

Black begins to crack under the strain of the wicked cross examination and finds himself salving wounds across his kingside. Now White seizes a clear strategic advantage. For the time being, Black's king refuses to commit himself to either wing and his strategy is to remain close to a door just in case fate necessitates a quick exit. Perhaps Black should consider a more forceful approach with 13...c5! 14 gxf5 c4 15 fxe6 fxe6 16 ♕e4 0-0-0 17 ♗c2 ♗b7 18 ♕g4 b4 19 ♘e4 b3 20 ♗b1 and it's anybody's game.

14 ♘g5

Rabble rousing begins on the kingside. Hodgson prefers to complicate rather than the strategic choice of clamping down on the ...c5 break with 14 ♘e4.

14...♘f8

Covering against e6-sacs, at the cost of discombobulating his knight. Black finds himself outnumbered, and decides to settle into a single spot and dig in.

15 ♘ce4 h6

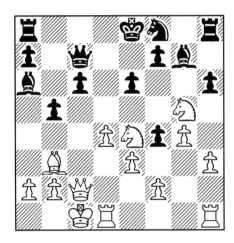

Exercise (critical decision): Black's visibly distressed king shifts uncomfortably on his throne. White holds a clear strategic advantage if he retreats his knight back to f3. But is there more in the position? We must also consider the tempting sacrifice on f7. Is it sound? Calculate its consequences and make a decision.

Answer: Black's king position is structurally unsound, made painfully evident by the falling plaster from the ceiling. The sacrifice gives White a winning attack but its ramifications are not at all easy for work out.

16 ♘xf7!!

White is in the market for a good assassin to eradicate the e8-nuisance, who from this point gets yanked about like a gaffed swordfish.

16...♔xf7 17 d5!

A nasty line opening. Only with this addition does White's combination find itself on the credit side of the ledger.

17...♗e5

After 17...♗c8 18 d6 ♕b6 19 ♘c5 the trouble for Black is 19...♗d7? is met with 20 ♘xd7 ♘xd7 21 ♗xe6+!, which is even stronger than the check on f5.

18 dxe6+ ♔g7 19 ♕c5!

Another consignment of fresh attackers is ready for delivery.

19...♗c8

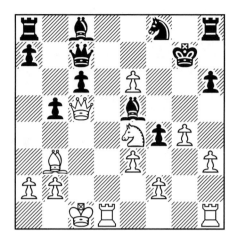

Exercise (combination alert): Black walked into a mating
net on his last move. How would you continue the attack?

Answer: Interference. White's attack clearly doesn't suffer a cash-flow shortage.
20 ♖d7+! ♗xd7

20...♔g6 21 ♕e7 also forces mate.

21 ♕e7+ ♔g8 22 ♕f7 mate 1-0

Summary: Black can also adopt a Slav/Stonewall Dutch Formation in this variation. Remember the h3 and g4 prying idea.

Chapter Five
The Vaganian Gambit

1 d4 ♘f6 2 ♗g5 c5 3 d5 ♕b6 4 ♘c3

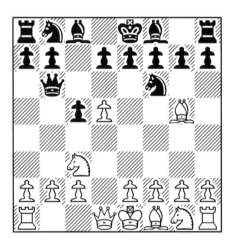

Don't get nervous about that "gambit" word in the chapter title. GM Aaron Summerscale describes the Vaganian Gambit as "one of Black's most ambitious lines against the Tromp, but at the same time, one of the riskiest. Black loses significant time getting his queen back to safety."

Here we go: the old immovable object versus irresistible force argument again. White offers b2, yet this isn't a case of Black sipping the poisoned Kool-Aid. Black can and often does accept, handing us space and initiative for a long time to come. After feigning polite incomprehension at Black's 'threat' to take b2, we offer a dangerous gambit for a massive development lead. This is what we get in a few moves:

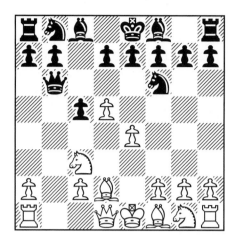

Let's gambit and subject our opponent's greedy streak to a rigorous behavioural modification regimen. Not only do we get to chase Black's queen with ♖b1 later on, we threaten a King's Indian Four Pawn (three in our case) Attack with f4 and e5. I, for one, think the sacrifice is sound, since we receive a sustained initiative/attack for the pawn.

Game 32
A.Lahiri-A.Tukhaev
Alushta 2005

1 d4 ♘f6 2 ♗g5 c5

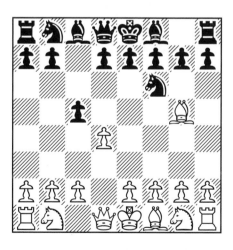

3 d5

I wish we had room in the book for 3 ♗xf6 gxf6 4 d5 ♕b6 5 ♕c1. My haunting regret from the 2004 U.S. Championship was that I had an opportunity to try the Vaganian Gambit on super-GM Hikaru Nakamura, and I chickened out and played this way:

a) 5...♗g7 (in the book's introduction we covered the psycho line 5...f5 6 e3 ♗h6 7 c4 f4 8 exf4 ♗xf4 9 ♕xf4 ♕xb2 10 ♘e2 ♕xa1 11 ♘ec3) 6 g3 d6 7 ♗g2 f5 8 c3 ♘d7 9 ♘d2 ♘f6 10 ♘h3 h5 11 ♕c2 ♗d7 12 a4 h4 13 ♘f4 hxg3 14 hxg3 ♖xh1+ 15 ♗xh1 0-0-0 16 ♘c4 ♕a6 17 ♕d3 ♖h8 18 ♗g2 ♔c7!. Now both ...b5 and ...e5 are in the air and Black already stands slightly better, C.Lakdawala-H.Nakamura, U.S. Championship, La Jolla 2004.

b) 3 ♘c3 cxd4 4 ♕xd4 ♘c6 5 ♕h4 leads to Open Sicilian/Veresov-style play, which we don't cover in the book.

3...♕b6

A reminder:

a) 3...♘e4 can transpose to Chapter One after 4 ♗f4 ♕b6 5 ♗c1 (we examine 5 ♘d2 in the final chapter of the book; instead, 5 b3?? walks into the embarrassing tactic 5...♕f6!).

b) 3...g6 and 3...d6 can lead to Schmidt Benoni structures: for example, 3...g6 4 ♘c3 (4 c4 ♘e4 looks risky for White, who may be vulnerable along the a1-h8 diagonal, in conjunction with ...♕a5+) 4...♗g7 5 ♘f3 d6 6 e4 0-0 7 ♗e2 ♘a6 8 0-0 ♘c7 9 a4 b6 10 ♖e1 ♗b7 11 ♗c4 ♘d7 12 ♕d2 ♖e8 13 ♖ad1 ♕c8 14 ♗f4 and White's central space gave him the edge, since e5 is coming, R.Siddharth-Ni Hua, Kolkata 2012.

4 ♘c3

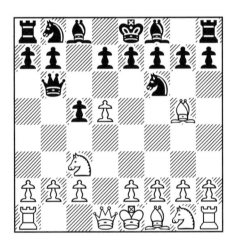

Our starting position in the line.

Question: You just allow Black to chop b2?

Answer: When we engage in the Vaganian Gambit, we scatter temptation like bird seed by offering b2. Clint Eastwood would agree with our sentiments: "Go ahead. Make my day!" It's easy to endure a little suffering when our cause is just. In this case I believe in White's compensation and am willing to back it up with hard currency.

4...♛xb2

Black accepts the challenge. We examine the declined line at the end of the chapter.

5 ♗d2

With the deadly threat of ♖b1, followed by ♘b5, winning on the spot. So Black's next move is forced.

5...♛b6

> *Question:* How do we proceed if Black plays 5...♛b4?

Answer: Keep chasing her around! After 6 ♖b1 ♛g4 7 f3 ♛h4+ 8 g3 ♛h5 9 e4 Black has lost a huge amount of time and the queen looks far more vulnerable here than on c7 or d8.

6 e4

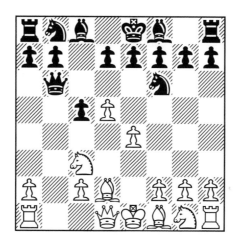

> *Question:* Earlier White wasted a tempo, taking two moves
> with his bishop to reach d2. What do we get for the pawn?

Answer: Black's queen also moved three times and will most certainly move again, since she is vulnerable on b6. Let's not underestimate the fact that Black's game suffers grave defects:

1. We are essentially up two extra tempi in an open position, which means Black's king may be in grave danger in the coming moves.

2. White, if given time, plans to overwhelm Black in King's Indian Four Pawns (well, okay, three in our case) Attack-style, with f4 and e5.

3. White gets the open b-file pressure which ensures Black's king won't castle queen-side.

Conclusion: White enjoys a sustaining initiative and, in my opinion, full compensation for the pawn.

6...e5

A popular set-up, suggested by Yelena Dembo in *Fighting the Anti-King's Indians*. Black, behind in development, wisely attempts to block the position in Czech Benoni fashion. Black often plays the move order 6...d6 7 f4 e5 8 f5, transposing.

7 f4 d6 8 f5!

This paradoxical option hands Black difficult strategic problems to solve and the precedents are encouraging for our side. White's last move is judged best by GMs Peter Wells and Eric Prié, and for what it's worth, your writer as well.

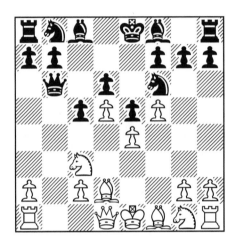

Question: Wait a minute! We sac'ed a pawn to attain a development lead, and then abruptly violated the principle: don't close the game when leading in development. Why?

Answer: Well, I did say "paradoxical option". Admittedly, at first glance, our brain reels from such a flagrant breech of opening protocol. You are correct in that it violates the principle stated, yet I think the move is fully justified for the following reasons:

1. Black's king will either remain in the centre or castle kingside, since the b-file is open and in our possession. This means we plan to follow with g4, if allowed, increasing our territorial advantage to alarming (for Black) levels and also make Black's king very, very nervous if he decides to castle into it.

2. Playing f5 and g4 renders Black's light-squared bishop nearly worthless.

3. Black lacks an obvious site of counterplay. If he or she tries ...c4!? later on, to clear c5, then we regain our sacrificed pawn.

Wells writes of your concerns: "I think it is quite possible that the only barrier to White scoring very heavily here is the gambiteer's psychological or stylistic aversion to this type of blocked position!"

Here is an example of White playing to open the game: 8 fxe5 dxe5 9 ♘f3 ♗d6 10 ♖b1

♕d8 11 ♗b5+?! (this is White's main move in the position, but today I consider it superficial, since White eventually wastes a tempo, moving it back to d3; I think White should play the immediate 11 ♗d3! which saves a tempo) 11...♘bd7 12 a4 0-0 13 0-0 a6 14 ♗d3 ♕c7 15 ♕e2 b6 16 ♘h4.

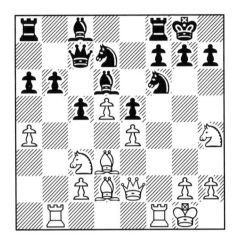

This probing move creates dark-square weakness in Black's camp. After 16...g6 17 ♗h6 ♖e8 18 ♘d1 (transferring force to the kingside) 18...♘h5 19 g3 ♘df6 20 ♘e3 ♗h3 21 ♖f2 c4 (Black returns the pawn to activate his dark-squared bishop and win material; the trouble is White still stands better at the end of the line) 22 ♘xc4 ♘g4 23 ♘xd6 ♕xd6 24 ♗e3 ♘xf2 25 ♕xf2 (White has enormous compensation for the exchange, since b6 falls, handing him two central passed pawns) 25...♖eb8 26 ♘f3 (threatening a cheapo on g5) 26...♗d7 27 ♗xb6 ♘f6 28 a5 ♘g4 29 ♕d2 ♗b5?! (Black should disrupt with 29...f5 30 c4 fxe4 31 ♗xe4 ♘f6) 30 c4 ♖xb6 (desperation) 31 axb6 ♗xc4 32 b7 ♖b8 33 ♗xc4 ♕c5+ 34 ♔g2 ♕xc4 in C.Lakdawala-G.Hernandez, Internet (blitz) 2000, your incompetent writer missed the simple and crushing 35 ♖c1! and later allowed a perpetual check.

8...♗e7

Black's last move may not be correct, since it allows White's space advantage to get completely out of control.

> ***Question:*** How can Black prevent the coming g4?

Answer: Black can try 8...h5, semi-thwarting our plan, may be a better try.

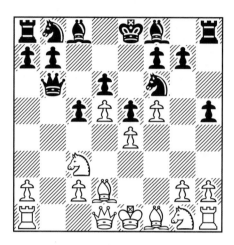

I still prefer White after 9 ♘f3 ♗e7.

> **Question:** Why doesn't Black continue to undermine with 9...g6?

Answer: A strategic error. White seizes control over e6, starting with 10 ♗b5+! ♗d7 11 ♖b1 ♗xb5 12 ♖xb5 ♕c7 13 fxg6, as in J.Bellon Lopez-M.Rodriguez Costa. Black is busted, since 13...fxg6 is met with 14 ♘g5 a6 15 ♘e6. With the seizure of e6, White takes control over the power grid: 15...♕c8 16 0-0! ♘bd7 17 ♖b1 b5 18 ♗g5 ♗e7 19 ♕e1 menacing both ♕h4 and ♕g3, with crushing pressure.

After 9...♗e7, 10 ♗c4 (I like this square for the bishop since it discourages ...c4 ideas) 10...♘bd7 11 ♕e2 ♕c7 12 a4 ♘b6 (going after c4, but this move misaligns the knight) 13 ♗b5+ ♗d7 14 a5 ♘c8 15 a6! (now White retains eternal control over b5) 15...bxa6 16 ♗xd7+ ♘xd7 17 ♕xa6 ♘db6 18 ♕b5+ ♕d7 19 ♔e2! (after this flexible decision, White decides there is no worthwhile objective to be achieved on the kingside and begins to shift focus to the weakened queenside; White doesn't always have to play for mate in this line and sometimes we don't fear a queen swap, even a pawn down) 19...♗d8 20 ♖hb1 g6 21 fxg6 fxg6 22 ♗g5! ♖f8 23 h4 ♗e7 24 ♖a6 ♔d8 25 ♕xd7+ ♔xd7 26 ♘b5 ♗d8 27 ♗xd8 ♔xd8 28 ♘g5 Hello e6! 28...♖f6 29 g3 ♔d7 30 ♖ba1 ♔e7 31 ♘e6 the a7-pawn is doomed, after which Black hangs on by a thread, S.Soors-N.Navalgund, Chennai 2011.

Otherwise, after 8...a6 9 g4 h6 10 h4 ♕d8 11 a4 ♗e7 12 ♕f3 ♘fd7?! (even worse a square than h7, since a future g5 break can't be held back) 13 ♕g3 f6 14 ♘f3 Black's tangled mess of a position isn't worth a lone pawn, C.Lakdawala-R.Mendoza, Internet (blitz) 2013.

9 g4!

Our philosophy: I want more!; our thuggish plan: steamroll Black off the board.

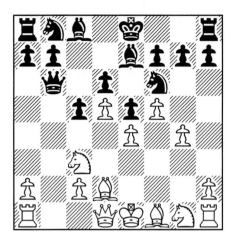

9...h6 10 h4

The pawns continue to flow upward, as if a seeping gas leak.

10...♛d8

The queen returns from her one-woman war on the queenside in disgrace, and probably shouldn't have had her heart set on a 21-gun homecoming salute.

11 ♛f3! ♞h7

Black, refusing to be out-paranoided by anyone, attempts a dark-square fortress, with the g5-square at ground zero.

12 ♛g3 ♜g8 13 ♞f3

Intending g5, which induces Black's awful-looking next move.

13...f6

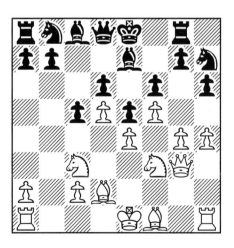

Gulp! Even the e7-bishop's and h7-knight's own mothers don't claim they are handsome children. *Houdini* suggests 13...g6!?, challenging White's kingside hegemony. After 14

♕h3 a6 15 a4 gxf5 16 exf5 it claims the game is dead even, but I still like White's chances. At least in this version, Black loosened White's central grip and has some chances of over-extending his opponent.

14 ♗h3?!

The wrong diagonal. An ugly smear stains the once pristine landscape. White's superior options:

a) 14 ♗e2 (keeping an eye on Black's ...b5 and ...c4 breaks) 14...♘a6 15 ♖b1 ♘c7 16 a4 b6 17 ♔f2 ♖b8 18 ♖bg1 a6 19 g5 fxg5 20 hxg5 ♘xg5 21 ♘xg5 ♗xg5 22 ♗xg5 ♕xg5 23 ♕d3 ♕f6 24 ♖g6 ♕f8 25 ♕g3 ♔d8 26 ♖hxh6 ♘e8 27 ♖h7, although maybe Black can still hang on here.

b) 14 ♖b1 a6 15 a4 ♘d7 16 ♘d1! b6 17 ♘e3 ♖b8 18 ♗e2 (the correct diagonal) 18...♘df8 19 ♔f2 ♕d7 20 ♘c4 ♕xa4? (wretched as it seems, Black had to grovel with 20...♕a7) 21 ♖xb6 ♖xb6 22 ♘xb6 ♕xc2 23 ♘xc8 ♕xe4 24 ♗xa6 ♕xd5 25 ♗b5+ ♔d8 26 ♘b6 ♕b3 27 ♗c4 and Black's three extra pawns don't even come close to compensating for the lost rook, D.Sahovic-L.Degerman, Biel 1990.

14...♘d7?!

After this rote move Black's plan is a little bit here, a little bit there, a little bit every-where, and now harbours little chance of achieving ...b5. Black should go for the plan mentioned in the above note with 14...♘a6.

15 ♔f2

The long submerged king re-emerges, like a pond's bullfrog coming up for a breather.

15...♖b8 16 a4

Oh, no you don't. Of course, White must at least stall the ...b5 break.

16...♘b6

Threatening to sneak into c4.

17 ♗f1

An admission that his 14th move was inaccurate. At last, White, sensing misgivings about his earlier dubious decision to post to h3, regains the mandate of heaven by re-routing the light-squared bishop back to its proper diagonal.

17...♘a8

Boy, that is a convoluted pathway to c7. Black decides the ...b5 plan repays inspection. The oddball knight isn't going to retrieve a portion of her lost status by moving a few notches down to a8.

18 ♗e2

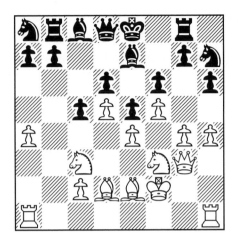

18...b6 19 ♖ag1 ♘c7

Eric Prié comments that this knight wishes it could reach f7.

20 g5 fxg5 21 hxg5 ♘xg5 22 ♗xg5 ♗xg5 23 ♘xg5 ♕xg5 24 ♕xg5 hxg5 25 ♖xg5 ♔e7

25...♔f8 26 ♘b5 ♘xb5 27 axb5 ♖b7 28 ♖g6 ♖d7 29 ♖h7 is zugzwang. For example:

a) 29...♖d8 30 f6 ♖d7 31 ♗g4 ♖c7 32 ♗e6 wins.

b) 29...♗b7 30 ♗h5 ♗c8 31 ♖e6 g6 32 ♖f6+ ♔e8 33 fxg6 ♔d8 34 ♗g4 ♖dg7 35 ♖xg7 ♖xg7 36 ♖f8+ and the c8-bishop falls.

c) 29...♔e8 30 ♗g4 with the nasty threat of f6 next, and Black collapses. The greedy bishop demands a hefty tithe from an already cash-strapped black populace.

26 ♖hg1 ♔f8

26...♘e8 27 ♗h5 ♗d7 28 ♗xe8 ♗xe8 29 ♖xg7+ ♖xg7 30 ♖xg7+ ♗f7 31 ♘b5 a6 32 ♘xd6 gets the job done too.

27 ♗h5 ♖b7

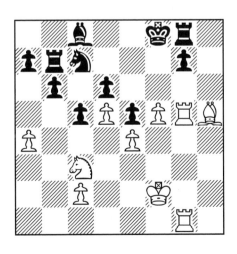

> *Exercise (combination alert):* Black's king looks uneasy with those three white gargoyles staring at him on the kingside. All but a single plan is tailored to fit the position's requirements. How did White proceed?

Answer: Pin.

28 f6 ♘e8 29 ♗xe8 ♔xe8

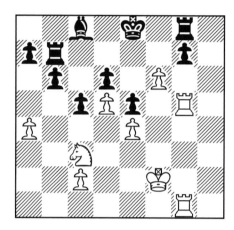

> *Exercise (combinational alert):* White can pick off g7, but he has something even better. What is it?

Answer:

Step 1: Lure Black's rook to the defence of d6.

30 ♘b5! ♖d7

Step 2: Take control of the seventh rank.

31 ♖xg7 ♖f8

Step 3: Knight fork.

32 ♘c7+! ♖xc7

Or 32...♔d8 33 ♘e6+.

33 ♖xc7 ♖xf6+ 34 ♔e3 1-0

Summary: Black's ...e5 plan always bothered me in the Vaganian Gambit – until now. I am switching to the counterintuitive 8 f5! and I urge you to do the same.

Game 33
V.Moskalenko-M.Erdogdu
Angora 2010

1 d4 ♘f6 2 ♗g5 c5 3 d5 ♛b6 4 ♘c3 ♛xb2

If you swallow a poisoned pawn, you run the risk of vomiting the decision later in the game. The strange fact that Black doesn't get mated 100% of the time is one of the mysterious vagaries of this line.

5 ♗d2 ♛b6 6 e4 d6 7 f4 e6

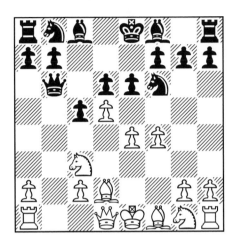

With this move Black gives a direct challenge to our impressive pawn centre, but at a cost.

Question: What cost? How can challenging an opponent's central space be wrong?

Answer: Black's move is in direct violation of the principle: don't allow the position to open when behind in development.

8 ♖b1

White's most common move. GM Viktor Moskalenko considers 8 ♘f3 an improvement.

Question: Why would White want to avoid the tempo-gaining ♖b1?

Answer: It's not a matter of avoiding the move, since it's always there for us. The reason Moskalenko prefers the immediate ♘f3 is to keep Black's queen on b6, where she may be vulnerable to ♘xd5 later on, after chasing Black's knight from f6 with e5: 8...exd5 9 e5 (White's point) 9...dxe5 (9...d4 10 exf6 dxc3 11 ♛e2+ ♔d7 12 ♗xc3 gxf6 13 ♛d2 doesn't look very healthy for Black's king) 10 fxe5 ♘e4 (Black fell too far behind in development after 10...♛e6 11 ♗b5+ ♘fd7 12 0-0 h6 13 ♘e2 g5 14 h4; I don't like Black's chances to survive the next dozen moves, M.Thuesen-P.Munck Mortensen, Denmark 1988) 11 ♘xd5 ♛d8 12 c4 ♗g4 13 ♛b1 (double attack on e4 and b7) 13...♘xd2 14 ♛xb7 ♘xf3+ 15 gxf3 ♗xf3 16 ♘c7+ ♔e7 17 ♘d5+ ♔e8 18 ♘c7+ ♔e7 19 ♘d5+ with perpetual check, L.McShane-Ni Hua, Bled Olympiad 2002.

8...♛c7!

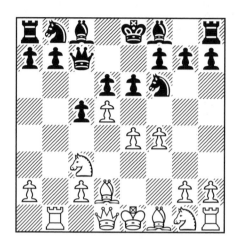

> *Question:* Why would Black retreat to c7, rather
> than d8, when White's knight has access to b5?

Answer: First, ♘b5 isn't a real tempo gain since after ...♛d8, Black regains the tempo with a
future ...a6. Secondly, Black fights for e5, since after 8...♛d8?! 9 ♗b5+ (or 9 dxe6 fxe6 10
♗d3 ♘c6 11 ♘f3 ♗e7 12 e5 ♘d5 13 ♘e4 ♘d4? 14 ♘xd4 cxd4 15 ♛h5+ g6 16 ♛h6 ♗f8 17
♛h3 a6 18 0-0 b5 19 ♘g5 ♘e7 20 ♘xh7! ♗g7 21 ♛g4! ♚d7 22 ♘g5 ♛g8 23 exd6 ♘f5 24 a4
♘xd6 25 axb5 axb5 26 ♖fe1 ♚c7 27 ♘xe6+ when Black's king is fried, C.Lakdawala-
J.Humphrey, San Diego (rapid) 2013) 9...♗d7 10 dxe6 fxe6 Hodgson disrupted with 11 e5!.
This move is only possible if Black plays 8...♛d8. After 11...♘d5 12 ♛h5+ (weakening the
dark squares around Black's king) 12...g6 13 ♛g4 (threat: ♛xe6+) 13...♘c6 14 ♘e4 dxe5 15
fxe5 ♛c7 16 c4 ♛xe5 17 ♘f3 ♛f5 18 cxd5! (White's queen isn't really hanging due to the
f6-fork) 18...exd5 19 ♛xf5 ♗xf5 20 ♘f6+ ♚f7 21 ♘xd5 ♗xb1 22 0-0 amazingly, White's attack rages on, despite the absence of queens on the board and White down the equivalent
of a full rook. Hodgson goes on to give us a grandmasterful demonstration of how to conduct a queenless attack: 22...♗f5 (22...♗xa2 23 ♘c3 ♗b3 24 ♘d4+ picks off the bishop) 23
g4! ♖d8 24 gxf5 ♖xd5 25 ♗c4 ♘e7 26 f6! b5 27 ♘g5+ ♚e8 28 ♗xb5+ ♚d8 29 ♘e6+ ♚c8 30
♘xf8 ♘f5 31 ♗a6+ ♚d8 32 ♗a5+ (clearly Black's long-suffering king is in urgent need of
first-aid attention) 32...♚e8 33 ♘e6 (with a fork threat on c7) 33...♚d7 34 ♘f4 ♖d6 35 ♗b5+
♚c8 36 ♗c3 ♖f8 37 ♗e5 ♖b6 38 ♗c4 ♘e3 39 ♗e6+ ♚b7 40 ♖e1 g5 41 ♖xe3 gxf4 42 ♗d5+ 1-
0, J.Hodgson-P.Glavina Rossi, Spanish Team Championship 1993.
9 ♘f3

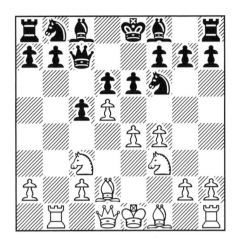

9...a6

Covering b5. Wise, as we can see from:

a) 9...♗e7 10 ♗b5+ ♗d7 11 0-0 0-0 12 ♕e2 a6 13 ♗xd7 ♕xd7 14 dxe6 fxe6 15 e5 ♘d5 16 ♘xd5 exd5 17 e6 ♕c7 18 ♕d3 d4 was A.Kinsman-F.Kwiatkowski, British League 1999. I like the look of White's position after 19 f5 ♘c6 20 ♘g5 ♘e5 21 ♕e4 ♕c6 22 ♖xb7 ♕xe4 23 ♘xe4 d5 24 ♘g3 ♘c6 25 ♖fb1.

b) 9...exd5?! is strongly met with 10 e5 dxe5 11 fxe5 ♘e4 12 ♘xd5 ♕d8 13 ♗f4 ♗e6 14 c4 ♕a5+ 15 ♘d2 ♘xd2 16 ♕xd2 ♕xd2+ 17 ♔xd2 ♘a6 18 ♖xb7 with a clear advantage to White, who retains a massive development lead and a rook on the seventh rank.

10 dxe6 fxe6

> ***Question:*** Since Black is so dangerously behind in development, can he try 10...♗xe6?

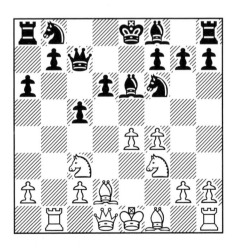

Answer: Your suggestion has never been tried. Let's look: 11 f5 ♗d7 12 ♗g5 ♗e7 13 ♗xf6 ♗xf6 14 ♘d5 ♕a5+ 15 ♔f2 ♗d8 16 ♖xb7 ♗c6 17 ♖b3 ♘d7 18 ♗c4 and *Houdini* assesses at even. So perhaps your suggested theoretical novelty is playable.

11 e5

Thematic and strong.

11...dxe5 12 fxe5 ♘g4

A new move:

a) 12...♘fd7 was P.Chakov-T.Todorov, Varna 1995. At this point, I would offer e5 and continue 13 ♘e4 ♘xe5 14 ♗c3 with a scary development lead for the two-pawn investment.

b) 12...♘d5 is unplayed so far. I would continue 13 ♘xd5 exd5 14 c4 d4 15 ♗d3 ♘c6 16 0-0 ♗e7 17 ♕c2 with a strong attack.

13 ♗d3!

Moskalenko, who has been known to express himself in acts of violence from far lesser provocations, increases his fervour to attack, and raises the stakes to dangerous levels – both for himself and for his opponent. His level of generosity refuses to ebb. So he correctly enhances his already considerable development lead with a secondary pawn sacrifice. His move looks better than the passive 13 ♗f4.

13...♘xe5

The knight, who is resolved to proceed with his fiscal dreams, despite the fearful risk involved, seeks redress to what he considers White's sacrificial excesses.

14 ♗e4!

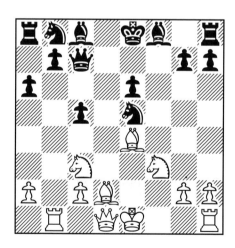

The bishop radiates strength from e4.

14...♘bd7 15 0-0 ♘f7?

After this move there is no pathway for Black to pre-empt inevitability. It wasn't any of his multiple murders which tagged Al Capone. He was sent to prison for tax evasion, like some white-collar criminal. Moral: inattention to details can be as fatal as messing up on the big plans. *Houdini* suggests 15...♘f6 16 ♘xe5 ♕xe5 17 ♗xb7. I still think Black is in trouble here, but less so than in the game.

16 ♘g5

Black finds himself too far behind in development and can't survive the coming assault.

16...♘f6 17 ♗f4!

Moskalenko is determined to enforce the law on what was previously thought to be un-governable territory.

17...e5

Black's options:

a) 17...♗d6? 18 ♘xf7 ♗xf4 19 ♘xh8 ♗e5 20 ♕f3 ♗xc3 21 ♗g6+! hxg6 22 ♕xc3 ♗d7 23 ♕d3! 0-0-0 24 ♘f7 with killing threats on d6 and d8.

b) 17...♕d8! (Black's best chance) 18 ♗xb7 ♗xb7 19 ♘xe6 ♕xd1 20 ♖fxd1 ♗c6 21 ♘c7+ ♔e7 22 ♘xa8 ♗xa8 23 ♖b6 ♘d7 24 ♖xa6 ♗b7 25 ♖a7 ♗c6 26 ♖c7 winning.

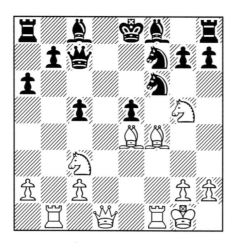

With his last move, Black hopes to nudge the intruder with a sharp elbow to the ribs. Is it just me, or does Black's dishevelled position remind you of Keith Richard's hair?

> **Exercise (combination alert):** Air surveillance photographs
> indicate the continued presence of hostiles in the area.
> We sense a winning combination for White. Where is it?

Answer: Principle: create confrontation when leading in development. The knight compels obedience, as if to a violated international treaty.

18 ♘d5! ♕d7

After 18...♘xd5 19 ♗xd5 ♘d8 20 ♗xe5 Black can resign.

19 ♘xf7 ♔xf7 20 ♗xe5

The attackers work hard, chipping away at f6 like industrious beavers.

20...♗e7 21 ♕h5+

The queen only enforces the laws which act against her own interests. "I am a liberator," she declares, when she knows perfectly well she is merely a conscienceless oppressor.

21...♔g8

The wobbly-legged king, who feels as if he has just been kicked in the head by a mule, backs into a wall and slowly slides to the ground, in a symbolic 'I-give-up' gesture.

22 ♗xf6 gxf6 23 ♖xf6! 1-0

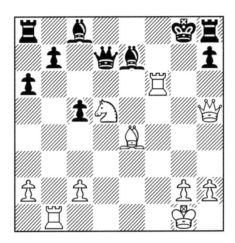

Defenders flutter every which way, like startled sparrows upon sighting the neighbourhood hawk.

Summary: 7...e6 is a popular idea. I don't trust it since it allows White to open the game favourably, when leading in development, and the resulting positions are an attacker's paradise.

Game 34
R.Vaganian-V.Jansa
Kragujevac 1974

GM Rafael Vaganian's eye-opening games were my first exposure to the Trompowsky. As I recall, this was the first Trompowsky game I ever played over.

1 d4 ♘f6 2 ♗g5 c5 3 d5 ♕b6 4 ♘c3 ♕xb2 5 ♗d2 ♕b6 6 e4 d6 7 f4 g6?!

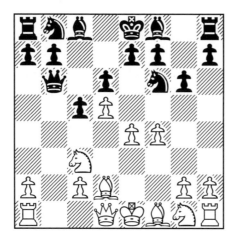

Answer: With his last move Black refuses to meet us halfway. His move essentially pro-claims: I have stolen a pawn, so "Now do your worst!" Black is un-intimidated by the coming e5 and plays leisurely, in pure Pirc/King's Indian Four Pawns Attack-style. In reality, his last move is one of the worst methods of meeting the Vaganian Gambit and I would place it in the category of the barely playable.

8 e5!

Vaganian is a man constitutionally incapable of remaining calm under such provocations. The good news: this is not some wild lunge from our side. White scores a whopping 78.6 percent from this position.

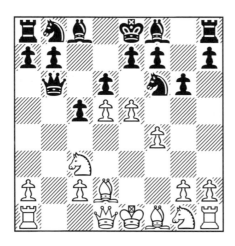

8...♘fd7

Question: Shouldn't Black exchange first on e5?

Answer: I think swapping on e5 is overly optimistic. By trading, Black opens the game further and hands White the f-file to attack: 8...dxe5?! 9 fxe5 ♘fd7 10 ♘f3 ♗g7 11 ♖b1 ♕d8 12 e6 (of course) 12...fxe6 13 ♘g5! ♘f6 14 ♗b5+ ♔f8 15 dxe6 a6 16 ♗e3! ♕a5 17 0-0! h6 (Black gets slaughtered if he accepts the gift: 17...axb5 18 ♖xb5 ♕c7 19 ♘d5 ♕d8 20 ♗xc5 ♘c6 21 c4 ♖xa2 22 ♘f7 ♕e8 23 ♘xf6 ♗xf6 24 ♖xf6 and Black is crushed) 18 ♕d3!! (going after g6) 18...♔g8 19 ♕xg6 ♗xe6 20 ♘xe6 ♖h7 21 ♖xf6! ♘d7 (21...exf6 22 ♕e8+ ♗f8 23 ♕xf8 is mate) 22 ♗xd7 1-0, R.Vaganian-V.Kupreichik, USSR Championship, Leningrad 1974. This game is annotated in *Play the London System*.

9 ♘f3 ♗g7 10 ♖b1 ♕d8

Black remains one move away from castling, so Vaganian disrupts the flow of events just in time.

11 e6! fxe6

Black also has a devil of a time unravelling after 11...♘f6 12 ♗b5+ ♔f8 13 ♘g5 fxe6 14 dxe6, as in A.Pixton-P.Stefano, Philadelphia 2000. Black remains in a terrible bind after 14...♘c6 15 0-0 ♘d4 16 f5! gxf5 17 Bc,4 but this is far more survivable for Black than the version he got in the game.

12 ♘g5!

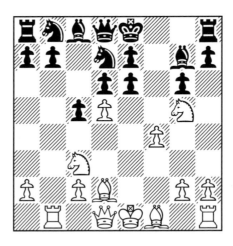

The knight realizes e6 is arable land, ripe for occupation.

Question: Is this attack sound? It looks to me as if White pushes to the fringes of reason and is in grave danger of overextension.

Answer: It is no easy matter to overcome our natural prejudices. In some positions we are obliged to play a move which contradicts our natural style. I realize that this is jarring stuff and White's play may remind us of a one-year-old's random pecks at a toy piano keyboard. If we examine it through the unbiased lens of the computer, it tells us that White stands clearly better. Such positions get less and less scary, the more we play them and the more we familiarize ourselves with the position's consequences.

12...♘f8?!

Jansa is utterly unprepared for his opponent's unrehearsed infusion of chaos. His last move fails to square matters in conjunction with e6. Black had to transpose to the Pixton-Stefano variation with 12...♘f6 13 ♗b5+ ♔f8 14 dxe6 when White's advantage was less marked than in the Vaganian-Jansa game.

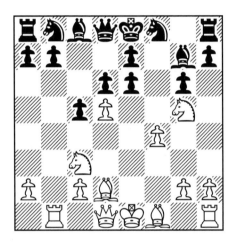

> *Exercise (combination alert):* Black's knight flops and tumbles loudly, like our dryer with a pair of tennis shoes in it. By posting the knight to f8, Jansa mistakenly agreed to contort to retain control over e6. How did Vaganian cross up this plan?

Answer: Pin/interference.

13 ♗b5+! ♗d7 14 dxe6 ♗xb5 15 ♘xb5 ♕c8

The dazed queen sprawls on c8, a woman who hears voices in her head and sees terrible visions of her own death.

> *Question:* It feels to me like Black is overreacting to White's ♘f7 threat. Why not just give up the exchange and bring out pieces with 15...♘c6?

Answer: The scent of impending danger permeates the air around Black's king and queen couple, and Black's extra pawn isn't much of a consolation prize when we examine his numerous problems:

1. Black is tangled up and behind in development and enveloped with threats.

2. It's not just an exchange Black is worried about. White forces the win of the queen with 16 ♘f7 ♛b8 (16...♛c8?? hangs the queen to 17 ♘bxd6+) 17 ♘bxd6+! exd6.

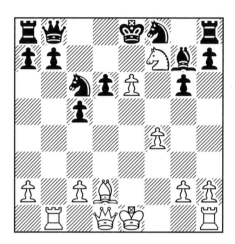

Now let's turn this position into an exercise.

> *Exercise: (combination alert):* White to play and force the win of Black's queen.

Answer: Attraction/knight fork: 18 ♖xb7! and Black's queen runs out of safe havens.

16 0-0 a6

Alternatively, 16...♛c6 17 f5 ♘a6 18 ♗c3 ♗xc3 19 ♘xc3 ♘c7 20 f6! exf6 21 ♖xf6 d5 22 ♛f3 ♘fxe6 23 ♘xe6 ♘xe6 was A.Zubarev-Y.Zinchenko, Rethymnon 2011. Now White's strongest move is 24 ♘xd5! threatening ♖xe6+, followed by ♘c7+. If 24...♖c8 25 ♖e1 ends all resistance.

17 ♗c3!

Removing Black's only active piece from the board. Vaganian skilfully weaves his way through a baffling capillary system of side streets, back alleys and hidden passages, always inching closer to Black's king.

17...axb5

No choice, since 17...♗xc3 18 ♘xc3 h6 19 ♘ge4 ♘xe6 20 ♘d5 ♘d7 21 ♘xe7! ♚xe7 22 ♛xd6+ ♚f7 23 f5 is crushing.

18 ♗xg7 ♖g8 19 ♗xf8

The human move. *Houdini* uncovered the impossible-to-see 19 f5!! ♖xg7 20 f6 exf6 21 ♖xf6 ♖e7 22 ♛f3 ♘bd7 23 exd7+ ♘xd7 24 ♘e4! (threatening a king/queen fork) 24...♖a6 25 ♘xd6+ ♖xd6 26 ♖xd6 when Black has no chance of survival.

19...♖xf8 20 ♘xh7 ♖g8

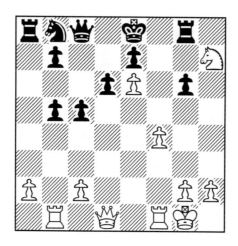

21 f5

Not the best method of continuing the attack. Possibly more accurate was 21 ♖xb5!, and if 21...♕xe6? 22 ♖e1 ♕c4 23 ♕xd6 ♘c6 24 ♖xb7 ♕d4+ 25 ♕xd4 cxd4 26 ♘f6+ ending the game.

21...gxf5 22 ♕h5+ ♚d8

This turns out to be a bloodless coup, as Black's king flees the borders of the kingside, and deposits himself to the relative safety – or so he hopes – of the queenside.

23 ♕f7 ♖e8 24 ♖xf5?!

Threat: ♕xe8+!. However, White missed the stronger continuation 24 ♖xb5! ♘a6 25 ♖b6! (threat: ♘f6!) 25...♘c7 (after 25...♚c7 26 ♖xa6! bxa6 27 ♘f6 ♖b8 28 h4! ♚c6 29 ♘xe8 ♕xe8 30 ♕xf5 White's kingside passers decide the game) 26 ♘f6! ♕xe6 27 ♕xe6 ♘xe6 28 ♘xe8 ♚xe8 29 ♖xf5 and, again, White's kingside passers decide the game.

24...♕c6!

Jansa fights back. Desperation is that invigorating tonic which jolts our apathy back to normalcy and beyond. Undoubtedly, Vaganian prayed for 24...♘c6?? 25 ♕xe8+! when Black is unable to recapture.

25 ♖e1

For now, the position resembles an abstractionist painting and hovers in a definitionless, neutral grey zone, free from clarity – until Black's next move.

25...♖xa2?

If Black had found 25...♖a4! the position would have remained an unclear mess.

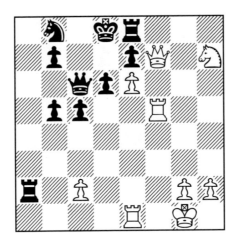

Answer: Discovered attack.

26 ♘f6! ♖xc2

Otherwise, 26...exf6 is met with 27 e7+ ♔c7 28 ♕xa2, while 26...♖h8? is met with 27 ♕g7 ♖h4 28 ♕f8+ ♔c7 29 ♘d5+! which wins the house.

27 ♕xe8+ ♕xe8 28 ♘xe8 ♔xe8 29 h4!

As it turns out, White is faster in the queening race, since his e1-rook can sacrifice for one of Black's passers.

29...♖c4

The roving rook hopes to sabotage enemy installations, behind the lines. The trouble with 29...b4 30 h5 b3 31 h6 b2 32 h7 is, of course, that White queens with check.

30 h5 ♘c6

30...♖g4 31 ♖ef1 ♔d8 32 ♖1f4! and the h-pawn promotes.

31 ♖ef1

Threatening mate on the move.

31...♔d8 32 ♖5f4!

Vaganian blocks out Black's rook and won't even allow a sacrifice for the surging h-pawn.

32...♘d4 33 ♔h2

Avoiding a cheapo on e2.

33...♘xe6 34 ♖xc4 bxc4 35 h6 ♘g5

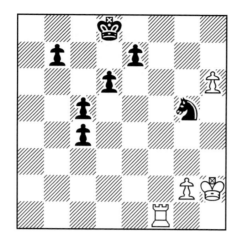

Exercise (planning/critical decision): No time for dry runs or rehearsals. A decision must be made immediately, upon which our future hangs in the balance. White has two available plans:

A) Chase Black's knight down with 36 ♖f5.

B) Leave the rook where it is to defend against Black's surging passers and hunt down the knight with White's king, with 36 ♔g3 and ♔g4.

Think carefully before you decide. Only one of the plans works and the margin is razor thin; White wins by a single tempo.

Answer: Only plan B is correct. Now all issues resolve into perfect solutional fits, as if by magic.

36 ♔g3!

36 ♖f5? allows Black a draw after 36...♘h7 37 ♖f7 c3 38 ♖f3 (38 ♖xh7?? loses to 38...c2 39 ♖h8+ ♔d7 40 h7 c1♛ 41 ♖d8+ ♔xd8 42 h8♛+ ♔c7) 38...b5 39 ♖xc3 b4 40 ♖c1 ♔e8 41 ♖f1 c4 42 ♔g3 b3 43 ♔f3 d5 44 ♔e3 e5 45 ♔d2 d4 46 ♖e1 ♔f7 47 ♖xe5 c3+ 48 ♔d3 b2 49 ♖b5 ♘f6 50 ♔c2 ♔g6 51 ♖b6 ♔f5 52 g4+ ♔g5 53 ♖b4 ♔xh6 54 ♖xd4 ♔g5 55 ♖b4 ♘xg4 56 ♔xc3 is drawn, since rook and king can't beat king and knight.

36...b5 37 ♔g4 c3

White wins by one tempo after 37...♘h7 (seeds of disenchantment with the knight's lot in life take root on h7) 38 ♔h5 c3 39 ♔g6 ♘f6 (the powerless knight can do nothing more than spew muffled oaths at the king's rude intrusion into his personal space) 40 ♖xf6! exf6 41 h7.

38 ♔xg5 1-0

Summary: Surprisingly, the comps worked out the position after 7...g6?! 8 e5! to a clear advantage for White, who enjoys a kind of KID Four Pawns Attack on steroids.

Game 35
J.Hodgson-R.Pert
British Rapidplay Championship, Bradford 2001

1 d4 ♘f6 2 ♗g5 c5 3 d5 ♕b6 4 ♘c3 ♕xb2

Once again we reach a state of unbridgeable philosophical differences: our side believes it is better to give than to receive, while Black's camp takes the opposing view. Once again, Black openly violates Morphy's terms of the opening contract: don't fall behind in development in an open position.

5 ♗d2 ♕b6 6 e4 d6 7 f4 ♗g4?!

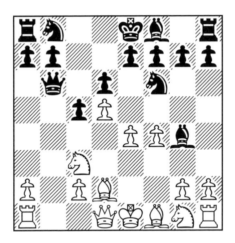

This natural move, played often at the club level, is actually quite rotten for Black and may actually deserve a full question mark.

8 ♗e2!

The best response. White, by swapping bishops, actually increases the energy potential of his position, since his queen on e2 is perfectly placed to enforce a coming disruptive e5 break. In a weird coincidence, White wins at a 78.6 % ratio from this position – exactly to the decimal the same as the stats last game after White's 8th move!

> **Question:** Isn't 8 ♘f3 stronger, since Black hands over the bishop-pair when White later plays h3?

Answer: This position requires not a strategic tweak, but a sledgehammer blow. Hodgson's choice is far more energetic and also just stronger. After 8...♘bd7 9 ♖b1 ♕c7 10 h3 ♗xf3 11 ♕xf3 g6 I don't believe White gets full compensation for the pawn, since the e5-break is going to be very difficult, if not impossible to achieve, S.Grimm-D.Sermek, Passau 1998.

8...♗xe2 9 ♕xe2

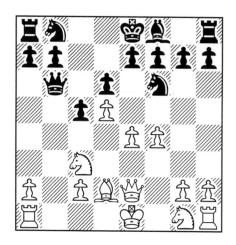

9...a6?!

One gets the impression that Black's king certainly doesn't appreciate his defender's laid-back management style. This is just too slow and Black soon gets pushed off the board.

> **Question:** Why would Black take time out to play ...a6 when so far behind in development?

Answer: The trouble is White threatens to regain the lost pawn with a clear advantage with ♖b1, followed by ♕b5+. Black shuts down this possibility, at the cost of further lagging, which he just can't afford:

a) 9...e6?! 10 ♘f3 ♗e7 (10...exd5? 11 e5 dxe5 12 fxe5 ♘fd7 13 ♘xd5 ♕c6 14 e6! fxe6 15 ♘f4 with a winning attack for White) was N.Tavoularis-T.Kett, Budapest 2010. Now White should continue with 11 ♖b1 ♕c7 12 ♕b5+, regaining the pawn with clear advantage. Following 12...♕d7 (12...♘bd7 13 dxe6 fxe6 14 ♘g5 is not going to be comfortable for Black) 13 ♕xb7 ♕xb7 14 ♖xb7 exd5 15 exd5 ♘bd7 16 0-0 0-0 17 g4! ♖fb8 18 ♖fb1 ♖xb7 19 ♖xb7 ♖b8 20 ♖xa7 Black is the one down a pawn and hanging on for dear life.

b) 9...♘fd7?! 10 ♘f3 g6 11 ♖b1 ♕c7 12 e5 dxe5 13 fxe5 ♗g7 14 d6! ♕c6 15 dxe7 ♔xe7 16 0-0 h6 was V.Vaisman-G.Miralles, French League 1992. Black is hopelessly busted after 17 ♘e4 intending ♘d6.

c) 9...e5! is *Houdini*'s recommendation, which restores some measure of composure to Black's otherwise rapidly destabilizing situation. After 10 ♖b1 ♕c7 11 ♕b5+ ♘bd7 12 ♕xb7 ♕xb7 13 ♖xb7 exf4 14 ♗xf4 a6 15 ♘f3 Black stands clearly worse, but at least he can play on, unlike with other choices.

10 ♖b1 ♕c7 11 e5

Of course. Principles: open the position and create confrontation when leading in development. The thought of Hodgson swearing off attacks is a little like the alcoholic asking the bartender for one 'last' drink.

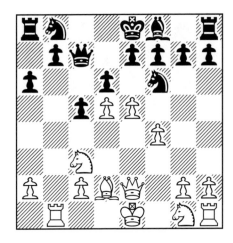

11...dxe5

> **Question:** Why open the game further when lagging
> in development? Can Black get away with 11...♘fd7?

Answer: Black landed in one of those dreaded, damned-if-you-do-and-damned-if-you-don't contradictions. He gets killed here as well after 12 ♘f3. Now if 12...g6 13 ♘e4! (threat: ♘xd6+) 13...dxe5 14 fxe5 e6 (14...♘xe5?? 15 ♘xe5 ♕xe5 16 ♗c3 spears a rook) 15 ♗c3 h6 16 dxe6 fxe6 17 ♘d6+ ♔e7 18 ♖xb7 ♕c6 19 ♘h4 when Black can comfortably resign.

12 fxe5 ♘fd7 13 ♘f3 e6

Alternatively, 13...g6 14 0-0 ♗g7 15 e6 fxe6 16 ♘g5 ♕e5 17 ♘xe6 ♖a7 18 ♘e4 when White's numerous threats overwhelm Black, N.Povah-S.Jackson, British League 2000.

14 0-0

White's development lead has gotten completely out of control.

14...exd5

Opening further, but the problem is 14...♗e7 is met with 15 d6.

15 e6!

A move which dispels all remaining doubt of the colossal wretchedness inherent in Black's position, after which the defence droops in distress. The coming weakness of the light squares is merely the symptom of Black's concern, but not the cause, which was his seventh move, which traded away the defender of that colour.

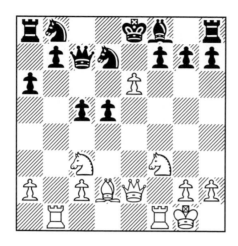

15...fxe6

If 15...♘f6 16 ♘xd5! (a strong gust of the knight's petulance comes Black's way) 16...♘xd5 17 exf7+ (*Houdini* announces a forced mate in seven moves from this point) 17...♔d7 (17...♔xf7 18 ♘g5+ ♔g6 19 ♕e6+ ♘f6 20 ♕f5+ ♔h5 21 ♘f3+ g5 22 ♕xg5 is mate) 18 ♕e8+ ♔d6 19 ♗f4+! ♘xf4 20 ♖fd1+ ♘d5 21 ♖xd5+! ♔xd5 22 ♖d1+ ♔c4 23 ♕a4+ ♔c3 (White's queen and the black king have a difference of opinion: Black's king is anti-execution, whereas White's queen, unfortunately, remains firmly entrenched in the pro-execution camp) 24 ♕b3 mate.

16 ♕xe6+ ♗e7 17 ♘xd5

The incision along the central light squares grows in the wake of the surgeon's scalpel.

17...♕d6 18 ♘g5!

The knight infestation continues, and the black king and queen's faces simultaneously register deep anguish. Less flashy but just as effective is 18 ♖xb7! ♕xe6 19 ♘c7+, and if 19...♔f7 20 ♘g5+ ♔g6 21 ♘gxe6.

18...♘c6

Otherwise, 18...♕xe6 19 ♘xe6, and if 19...♖a7 side-stepping the fork, then comes 20 ♘dc7 mate.

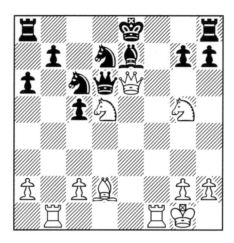

Exercise (combination alert): The possession of an overwhelming position isn't a written guarantee of a point on the wall chart. White must still deal with the dangling loose end of actually forcing the win. Tortured shapes, demons sent to the corporeal world on an errand, float menacingly over Black's king. White has two methods of winning. Find one of them:

Answer: Attraction/knight fork.

19 ♘c7+!

Black's queen finds herself at the mercy of White's irrational knights, who continue to make outrageous ransom demands. Also crushing was 19 ♕f7+ ♔d8 20 ♗f4 ♘de5 21 ♗xe5 ♘xe5 22 ♘e6+ ♔d7 23 ♖xb7+ (the attacking debauch continues unabated) 23...♔c8 24 ♘xe7+ ♔xb7 25 ♖b1+ forcing mate.

19...♕xc7 20 ♕f7+

The point. White forces Black's king to the fork square on d8.

20...♔d8 21 ♘e6+

The knight stares raptly at Black's queen, the way a homely, pimple-faced high school teen gazes lovingly at the cheerleader who walks by in the hallway.

21...♔c8 22 ♘xc7 ♔xc7 23 ♗f4+ 1-0

"Soon, very soon, you will be no more than an unpleasant memory," White's bishop tells his brother on c7.

Summary: The natural 7...♗g4? (yes, I downgraded the move to the full question mark it deserves) comes close to being labelled a losing move for Black. More good news: the move is commonly played at the club level, so be ready for it.

Game 36
C.Lakdawala-J.Funderburg
San Diego (rapid) 2007

1 d4 ♘f6 2 ♗g5 c5 3 d5 ♕b6

My old student, John Funderburg, is a three-time San Diego Chess Club Champion and maintains a solid master's rating.

4 ♘c3

Civil disobedience commences, proving that your writer is indeed a worthy son of Gandhi. From time to time, annoying religious pamphleteers ignore the 'No Solicitors' sign prominently displayed on my front door and ring the doorbell, in their efforts to save me from eternal damnation. I normally politely send them on their way. But some days, when in an ornery mood, I welcome them in with: "Om mani padme hum! May universal blessings bring peace upon you, brothers and sisters!" It was in one of these latter moods that I offered to play the Vaganian Gambit. The b2-pawn is once again the unwanted infant left on Black's doorstep.

4...e5!?

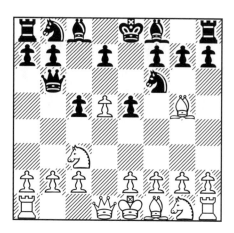

Any citizen of Troy will tell you: sometimes a gift is no gift.

Question: Speaking of chicken, why play ...♕b6 and then not take b2?

Answer: I wouldn't call it chicken, as much as caution battling ambition, and winning. It beats me why players bother with ...♕b6 and then don't take, but I have had two masters do just that against me. So we have to be ready for the declined line as well. Also, GM Timur Gareev – ranked fourth in the U.S. – who now lives in San Diego, showed up one morning at our Saturday Gambito rapid tournaments. We started a blitz game and he played 4...e5 on me as well. Gareev plays the Trompowsky as White so this was a deliberate choice on his part. Unfortunately, the round began and we had to abandon the blitz game, so I don't know what he intended against our approach.

Question: What kind of a set-up is Black looking for with his last move?

Answer: The idea is to play a kind of Czech Benoni where the white bishop on g5 may later be vulnerable to swaps for Black's e7-bishop and also ...♘xd5 tactical shots. However, in the normal Czech Benoni, White's c-pawn is already on c4. In this version c4 is available for our pieces, especially a knight, so I think we get a decent deal in this trade-off: 4...d6 5 e4 g6 6 ♗b5+ ♗d7 (possibly inaccurate since the swap of light-squared bishops only helps White; after 6...♘bd7 7 a4 ♕a5 8 ♗d2 ♕c7 9 ♘f3 ♗g7 10 0-0 0-0 11 h3 a6 12 ♗e2 b6 13 ♗f4 ♗b7 14 ♖e1 ♖ad8 15 ♗c4 Black has yet to neutralize White's extra space, M.Orr-K.Jorrit, Bled Olympiad 2002) 7 ♗xf6! (or 7 a4 ♗g7 8 ♘f3 a6 9 a5 ♕c7 10 ♗e2 b5 11 axb6 ♕xb6 12 ♖a2 h6 13 ♗d2 0-0 and White's central space gave him the edge, S.Lputian-Wang Zili, Moscow Olympiad 1994) 7...exf6 8 a4 (a new move and I believe an improvement over the previously played 8 ♗xd7+ and 8 ♕d3) 8...♗g7 9 ♘ge2 (if Black catches up in development and achieves ...f5 he stands better; fortunately, he can't achieve it) 9...0-0 10 0-0 ♕c7 11 ♘g3! (preventing ...f5) 11...a6 12 ♗e2 (he is cramped, so exchanges only help Black) 12...b6 13 f4 ♕c8 (intending...f5) 14 f5!.

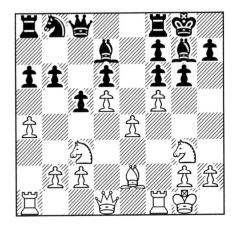

Question: Doesn't this move violate two principles? It:
1. Fixes pawns on the same colour of your remaining bishop.
2. Creates a gaping hole on e5.

Answer: All true, but this is secondary to the cramping effect of f4-f5: 14...♗e8 (more accurate was 14...♗h6, activating his dark-squared bishop) 15 ♕d2 ♘d7 16 h4! ♘e5 17 h5 g5?! 18 h6! ♗h8?? (strategic suicide, as Black is effectively down a piece from this point on; he had to brave the white attack down the h-file and take with 18...♗xh6 19 ♘d1 c4 20 ♘h5

♕c5+ 21 ♘f2 ♗g7 22 b4 ♕c7 when I planned an eventual ♔h2 and maybe even ♔g3!?, followed by doubling rooks on the h-file, with a strong attack) 19 b3 (Black is hopelessly busted; all White has to do is to open the position on the queenside and he is effectively a piece up) 19...♕b7 20 ♘d1 b5 21 axb5 axb5 22 ♘f2 (idea: ♘h3 and ♘xg5) 22...♗d7 23 ♘h3 (perhaps it was better to remove his only good piece with 23 ♘d3!? ♘xd3 24 ♗xd3) 23...♖xa1 24 ♖xa1 ♖a8 25 ♖a5 c4 (a cheapo, threatening ...♕b6+) 26 ♔h2 ♖c8 27 b4 ♔f8 28 ♕e1 ♕b6 29 ♕g1 ♕xg1+ (29...♕d8 30 ♖a6 is also hopeless for Black) 30 ♔xg1 ♔e7.

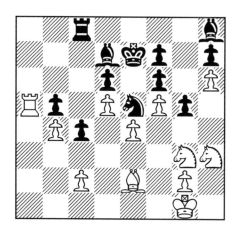

Exercise (planning): Come up with a clear winning plan for White:

Answer: Target b5, the weak link, by transferring the knights to c3 and d4, and then picking off b5: 31 ♘f2! ♔e8 (Black has nothing better to do than wait) 32 ♘d1 ♔e7 33 ♘c3 ♖b8 34 ♔f2 ♔e8 35 ♗h5! (intending ♘e2 and ♘d4 without allowing Black ...♘g4+ tricks) 35...♔e7 36 ♘ge2 ♗e8 37 ♘d4 1-0, C.Lakdawala-K.Wagner, San Diego G/15 Championship 2010.

Returning to 4...e5:

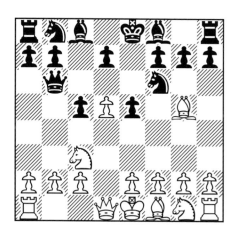

5 ⬜b1

Played with a huge sigh of relief.

Question: Can you play 5 e4 here?

Answer: Sure, but the chicken in me returned and I eagerly protected b2. Play may transpose after 5...♕xb2 6 ♗d2 ♕b6 7 f4 d6 8 f5 which we looked at in the first game of the chapter.

5...♗e7 6 e4 d6 7 ♘f3 ♘bd7

Question: Why would Black block in his bishop like this?

Answer: Black's light-squared bishop is his good model, and he doesn't want to risk swapping it away after 7...♗g4?! 8 ♗e2 0-0 9 ♘d2, when he either agrees to an unfavourable trade or loses time backing off the bishop.

8 ♘d2 a6

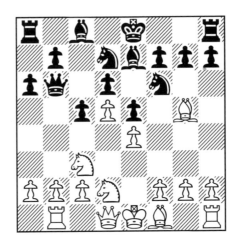

9 ♗e3!

Question: This move makes no sense to me. Didn't you just lose a tempo?

Answer: I avoided the line 9 ♗e2?! ♕d8! 10 a4 ♘xd5! (we must watch out for this dirty trick when our bishop sits unguarded on g5) 11 ♗xe7 ♘xe7 12 ♘c4 0-0 13 ♕xd6 ♘c6. Right or wrong, I felt Black equalized here.

9...♕c7 10 a4 b6 11 ♗d3 ♘f8

Strategic threat: ...♘g4. After 11...0-0 I intended 12 g4!? continuing my kingside expansion ambitions.

12 f3 ♘g6 13 g3 h6 14 ♕e2

Suppressing the ...c4 and ...b5 breaks, while keeping Black tied down to the defence of a6.

14...♘h7

Intention: ...♗g5.

15 h4!

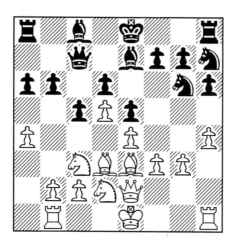

Oh, no you don't! Black walks into work one day and discovers his once spacious office converted into a broom closet. He contrives to ignore the white elephant in the room: the fact that his solidity doesn't make up for cramped quarters and a lack of counterplay.

15...♘f6 16 ♗f2

Clearing e3 for a knight.

16...h5 17 ♘c4 ♘d7 18 ♘e3

The knight tacks and weaves his way to its optimal square on e3. Note that Black's ...b5, ...c4 and ...f5 breaks have all be squelched.

18...♗f8!

Black realizes his pieces sprawl awkwardly and reroutes, planning: ...♘e7, ...g6, ...♗g7 and, maybe one day, ...f5.

19 ♔f1

The king roams about as if he owned the place. I walk my king to g2, since the rook already belongs on h1, in case Black tries ...g5 breaks.

19...♘e7 20 ♔g2 g6

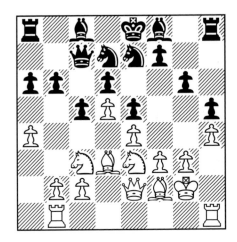

21 ♖bf1

Answer: Plan A: Play for f4 after due preparation.

The alternative was Plan B: Play for a b4 break, like this: 21 ♘c4 ♗h6 (21...♖b8 22 b4 b5
23 axb5 axb5 24 ♘xd6+! ♕xd6 25 bxc5 ♘xc5 26 ♘xb5 leaves Black busted) 22 b4 0-0 23
bxc5 bxc5 24 ♗e3 ♗xe3 25 ♕xe3 ♔g7 26 a5 with queenside pressure.

21...♗g7 22 b3 ♘f6 23 ♗e1!

Heading to c3 to magnify the effect of f4.

23...♗h6 24 ♗d2 ♔f8

Played with the same logic applied to my earlier ♔f1, ♔g2 sequence.

25 ♖f2 ♔g7 26 ♖hf1 ♕d7!

What a nuisance. I must cover the infiltration threat to h3.

27 ♖h1 ♘e8 28 ♘b1

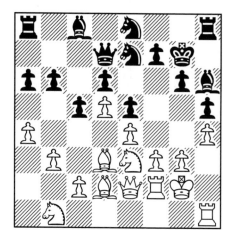

Heading for a3 and clearing c3 for my bishop.

28...♘c7

Hoping to achieve ...b5 someday.

> **Question:** Black has enough force to engineer ...f5. Why not play it now?

Answer: White still retains a clear strategic advantage if Black decides to open the position after 28...f5! 29 ♘c4 ♕c7 30 a5 b5 31 ♘b6 ♖b8 32 c4 b4 33 ♘xc8 ♖xc8 34 f4! fxe4 35 ♗xe4 when Black's exposed king remains in grave danger.

29 ♘a3 ♖b8 30 c4

I wanted to seal the queenside to concentrate my fire on the other wing without distraction. My opponent carefully retains the tension, however.

30...♗b7 31 ♗c3 f6 32 f4

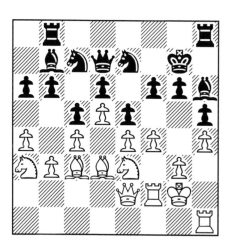

At long last. Plateaus can turn into comfortable, unchanging prisons if we let them. White finally takes action and achieves the desired break.

32...♖bf8

> **Question:** Can Black generate central counterplay with 32...exf4 33 gxf4 ♖be8?

Answer: White's centre remains stable and Black's king looks like he is in a bad way after 34 ♖g1, intending an eventual f5 break.

33 ♘ac2 ♗c8 34 f5

Weakening f5 and h5.

34...♕e8 35 ♖hf1 g5 36 ♖h1! ♖fg8

> **Question:** Your last move looks like an error to me. Why can't Black seal the kingside with 36...g4?

Answer: By doing so, Black swaps one problem for another. I would respond with 37 a5!, blasting open the queenside when Black isn't prepared for it, and if 37...b5 38 b4!. With this frictionless pivoting, we seamlessly swap Plan A for Plan B, with zero wasted motion.

37 hxg5 ♗xg5 38 ♔f1

Threat: ♖fh2, going after h5.

38...♖h6 39 ♖fh2 ♖gh8

Black searched every avenue for counterplay – the maybes, the probables, the possibles, and even looked into the highly unlikelies and even the impossibles – without finding a solution, since none exists.

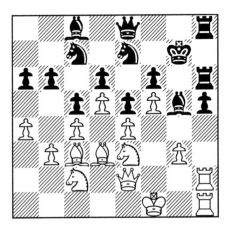

> **Exercise (planning):** White has access to two methods which increase advantage. Find them:

Answer: Transfer the knight to f3. Not only is h5 weak, but X-rays spot a secondary metas-tatic growth appearing on g5. Black, who had hopes of containing the chronic weakness, is doomed by the appearance of a malignant twin.

40 ♘e1!

The key to victory is to eliminate Black's 'bad' bishop, who happens to be the steward of the kingside dark squares. Also strong is 40 a5! b5 41 b4!, favourably prying open the queenside.

40...♗xe3

We now add weak dark squares, denoting Black's growing list of phobic stressors. 40...♗d7 41 ♘f3 nails the bishop anyway.

41 ♕xe3 b5

I give little credence to this attempted distraction and proceed on course on the king-side.

42 axb5 axb5 43 ♘f3 ♗d7

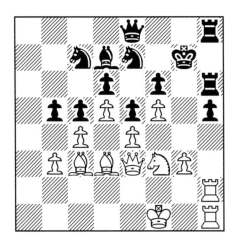

> **Exercise (planning):** Black's position nears the breaking point.
> Find the expedient which pushes it over the edge:

Answer: Pin. The coming g5 destroys Black's resistance.

44 g4 bxc4 45 bxc4 ♕f7 46 ♗d2

Queen and bishop remain at a distance, yet involved in the proceedings on the kingside, in a kind of supervisory contact. Your business savvy writer rarely applies a combinational solution in a rapid game when the simple, mundane one will do – even if I see the flashy one over the board. White can also play 46 g5! fxg5 47 ♗xe5+! dxe5 48 ♘xe5 ♕e8 49 ♕xg5+ ♔f8 50 ♖xh5!, and if 50...♖xh5 51 ♕f6+ ♔g8 52 ♖g1+ forces mate.

46...♔f8 47 g5

The g5-square is the distillation point, from which all which is rotten in Black's position spews forth. 47 ♕xh6+ ♖xh6 48 ♗xh6+ ♔g8 49 ♖xh5 is also hopeless for Black.

47...fxg5 48 ♕xg5

The queen broods over g5 like an overbearing mother. 48 ♘xg5, intending to eventually sink the knight into e6, was also awfully tempting.

48...♕f6

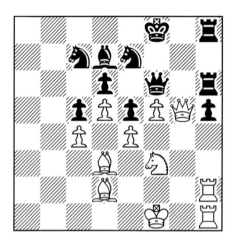

> ***Exercise (combination alert):*** I missed a
> combination here. How can White win the exchange?

49 ♕xf6+

Still winning, but slightly stronger was:

Answer: Overload/zwischenzug: 49 ♕h4! ♕xh4 50 ♗xh6+ ♖xh6 51 ♖xh4. This is one of those combinations which shows little evidence of design, and just happens to be there.

49...♖xf6 50 ♖xh5 ♖xh5 51 ♖xh5 ♔g7 52 ♗g5 1-0

One look at the bishop and we are reminded of the spider who hangs upside down, patiently awaiting the neighbourhood fly's arrival in his net. After 52...♖f7 53 f6+ ♖xf6 54 ♗xf6+ ♔xf6 Black's fortress dreams are ruined by the line 55 ♖h6+ ♘g6 56 ♘h4 ♗e8 57 ♘f5 when d6 falls.

Here 52 ♘g5!, intending ♖h7+, may be even stronger than winning material. The knight leaves a trail of slime in his wake, like your now standard movie alien while in pursuit of Sigourney Weaver.

Summary: If Black declines the Vaganian Gambit, then squeeze your opponent with your territorial advantage.

Chapter Six
Trompowsky versus King's Indian

1 d4 ♞f6 2 ♗g5 g6 3 ♗xf6 exf6

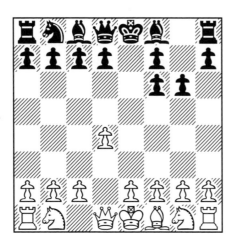

Structurally, this chapter is similar to and may even transpose to the positions we examined in Chapter Four, so it isn't exactly a leap into the darkness of the unknown – for us. On the other hand, for your KID-loving opponent, this will probably be all new territory for him or her. We once again exert our will upon the position and force our opponents to play in our backyard, not theirs.

> *Game 37*
> **G.Kasparov-J.Salzberg**
> New York (simul) 2000

1 d4 ♘f6 2 ♗g5 g6

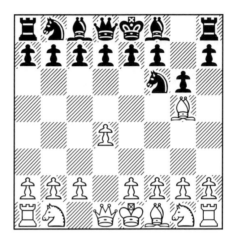

A move which declares: "I'm a King's Indian player, and your second move isn't going to change that!" Yet with our third move, we do indeed alter matters.

3 ♗xf6

This is the most Trompowskyish move you can play. Of course, you have a million other choices, like Torre Attack and transposition to normal KID lines which include ♗g5.

3...exf6 4 e3

I have thought about pre-empting ...d5, by tossing in an immediate 4 c4. Play may follow with: 4...♗g7 (4...♗b4+ 5 ♘d2 doesn't bother White) 5 ♘c3 f5 6 e3 0-0 7 ♘ge2 (keeping an eye out for ...f4 tricks) 7...d6 8 g3 (we can also play the Catalan-Trompowsky against the KID) 8...h5 9 h4 ♘d7 10 ♗g2 ♘f6 11 0-0 ♘g4 12 ♘f4 ♗h6 13 b4 ♖e8 14 ♖b1, S.Ionov-R.Mamedov, Loo 2013. It's easy to see that White will continue to make queenside spatial gains, and I'm not really sure how Black proceeds on the kingside.

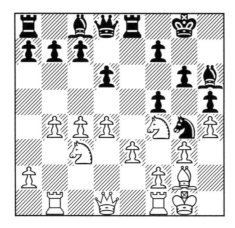

Question: How do we defend if Black goes psycho on us and lashes out with 14...g5?

Answer: We should have adequate resources to defend against the attack after 15 hxg5
♕xg5 (or 15...♗xg5 16 ♘xh5 ♖xe3 17 ♘d5! ♖e6 18 ♕d3 ♖h6 19 ♘df4 c6 20 b5 ♕c7 21 bxc6
bxc6 22 ♖b2 and at this stage I don't see how Black continues with the attack; meanwhile,
White seriously damaged Black's structure and earns queenside gains) 16 ♘cd5 h4 17
♘xc7 hxg3 18 ♘xe8 ♕h4 19 ♘f6+! (deflection) 19...♕xf6 20 ♕f3 gxf2+ 21 ♖xf2 (I don't believe in Black's attack if he or she refuses f2) 21...♘xf2 22 ♔xf2 when Black's pawn structure is a wreck and White dominates d5, with a clear advantage.

4...♗g7

Question: How is the position any different from the
3...exf6 lines of Chapter Four, after Black plays 4...d5?

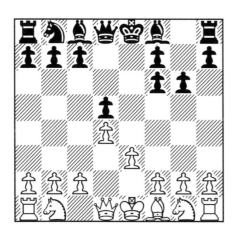

Answer: Not much different. In fact, we may directly transpose. The only slight alteration is that in this chapter's version, Black commits to an early ...g6, which he or she doesn't necessarily have to play in the Chapter Four versions. We examine ...d5 lines later in this chapter, but with Black's bishop on g7, rather than on d6, which we covered in Chapter Four.

5 h4

The thought of delivering checkmate acts upon us all as a potent stimulant. This may be the most annoying move for Black if he or she is a KID purist. Black can either weaken the kingside with ...h5, or allow us the potential to open the h-file if we are allowed h5.

5...d6

Black refuses to alter course and sticks with a pure KID set-up. We examine 5...h5 later in the chapter.

6 h5 f5 7 ♘e2

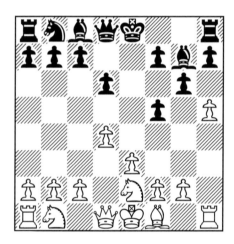

This move scores 100% from four games in my database.

> **Question:** Why e2 rather than f3?

Answer: For the same reasons we normally play to e2 in the 3...exf6 lines of Chapter Four: e2 is the knight's most flexible square, from which it may head for f4.

7...0-0!?

> **Question:** Castling into it?

Answer: One does get the feeling that Black is a man of a carefree disposition. Have you noticed that Kasparov's simul opponents in this book don't seem to believe in his attacking powers? Black's confident, some would proclaim overconfident move is obviously a high-risk proposition, made even more so with Kasparov at the attacking end.

Answer: Going ...g5, now or later, loosens Black's kingside structure. An example: 7...♘d7 8 ♘f4 c6 9 ♘d2 ♕e7 10 c3 ♘f6 11 ♗e2 g5 12 h6! ♗f8 13 ♘h5 ♗xh6 14 ♘g3 ♗g7 15 ♕c2 f4 (Black falls too far behind in development after 15...♕e6 16 ♗d3 f4 17 ♘f5 ♗f8 18 0-0) 16 exf4 gxf4 17 ♘f5 ♗xf5 18 ♕xf5 ♕e6 19 ♕xf4 0-0-0 20 ♔f1 h5 21 ♗d3 when White stood better due to superior pawn structure and better bishop, A.Girish-V.Antonio, New Delhi 2010.

8 ♘d2 ♘d7 9 ♘f4 ♘f6 10 g3

Kasparov switches to the more positional Catalan-Trompowsky version, seeing his bishop is better off on g2, rather than d3, where it hits a wall on f5.

10...♖e8 11 ♗g2 ♘e4

Black makes use of his trump: control over e4. Now ...♗xd4 is in the air.

12 c3 ♘xd2?!

Black's knight inexplicably weakens its adhesive grip over e4. This looks rather convenient for White. Black's unnecessary concession violates the principle: don't be the one to release the central tension without good reason. Black looks okay after 12...c6 13 hxg6 hxg6 14 ♘xe4 (Black also looks fine after 14 ♕c2 ♕e7) 14...fxe4 15 ♕c2 ♕e7 16 ♗h3 a5 17 ♗xc8 ♖axc8 18 0-0-0 b5 19 ♔b1.

13 ♕xd2 c5?!

Enthusiasm alone isn't enough to overlook a strategic sin. Black passes a demarcation point between need and desire. He weakens d5 in an abstract desire to remain active, for no good reason. He should play 13...c6 14 hxg6 hxg6 15 0-0-0 a5 with a sharp position.

14 ♔f1 ♖b8 15 ♗d5

The result of Black's ...c5 outburst: White's pieces roost on d5, placid and content as well-fed cows in their bovine happiness.

15...♗e6?

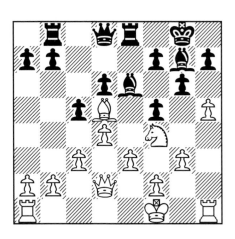

> *Exercise (combination alert):* Black, already in deep strategic trouble,
> just blundered on his last move. White to play and win material:

Answer: Deflection, so that g6 hangs.

16 hxg6 hxg6 17 ♖d1?!

Hey, I said "g6 hangs". Ah, yes, the simul disease – lack of alertness, mingled with inexplicable assessments – afflicts even the Kasparovs of the world. He either missed the simple combination in a distracted, simul state of mind, or, unmoved by sordid mercenary motivations, deliberately declined the pawn in order not to fix Black's structure. Whatever the motivation, it looks mistaken. 17 ♗xe6 fxe6 18 ♘xg6 simply picks off a pawn. Who knows, perhaps Kasparov liked the position he got in the game better than this pawn-up version.

17...♗xd5

Black eliminates the combination and we reach a classic dominant knight versus not-so-wonderful bishop situation.

18 ♘xd5 ♖c8?!

Black would be much better off closing the d-file with 18...cxd4 19 cxd4.

19 dxc5 dxc5 20 c4

Now the knight's radial authority extends in surrounding spokes of power.

20...♖e4

I'm not sure what the rook is fishing for here. I would play 20...♕d6 and just wait.

21 b3 ♕g5?

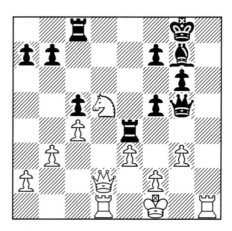

> *Exercise (combination alert):* The white queen's dark analogue
> mistakenly decides to assert her authority upon the kingside.
> Black's last move, which indulges in an oblique gesture, more for
> show than substance, hangs material. White to play and win material:

22 ♔g2?!

Answer: We don't always have to win our Tromps with mating attacks, ending with a cascade of sacs. Vulgar as it sounds, sometimes we can just steal a pawn or two to get the job done. Kasparov, probably focused on Black's king, missed 22 ♕a5! a6 23 ♕b6 ♖b8 24 ♕xc5 winning an important pawn.

22...♗f6??

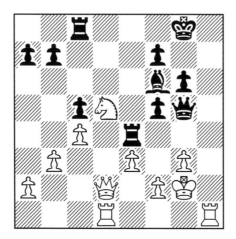

> ***Exercise (combination alert):*** Black's bishop gets ahead of himself, like
> an overeager singer who finds himself three bars ahead of the musician's
> accompaniment. After Black's last move, a monster error, the *Houdini*
> evaluation rockets to +15.66, and Black's assertion – whatever it may be –
> receives a jarring behavioural modification. What did he miss?

Answer: Queen trap/fork.

23 f4!

What luck. Kasparov must be the king of kismet to have such good fortune fall before him. The f-pawn expresses his feelings with generous portions toward the g5-pest, and now the solid earth begins to crumble, crack and open beneath Black's feet.

23...♗c3

There is no worse feeling in chess than that euphoric/dysphoric manic swing, from a playable (even worse is when you are winning! to a losing position in the space of a single move. The bishop's craving for justice is denied, so he settles for simple vindictiveness. The surly bishop reminds us of the Chihuahua, robbed of his bone by the Great Dane, but still up for a fight against his infinitely larger foe. Somehow I get the feeling this won't get Black off the hook and I freely admit this game falls short from being described as a feast of reason.

After 23...♕g4 24 ♘xf6+ the knight decides that the time has come to abolish the monarchy, execute Black's queen and install a democratic republic, with himself in the role of dictator for life. "How peaceful she looks," murmurs the knight, upon viewing his freshly murdered sister's bloody corpse on g4 after 24...♔g7 25 ♘xg4.

24 ♕xc3 1-0

Summary: A quick h4 is generally effective versus a die-hard KID opponent, since most of them refuse to respond with ...h5. This in turn allows us h5, with slight but nagging pressure.

1 d4 ♘f6 2 ♗g5 g6 3 ♗xf6 exf6 4 e3 ♗g7 5 h4 0-0!?

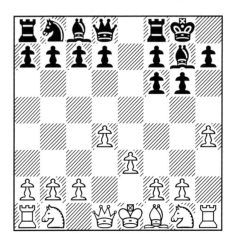

Answer: Yes, that exact thought crossed my mind as well. Once again, Black allows h5. Next game we look at 5...h5.

6 h5 h6?!

This potentially weakens g6 and the light squares around Black's king. Superior options are:

a) 6...f5 and now White should avoid 7 c4? discouraging ...d5 but also weakening the central dark square: 7...c5 8 ♘e2 ♘c6 9 ♘bc3 cxd4 10 ♘xd4 was A.Gulko-Y.Vovk, Internet (blitz) 2009. Now Black should continue 10...♘xd4 11 exd4 ♕b6, double attacking b2 and d4, with a clear advantage. One of the tricks of this line is to know when you can get away with c4, and when you can't. This is a clear case of can't.

b) 6...d6 7 ♘e2 c5 8 ♘bc3 ♘c6 9 hxg6 hxg6 10 ♕d2 f5 11 0-0-0 cxd4 12 exd4 d5 13 g3 ♗e6 14 ♗g2 ♖c8 15 ♔b1 b5 16 ♘f4 ♘xd4 17 ♘xe6 ♘xe6 (17...fxe6 18 ♕e3 ♕b6 19 ♘xd5! ♕c5 20 c3 also favours White) 18 ♘xd5 and I like White's chances due to that powerfully posted d5-knight, D.Lima-N.Delgado Ramirez, Rio de Janeiro 2004.

7 ♗d3 f5 8 ♘e2 ♕g5?!

Our recourses in any crisis: fight or flight. In this instance, Black mistakenly chooses the former as my opponent's newly found belligerence telepathically wafts over to the king-side. Yet this plan swerves from the position's core truth. A vaguely aggressive, scattershot strategy won't do in such a position, which clearly doesn't warrant it. Black's last move, although externally attractive, lacks functionality, loses the ...g5 option, walks into a future ♘f3 and actually endangers Black's queen if ...♘f6 follows later on. Black should play 8...d5.

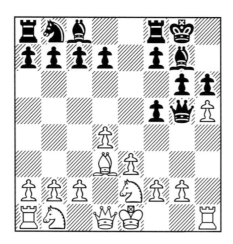

9 ♔f1!?

> *Question:* Why move your king when you can play 9 ♘f4?

Answer: I feared 9...♗xd4?, but missed the fact that the line favours White after 10 hxg6 ♗xb2 11 ♖h5 ♕e7 12 ♘d2. Your suggested line is not a line conducive for a simul.

> *Question:* Are you suggesting that the player
> giving the simul should alter his or her style?

Answer: Exactly correct. I tend to score very well (better than my rating) in simuls because I avoid the mistake other titled players make, which is to complicate. My simul philosophy has always been:

1. Keep it simple and play like a chicken. Miscalculation due to complications is the great enemy of the simul-giver.

2. Don't hang anything. Add fatigue to the equation and number two isn't so easy to achieve – unless, of course, the positions remains simple. So the rule is to distil your opponent's attempt to invoke chaos into recognizable patterns, in order to keep disorientation at bay.

3. Technique them out. I have found that even exhausted, I can still beat even strong players in a simul, as long as the situation is strategically clear, or it's a technical ending.

4. Ingest huge quantities of that blessed nectar, caffeine.

9...b6 10 ♘d2 ♗b7 11 ♖h2!?

Once again, I avoid 11 ♘f4 fearing 11...♗xd4?? and miss that White wins after 12 ♘f3.

11...d6 12 c3 ♘d7 13 ♘f4 ♘f6?

Black should backtrack and play 13...♕f6.

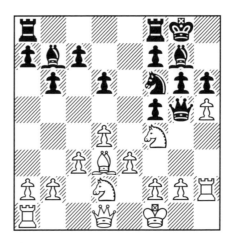

Exercise (combination alert): On his last move, a blunder,
Black clearly came down with a case of concentratus
interruptus. This one is easy. White to play and win material:

Answer: Deflection/knight fork. Black can't recapture, since e6 bulges herniatically, in an otherwise healthy structure.

14 hxg6 ♖ae8

If 14...fxg6?? (a lurking presence remains on f4, just outside the black queen's line of sight) 15 ♘e6 ♕g4 and now the simplest is 16 ♗e2! when Black must hand over even more material to save his queen.

15 gxf7+ ♖xf7

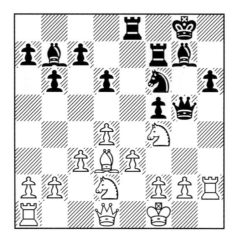

16 ♘f3

White still has a completely winning game after this move, but slightly stronger was:
Answer: 16 ♗c4! d5 17 ♘f3! (the hostile witness on g5 is instructed to answer unpleasant questions under cross examination) 17...♕g4 18 ♗b5 c6 19 ♖h4 trapping the queen.

16...♗xf3

This move certainly doesn't help, since weak light squares embody Black's woes, but the problem is 16...♕g4 is met with 17 ♗c4 d5 18 ♗b5 c6 19 ♖h4, trapping the wayward queen.

17 gxf3

Black's game is a wreck.

17...♖fe7 18 ♕d2

Admittedly paranoid (keep in mind, though, that paranoia represents a virtue in a simul game), but I was watching for sacrifices on e3.

18...c6 19 ♖e1 d5

> **Question:** Can Black put up a fight an exchange down after
> 19...♕xf4 20 exf4 ♖xe1+ 21 ♕xe1 ♖xe1+ 22 ♔xe1 ♘d5?

Answer: I was hoping for that line. The simplifying 23 ♗c4 is also lost for black.

20 ♖g2 ♕h4 21 ♗xf5 ♘h5

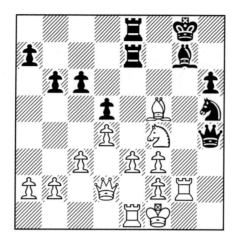

Exercise (calculation): Analyze 22 ♘g6. Does it work?

Answer: It sure does.

22 ♘g6 ♕h1+ 23 ♖g1 ♘g3+

Black fires the final shot in his clip. The knight bursts upon the scene with an entrance which would warm the heart of any scene-stealing stage actor. In situations of utter desperation, sang froid tends to enjoy an extended holiday and the sober keeping of accounts also sneaks out through the back door. Black keeps sac'ing in the vague hope of keeping his initiative alive. Clearly, the capering knight's diminishing circles to nowhere is some kind of modern interpretative dance, the meaning of which is only understood by my opponent. This desperado shouldn't have come as a surprise to you, and the hoped-for shot fails to detonate upon contact.

23...♕xf3 24 ♗g4! Also wins.

24 fxg3

I continue to feed with a voracious appetite.

24...♕xf3+ 25 ♕f2 ♖xe3 26 ♖xe3 ♖xe3

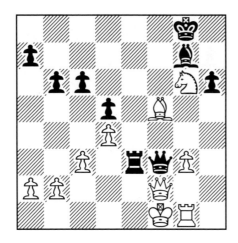

Exercise (combination alert): White to play and win.

Answer: Simplification/ knight fork.

27 ♕xf3! ♖xf3+ 28 ♔e2 1-0

28...♖xf5 (Black's disoriented rook asks: "Am I dreaming you, or did you dream me?") 29 ♘e7+ forks king and rook with a pickpocket's surreptitious agility.

Summary: I think Black is better off tossing in ...h5 in response to h4, as he does next game.

Game 39
A.Kireev-K.Rakay
Stare Mesto 2005

Enough of simul games! This is the first tournament game of the chapter.

1 d4 ♘f6 2 ♗g5 g6 3 ♗xf6 exf6 4 e3

At the next opportunity, I will try 4 c4!?, and if 4...♗g7 5 e3 0-0 6 ♘c3 c5 7 dxc5 f5 8 ♘ge2 when I prefer White, who looks structurally great, but still lags in development.

4...♗g7

Also possible is 4...d5 5 h4 h5 6 c4 dxc4 7 ♗xc4 ♗d6 8 ♘c3 c6.

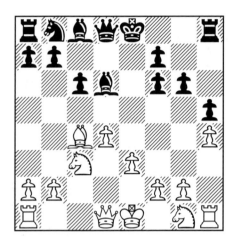

Question: Doesn't this position look an awful
lot like the ones we covered in Chapter Four?

Answer: Correct. Positions from this chapter can even directly transpose to the 3...exf6 lines
of Chapter Four. Following 9 ♕c2 ♕e7 (one can only pray for 9...0-0?? 10 ♕xg6+) 10 ♘ge2
♘d7 11 0-0-0 ♘b6 12 ♗b3 ♗e6 13 ♔b1 ♗xb3 14 ♕xb3 0-0-0 (an interesting plan by my
opponent, who cheated me out of an opposite-wings castling position) 15 ♖c1 ♔b8 16 ♔a1
f5 17 g3 ♖he8 18 ♖hd1 ♗c7 19 ♘a4 ♘xa4 20 ♕xa4 ♕e4 21 ♕c2 ♕f3 22 ♘c3 ♗xg3? (overly
ambitious; 22...f6 is equal) 23 fxg3 ♕xg3 24 d5! cxd5 25 ♖xd5?! (*Houdini* claims 25 ♘xd5!
♖c8 26 ♕a4 is stronger) 25...♖c8?! (Black had better chances to hold the game after
25...♕xe3) 26 ♖d7 ♖c7 27 ♖xc7 ♕xc7 28 ♕f2 a6 29 a3 ♕c5 30 ♖e1 ♖d8 31 ♕f4+ ♔a8 32 e4
♖d3 33 exf5! ♖xc3 34 ♖e8+ ♔a7 35 ♕b8+ ♔b6 36 ♕d8+ ♔a7 37 bxc3 ♕xa3+ 38 ♔b1 ♕b3+
39 ♔c1 ♕xc3+ 40 ♔d1 ♕f3+ 41 ♖e2 White evaded perpetual check and won a queening
race by one tempo (it is my fate in life that my victories always come on move 100, by a
single tempo; I look with eyes of longing toward players who are able to win miniatures),
C.Lakdawala-B.Baker, San Diego (rapid) 2013.
5 h4 h5

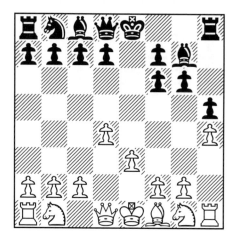

6 ♘e2

Question: Is 6 c4, which discourages Black's next move, the more accurate choice?

Answer: It's fine, as long as you correctly factor in early ...c5 ideas: 6...d6 (after 6...c5 7 ♘e2 0-0 8 dxc5 f5 9 ♘bc3 ♘a6 10 g3 ♘xc5 11 ♗g2 I prefer White's structure and control over d5, over Black's bishops) 7 ♘c3 ♘d7 8 ♘f3 (I would have developed this knight to e2) 8...c6 9 g3 0-0 10 ♗g2 ♘b6 11 b3 ♗g4 12 0-0 ♖e8 13 ♖e1 ♘d7 14 ♕d3 ♗xf3 15 ♗xf3 f5 16 b4. It feels like White's queenside chances are slightly preferable to Black's on the kingside, A.Botsari-M.Kouvatsou, Volos 1996.

6...d5 7 c4 c6

A new move in the position, but 7...dxc4 looks more logical: 8 ♘f4 c5 9 d5!? (this move looks strategically incorrect, but the mysterious property of genius tends to play by its own rules; perhaps better was 9 ♗xc4 cxd4 10 ♕b3 ♕d7 11 0-0 ♘c6 12 ♖d1 ♘a5 13 ♕b5 ♘xc4 14 ♕xc4 f5 15 ♘c3 ♕c6 16 ♖xd4! ♕xc4! 17 ♖xc4 0-0 18 ♖d1, which *Houdini* says is even, while I prefer White's development lead over Black's bishops) 9...f5 10 ♘c3 b5! 11 d6!? (I would have broken up the queenside pawns with 11 ♘xb5!? ♕a5+ 12 ♘c3 ♗xc3+ 13 bxc3 ♕xc3+ 14 ♔e2) 11...0-0 12 ♗e2 (I don't trust White's position if he gets greedy with 12 ♕d5 ♕a5) 12...b4 13 ♘b5 with an unclear mess which, intuitively, appears to favour Black, H.Nakamura-G.Ginsburg, Internet (blitz) 2006.

8 cxd5 ♕xd5

In Chapter Four we discussed the demerits of the inferior ...cxd5 captures.

9 ♘bc3 ♕a5 10 ♘f4 f5

After 10...0-0 11 ♗c4 ♔h8 12 ♕b3 ♕c7 13 a4 a5 14 d5 ♘a6 15 d6! ♕d7 16 ♖d1 f5 White enjoys enduring pressure due to the cramping pressure of his deeply advanced d-pawn.

11 ♕b3 ♕b6

Always be on the lookout for 11...0-0?? 12 ♘xg6, just in case your opponent is napping.

12 ♕c2 ♘d7 13 ♗c4 ♗h6 14 ♘d3 0-0 15 0-0 ♔g7 16 g3 f4?!

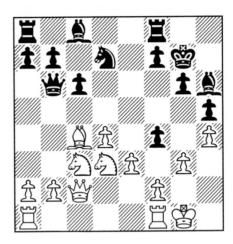

Treachery loves a power vacuum. Black, dissatisfied with his position, mistakenly attempts to reshape it to his will. He may have felt his game was starved of expressions of protest and now seeks to remedy the issue. Yet there is no sense in starting handicapped by picking a fight while ill-equipped and understaffed. In my younger days I had a friend, who although in his late teens, looked like a 12-year-old. To alleviate the dilemma he grew a beard, which in turn, made him look like a 12-year-old with a beard. Moral: sometimes we make a problem worse by attempting to fix it.

Question: Why did Black give away a pawn?

Answer: It isn't a real sacrifice since Black regains the pawn in every version. But just because a tricky move is playable, doesn't necessarily mean it is also wise. At the end of the variation, Black allows White open lines to his king.

17 gxf4!

The most devious variety of traps is to deliberately misunderstand and 'fall' into the opponent's 'trap', having perceived that it is flawed in some manner.

17...♕d8

The queen sticks her oar into the argument, the point being that Black regains the sacrificed pawn. The trouble is Black's position deteriorates from its pre-sacrifice levels.

18 ♔g2 ♕xh4 19 ♖h1 ♕g4+ 20 ♔f1

Houdini assesses at equal, but I feel White enjoys a clear edge due to his central dominance and the open g-file for his rooks.

20...♖e8 21 ♖g1 ♕h3+ 22 ♔e1 ♘b6?

22...♖e7 looks necessary, but even then I still like White's attacking chances on the kingside: 23 ♔d2 ♕f5 24 ♖g2 a5 25 ♖ag1! (threat: ♗xf7!) 25...♔f8 26 ♗b3, although *Houdini* stubbornly insists the game remains even.

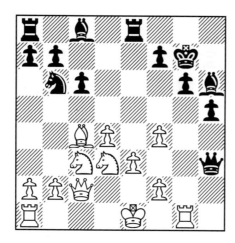

> *Exercise (combination alert):* Black inadvertently pushes a button which activates a vast machinery in motion. A seemingly trivial cause may trigger a huge transformation. This move induces a chain reaction, similar to billiards, when one ball hits another, which hits another. What did Black overlook on his last move?

Answer: Demolition of the king's position. The bishop sacrifice bores into the now gelatinous defensive barrier.

23 ♗xf7!

The bishop slides uninvited into the chair next to Black's king and it becomes obvious that Black's counterattack goes off course, with pieces veering erratically in jagged directions and without a sense of unified intent.

23...♖xe3+

The greatest of delusions is the slave who believes he or she is free. Do you sense a marked increase in Black's decrease about now? This move is absolute desperation, but who can blame Black for going with the maximalist argument and engaging in an act of arson over the board? I suppose when we are in need, excess always appeals as a cure.

23...♗f5 24 ♗xg6! ♗xg6 25 ♘e5 is also a game-ender, as is 23...♔xf7 24 ♘e5+ (White's gaze of displeasure is painfully emblazoned upon g6) 24...♔e7 25 ♕xg6 ♕e6 26 ♕h7+ ♔d8 27 ♖g6.

24 fxe3 ♕xe3+ 25 ♘e2

Conveniently covering g1, while blocking Black's check. The knight entwines, blocking Black's counterplay avenues, like a garter snake wrapping itself around a tree branch.

25...♗f5

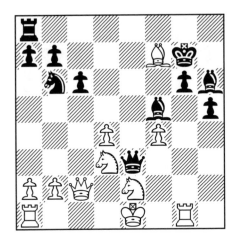

Exercise (combination alert): It appears as if Black mustered quite a ferocious attack for his investment. However, find one powerful idea and Black's 'attack' is a spent force.

Answer: X-ray defence/pin.

26 ♗xg6!

The wizard makes a spell-casting flourish with his hands in the direction of Black's king, who, a few hours later, mysteriously sickens to fatal levels.

26...♗xg6 27 f5

Black's initiative is a car's engineless hull, destined to go nowhere.

27...♖e8

After 27...♗g5 28 ♘df4! is the most efficient consolidation method.

28 ♖xg6+ ♚h7 29 ♘e5 1-0

Summary: When Black responds to an early h4 with ...h5, be on the constant lookout for sacrifices which undermine g6.

Game 40
J.Piket-L.Espig
German League 2000

1 d4 ♘f6 2 ♗g5 g6 3 ♗xf6 exf6 4 e3 ♗g7 5 h4 h5 6 ♘e2 d6

This tends to be the choice of the King's Indian purist who avoids ...d5.

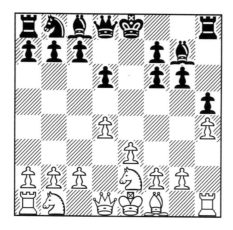

7 c3

> **Question:** Could White do without this move and
> proceed as he did in the game, but play c4 in one go?

Answer: White probably directed the reinforcing c3 against ...c5. Let's see what happens if he avoids c3: 7 g3 0-0 (7...c5?! is premature: 8 dxc5 ♕a5+ 9 ♘bc3 dxc5 10 ♕d6! f5 11 0-0-0 ♕b6 12 ♘b5! ♕xd6 13 ♘xd6+ ♔e7 14 ♗g2 ♘c6 15 e4! fxe4 16 ♘xe4 c4 17 ♘f4 ♗h6 18 ♖he1 ♗xf4+ 19 gxf4 with a scary looking development lead) 8 ♗g2 c5. At this point, it feels like 9 c4 is loosening and gives Black excellent dark-square counterplay after 9...♘c6 10 ♘bc3 ♗g4 11 ♕d2 ♕a5. *Houdini* rates this position at even, but I prefer Black, who applies unpleasant pressure on the dark squares.

7...f5 8 ♘d2 ♘d7 9 g3

If you will recall, this is the Catalan-Trompowsky plan we looked at in Chapter Four.

9...♘f6 10 ♗g2 0-0 11 a4

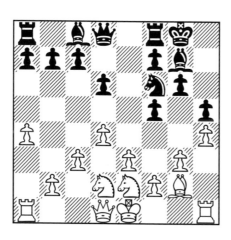

Answer: White's general plan in the Catalan-Trompowsky is to simply increase queenside gains. With his logical last move, White does just that.

11...♖e8 12 a5 ♖b8 13 0-0 ♘e4 14 ♕c2 ♕e7 15 ♘f4 c6 16 c4

Finally, White feels comfortable enough to play this space-gaining, yet slightly loosening move, since he no longer fears ...c5, as his knight is ready for occupation of d5.

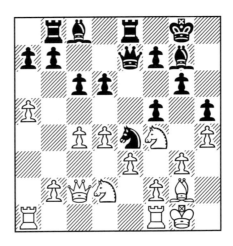

16...♗d7

Answer: It isn't so tempting, since the move violates the principle: an extra piece generally outweighs three pawns in a crowded middlegame, since pawns tend to have lesser influence in this part of the game.

Answer: Correct. Pawns gain, while the piece tends to decrease in value as the ending nears, since pawns begin to generate promotion threats in an ending.

After 17 fxg3 ♕xe3+ 18 ♔h2 ♕xd4 19 ♖ab1 White stands clearly better.

17 ♖a3

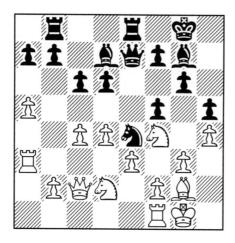

Question: You just said that the ...♘xg3 sacrifice was virtually unplayable for Black, and yet here we clearly note that White played his last move to prevent it. How do you reconcile this contradiction?

Answer: I think White played his last move, not because he was afraid of the sacrifice, but because he didn't want to deal with the bother of calculating its consequences on every move. Sometimes a move is played not for its inherent strength, but for its practical value.

17...♗h6 18 ♘f3 ♕d8 19 ♖fa1 ♗g7

Black seems to be out of ideas and decides to simply wait. Piket tacks about as well before committing to a plan.

20 ♘d2 ♕e7 21 ♖d1 ♗h6 22 ♘f3 ♗g7 23 ♘d3

Contemplating c5.

23...♕d8 24 c5

White finally abandons his isolationist policy and engages the enemy by altering the structure and breaking the queenside stasis.

24...dxc5

24...d5 25 a6 b6 26 cxb6 ♖xb6 27 ♘fe5 looks slightly unpleasant for Black, who must worry about c6, and also potential problems on c5 and e5.

25 ♘xc5 ♘xc5 26 dxc5

White managed to rid himself of the e4 pest.

26...♕c7 27 ♘g5

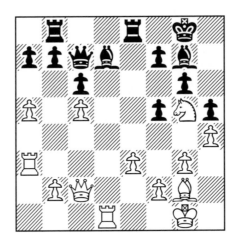

Piket accrued strategic gains and his position looks a tad better than Black's.

27...♖e7 28 ♖ad3 ♗e8 29 ♕d2 ♗f6?!

Black should strive to chip away at the bind with 29...b6.

30 ♖d6! ♗e5

'Threatening' to not take the rook. Black finds he can't rid himself of the annoying d6-rook, who remains where he is, like an overly tight ring on an obese person's finger.

31 f4?!

An impractical idea, reminding me of the time I ordered ice cream through the mail. This looks hasty. White continues to apply queenside and central pressure after 31 b4! b6 32 ♕a2 (threat: ♖xg6+) 32...♔h8 33 ♘f3 ♗g7 34 ♘d4.

31...♗g7

Now e3 is a target. Of course d6 remains immune.

32 b4 b6

Black correctly takes action and attempts to dissolve the bind through exchanges.

33 cxb6 axb6 34 a6!

The queenside becomes a vast breeding ground of White's vast ambition. Good judgement. The artificially isolated yet passed a-pawn is more a source of strength than a weakness.

34...b5 35 ♔h2?!

Black's position grows critical after 35 ♕a2! ♔h8 (if 35...♔f8?? 36 ♖xg6!, and if 36...fxg6?? 37 ♘h7 mate) 36 ♗xc6! ♗xc6 37 ♕c2 ♖c8 38 ♖xc6! ♕xc6 39 ♖d8+. Deflection, and wins.

35...♖a8 36 ♕a2 ♕b6 37 ♖xg6

The beast drips slaver, just imagining the taste of the black king's tender flesh and succulent marrow.

37...♕xa6

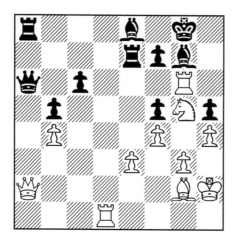

Black decides to co-opt White's queenside ambitions and make them his own. This is a much better version for Black than the line mentioned in the above note.

38 ♕xa6?!

In such critical positions, even a trivial-looking inaccuracy may lead to unwanted ramifications. This move looks like a misguided winning attempt (although Piket did win in the end!).

Objectively, White should enter the forcing line 38 ♖xg7+! (a flaring eruption smites the black king's eyes) 38...♔xg7 39 ♕c2 f6 40 ♕xf5! fxg5 (40...♗g6? is met with 41 ♕c5) 41 ♕xg5+ ♔f8 42 ♕f6+ and Black must accept perpetual check: 42...♖f7 (42...♗f7?? 43 ♕h8+ ♗g8 44 ♕h6+ ♔f7 45 ♗f3! wins) 43 ♕h8+ ♔e7 44 ♕e5+ ♔f8 when Black's king rocks back and forth between f8 and e7.

38...♖xa6 39 ♖gd6 ♖xe3

Black is up a pawn and the one with the winning chances.

40 ♖1d3 ♖e2 41 ♖d2 ♖xd2 42 ♖xd2 ♗c3 43 ♖d8 ♔f8 44 ♗f3 ♔e7 45 ♖b8 f6?!

Black's energy begins to invert from hot to cold. I don't think White survives the passers after 45...♖a7! 46 ♗xh5 ♗xb4.

46 ♘e6!

After many painfully abstinent moves on the defensive, Piket finally engages in a vigorous attempt to snatch the initiative. Threat: ♖xe8+. The knight begins to insinuate himself into the proceedings.

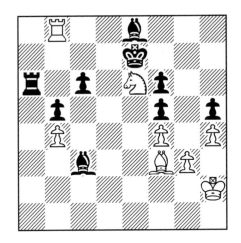

46...罝a2+ 47 含h3 奧xb4

47...含xe6 48 罝xe8+ 含d7 49 奧xc6+! 含xc6 50 罝c8+ 含d5 51 罝xc3 罝b2 52 罝c5+ 含e4 53 罝xb5 罝b1 54 含g2 罝b2+ 55 含h3 罝b1 is drawn.

48 包d4

Piket aligns his forces in harmony. All of a sudden, many of Black's pawns dangle en prise.

48...奧c5?!

Now Black risks losing. 48...罝a6! 49 罝b7+ 含d8 50 罝b8+ 含e7 51 罝b7+ 含d6 52 包xf5+ 含c5 53 包g7 罝a8 54 罝e7 罝a3 55 奧e4 奧e1 56 包xe8 奧xg3 57 含g2 奧xf4 58 包xf6 罝g3+ 59 含f2 罝h3 should be drawn.

49 包xf5+ 含d7 50 包g7 罝a3 51 奧e4

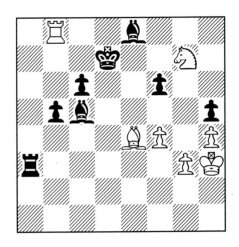

> ***Exercise (critical decision):*** A frantic battle for sole rights
> to ever after erupts. Let's tackle a rigorous analytical challenge.
> Black has the choice of the following candidate moves:
> a) 51...♗f7, removing the bishop from harm's way.
> b) 51...♗f2, going after g3.
> c) 51...♗d6, threatening both b8 and f4. The elemental
> step in fixing a problem is to first identify its source.
> Two of the choices lose; Black draws in the other. Which one would you play?

51...♗d6??

Black fails to discover a plan which maximizes utilization of available resources, without an iota of redundancy.

Answer: 51...♗f2! is the only move. The sectors in the sliced pie all converge with lines of force to g3. After 52 ♔g2 ♗xg3 White's kingside structure has that denuded, plucked chicken look: 53 ♖xe8 ♗xf4 54 ♗f5+ ♔c7 55 ♘e6+ ♔d7 56 ♖h8 ♗e5 57 ♖xh5 ♖a2+ 58 ♔f3 ♖a3+ 59 ♔e4 ♖a4+ 60 ♔d3 ♖a3+ 61 ♔c2 ♖a2+ 62 ♔b3 ♖b2+ 63 ♔a3 ♔d6. Black's pieces radiate super-activity and his pawns are ready to roll forward. I don't think White holds an advantage here and either side may win.

For the record, 51...♗f7?? hangs the bishop to 52 ♖b7+.

52 ♗f5+

Black's harassed king is forced to mingle with the common rabble with dignified distaste.

52...♔c7 53 ♖xe8 ♗xf4 54 ♘xh5

The knight is the lever which tips the balance White's way. How annoying. The geometry conspires against Black, since g3 is held and the extra piece proves decisive, with White's h-pawn ready to roll forward.

54...♗e5 55 ♔g4!

Unravelling, in preparation for ♘f4 and h5. White's king, sick and tired of a subordinate position in the firm, decides to assert himself.

55...b4 56 ♘f4 b3 57 h5 1-0

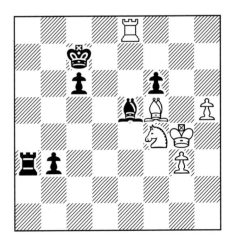

57...♖a2 58 h6 ♖h2 59 ♘h5 ends the discussion.

Summary: The Catalan-Tromp plan works in this chapter, as well as the fourth. Also, one of our most difficult opening decisions is if White can improve and save a tempo by omitting c3 and later playing for c4 in one jump.

Chapter Seven
The Pseudo-Tromp

1 d4 d5 2 ♗g5

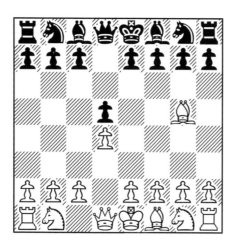

Our bishop reaches g5 like a nervous teen at a high school dance, who valiantly approaches the terrifying prom queen in the pink chiffon dress, for a dance. This chapter comes with a warning label: Danger – Play at your own risk!

White's task of securing an edge is more difficult here than in the 1...♘f6 2 ♗g5 lines. In fact, some Trompowsky authorities, like GM Eric Prié, hint that the Trompowsky may actually be dubious against 1...d5 and view it as a dangerous, irrevocable venture. I don't believe this is correct, and the parties should emerge from the complications with equivalent potentialities for success or disaster. However, I do agree that 1...d5 represents our biggest theoretical challenge of the book. Our expectations should be lowered, to just disarrange and confound, rather than insist on an opening edge.

If you don't like the positions we reach from this chapter, then you may consider playing Trompowsky only on the 1...♘f6 move order, and on 1...d5, go for the Queen's Gambit, London System, Torre Attack or Colle System. In my opinion, there is nothing disreputable or unsound about White's side in the Pseudo-Tromp – but we do come close.

Key battlegrounds we reach in this chapter:

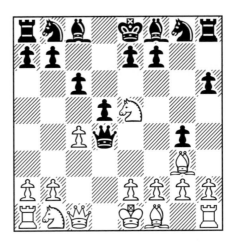

Another gambit, where we receive development lead and a loosening of Black's structure for the pawn.

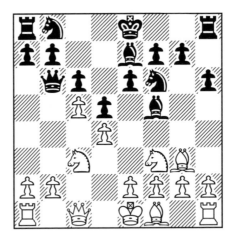

Black can also play in Slav-fashion, with theoretically balanced chances.

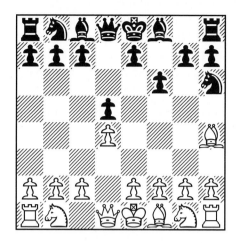

With 2...f6 3 ♗h4 ♘h6, Black simply intends to hunt down our wayward bishop with ...♘f5 and pocket the bishop-pair. We respond with f3, offering air to our bishop, which leads to structurally alien landscapes.

> ## Game 41
> ## **J.Hodgson-B.Lalic**
> ### British Championship, Scarborough 1999

1 d4 d5 2 ♗g5

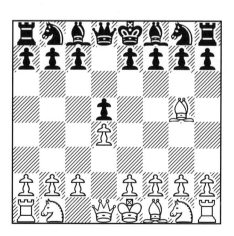

> **Question:** The Pseudo-Tromp may come with a warning label, but are there any black systems where should we avoid the Trompowsky?

Answer: I would avoid the Trompowsky against 1...f5, 1...g6, 1...d6, 1...c6 and, of course, 1...e6, since 2 ♗g5?? ♛xg5 works out quite well for Black. When not to play the Trompowsky is explained in the book, *The Modern Defence: Move by Move.*

Answer: Modesty prevents me from mentioning the writer's name, but I would like to add that many consider him one of the great chess thinkers of our era.

2...h6

Black can also reach our position with the move order 2...c6 3 ♘f3 h6.

3 ♗h4

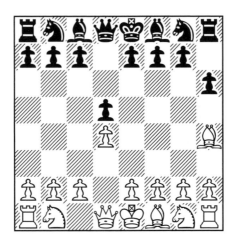

3...c6

Question: Won't this just transpose to some kind of Slav?

Answer: Probably not. Black plans ...♛b6 next, targeting b2, which makes the game Slav-like, but not a real Slav.

Instead, after 3...c5 4 dxc5 (principle: open the game when leading in development) 4...♘c6 5 c3 g5 6 ♗g3 e5 7 ♘f3 f6, as in A.Fier-B.Grachev, Jurmala 2013, I would try 8 b4. The position is a kind of wigged out, Reversed Slav Geller Gambit: 8...a5 9 b5 ♘a7 10 e4! dxe4 11 ♘fd2 h5 12 h4 with complications favouring White.

4 ♘f3

I prefer this move order over 4 e3, for the simple reason that it makes it harder for Black to achieve the ...e5 break.

Question: How does Black achieve ...e5 after 4 e3?

Answer: Like this: 4...♕b6 5 ♕c1 e5! 6 ♘f3 (Black's clever tactical point is that e5 is untouchable, since 6 dxe5?? hangs a piece to 6...♕b4+ 7 ♘d2 ♕xh4) 6...e4 (if Black always played this move I would be okay with the 4 e3 move order; the position I want to avoid is this one: 6...exd4 7 exd4 ♗e7 which essentially turns the game into a dry Exchange French-like position) 7 ♘fd2 ♗e6 8 c4 ♘d7 9 ♘c3 ♘e7 10 c5 ♕a5?! (a waste of time, since b4 follows with tempo) 11 ♖b1 ♘f5 12 b4 ♕c7 13 ♗g3 ♘xg3 14 hxg3 b5 15 a4 a6 16 ♖a1 ♖b8 17 axb5 axb5 18 ♗e2 ♗e7 19 ♖a6 0-0 20 0-0 f5?? was C.Lakdawala-R.Scherbakov, Internet (blitz) 2000.

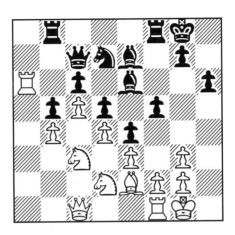

> ***Exercise (combination alert):*** In this position, your
> innocent-minded writer missed a simple win. Do you see it?

Answer: Deflection/clearance: 21 ♘xb5! wins on the spot. Instead I later sac'ed on b5 and the game was drawn.
4...♕b6 5 ♕c1!?

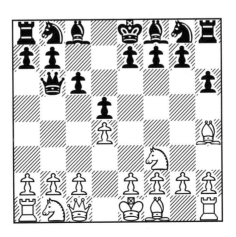

5 b3 is a lot safer, but we don't have room in the book to cover both lines, so let's go with the riskier choice.

Answer: 5 ♕c1 is actually a gambit. Please see Black's next move to discover why. After 5 b3 ♗f5 6 e3 e6 7 ♗d3 ♗xd3 8 ♕xd3 ♗e7 9 ♗g3 ♘d7 10 0-0 ♘gf6 11 c4 0-0 12 ♘c3 a5 13 ♖fd1, as in V.Kramnik-B.Gelfand, Moscow (blitz) 2008, Black looks fine after 13...♕a6.

5...g5!?

Ambition is synonymous with risk. Prié calls this move "the critical continuation". Black undermines the defender of d4 and places the burden on us to prove compensation.

6 ♗g3 g4 7 ♘e5 ♕xd4

A tyrannical authority doesn't require hard evidence to convict. Mere suspicion is enough to condemn. Black's point: he snatches a pawn, to the detriment of development and structure. In this line we push past the boundaries of eccentric idiosyncrasy and enter just plain weird.

8 c4

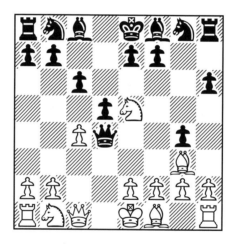

A critical tabiya position for us in this chapter. There is no benefit in negotiation with an implacable foe. Black's risky (for us as well as our opponent) pawn grab is an open declaration of war, and our job is to destroy him before he does the same to us. Principles: open the position and create confrontation when leading in development. Our starting position in the gambit line, where we enter a grey area, somewhere between substance and shadow.

Answer: White gets the following compensation for the pawn:

1. A big development lead in an open position, with chances to increase it, since Black loses even more time with a vulnerable queen.

2. In order to win the pawn, Black defaced his kingside structure, which ensures our side a rich supply of confrontation targets and prying mechanisms, like h3 or even f3.

3. One thing to keep in mind, though, is that Black actually controls a greater chunk of the centre. If we allow him or her to catch up in development, consolidate and achieve ...f6 and ...e5, then we are in danger of losing.

Houdini assesses at about even, so the better prepared side (us, of course!) will be the favourite to take the point. The world isn't big enough for two Caesars or two Alexander the Greats. In this variation, one must conquer the other. To my mind, this looks like a 50-50 proposition – a rock in a river, which either gets worn down by time and water, or emerges the winner after a few millennia when the river runs dry.

8 e3 can lead to similar play: for example, ♕c5 9 c4 ♗g7 10 ♘c3 d4!? (after 10...♘d7 11 ♘xd7 ♗xd7 12 cxd5 cxd5 13 ♕d2 e6 14 ♖c1 ♖c8 15 ♗e2 ♘f6 16 0-0 0-0 17 ♗e5 Black's loose kingside structure offers White full compensation for the pawn) 11 exd4 ♕xd4 12 ♕c2! ♘a6 (12...♗xe5!? 13 ♖d1 ♕c5 14 b4! ♕xb4 15 ♗xe5 looks very dangerous for Black, who gave up control over the dark squares for a second pawn) 13 ♖d1 ♕c5 14 a3! ♕a5 15 c5! ♗e6 was I.Miladinovic-M.Godena, Bratto 2004. White gets a vicious attack for the material after (if 15...♕xc5?? 16 b4, and if 16...♕b6?? 17 ♗c4 ♗xe5 18 ♗xe5 ♘f6 19 0-0! and Black has no hope to survive the coming assault) 16 ♗c4! ♗xc4 17 ♘xc4 ♕xc5 18 ♘e4 ♕h5 19 ♕b3 b5 20 0-0! ♘f6 21 ♘cd6+! exd6 22 ♕c3 with a powerful initiative in the works.

8...♘d7

Black logically strives to swap, since he is up a pawn. Other options:

a) 8...♗g7 9 e3 ♕c5 transposes to the Miladinovic-Godena game from the note above. Instead, 9...♕b6 10 cxd5 ♘d7 11 ♘c4 ♕b4+ 12 ♘c3 cxd5 13 ♘d2 ♘gf6 14 ♘b5 0-0 15 a3 ♕c5 16 ♕xc5 ♘xc5 17 ♘c7 ♖b8 18 ♘xd5 ♘xd5 19 ♗xb8 ♗xb2 20 ♖a2 ♗c3 21 ♗xa7 ♘e4 22 ♗d4 ♗a5 23 ♗d3 ♘xd2 24 ♖xd2 ♖d8 25 ♔e2 ♗xd2 26 ♔xd2 ♘f4 27 exf4 ♖xd4 28 ♔e3 ♖a4 29 ♖c1 ♗d7 30 ♖c3 led to an even ending in A.Stefanova-M.Chiburdanidze, Elista 2004.

b) Next game we look at 8...♘f6.

9 e3 ♕c5 10 ♘d2

10 ♘xg4? is too slow, since White loses the initiative after 10...♗g7 (threat: ...h5) 11 h3 h5 12 ♘h2 ♕b6 13 ♘c3 h4 14 ♗f4 e5 15 ♗g5 f6 snagging a piece.

10...♗g7 11 ♘d3 ♕b6 12 a4!

A novelty at the time and probably White's best move. The disruptive a5 is in the air, and White also plans cxd5 and, after Black recaptures, the a4-pawn may be utilized as a hook, with ♗b5+. White has a quieter option with 12 ♗e2 h5 13 cxd5 cxd5 14 ♕c2 e5 15 ♗h4 ♘e7 16 ♗xe7 ♔xe7 17 0-0, but I have a bad feeling White just doesn't have enough for the pawn, since Black owns strategic trumps like central control and bishop-pair.

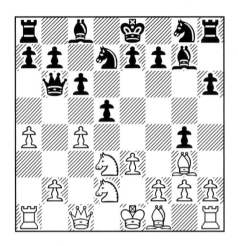

12...♘c5!

Black seeks to undermine b2. Lalic actually punished his own move with a question mark, but I don't understand why. It looks to me like it's Black's best move. Lalic's suggestion 12...a5 is still untried. Play may continue 13 ♗e2 h5 14 cxd5 cxd5 15 0-0 e5 16 ♗h4 ♘e7 17 ♗xe7 ♔xe7 18 e4 d4 19 b4! axb4 20 ♘c4 ♕h6 21 ♕b2 ♔f8 22 ♘xb4. It feels like White gets full compensation for the pawn, since Black's game remains scattered and White can think about f3, prying open the f-file.

13 cxd5 ♘xd3+ 14 ♗xd3

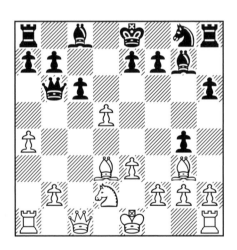

14...♗xb2!?

Rather than this optimistic capture, Black can put the gambit to the test with:

a) 14...cxd5 15 ♗b5+ ♔f8 16 0-0 ♗f5 (the 16...a6 of J.Hodgson-M.Krasenkow, German League 1998, should be met with 17 ♗c7 ♕f6 18 ♕c5!! with compensation; amazingly, if 18...axb5 19 axb5 ♖xa1 20 ♖xa1 ♕xb2 21 ♖a8 ♗c3 22 ♗g3 ♕xd2 23 ♕xc8+ ♔g7 24 ♕xg4+

♔h7 25 ♕f5+ ends in perpetual check) 17 ♗c7 ♕g6 18 ♕c5 and *Houdini* rates this position at dead even, J.Hodgson-M.Godena, Mondariz 2000.

b) 14...♕xb2 15 ♕xb2 ♗xb2 16 ♖b1 ♗g7 17 dxc6 bxc6 18 ♔e2 followed by ♖fc1, with loads of targets for a mere pawn.

15 a5!

Now we see yet another clever point behind 12 a4. In positions of this level of complexity, we can't possibly know how things will turn out. So just ride the currents and go where fate takes us.

15...♕b4!

15...♗xc1?? fails to 16 axb6 ♗xd2+ 17 ♔xd2 a6 18 ♗xa6!! bxa6 19 dxc6 when Black loses massive material after the coming b7.

16 ♕b1 ♘f6

16...♗c3?! is met with the nonchalant 17 dxc6!! ♗xd2+ 18 ♔e2 ♕xb1 19 ♖axb1 bxc6 20 ♔xd2 ♘f6 21 ♖hc1, and if 21...♗d7? 22 ♖b8+! ♖xb8 23 ♗xb8. Black's a-pawn falls, leaving him busted.

17 ♖a4!

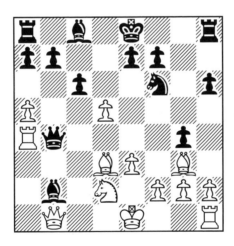

Very few of our plans are ironclad on the chessboard. An uncertainty principle – the anomaly factor – is the great disrupter of our most cherished futures. This startling shot wrests control over the initiative and offers White full compensation for the sac'ed material. However, White achieves his aim at frightful cost materially. Also possible is the calmer and safer line 17 dxc6 bxc6 18 0-0 ♗e6 19 ♘c4! ♗c3 20 ♖c1 ♗xc4 21 ♕xb4 ♗xb4 22 ♖xc4 c5 23 ♗e5 when White gets full compensation for the pawn.

17...♕xa4!

Black looks worse if he chickens out with 17...♕c3!? 18 dxc6 bxc6 19 0-0! ♕xd2 20 ♖a2 0-0 21 ♖d1 ♕c3 22 ♖xb2 ♕xa5 23 e4, with a strong attack to follow.

18 ♕xb2 ♕xa5

It's difficult to put a finger on who is winning or losing, since in the midst of such chaos, we lack standards of comparison to rational patterns. Options:

a) 18...cxd5?? 19 ♗b5+ winning the queen.

b) 18...0-0! may be Black's best move, but it takes a comp to know why: 19 d6 ♘d5 20 dxe7 ♖e8! (20...♘xe7 21 ♗f4 offers White full compensation for his investment) 21 ♗d6 ♕xa5 22 h3 g3 23 0-0 ♕c3 24 ♕xc3 ♘xc3 25 fxg3 with a position very difficult to assess. White's attack rages on, despite the absence of queens. I played out several *Houdini* scenarios and for some strange reason they all worked out to draws.

19 d6!

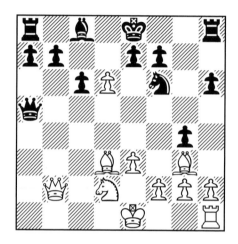

So shrewd is Hodgson's plan, that even deep into it, we find difficulty discerning any evidence of deliberate design. What first appeared as crude bluster on White's part, now transforms into something far more subtle and dangerous: Black's dark squares border on collapse, but then again, he enjoys a massive surplus of material.

19...♗f5?

This move loses the initiative. Black's only chance to survive lay in 19...♕d8! 20 ♗b1 ♖g8 21 0-0. I like White's attacking chances in what is objectively a dynamically balanced game.

20 e4 ♗xe4

Neither can Black survive 20...♗e6 21 dxe7 ♕g5 22 ♕xb7.

21 ♗xe4 ♘xe4

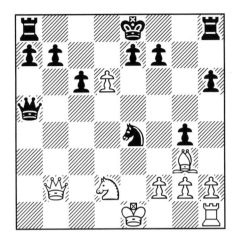

Exercise (critical decision): Our collective heads spin from the complications. From what feels like innumerable potential constructs and plans, there hides White's only path to victory. He has three choices:

a) 22 d7+, going after Black's king.

b) 22 ♕xh8+, grabbing the free rook.

c) 22 0-0, nonchalantly castling before undertaking anything else.

This is not the time to waver. Only one line wins, but which one?

Answer: After castling ('c'), all of White's tactics work to perfection.

22 0-0!!

Despite arithmetically impossible odds, Hodgson clarifies that which is outwardly indefinable into luminous transparency. This was the only way:

a) If 22 d7+?? ♔xd7 23 ♕xb7+ ♔e6 24 ♕xc6+ ♘d6 White's attack runs out of gas and he is completely busted.

b) 22 ♕xh8+? ♔d7 23 ♕d4 ♕xd2+ 24 ♕xd2 ♘xd2 25 ♔xd2 exd6 when White is the one struggling, with only one piece for Black's four pawns.

22...♘xg3

More alternatives:

a) 22...♘c3?? 23 dxe7! ♔xe7 24 ♘c4 disconnects the queen's connection to the c3-knight.

b) 22...♘xd2?? 23 ♕xh8+ ♔d7 24 ♕xa8 ♘xf1 25 ♕xb7+ ♔e6 26 dxe7 forces mate.

c) 22...0-0-0 23 ♘xe4 and Black has very low chances to survive the coming assault.

23 ♕xh8+ ♔d7

The king has no time to mourn and hastily buries his loved ones in unmarked graves on h8 and a8.

24 ♕xa8 ♘e2+

24...♘xf1?? 25 ♕xb7+ ♔xd6 26 ♘c4+ forks.

25 ♔h1 ♕xd2 26 dxe7 ♔xe7 27 ♕xb7+ ♔f6 28 ♕xc6+ ♔g7 29 ♕e4!

Houdini thinks this move is even stronger than 29 ♕a4!, double attacking g4 and a7.

29...h5 30 ♕e5+

Slightly more accurate is 30 f4!.

30...♔g6 31 f4! gxf3 32 ♕e4+ f5 33 ♕c6+ ♔g5 34 ♕xf3 f4 35 g3?!

Perhaps a time trouble inaccuracy. Much stronger is 35 ♕a3! ♕e3 36 ♕xe3 fxe3 37 ♖e1 which is decisive.

35...h4! 36 gxf4+ ♘xf4 37 ♖d1 ♕a5?!

Better is 37...♕b4!.

38 ♖g1+ ♔f5 39 ♕g4+ ♔e4

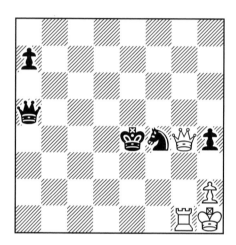

Exercise (critical decision): Should White take time out to grab h4?

40 ♖f1?!

An inaccuracy.

Answer: No: 40 ♕xh4?? is met with 40...♕d5!! 41 ♕g5 ♕c6! 42 h4 ♔e3+ 43 ♔h2 ♕c2+ 44 ♔h1 ♕e4+ and the pieces lock in an eternally recursive loop, resulting in perpetual check.

According to *Houdini*, White's most accurate move was 40 ♖c1! ♕d5 41 ♖e1+ ♔d3+ 42 ♔g1 ♕c5+ 43 ♔f1 ♕c4 44 ♔f2 ♕c5+ 45 ♔f3 ♔d2 46 ♕g1!, forcing queens off the board. Now Black's initiative – like a neighbour who drops in for a minute to say hello – came and went: 46...♕xg1 47 ♖xg1 and Black drops a7 after the coming ♖a1.

40...♕d2! 41 ♕f3+ ♔e5 42 h3 a5 43 ♖f2 ♕d4 44 ♖f1 ♕b4!?

Lalic divulges a dark secret one normally reserves for the diary: he may be playing for the win. A more pragmatic player would repeat with 44...♕d2, asking White how he intends to make progress.

45 ♕e3+ ♔f5 46 ♔h2 a4 47 ♖f2 ♕e4!

47...a3? is decisively met with 48 ♕e8! intending ♕h5+ and ♕xh4.

48 ♕xe4+ ♚xe4 49 ♖a2 ♚f5 50 ♖xa4

This is not going to be so easy to win, since White is tied down to h3.

50...♚g5 51 ♖a5+ ♚g6 52 ♖a1 ♚h5 53 ♖g1 ♘e6 54 ♖g4 ♘g5 55 ♚g2 ♘e6 56 ♚f3! ♘g5+ 57 ♚f4!

Otherwise White is unable to make progress. A similar plan would be 57 ♚g2! ♘e6 58 ♖e4 ♘g5 59 ♖e8 ♘f7 60 ♚f3 ♘g5+ 61 ♚f4! ♘xh3+ 62 ♚f5 ♚h6 63 ♖h8+ ♚g7 64 ♖xh4 ♘f2 65 ♖d4 when the knight is trapped.

57...♘xh3+ 58 ♚f5 ♘f2 59 ♖g8

Threatening mate.

59...♚h6 60 ♖h8+ ♚g7 61 ♖xh4

Houdini announces forced mate in 29 moves.

> **Question:** Earlier in the book you said rook versus knight is an
> easy draw for the knight side. What changed in this position?

Answer: Endgame principle: a knight easily holds off a rook, but only if it is near its king.
When the knight and king get separated by huge distances, as in this case, the king/rook
team may further isolate and finally trap the knight. The remaining moves are instructive.

61...♘d3 62 ♖d4 ♘c5 63 ♖c4 ♘b3

Or 63...♘d3 64 ♖c3 ♘b4 65 ♔e4 ♔f7 66 ♖c7+ ♔e6 67 ♖c4! ♘a2 68 ♔e3! ♔d5 69 ♔d3
(zugzwang) 69...♔e6 70 ♔d2 ♔d5 71 ♖a4 trapping the knight.

64 ♖c7+ ♔f8 65 ♖c3!

White king and rook watch the frantic knight's ill-concealed efforts to escape their
clutches with vast, malicious amusement.

65...♘d4+ 66 ♔e5 ♘b5

After 66...♘e2 67 ♖e3 ♘c1 68 ♔f6! ♔g8 69 ♖g3+ ♔h7 70 ♖g7+ ♔h6 71 ♖g1! both the
knight and mate are simultaneously threatened.

67 ♖c5 ♘a3 68 ♔d4 ♔e7

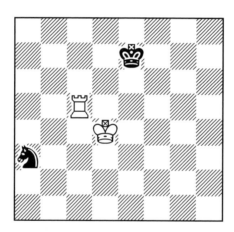

> **Exercise (combination alert):** "That which does not kill me, makes me stronger,"
> declares the knight. Ironically, these were the final words of his life. White's
> lengthy ministrations finally bear fruit. The knight is trapped. Work out the finish.

Answer: 69 ♔d3!

Also highly effective is 69 ♖a5! ♘b1 70 ♔d3 ♔d6 71 ♖a1.

69...♔d6 70 ♖a5 1-0

"My mercy has its limits," says the rook to the knight.

Summary: The crazy position which arises after 5 ♕c1 g5!? may be one of our biggest tests
of this chapter. If you don't like it, you can always switch to the quieter 5 b3 line.

Game 42
J.Hodgson-R.Ziatdinov
Guernsey 1991

1 d4 d5 2 ♗g5 h6 3 ♗h4 c6 4 ♘f3

I beat GM Ziatdinov in 1999 in a wild game with the line 4 e3 ♛b6 5 ♛c1 e5 6 ♘f3 e4 (as mentioned last game, the killjoy move 6...exd4 ruins this line for White if we looked forward to a fight) 7 ♘fd2 which we don't cover in this book.

4...♛b6 5 ♛c1 g5

With a venture like this comes an irrevocability clause: There is no turning back and there is only one certainty: both parties won't win.

6 ♗g3 g4 7 ♘e5 ♛xd4 8 c4 ♘f6

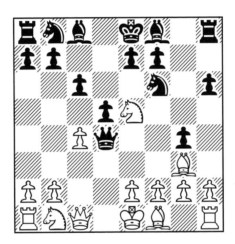

Question: What is Black's reasoning behind his last move?

Answer: Unlike last game, where Black immediately issued a challenge to the e5-knight, in this case Black ignores it, calmly developing, while reinforcing d5.

9 ♘c3

Question: Is 9 cxd5 possible, since Black can't recapture with his c6-pawn?

Answer: Your suggestion has never been tried. *Houdini* approves and assesses at even after 9...♘bd7 (or 9...♘xd5 10 e3 ♛b4+ 11 ♘d2 ♗g7 12 ♛c2 when, intuitively, it feels like White gets full compensation for the pawn) 10 e3 ♛xd5 11 ♘c3 ♛e6 12 ♘d3. Black's position is loose and he continues to lag behind in development. These two factors should give White enough for the pawn.

9...♗e6

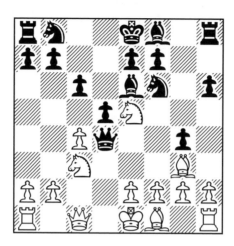

Question: Isn't Black's last move unnatural, since it gums up his e-pawn?

Answer: I think the move is fine. Black's dark-squared bishop emerges on g7, so blocking the e7-pawn isn't much of a factor.

10 e3 ♕b6 11 cxd5

More accurate than 11 ♗e2, since after Hodgson's move, White's bishop may check on b5. Here 11...h5 12 0-0 ♗h6?! (12...♗g7 looks better) 13 cxd5 cxd5 was T.Clarke-D.Guthrie, Edinburgh 2003. I prefer White's game after 14 ♘a4, intending ♘c5, with nagging pressure.

11...cxd5 12 ♗b5+

White also looks slightly better after 12 ♘b5 ♘a6 13 ♘d4 ♕b4+ 14 ♕c3 ♕xc3+ 15 bxc3 ♗d7 16 ♖b1 ♘c5 17 ♘b5 ♘e6 18 c4 ♗c6 19 cxd5 ♘xd5 20 e4 ♘b6 21 ♘xa7 ♖xa7 22 ♘xc6 bxc6 23 ♖xb6.

12...♘c6 13 a4

Just like last game. Threat: a5 and a6. Apparently this move is Hodgson's favourite idea in this variation.

13...a5 14 ♘e2

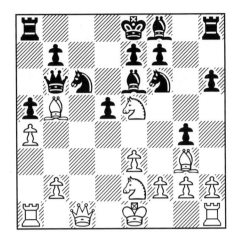

Intending to transfer to d4, adding pressure to the pin, but perhaps also leaving open ♘f4 options.

14...♗d7!?

Ziatdinov has had enough of the pin and agrees to a clear concession. The alternative: 14...♖c8 15 ♕d1 ♗g7 16 ♘f4 0-0 17 ♘xe6 fxe6 18 ♘g6 ♖fd8 19 0-0 ♔f7 20 ♗xc6 ♔xg6 21 ♗b5 with a '0.00' assessment from *Houdini*. I actually slightly prefer White, who owns the bishop-pair, control over the light squares and potential attacking chances against Black's wandering king.

15 ♘xd7 ♘xd7 16 0-0 ♗g7 17 ♘f4

White can also try 17 ♘d4!? ♗xd4 18 exd4 ♘xd4 19 ♗xd7+ ♔xd7 20 ♕e3 f6 21 ♖ad1 e5 22 ♗xe5! ♘f3+! (Black can't survive 22...fxe5?? 23 ♕xe5) 23 gxf3 ♕xe3 24 fxe3 fxe5 25 ♖xd5+ ♔e6 26 ♖b5 gxf3 27 ♖xf3. White has all the winning chances, but Black should probably hold the game.

17...♘f6

17...e6 18 ♘h5 ♗e5 19 ♗xe5 ♘dxe5 20 ♕c3 looks quite dangerous for Black.

18 ♗h4 e6 19 ♕c3! ♘h5 20 ♕a3!

With a sneaky mate threat on e7. The queen nears with silent yet dangerous reproach, acting as a pestle, which grinds away at the dark squares. We get the feeling that over the last ten moves, White achieved more than his probable expectations, while Black got stuck with a lot less than he hoped for.

20...♗f6

Question: Why not kick the queen off the diagonal with 20...♗f8?

Answer: It's a trap. In fact, let's turn this into an exercise:

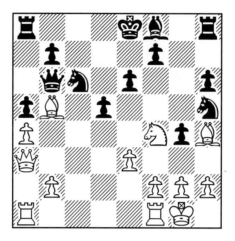

Answer: Knight fork: 21 ♘xh5! ♗xa3 22 ♘f6+ and White forks, regaining the queen with interest, no matter which square Black picks for his king.

21 ♗xf6 ♘xf6 22 ♖ac1

The comps say the position is even. I disagree and prefer White for the following reasons:

1. Black's king lacks a safe haven anywhere on the board.

2. Black continues to lag badly in development, mainly because he has no easy way to connect his rooks.

3. White's queen dominates the dark squares and continues to heckle Black's king from a distance.

4. Black suffers an unpleasant pin on c6.

Conclusion: This looks like too much suffering for only one pawn.

22...♘e4 23 ♖c2 ♖c8 24 ♖fc1 ♖c7 25 ♘d3

I don't see Black surviving 25 b4!: for example, 25...0-0 (Black is busted after 25...axb4? 26 ♕xb4 ♔d8 27 ♕b2 ♖h7 28 ♘h5) 26 bxa5 ♕xa5 27 ♕b2 ♔h7 28 ♗d3! (threat: f3) 28...♖fc8 (28...♔g8? 29 ♗xe4 dxe4 30 ♖c5 ♕a8 31 ♕f6 ♕d8 32 ♕xh6 e5 33 ♘d5 wins) 29 f3 ♘e5 30 ♖xc7 ♖xc7 31 fxe4 ♘xd3 32 ♘xd3 ♖xc1+ 33 ♕xc1 dxe4 34 ♘c5 when White should be able to convert the extra piece.

25...f6 26 ♘f4 ♔f7 27 ♕d3

Threat: ♘xd5!.

27...♖d8

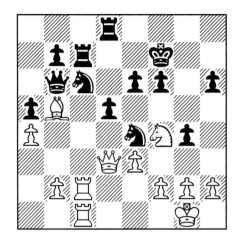

Exercise (planning): Black's position looks awfully loose and our intuition indicates that his king is in grave danger. Find White's best method of continuing the attack:

28 ♕e2?

After this move the glow of attack which sustained White's optimism, grows dim. This looks like a distorted echo of the correct idea. White declines an attainable goal to chase a mirage and now his intended attack never really gets past the larval stage of development. Why utilize subtlety when you possess overwhelming force?

Answer: White can expedite the process with 28 f3!. Before we work out a plan or sort variables, we must first identify a strategic or tactical marker which gives us direction. In this case, White's queen is granted entry to g6, from which her intended mischief grows exponentially: 28...gxf3 29 gxf3 ♘g5 30 ♕g6+ ♔e7 31 ♖c5! ♖f8 (or 31...♘xf3+ 32 ♔h1 ♘g5 33 ♕g7+ ♘f7 34 ♗xc6 bxc6 35 ♘g6+ ♔d6 36 ♕xf6 ♖e8 37 e4! with a winning attack) 32 ♕xh6 ♘xf3+ 33 ♔h1 (a criminal on the run sees a crowd as a means of making himself invisible to the authorities) 33...♘fe5 34 ♖xd5! (the rook is untouchable) 34...♖f7 35 ♕h3! (the queen's enemies are forced to exist in a state of eternal vigilance from her assassination attempts) 35...♘d4 (35...♘d8 36 ♖cd1 is curtains for Black, since 36...♖c8 walks into mate after 37 ♖d7+ ♔e8 38 ♕h8+ ♖f8 39 ♖xd8+) 36 ♖d1! ♘xb5 37 ♖xe5! fxe5 38 ♕h4+ ♖f6 39 ♘g6+ ♔f7 (Black's king writhes in agitation, under the heel of his sister's tyranny) 40 ♕h7+ ♔e8 41 ♕g8+ ♖f8 42 ♕xf8 mate.

28...♖g8 29 f3 gxf3 30 ♕xf3 ♖g5!

Alertly covering h5 infiltration.

31 ♔h1 ♖e7 32 ♗xc6

Or 32 ♕h3 h5 33 ♖f1 f5 34 ♕h4 ♖e8 35 ♗e2 ♖h8 when chances remain even.

32...bxc6 33 h4?!

Necessary was 33 ♖xc6 ♕xb2.

33...♖g3 34 ♕h5+ ♔g7 35 ♖xc6 ♕xe3?!

Now the game should be drawn. Black missed 35...♘f2+! 36 ♔h2 ♕xe3 37 ♖1c3 ♘g4+ 38 ♕xg4+ ♖xg4 39 ♘h5+ ♔g6 40 ♖xe3 ♔xh5 41 ♖exe6 ♖xe6 42 ♖xe6 ♖xh4+ 43 ♔g1 ♖xa4 44 ♖xf6 when White is the one struggling for the draw.

36 ♘xe6+

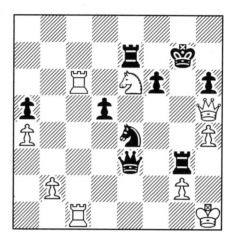

> **Exercise (critical decision):** Black is presented with a narrow window of opportunity. His choices: a) 36...♖xe6, eliminating the pest to begin his own attack. b) 36...♔h7, exercising patience. What should Black play here?

36...♖xe6??

It's never a pleasant meeting when we confront our own powerlessness. Apparently the fact that Black's nervous system hasn't completely been restored is made manifestly clear by this jittery action. Now Ziatdinov's dreams of mate bubble up on himself. All we can do is play the hand we are dealt. Go past what natural resources and limits can bear, and we court self-destruction.

Answer: Correct was 'b': 36...♔h7! 37 ♕f5+ ♖g6! (threat: ...♘g3+, forking king and queen) 38 ♘f8+ ♔g8 39 ♕xd5+! ♖f7 40 ♘xg6 ♘f2+ 41 ♔g1 ♘g4+ 42 ♔h1 ♘f2+ with perpetual check.

37 ♖c7+!

White's mating attack, now in full swing, has no need for the assistance of faith or hope, when it so obviously works to capacity. It is Black who gets mated. Ziatdinov, un-doubtedly in time pressure, hoped for 37 ♖xe6?? ♖h3+ 38 gxh3 ♕xh3+ 39 ♔g1 ♕g3+ 40 ♔h1 ♘f2 mate.

37...♔h8 38 ♖c8+ ♔h7 39 ♖1c7+ 1-0

It's mate with 39...♖g7 40 ♕f5.

Summary: We must also be prepared to deal with 8...♘f6, where Black refuses early con-frontation and simply hopes to catch up in development while retaining the extra pawn.

Game 43
J.Hodgson-T.Thorhallsson
Istanbul Olympiad 2000

1 d4 d5 2 ♗g5 h6

As mentioned earlier, it makes no difference if Black plays ...c6 or ...h6 first. After 2...c6 3 ♘f3 ♛b6 4 ♕c1 ♗f5 5 e3 h6 6 ♗h4 e6 7 ♗e2 ♘d7 8 0-0 ♘gf6 9 c4 dxc4!? (Black is better off avoiding this swap, since it hands White a slight central edge) 10 ♘bd2 ♗e7 11 ♘xc4 ♛d8 12 a3 0-0 (12...c5?! looks premature: White stands clearly better after 13 ♖d1) 13 b4 (clamping down on both ...a5 and ...c5) 13...♘e4 14 ♗xe7 ♛xe7 15 ♕b2 (our queen often ends up on b2 in this line) 15...a6 16 ♖ac1 ♖fd8 17 ♘a5 White exerts slight yet nagging pressure, C.Lakdawala-'DeadManWalking', Internet (blitz) 2013.

3 ♗h4 c6 4 ♘f3 ♛b6 5 ♕c1 ♗f5

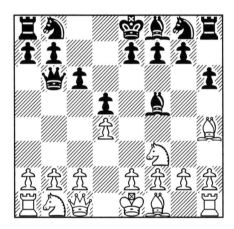

This move is what you are most likely to see from most of your club-level opponents, who know little to zero Trompowsky theory and just bang this move out because it looks natural and sound. Black wants no part of ...g5, ...g4 and ...♛xd4 adventures (or more likely, the concept never even occurs to our opponents), and trusts in the solidity of a Slav-like set-up.

> ***Question:*** Why Slav-like? Isn't the position essentially a Slav?

Answer: Almost, but with these differences:

1. White's queen sits on c1, not a normal Slav square.
2. Black's queen posts on b6, a vulnerable square.

> ***Question:*** Why vulnerable? Black's queen looks like she exerts pressure from b6.

Answer: The trouble is White's main plan in this Tromp version is to blanket the queenside with a pawn storm with c4 and c5, which happens to directly hit Black's current queen's position. This means Black loses time, usually heading back to d8, handing back tempi. White, on the other hand, when he moves his queen, doesn't necessarily have to move to d1. That means White essentially earns a tempo in this trade off.

6 c4 e6 7 ♘c3

After 7 c5 ♕a5+ 8 ♕d2 ♕xd2+ 9 ♘bxd2 ♘d7 10 e3 ♘gf6 11 b4 g5 12 ♗g3 ♘h5 13 ♘b3 ♘xg3 14 hxg3 ♗e7 15 ♗e2 ♔f8 16 ♘a5 ♖b8 17 b5 cxb5 18 ♗xb5 ♗d8?! (Black looks okay after 18...b6 19 ♗xd7 bxa5 20 ♘e5 ♖b2 21 0-0 when his active rook and control over b1 should compensate for White's protected passed c-pawn) 19 ♘b3 ♘f6 20 ♘xg5 White picked off a pawn and converted, M.Turner-M.Ferguson, Tromsø 2010.

7...♗e7 8 ♗g3 ♘f6 9 c5

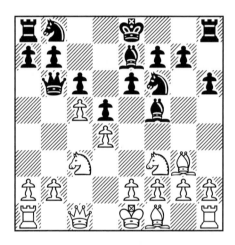

> **Question:** Doesn't this move violate the principle: don't relieve central tension without good reason?

Answer: No, because there is a good reason. As mentioned earlier, our plan against Slav set-ups is nearly always c5, followed by b4 and eventually the b5-break. The reason is that our awkward queen conveniently transfers to b2 or c3, where it helps our b5 break and also watches over the important e5-square, since Black often generates counterplay with an ...e5 central counter. Chances tend to be balanced, but having played these systems, I prefer White stylistically, mainly because our plan is so straightforward and easy to follow.

9...♕d8

9...♕a5?! makes no sense since White gains another tempo with 10 a3 intending b4.

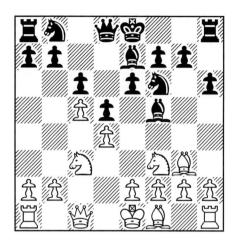

10 e3

> **Question:** Since Black may plan an eventual ...♘h5, or ...♘e4 and then
> ...♘xg3, should we toss in 10 h3 to preserve our dark-squared bishop?

Answer: That would be desirable, but the move looks premature and we don't have time;
h3 has to be timed correctly. Black looks better after 10...b6! and if we insist on maintaining our queenside space edge with 11 b4, Black responds with 11...♘e4, and if 12 ♗h2?
bxc5 13 dxc5 (13 bxc5?? loses to 13...♕a5) 13...♗f6 14 ♘xe4 ♗xe4 15 ♘e5 ♕c8, intending
...♘d7 next, when White is behind in development and under pressure from the e5-pin.

10...♘bd7

Others:

a) 10...0-0 11 h3 (now the move is okay) 11...b6 12 b4 a5 13 a3 ♕c8 14 ♗e2 ♘bd7 15 0-0
and perhaps White can claim a tiny edge due to the extra queenside space, J.Hodgson-
U.Boensch, German League 2002.

b) No one has tried your suggestion 10...♘h5, which does look playable for Black, although after 11 ♗e5 ♘d7 12 ♗e2 0-0 13 0-0 ♘xe5 14 dxe5 g5 15 h3 ♘g7 16 b4 ♕c7 17 ♕d2
b6 18 ♘a4 f6 19 exf6 ♗xf6 20 ♘d4 I still prefer White in this sharp position.

11 h3

Correctly timed to alleviate ...♘h5 worries.

11...0-0 12 b4 ♘e4

12...a6 13 ♗e2 ♘e4 14 ♘xe4 ♗xe4 15 0-0 g5!? was D.Kosic-R.Simic, Sveti Sava 1994. This
isn't just bluster, and we must give such attacks (even shady ones) due respect, and counterattack with accuracy: 16 a4 and dare Black to do his worst on the kingside. Such attacks
are vulnerable to strong queenside counters, since White owns a sound structure around
his king. Let's look at an attacking scenario against *Houdini*: 16...♗h7 17 b5 f5 18 bxc6 bxc6
19 ♗d3 h5 20 ♖b1 ♗f6 21 ♗d6 ♖f7 22 ♕c3 g4 23 hxg4 fxg4 24 ♘d2 h4 25 ♖b7 ♕e8 26 ♗c7

♖c8 27 ♖a7 e5 28 ♗xa6 ♖d8 29 dxe5 ♘xe5 30 ♖xf7! ♔xf7 (30...♘f3+? 31 ♘xf3 ♗xc3 32 ♘g5 ♗g7 33 ♗e2 gives White too powerful an initiative for the queen) 31 ♕b4 h3 32 ♗e2 hxg2 33 ♔xg2 when White is up a pawn and his king looks safer than Black's.

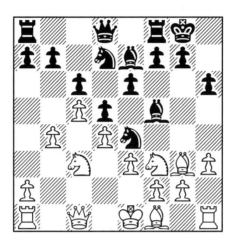

13 ♘xe4 ♗xe4

The bishop attaches itself to the now vacant e4-square, going after a piece which controls the key e5-square.

> **Question:** Can Black recapture with the pawn?

Answer: 13...dxe4!? is untried, but may be playable: 14 ♘e5 (or 14 ♘d2 intending ♘c4; now *Houdini* likes 14...e5!? 15 dxe5 a5 16 a3 axb4 17 axb4 ♖xa1 18 ♕xa1 b6 19 ♕c3 bxc5 20 b5! cxb5 21 ♗xb5 ♕b6 22 ♗xd7 ♗xd7 23 0-0 ♕c6 24 ♕c2 ♗f5 25 ♖c1 when the game looks even) 14...♘xe5 15 ♗xe5 ♗f6 16 ♗d6 ♖e8 17 ♕c3 ♗e7 18 ♗h2 and White may have a microbe of an edge, since Black has yet to achieve ...e5 and White can play for the b5 break.

14 ♘d2

14 ♗e2 allows Black an immediate 14...e5! break: 15 dxe5 a5 16 a3 ♗xf3 17 ♗xf3 ♗h4 18 ♗h2 ♖e8 regaining the pawn, with equality.

14...♗h7

Leaving open ...g5!? potential. After 14...♗g6 15 ♕c3 ♗f6 16 ♘b3 ♖e8 17 ♗d3 ♗xd3 18 ♕xd3 e5 19 0-0 a6 20 a4 ♕e7 21 ♘a5 exd4 22 exd4 ♘f8 23 ♗d6 ♕d7 24 ♖ae1 it's a balanced game. The weakness of d4 makes up for White's b5 potential, J.Hodgson-A.Naumann, German League 2003.

15 ♕c3

Intending ♗d3.

15...♖e8

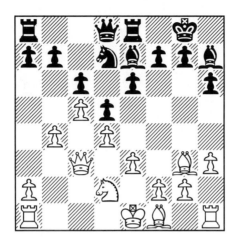

16 ♗d3

Answer: The trouble was Black's h7-bishop controlled the key b1-square, which White needs for a rook to enforce b5 and hopefully infiltrate down the file later on.

16...♗xd3 17 ♕xd3 ♗h4 18 ♗d6 e5

Black achieves his thematic central break.

19 0-0 ♗f6

Black has conducted a model defence and equalized.

20 a4 a6

Played under the theory that the more queenside pawns traded, the better for Black. However, I think White may actually hold a tiny edge after this move. Black achieves absolute equality with the plan 20...♖e6! 21 b5 ♗e7! 22 ♗xe7 ♕xe7 23 ♖ab1 exd4 24 exd4 b6!. The game is soon drawn when Black clears away the queenside pawns: for example, 25 ♘b3 bxc5 26 dxc5 ♘xc5 27 ♘xc5 ♕xc5 28 ♖fc1 ♕b6 29 bxc6 ♖xc6! 30 ♕xd5 ♖xc1+ 31 ♖xc1 ♖d8 with a near certain draw.

21 b5 axb5 22 axb5 ♖xa1 23 ♖xa1 exd4 24 exd4

So far the queenside has proven to be a somewhat barren playground for White's dreams. Black is under no more than just a shade of pressure there, since his pawns remain safe, outside the jurisdiction of White's queen. Also, the presence of the weak d4-pawn places an awkward constraint upon White's queenside ambitions. So far, it feels as if both sides drift about, doing this and that, navigating the position in a peaceful trance, and nobody can claim the game has been prolific with incident. All that is about to change.

24...cxb5?

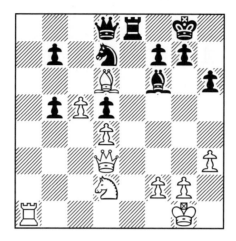

When we play directionless moves, without an overall plan, our tendency is to simply react, from crisis to crisis. Even worse though, is when we follow an incorrect plan with great determination, as we see in this case. The enemy's gate opens just a crack and this concession turns out to be far more than just a minor amendment. Black, at the slightest encouragement goes off like fireworks, in his eagerness to stay active. So he mistakenly self-vandalizes his queenside pawns, under the impression he may be able to pull off a swap of all of them and earn a draw. Black's once perfectly playable game goes haywire, as if two or three key actors in the middle of a play, suddenly stop acting, sit on the stage couch and enjoy a leisurely coffee break. Now b5, b7 and d5 are grievous wounds which time refuses to heal.

Black only stands a shade worse after the correct 24...♘f8 25 ♘f3 ♘e6 26 ♖a7 ♕c8 27 b6 ♘g5.

25 ♘f3 b6?

Opportunity swirls, now circling the drain. Black continues to become inextricably entwined in a misconstrued side issue, to the detriment of his overall position. Now he allows White an unblockable, passed c-pawn. His last chance lay in 25...♕c8 26 ♕xb5 ♕c6 27 ♖b1 ♕xb5 28 ♖xb5 ♘b8 29 ♖xb7 ♘c6 30 ♖b1! when White hangs on to his extra pawn.

26 ♖a7 bxc5 27 ♕xb5

"A woman's work is never done," sighs the queen, as she realizes that she neglected to sign the freshly executed b5-pawn's death warrant. The bully continues to pick on Black's now wiped out queenside, her pickee of choice.

27...♘f8 28 dxc5

Material is even; the position is not. White's surging, passed c-pawn proves impossible to blockade.

28...♕c8 29 ♖b7

Threat: ♖b8.

29...♕a8

29...♛e6 is met by 30 ♖b8 ♞d7 31 ♖xe8+ ♛xe8 32 c6 ♞e5.

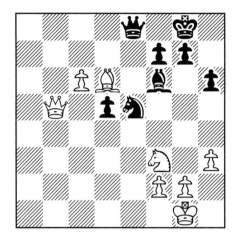

Exercise (combination alert): White to play and win.

Answer: Overload/deflection/pawn promotion. 33 ♗xe5 ♗xe5 34 c7! (what a visually stunning shot, overloading Black's queen) 34...♛xb5 35 c8♛+ ♚h7 36 ♛f5+ picks off a piece.

30 c6 ♛a1+

The queen, feeling hedged in by what she deems her social inferiors, decides to part company, and the population of able defenders grows sparser on the queenside. This last move appears rather random, like a person who picks a vacation destination by closing her eyes and tossing a dart at a wall map. The problem is nothing works: 30...♖c8 31 c7 and now what? White threatens ♖b8.

31 ♚h2 ♞e6 32 c7 1-0

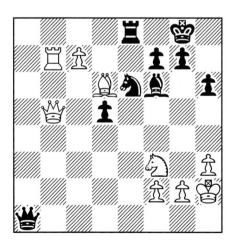

The passed c-pawn gazes at the c8-promotion square with a wistfully loving look, similar to when Moses, thirsty and craving both milk and honey, caught a fleeting glimpse of the Promised Land in the horizon. There is no good answer to the coming ♖b8. Note how autopilot and easy White's play looked.

Summary: The solid Slav line should be even if both sides understand their respective plans: our plan is c5, and eventually b5, while Black's is to play for an ...e5 central counter.

> ## Game 44
> ### J.Hodgson-M.Turner
> ### Kilkenny 1999

1 d4 d5 2 ♗g5 h6 3 ♗h4 c6 4 ♘f3 ♕b6 5 ♕c1 ♗f5 6 c4 e6 7 ♘c3 ♗e7! 8 ♗g3 ♘f6 9 c5 ♕d8 10 e3 0-0 11 h3 ♘bd7 12 b4 ♘e4 13 ♘xe4 ♗xe4 14 ♘d2 ♗g6 15 ♕c3 ♗h4

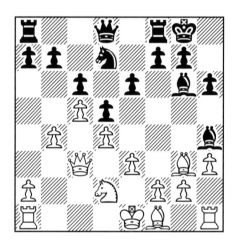

> ***Question:*** Is there much difference between this move and last game's 15...♖e8?

Answer: Not much, if any at all. Play proceeds pretty much the same way in both games.
16 ♗d6 ♖e8 17 ♗d3 ♗xd3 18 ♕xd3 e5 19 0-0 a6 20 a4 e4?!

Of course, such a move can't be interpreted as anything but an open declaration of war. Turner lays the foundation of a future kingside assault, but the trouble is it may be too slow. Black's infatuation with attack passes a barrier and enters into the danger zone. A move based on the premise: rebellion, if gaining a foothold on the population, tends to spread quickly across the map. The ambitious plan looks strategically suspect.

Safer and probably superior is the 20...exd4 21 exd4 plan we looked at last game. I actually love it when Black plays for ...e4, rather than ...exd4.

Answer: True, it slightly increases danger to our king, but I think more importantly, it re-moves all the pressure off our d4-pawn, which isn't the case in ...exd4 lines. This in turn allows us to attack the queenside without fear of dropping d4. And from my experience, White's queenside attack arrives faster than Black's corresponding kingside attack. For this reason, I debate against the advisability of a direct kingside assault for Black. 21...♘f8 fol-lowing last game's pattern should keep White's minuscule edge at bay.

21 ♕e2 ♖e6

Here they come.

22 b5 ♖g6

Alternatively, 22...axb5 23 axb5 ♖g6 24 ♖fb1 ♖xa1 25 ♖xa1 ♕g5 26 g3! (go ahead, make my day!) 26...♕f5 27 ♖a7! ♕xh3 28 ♖xb7 cxb5 29 ♘f1 ♘f6 30 ♕xb5.

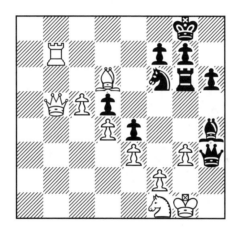

Answer: *Houdini* assessment: +3.69! – completely busted for Black. It is easy to misassess such a position. White's king may not be much to look at, but at least he remains alive. Black's pieces do indeed hover ominously over our king, but when we ask the essential question: "Where is Black's knockout combination?" we find it difficult to come up with an answer. I see no way for Black to increase the power of this attack. Meanwhile, White's passed c-pawn rams through. *Houdini*'s analysis continues: 30...h5 31 ♖b8+ ♔h7 32 c6 ♘g4 33 c7 (one move away) 33...♘xe3 34 ♘xe3 ♗xg3 35 ♗xg3 ♖xg3+ 36 fxg3 ♕xg3+ 37 ♘g2 and there is no perpetual check.

23 bxc6 bxc6 24 ♖ab1

As often in this line, b7 is an inviting infiltration square.

24...♘f8

Black really can't backtrack and defend here with 24...♖a7, since White simply plays 25 ♖b3 intending to double. Black's queenside is doomed and the only defence is to deliver checkmate on the other side of the board.

25 f3!

White acts vigorously to defend his borders. After this move Black's potential for the creation of mischief has been reduced. Principle: meet a wing attack with a central counter. Hodgson times f3 perfectly, since Black's knight no longer has access to f6.

25...exf3

25...f5?? fails miserably to 26 fxe4, winning material, no matter how Black plays it.

26 ♘xf3

Threat: ♘e5, targeting g6, f7 and c6.

26...♗f6 27 ♖b7!

To a person of honour, the keeping of secrets is an objectionable practice. Yet we as chess players do just that in virtually every game we play. This sneaky move in reality invites Black to fall into a cheapo.

27...♕c8

Double attack on b7 and h3. Or is it?

28 ♖fb1!

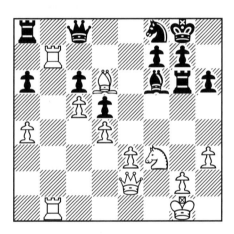

A move which thrusts Black's hopelessness upon him.

28...♘d7

Black's game takes a turn for the worse and relapses into its old state of sickly passivity. One senses the out-of-synchness in Black's game, which would tax the abilities of the ablest of attackers. The long-mute black would-be attackers strive for utterance yet still fail to express themselves. There simply is no method to progress the kingside attack.

> **Question:** This doesn't seem like the right time for kindly forbearance. What was wrong with 28...♕xh3?

Answer: The hoped-for rich source of counterplay begins to languish for Black. The trouble is White has his own, more potent threat with 29 ♖b8 ♖xb8 30 ♖xb8. Black's king takes deep breaths, mainly to clear his mind of violent thoughts about White's mocking rook and bishop. Black's knight hangs and there is no way to gin up his kingside threats.

29 ♖c7

The rook, upon viewing Black's queen (and c6), experiences that baffling yet exhilarating feeling: love at first sight.

29...♕e8 30 ♖xc6

The degradation of Black's queenside pawns spreads like a flu-contaminated sneeze in a crowded bus. Even stronger may be 30 ♖bb7.

30...♕e4 31 ♖f1

The kingside is a country at civil war between multiple autonomous republics, all striving for dominance. Hodgson decides not to get greedy with 31 ♖b7 and plays for consolidation.

31...♖e8 32 ♖xa6 ♘f8

The ending is completely resignable after 32...♕xe3+ 33 ♕xe3 ♖xe3 34 c6 ♘f8 35 ♖a8 ♗e7 36 c7.

33 ♗xf8

The more pieces off the board the better.

33...♔xf8 34 ♖b6 h5

The e3-pawn still remains taboo: 34...♕xe3+ 35 ♕xe3 ♖xe3 36 a5 ♖a3 37 ♖b8+ ♔e7 38 ♖e1+ ♔d7 39 ♖b7+ ♔c6 40 ♖eb1! ends the discussion.

35 a5 ♖g3

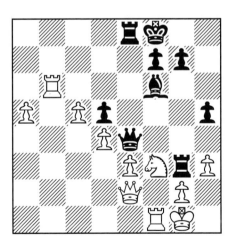

An empty gesture. It becomes obvious that the attack is about as lively as the actor who played the corpse in *Weekend at Bernie's*.

36 a6

Threat: a7 and ♖b8.

36...♖a8

Black plays on, but with an increasing feeling of desolation. His attacking attempts max out and there is no way to even make it close. If the attacking side is forced into a move like this, then it's time to resign.

37 ♕f2 h4 38 ♘e5! 1-0

The weakness of f7, like a flare-up of an old injury, resurfaces: 38...♔g8 39 ♘g4 ♗g5 40 ♕xf7+ ♔h8 41 ♖f2 ♗xe3 42 ♘xe3 ♕xe3 43 ♕h5+ ♔g8 44 ♕xd5+ gets the job done.

Summary: Surprisingly, the ...e4 plan is ineffective, since White is given a free hand on the queenside and Black's kingside attack appears slower.

Game 45
I.Popov-A.Grigoryan
Kirishi 2007

1 d4 d5 2 ♗g5 f6

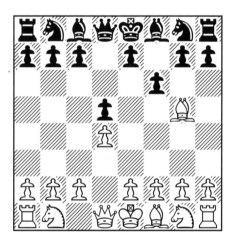

We arrive at our next giant challenge of the chapter. Be warned: Trompowsky expert Eric Prié actually thinks Black may stand slightly better at this point. Also IM Richard Pert gave Black's move an exclamation mark in his Trompowsky book.

Question: Do you agree?

Answer: No. This is the line I play against Trompowsky as Black, but I believe White's game is fully playable and there are sneaky methods for White to turn the position into an unclear mess, in which we will most likely seize the familiarity advantage.

3 ♗h4

Answer: Unfortunately, ...f6 may help Black more than harm, after 3...♘c6 (3...c5 is also very playable: 4 c3 ♘c6 5 ♘f3 ♕b6 and now Morozevich saw nothing better than the lame retreat 6 ♗c1, which wasn't exactly inspirational stuff for team Trompowsky, A.Morozevich-H.Nakamura, Biel 2012; 4 e3 looks better, but I'm not crazy about White's position after 4...♘c6 5 ♘f3 g5! 6 ♗g3 h5 7 h3) 4 ♘f3. Now 4...♗g4 is normally played, but Black has an attractive option in 4...g5!. This move is also given Pert's seal of approval (4...e5!? 5 dxe5 is also dangerous for our side since we directly transpose to a line of the Blackmar-Diemer Gambit, as we conveniently hand Black ...f6 for free), and after 5 ♗g3 h5 6 h3 ♘h6! 7 ♘c3 (7 e3 ♘f5 8 ♗d3 ♘xg3 9 ♗g6+ ♔d7 10 fxg3 ♖h6 11 ♗d3 e6 is an unclear mess; White's damaged structure and lack of a dark-squared bishop are compensated by Black's shaky king's position) 7...♘f5 8 e4! dxe4 (8...♘xg3 9 fxg3 dxe4 10 ♘xe4 ♕d5 11 ♕e2 ♖h6 12 ♘c3 ♕d6 13 0-0-0 gives White dangerous attacking chances) 9 ♘xe4 ♘cxd4 10 ♗d3 ♘c6 11 c3 ♗h6 12 ♕c2 ♔f8 13 ♖d1 *Houdini* says even, but I'm not so sure White gets full compensation for the pawn in the form of attacking chances, H.Kruse-D.Lafarga Santorroman, correspondence 2007.

3...♘h6

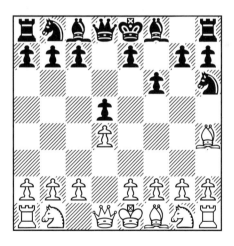

Answer: Black's move isn't so strange when we realize that Black's knight intends to chase our bishop down, with ...♘f5 next, bagging the bishop-pair.

4 f3

Thwarting Black's plan by offering our bishop a home on f2. 4 e3 is more common, but having played Black's side, I don't really want to enter the line 4...♘f5 5 ♗g3 (I think Black stands better after 5 ♗d3 ♘xh4 6 ♕h5+ g6 7 ♕xh4 ♗g7 when he obtains the bishop-pair and eventually plays for the ...e5 break after due preparation) 5...h5!. I tried to make this position work for White, but finally gave up. After 6 ♗e2 h4 7 ♗h5+ ♔d7 8 ♗f4 g5 9 e4 dxe4 10 ♗c1 Prié calls this line "inadequate" for White.

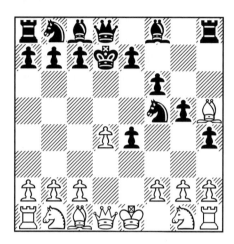

Question: Do you agree with him?

Answer: Unfortunately I do. I just don't believe in White's compensation for the pawn after 10...c6, although I do admit White gets practical chances due to Black's rather odd king's position. So let's bypass the main line 4 e3 and go with the lesser-known 4 f3 line, which may be White's best (or perhaps least worst?) choice.

4...c5

We look at 4...♘c6 a couple of games later in the chapter. Instead, 4...♘f5 5 ♗f2 ♘c6 6 c3 e5 7 e4 dxe4 8 fxe4 ♘d6 9 ♘d2 exd4 10 cxd4 ♘f7 11 ♘gf3 ♗g4 was J.Bonin-M.Grinman, New York 2003, where I like White's strong centre after 12 ♗c4.

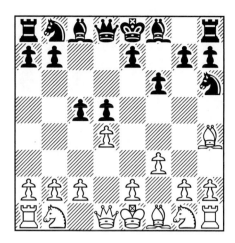

5 dxc5!?

Question: Why do we give up the centre like this?

Answer: We take on c5 with the intention of gaining time, since Black expends energy to regain the pawn, or failing that, remains down a pawn. 5 c3 is passive and playable as well, if somewhat un-inspirational: 5...cxd4 6 cxd4 ♘c6 7 e3 e5 8 ♘c3 ♘f5 9 ♗f2, Y.Lapshun-H.Nakamura, New York (rapid) 2002. I would rather take Black after 9...♗b4.

5...e5

Black dominates the centre and threatens to regain c5 with the superior position.

6 ♗f2 ♘c6

Next game we look at 6...d4.

7 e4

We seize our fair share of the centre, free our position and deny Black's pieces the use of f5.

7...dxe4

No one has tried 7...d4. We can respond with 8 ♗c4 (or 8 c3 ♗xc5 9 b4?! ♗b6 10 b5 ♘e7 11 cxd4 f5!, playing on the development lead by following the principle: create confrontation when leading in development; Black stands better) 8...♗xc5 9 ♘e2 ♕e7 10 0-0 ♗e6 11 ♗xe6 ♕xe6 12 c3 dxc3 13 ♘bxc3 ♗xf2+ 14 ♖xf2 ♖d8 15 ♘d5 0-0 16 ♕b3, with an even position.

8 ♕xd8+ ♔xd8

His unnatural sister's creepy touch makes the black king's skin crawl.

9 ♘c3!

9 fxe4?! walks into 9...♘g4.

9...exf3 10 0-0-0+ ♔e8

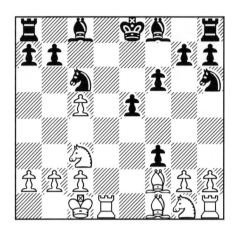

11 gxf3!?

White recaptures with the pawn to retain some central influence.

> *Question:* Can White recapture with the knight, relying on his development lead?

Answer: That is the route I would have taken. Let's take a look: 11 ♘xf3 ♗e6 12 ♗d3 ♗e7 13 h3 ♔f7 14 ♗e4 g6 15 g4 ♖hd8 16 ♘d5 ♖ac8 17 g5!. At this point *Houdini* likes White after 17...♘f5 18 ♘xe7 ♔xe7 19 gxf6+ ♔xf6.

11...♗e6 12 ♗b5 ♔f7 13 ♘ge2 ♗e7 14 ♘d5 a6

This brand of baffled fury does nothing to harm White and exerts a corrosive effect on Black's dark squares. Black may be better off without this move.

15 ♗a4 ♘d4!?

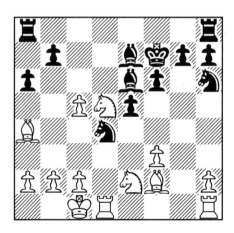

An interference trick.

16 ♘xd4

White can also try the risky exchange sacrifice 16 ♖xd4!? exd4 (16...♗xc5!? 17 ♖b4 ♗xf2 18 ♖xb7+ ♔g6 19 ♘e7+ ♔h5 20 ♗d7 looks playable for Black too, despite the strange positioning of his king) 17 ♘xe7 ♔xe7 18 ♘xd4 ♗d5 19 ♗g3 g6 20 ♗d6+ ♔f7 21 ♖d1 when it feels like he achieves full compensation with a pawn and bishop-pair for the exchange. **16...♗xd5 17 ♗b3! ♖hd8 18 ♗xd5+ ♖xd5 19 ♘b3 ♖xd1+ 20 ♖xd1**

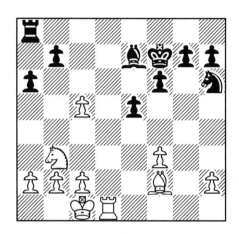

Question: Isn't Black better? After all, he owns the healthy majority.

Answer: We shouldn't refuse to sign a lucrative contract simply because a single clause is not to our liking. I don't believe Black stands better. His kingside pawn majority may look pleasing to the eye, but Black's queenside, especially b7, looks vulnerable to ♘a5 tricks.
20...♔e6?!

Inaccurate. Black has a better chance to hold the balance after 20...♔e8 21 ♘a5 ♖b8.
21 ♘a5 ♖b8?!

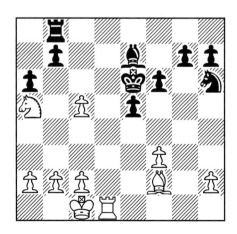

Answer: 22 ♖d3!

White's rook creeps forward, insinuating himself into Black's business like an advancing tide. There is no good defence to the coming ♖b3.

22...f5!

A souring position has a way of acting as a stimulant, urging us to action. Black activates his kingside pawn majority, hoping to repackage something new from the wreckage of the old, and avoids the trap 22...♘f7 23 ♖b3 ♘d8?? 24 c6! (pin/double attack). White wins since Black can't defend both b7 and the c7 threat.

23 ♖b3

White's rook and knight eye b7 with intense disfavour.

23...♗g5+ 24 ♔b1 ♖d8

Threatening a back-rank mate.

25 ♖b6+!

A necessary nuance.

25...♔f7 26 ♖xb7+ ♔e6 27 ♖b6+

The rook continues to shadow Black's king, never allowing him a moment's peace.

27...♔f7 28 b4!

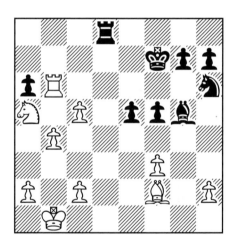

If you make your escape untraceable, you become impossible to kill. A multipurpose move:

1. White avoids the back-rank cheapo.

2. White activates his queenside majority.

The war doesn't end. It simply relocates to separate killing fields, now in the form of a queening race.

28...e4

28...♖d2? is too slow: 29 c6! ♗d8 30 ♖b8 e4 31 fxe4 fxe4 32 ♗h4! and the deflection wins.

29 ♘c4!

29 fxe4? ♘g4 allows Black back into the game.

29...♖d1+

29...exf3 is met with 30 ♘e5+ ♔e8 31 ♖e6+ ♔f8 32 ♘xf3 ♗f6 33 ♔c1, consolidating.

30 ♔b2 ♗f6+

White is faster in the queening race after 30...exf3 31 ♘e5+ ♔e8 32 ♖xa6! ♗c1+ 33 ♔b3 ♘g4 34 ♘xg4 fxg4 35 b5 ♗f4 36 ♖a8+ ♖d8 37 ♖a4 ♗xh2 38 ♖xg4 ♖d2 39 ♗h4 ♔f7 40 ♗g3!.

31 ♔b3 exf3 32 c6

Threat: c7. It's impossible to quarantine a disease once it reaches epidemic proportions. Black is forcibly reminded of the open sore on c6.

32...♘g8

32...♗d8 33 ♘e5+ ♔e8 34 ♖b8 ♔e7 35 ♘xf3 ♘g4 36 ♗h4+ ♘f6 37 ♖b7+ ♔e6 38 c7 wins.

33 c7

The salivating c-pawn is a lion, entering a den of many Daniels, each of whom has his faith sorely tested.

33...♘e7

The knight agrees to be harnessed to the yoke of c8.

34 ♗c5

It becomes apparent that the flimsy defenders are woefully unequal to the task of halting White's ambitious c-pawn.

34...♖d7 35 ♖b7 ♘c8 36 ♘b6

White ruthlessly targets all would-be blockaders.

36...♗e7

Black agrees to pay an extortionate cost, hoping to avoid White's promotion attempts.

37 ♘xc8 ♗xc5

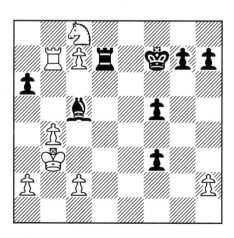

Exercise (combination alert): Black's last move fulfils an unfortunate function: the last straw, after which his game collapses. Previous to this point, White was just warming up. Now comes time for the finishing touch. White to play and win.

Answer: Clearance/pawn promotion.

38 ♘d6+! 1-0

White's c-pawn passes the stage of mere ambition and enters the early phase of megalomania.

Summary: At the time of writing, White's main line, 4 e3, doesn't seem to cut it. So let's take up the lesser-known, unclear alternative 4 f3.

Game 46
I.Miladinovic-T.Nabaty
Belgrade 2013

1 d4 d5 2 ♗g5 f6 3 ♗h4 ♘h6 4 f3 c5 5 dxc5 e5 6 ♗f2 d4

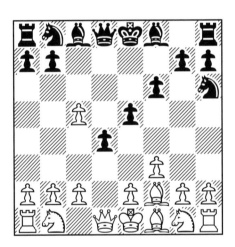

Black cuts off our bishop's communication to c5.

7 e3

The gargantuan centre must immediately be challenged.

Question: Can White think about 7 b4 to hang on to c5?

Answer: Not good. White can't hang on to the extra pawn and such a move is a self-inflicted wound to our structure: for example, 7...a5 8 e3 dxe3 9 ♕xd8+ ♔xd8 10 ♗xe3 ♘f5 11 ♗f2 axb4 and Black regained the pawn, while retaining the vastly superior pawn structure.

7...♗xc5

Question: Has anyone tried 7...♘f5?

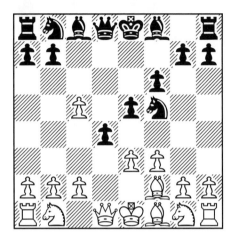

Answer: Your suggestion is a theoretical novelty and may be playable for Black: 8 exd4 ♘xd4 (after 8...exd4 9 ♕e2+ ♗e7 10 ♘d2 ♘d7 11 g4 ♘e3 12 ♗xe3 dxe3 13 ♕xe3 0-0 14 0-0-0 ♗xc5 15 ♕b3+ ♔h8 16 ♘e4 I don't think Black's bishop-pair and dark-square control fully compensate the missing pawn, mainly since White isn't behind in development and the e4-knight is excellently posted) 9 c3 ♘e6 10 ♕xd8+ ♔xd8 11 ♘d2 (White may be overextending after 11 b4!? a5 12 a3 axb4 13 cxb4 b6 14 ♘d2 bxc5 15 b5 ♘d4 16 ♗d3 ♗d7 17 b6 ♘bc6 18 ♘c4 ♗e6 when the b6-pawn is in grave danger) 11...♗xc5 12 ♖d1 ♔c7 13 ♗c4 looks about even.

8 exd4 ♗xd4

Otherwise, 8...exd4 9 ♗c4 ♘f5 10 ♘e2 ♘c6 11 c3 ♘e3 12 ♗xe3 dxe3 was G.Chepukaitis-V.Milov, Internet blitz) 2002. After 13 ♕xd8+ ♔xd8 14 ♘a3 ♗xa3 15 bxa3 ♘e5 16 0-0-0+ ♔c7 17 ♗b3 I'm not sure if e3 represents a liability or a strength for Black. *Houdini* rates it around even.

9 ♗xd4 exd4 10 ♗b5+ ♘c6 11 ♕e2+

Instead, 11 c3 0-0 12 ♘e2 ♖e8 13 cxd4 ♘f5 14 0-0 ♘e3 15 ♕b3+ ♔h8 16 ♖f2 ♘xd4 17 ♘xd4 ♕xd4 18 ♖d2 ♕c5 19 ♗xe8 ♘c2+?? (played in S.Drazic-M.Geenen, Milan 2002; instead, 19...♘g4+ 20 ♔f1 ♘e3+ should end in perpetual check, since 21 ♔e2!? ♘xg2 looks awfully risky for White, despite the extra material) 20 ♔h1! ♘xa1 21 ♕d1 ♗e6 22 ♗d7 ♗xa2 23 ♘c3 wins a piece.

11...♔d7?!

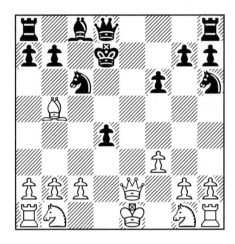

Threat: ...♖e8.

Question: What the hay!?

Answer: Sometimes we make deliberately stupid-looking moves to extract a perverse de-light in challenging our opponent's sense of incredulity. Yet one senses that Black, caught up in a sense of theatre, gets ensnared with the details. Do you get the feeling that the Trompowsky – a system conducive to extremes – isn't your standard-issue opening reper-toire? In a strange way, Black's unhinged-looking last move is perfectly natural, since he strives to keep queens on the board, due to his isolated d-pawn, but the king travelled in the wrong direction. This is not simply an isolated outbreak of crazy. Indeed, crazy begins to spread across the board, to both sides.

I think it's more logical to go the other direction with 11...♔f7! 12 ♗c4+ ♔f8 13 ♘d2 ♘f5 (Black's isolani clearly has its strong points; in this case e3 is a tender square for White, who must guard entry from hostiles) 14 ♘f1 g6 15 0-0-0 ♔g7 16 g4 ♖e8 17 ♕d2 ♘d6 18 ♗d5 and *Houdini* likes Black, while I feel it's anyone's game here.

12 ♕d2 ♔c7 13 ♘a3 ♘f5 14 ♘e2 ♕d5 15 0-0-0!?

Risky. I would deny Black play against the king, castle the other way with 15 0-0! and then play on the weakness of d4. *Houdini* gives White an edge with this plan.

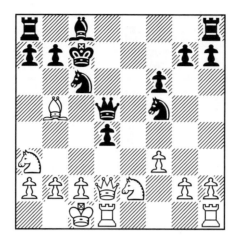

15...罩d8

Question: Why can't Black grab a2?

Answer: Firstly, it doesn't even win anything since Black drops d4. Secondly, Black's king is fatally exposed after 15...♕xa2?? 16 ♗xc6 ♕a1+ 17 ♘b1 bxc6 18 ♘xd4 (threat: ♘xf5 and ♕f4+). Now if 18...♘xd4 19 ♕f4+ ♔b7 20 罩xd4, threatening a nasty check on b4, as well as 罩a4, trapping Black's queen.

16 ♘c3

After 16 ♗xc6! bxc6 17 ♘f4! ♕c5 (17...♕xa2?? 18 ♕a5+ wins; White's queen visits her brother, when he dearly hoped for the separation to continue) 18 罩he1 a5 19 g4 ♘h4 20 ♕f2 ♘g6 21 ♘xg6 hxg6 22 c3! White wins a pawn.

16...♕e5?

Black should try 16...♕c5 17 ♗xc6 bxc6 18 ♘e4 ♕d5 19 c4! ♕e5 20 罩he1, although even then, White holds the initiative.

17 ♗xc6 bxc6 18 ♘c4 ♕c5 19 b3

Even stronger is 19 ♘e4! ♕xc4 20 ♕a5+ ♔d7 21 ♕xf5+ ♔e7 22 ♕xh7 ♔f8 23 ♕h8+ ♕g8 24 ♕xg8+ ♔xg8 with a solid extra pawn.

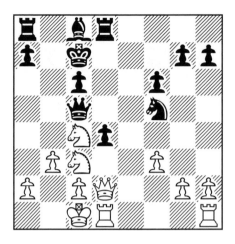

19...♘e3!?

Question: Doesn't this simply drop a pawn?

Answer: Reality jars Black, as if colliding with a telephone pole while daydreaming on a walk. He comes to the conclusion that little profit can be derived from his present path, and so switches direction to a difficult, if not lost ending. I agree that it isn't exactly a judicious decision, but I ask: can a move be a mistake if everything else loses?

Black rationalizes: to await a powerful enemy's approach without preparatory measures is tantamount to leaving a disease untreated and allowing it to progress to terminal levels. So he offers a pawn to remove queens from the board, worrying that White's attack may get out of control. It looks like an attempt to locate a silver lining to a plan gone sour. The trouble is the solution to one predicament can be the direct causal factor for another, equally serious one. If 19...♗e6 20 ♘e4 ♕d5 21 ♕f4+ ♚c8 22 ♖he1 c5 23 g4 g5 24 ♕d2 ♘h4 25 ♘xf6 when Black won't survive.

20 ♘xe3 ♕xc3 21 ♕xc3 dxc3 22 ♖xd8 ♚xd8 23 ♖d1+

"Actions speak louder than words," declares the rook, as he prepares to hand the c3-pawn a swift kick to the nether regions. There is nothing wrong either with the simple 23 ♘d1.

23...♚c7 24 ♖d3

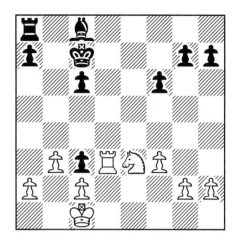

Black must bid adieu to c3.

24...♗a6 25 ♖xc3 ♖e8 26 a4 ♔b6 27 b4

Denying Black's king dark squares and following the principle: if you have a wing majority, push it.

27...♖d8 28 ♖c5 ♗e2 29 ♘f5

White seeks to provoke pawn weakness in Black's camp. Black can't allow White's knight to roost on f5 forever, and is soon induced into ...g6.

29...♖d7 30 ♔b2 g6 31 ♘g3 ♗a6 32 ♔c3

Covering d2.

32...♖d1

Black attempts a kingside raid with his rook.

33 ♘e4

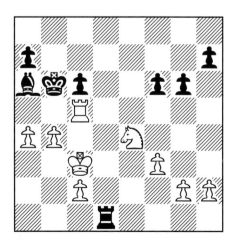

33...f5

> **Question:** Can Black skip this move and
> immediately go after White's kingside with 33...♖h1?

Answer: White looks faster in the race after 34 ♘xf6 ♖xh2 35 ♘d7+ ♔c7 36 ♖a5 ♔xd7 37
♖xa6 h5 38 ♖xa7+ ♔d6 39 a5 ♖xg2 40 a6 ♖f2 41 ♖f7 ♖f1 42 ♔b2 (cutting off ...♖a1)
42...♖e1 43 ♖g7 and wins.

34 ♘g5 ♗f1 35 g3 ♗g2 36 a5+ ♔b7

36...♔c7 is met with 37 b5.

37 ♖e5

Threatening a nasty check on e7.

37...h6 38 ♘e6 ♗xf3

Regaining the lost pawn doesn't mean much of a victory, since everything else in Black's
game swirls in a downward spiral.

39 ♘c5+ ♔c8 40 ♖e8+ ♖d8 41 ♖e7 ♔b8

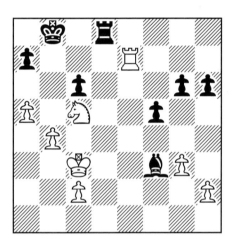

Black's monochromatic position runs at 50% capacity as White's efficiently ordered
forces press down with brutal logic. An assessment:

1. White's rook, knight and king all outwork their counterparts.

2. White dominates the seventh rank.

3. Black's kingside pawns are loose and remain in grave danger.

4. Security is unusually heavy around the black king's walled compound and rightly so,
since White's pieces have designs on Black's king, who isn't entirely safe from White's attacking ambitions, because there exist dangerous attacking geometries with rook, knight
and a-pawn.

Conclusion: The time for bubbly happiness ends for Black, as a new era of misery begins.
Even a novice entering his or her first tournament can tell us that everything that could
possibly go wrong, has gone wrong for Black.

> **Exercise (planning):** Come up with a clear plan
> for White, based on number four on our list:

42 a6

Answer: Simpler is 42 ♘a6+! when the knight and rook send a wave of bad vibes in the direction of Black's ill-tuned king: 42...♔a8 (if 42...♔c8 43 ♖c7 mate) 43 ♘c7+ ♔b8 (43...♔b7?? hangs material to 44 ♘e6+) 44 ♘e6 ♖c8 45 a6! (threatening ♖b7+, followed by ♘c7+; at this point, the black king surveys his rapidly shrinking kingdom with a fatalistic sigh and his sense of despair reaches the equivalent level of Napoleon's clinical depression during his stay at Elba) 45...c5 46 ♘xc5 when Black's pieces, devoid of purpose, continue to loaf aimlessly.

42...♗d5 43 ♖b7+ ♔a8 44 ♖h7 g5

Black has no way to hang on to his pawns: for example, 44...h5 45 ♘d3 ♖g8 46 ♘e5 ♗e4 47 ♖h6 and Black crumbles.

45 ♖xh6 f4 46 gxf4 gxf4 47 ♖f6 f3 48 ♘d7

Threat: ♘e5 and ♘xf3. Of course, the knight is immune due to the loose back rank.

48...♖e8 49 h4

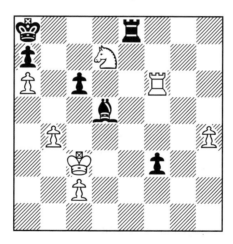

Black, hamstrung by a fatally weak back rank, can't do a thing. Meanwhile, White leisurely pushes his passed h-pawn. There is nothing wrong too with the immediate 49 ♘e5.

49...♗e6 50 ♘e5 ♗c8 51 ♘xf3 ♗xa6 52 h5 ♗e2 53 h6 c5 54 ♘g5

What's the rush? I would take time out to munch on a pawn first with 54 bxc5.

54...cxb4+ 55 ♔xb4 ♖b8+ 56 ♔c3 ♖c8+ 57 ♔d2 ♗c4 58 ♘f7!

Another winning plan is 58 h7 ♖h8 59 ♔c3 ♗a2 60 ♔b2 ♗d5 61 ♖d6 ♗g2 62 ♖d7 ♗c6 63 ♖g7 ♗d5 64 ♘f7.

58...♖f8

If 58...♗xf7 59 ♖xf7 and there isn't much Black can do about h7, ♖g7 and ♖g8.

59 h7 &xf7

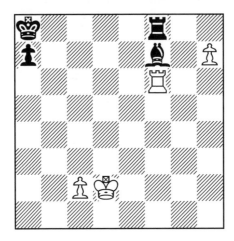

> ***Exercise (combination alert):*** Competence in finding combinations
> is simply pattern recognition, mixed with the art of spotting
> anomalies. In this instance we have the most elementary of combinations –
> in fact, maybe the easiest one in the book. White to play and win.

Answer: Overload.

60 &xf7

Black's rook can only watch helplessly as White forces promotion.

60...&xf7 1-0

Summary: Black can also go for an isolani position, where it's difficult to decide whether the d4 isolani is more a strength than a weakness.

> *Game 47*
> **V.Belikov-A.Raetsky**
> Voronezh 2007

1 d4 d5 2 &g5 f6 3 &h4 &h6 4 f3 &c6

This may be Black's best move in the position, as it now feels like our side barely maintains equality.

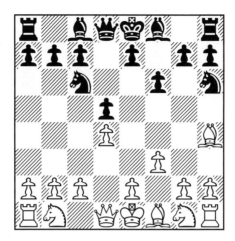

Question: Why does Black avoid ...c5?

Answer: In this version Black seeks to play in Reversed Veresov fashion.

Question: What are the moves to the Veresov?

Answer: White gets the Veresov after 1 d4 ♞f6 2 ♞c3 d5 ♝g5. Now in the Veresov, White often expends a tempo with f3, building for an e4-break. In the Trompowsky version, note that we gave Black the corresponding ...f6 for free. So in a sense, Black, up a tempo, plays a real Veresov, not merely a reversed facsimile.

5 c3

White reinforces d4.

Question: True, but why not develop and reinforce the centre with 5 e3?

Answer: That is also possible. The reason White played c3 over e3 is that he hoped to engineer e4 in one go, without wasting a tempo on e3. 5 e3 is playable as well, though: for example: 5...♞f5 6 ♝f2 e5 7 ♞c3 ♝b4 8 ♕d2 0-0 9 a3 exd4 10 exd4 ♖e8+ 11 ♞ge2 ♝xc3 (perhaps better is 11...♝a5! 12 0-0-0 b5 13 ♞f4 b4 14 axb4 ♞xb4 15 ♚b1 c6 16 g4 ♞d6 17 ♞a4 with a very sharp situation where Black clearly stands no worse due to the open b-file) 12 ♕xc3 ♕e7 13 0-0-0 with a tricky Exchange French/opposite-wing attack position where I favour White due to his strength on the dark squares, L.Rojas Keim-W.Pohl, Schwaebisch Gmuend 2010.

However, after 5 e4?! dxe4 6 d5 ♞f5 7 fxe4 ♞xh4 8 ♕h5+ ♞g6 9 dxc6, as in J. Acers-E.Sveshnikov, Kamena Vourla 2012.,Black looks clearly better after 9...♕d4!.

5...e5

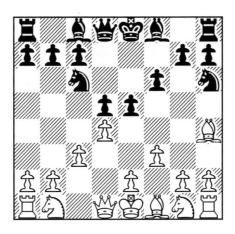

6 dxe5

White captures on e5 at a stage where Black can't recapture with his f-pawn. 6 e3 is more solid, if uninspiring: 6...♘f5 7 ♗f2 exd4 8 exd4 with equal chances, A.Sidenko-N.Knudsen, correspondence 2000.

6...♘xe5 7 ♗f2

This move is new and probably improves upon 7 e4?!, N.Ajrapetian-S.Surov, Anna 2012. Simplest for Black may be to swap into a pleasant ending with 7...dxe4 8 ♕xd8+ ♔xd8 9 fxe4 which saddles White with an isolani and gives Black control over e5.

7...♗e7 8 ♘d2 0-0

8....♗f5 hoping to suppress e4, doesn't succeed in its aim after 9 ♕a4+ c6 10 e4 dxe4 11 ♘xe4.

9 ♕c2

White plans to unwind by castling queenside, followed by e4.

9...c5 10 e4

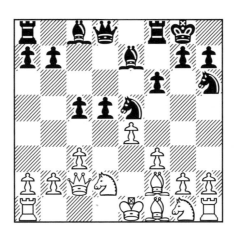

White finally challenges Black's centre.

10...♚h8

> *Question:* Should Black consider taking on an isolani with 10...d4?

Answer: The isolani quickly grows unstable after 11 cxd4 cxd4 12 ♘e2! d3 13 ♕b3+ ♘hf7 14 ♘f4. *Houdini* still thinks the game is pretty close to equal, but I feel like that advanced d-pawn is about to fall.

11 0-0-0

In this chapter, chaos is our gospel.

11...dxe4

> *Question:* Okay, now that White committed to queenside castling, I don't care if I lose the isolani. How about 11...d4?

Answer: Timing is everything in chess. And this time offering the isolani looks fine for Black after 12 ♘b3 ♗e6 13 ♔b1 ♖c8 14 ♘h3 a5 15 ♘f4 ♗g8 16 cxd4 cxd4 17 ♕d2 ♗b4 18 ♕xd4 ♗xb3 19 axb3 ♕c7 with reasonable compensation for the sac'ed pawn.

12 ♘c4

The knight's erratic swayings are designed to confuse. This looks more accurate than 12 ♘xe4 ♕a5 13 ♔b1 ♗e6 when Black holds a mild initiative.

12...♘d3+ 13 ♗xd3 exd3 14 ♖xd3 ♕e8 15 ♘e3

Covering against ...♗f5.

15...♕f7 16 c4!

Now follows a pitched battle for rights to d5.

16...b5!

The ominous sounds of an approaching attacker's echo in the distance.

17 ♘e2! bxc4 18 ♕xc4 ♗e6

This looks quite bad for White, but everything is under control as long as he controls the d5-square.

19 ♘d5

Played with a cheery optimism for one in a possibly inferior position. If the e6-bishop is the superhero, then White's d5-knight is the counterpart evil genius. A plan like this jars those of us (including your writer) with strategically orderly minds. Normally when one side is forced to self-pin, it is a key indicator that all may not be well. White, having been pushed around for so long, decides that silence on the matter is unendurable, and so takes the nuclear option and embraces a treacherous path. He manages to juggle simultaneous defensive issues, so far keeping each one at bay.

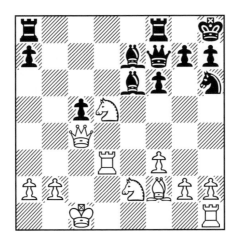

19...♖fd8

19...♗d6! looks better, since the bishop may later play to e5 and chop the back-up knight on c3: 20 g4 ♛b7 21 ♖hd1 ♘f7 22 ♖b3 ♛c6 23 h3 and Black looks slightly better here.

20 ♖hd1

20 ♘ef4! is more accurate.

20...♖d7

After 20...♗d6 21 ♗g3 ♘f5 22 ♘ef4 ♘xg3 23 hxg3 ♗xf4+ 24 gxf4 ♖d7 25 ♛xc5 I like White. A pawn, even a devalued one, is a pawn.

21 ♖3d2 ♘f5?!

Missing the final opportunity for 21...♗d6!.

22 ♘ef4

Pointing out an uncomfortable truth: the light-squared pest is removed from e6 and now the advantage swings to White who begins to take over on that colour. Frustratingly for Black, d5 creaks under its burden yet fails to break.

22...♖ad8?!

This inaccuracy loses material. Black had to enter an inferior ending with 22...♗xd5 23 ♘xd5 ♗f8 24 ♘e3 ♘xe3 25 ♛xf7 ♖xf7 26 ♗xe3 when c5 presents an inviting target.

23 ♘xe6 ♛xe6

Exercise (combination alert): White exploited the geometry
to force the win of a pawn. How did he accomplish it?

Answer: Removal of a key defender/overload. White's queen rejects the menial role allotted
to her on c4 and demands a more prominent position on e4.
24 ♕e4!
Suddenly, Black's initiative freezes in mid-stride, as if the victim of an evil spell.
24...♕xe4
No choice in the matter. Black's queen leaves in disgrace, followed by the cold glares of
the townsfolk. Now Black loses material.
25 fxe4 ♘d4
Once again forced, since 25...♘h6?? is met with 26 ♘xe7 when Black cannot recapture.
26 ♗xd4 cxd4

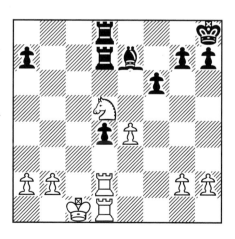

27 ♘xe7!?

Clearly, Belikov subscribes to the belief that the worst bishop is better than the best knight.

> **Question:** Why would White trade off his dominant knight for Black's bishop?

Answer: White traded perhaps for three reasons:

1. Black's bishop isn't such a bad piece and in endings, bishops tend to take on greater value than knights.

2. White's knight, although visually pleasing, really serves no function on d5 other than to impress, like a trophy won in a chess tournament.

3. Maybe White was concerned that Black could play for an ...f5 undermining plan.

Let's take a look and see what happens if White avoids the swap: 27 ♖xd4 ♗c5 28 ♖c4 ♗f8 29 ♔c2 f5 30 ♘c3 ♖xd1 31 ♘xd1 fxe4 32 ♖xe4 ♔g8. Obviously White retains good winning chances, but I'm not sure if he would be better off in a pure rook ending or this one, which risks Black's bishop outperforming the knight at a later stage. At the moment, the knight's competency or incapacity is not apparent when matched up with Black's bishop.

27...♖xe7 28 ♖xd4

Having been around dogs all my life, I have my finger on the pulse of their motivation and even consider myself a breed of honorary dog. Their universal philosophy: "What's mine is mine and I'm not sharing!". White wins a pawn and now in a spirit which would warm the greedy hearts of dogs worldwide, hangs on to it like a hard-won bone. When such turnarounds occur, there is a sense of overwhelming relief, the way a terminally ill patient discovers that her cancer inexplicably went into spontaneous remission.

28...♖c8+ 29 ♔d2

Endgame principle: centralize your king if you judge that there is no mating attack danger.

29...h5 30 ♖c1

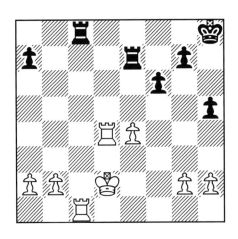

> *Exercise (critical decision):* Is Black better off with four rooks on the board or two? One path may lead to the draw, while the other looks very difficult to save. Make a decision: should Black swap rooks or not?

30...♖b8?!

Answer: Black may have been better off in a rook versus rook ending with 30...♖xc1! 31 ♔xc1 ♔g8 32 ♔d2 ♔f7 33 b4 ♖b7 34 ♔d3 ♔e6 35 a4 a6 36 ♖c4 h4 37 ♔c3 ♔e5 38 ♖c6 ♖a7 39 ♔c4 ♔xe4 40 a5 h3 41 gxh3 f5 42 ♖e6+ ♔f3 43 ♔c5 ♖a8 44 ♔b6 ♖b8+ 45 ♔xa6 ♖xb4 46 ♖b6 ♖a4 47 ♖b3+ ♔f2 48 ♖b7 f4 49 ♖xg7 f3 50 ♔b6 ♖b4+ 51 ♔c6 ♖a4 52 ♔b5 ♖a2 53 a6 ♔e2 54 a7 f2 55 ♖e7+ ♔d2 56 ♖f7 ♔e2 57 ♔b6 f1♕ 58 ♖xf1 ♔xf1 59 h4 ♖b2+ 60 ♔c6 ♖a2 61 ♔b7 ♖b2+ with a draw. Of course none of this is forced, but, intuitively, I feel that entering a single rook ending was Black's best drawing shot, since this path enables his king to help out on the queenside, unlike the game's continuation.

31 b3 ♔h7 32 ♖c5 ♔h6 33 ♔d3 ♖b6 34 ♖dd5 g6 35 ♖c4 g5 36 ♖dc5 ♖d6+ 37 ♖d5 ♖b6

Black can't afford to hand White a passer with 37...♖xd5+? 38 exd5.

38 h3 ♔g6 39 ♖cd4 ♖a6 40 a4

Ah, good, he heard me. White begins the process of advancing his majority.

40...♖b7 41 ♔c3 ♖c6+ 42 ♖c4 ♖e6 43 b4

At last, White begins to roll forward his queenside pawn majority. The fact that Black's king is unable to help out on the queenside is the decisive factor.

43...♖be7 44 ♔d3 h4 45 b5 a6

This makes matters worse. Why hand White a passer without making him work for it?

46 ♖b4

Endgame principle: post your rooks behind your passed pawn. Note the decisive factor: Black's king remains removed from the queenside sphere and may as well be the resident of another dimension.

46...♖b7 47 ♔d4 axb5 48 axb5 ♖be7

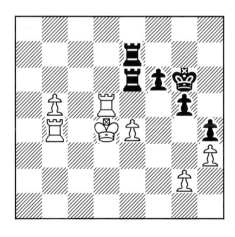

> ***Exercise (planning):*** How did White now make decisive progress?

Answer: Push the passer. The e4-pawn is meaningless since White is miles ahead in the queening race, which in reality is no race at all.

49 b6! ♖xe4+ 50 ♔c5 ♖e2 51 b7 ♖c2+ 52 ♔d6 1-0

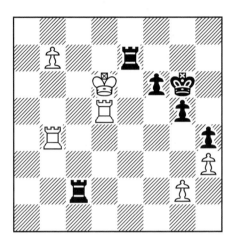

> ***Question:*** Did Black resign prematurely? After all
> he will be up two pawns which threaten to queen.

Answer: The extra rook easily beats the pawns, like this: 52...♖xb7 53 ♖xb7 ♖xg2 54 ♖d3 f5 55 ♖b6! (Black's king hears the muffled voices of conspirators all around him, since he virtually advertises his presence to the surrounding attackers) 55...g4 56 hxg4 fxg4 57 ♖d5! (White's rooks decide to perform a duet, serenading Black's king) 57...♔f7 (57...h3 58 ♔c7+ forces mate in two moves) 58 ♖f5+ ♔g7 59 ♔e6 (threat: ♖f7+ followed by mate next move) 59...♖e2+ 60 ♖e5 ♖xe5+ 61 ♔xe5 g3 62 ♖b4 and wins.

Summary: 4...♘c6 is an attractive option for Black. The best our side has may be equality.

Game 48
S.Drazic-N.Doric
Mogliano Veneto 2000

1 d4 d5 2 ♗g5

We continue to embrace a line in defiance of theoretical disapproval.

2...f6 3 ♗h4 ♘h6 4 f3 ♘f5

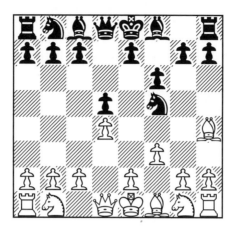

This move may be the worst of Black's fourth-move options.

Question: Why? It looks logical since it gains a tempo on White's bishop.

Answer: Does it? White's bishop wants to roost on f2 anyway. Also, e4 and g4 are in the air, so it may be White, not Black, who actually gains time.

5 ♗f2 e6

Better is 5...e5 6 dxe5 fxe5 7 e4 dxe4 8 ♕xd8+ ♔xd8 9 fxe4 ♘d4 10 ♗d3 when White may have a microbe of an edge due to his superior development in the ending, C.Depasquale-L.Jackson, Auckland 2010.

6 e4 ♘d6 7 ♘c3 c6 8 ♗d3 b6

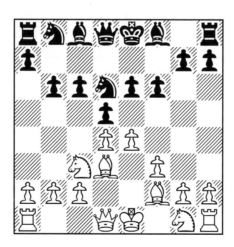

Question: Didn't we already look at this position in Chapter Two?

Answer: Not quite. The structure is similar, with two differences, both in our favour:

1. In this version we induced ...f6, which in turn weakens e6.

2. In this version, White's bishop sits on f2, supporting d4, and is a superior square to f4, as seen in Chapter Two, where the bishop tends to get in the way.

9 ♘ge2 ♗a6?

Sometimes in life we despise someone and then when they leave our lives we realize we desperately needed them. Black allows himself to get distracted with preoccupations, when he should strive to get his house in order.

> **Question:** Why would you punish this natural French Defence move, where Black rids himself of his bad bishop, with a question mark?

Answer: This is not a French, since Black tossed in the now highly undesirable ...f6, which weakens e6. Black actually needs the theoretically bad bishop to defend the tender square. While Black fights a cosmetic battle on the queenside, the real enemy continues to gather power and resources in the direction of e6.

10 ♘f4

The most difficult affair to conceal in a war is troop movements. The knight glares at e6 with ill-concealed contempt.

10...♔f7 11 0-0 ♗e7 12 ♖e1 ♗xd3

If 12...g5 13 ♘h5 ♕d7 14 ♕e2 ♗xd3 15 ♕xd3 and Black's position is too loose to survive.

13 ♕xd3 ♘d7

After 13...g5 14 exd5! gxf4 15 ♖xe6 cxd5 16 ♖ae1 ♗f8 17 ♘xd5 ♘d7 18 ♘xf4 White threatens both ♕b3, and also ♖xd6 followed by ♕b3+ and a then a knight fork on e6.

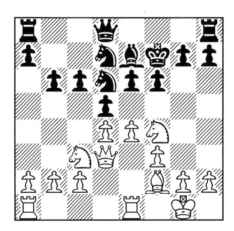

> **Exercise (combination alert):** A creeping sense of chill apprehension envelops the area around Black's king and long disuse renders the defenders barely operational. Find White's crushing breakthrough.

Answer: Attraction/double attack/demolition of king's structure.

14 ♘xe6!

To the king's consternation, this shot sends a jarring note into his formally tranquil world.

14...♔xe6

Obviously the king resents the intrusion into his personal space. This is a little like a man who marries a woman he doesn't love, solely for her money, and then discovers she is broke. It's too late to turn back now, with belated expressions of remorse for an irrevocably made past decision. I bet at this point Black very much missed his light-squared bishop.

15 exd5+ ♔f7 16 dxc6 ♘b8

Possible too was 16...♘f8 17 ♘d5 ♘c8 18 ♕b3 ♔g6 19 ♘f4+ ♔h6 20 ♕f7 (threatening mate on the move) 20...g6.

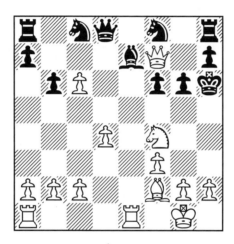

> *Exercise (combination alert):* Black's king swirls around like a
> storm-driven ship. How do we track him down in his hiding place?

Answer: Attraction. It becomes apparent that the knight/queen attacking pair is the true power behind the throne. 21 ♘h5!! (threat: ♕g7+) 21...♔xh5 (do you think it's possible that just a touch of anxiety weighs upon the black king's mind?) 22 ♕g7! entering g7, merely an annex to Black's king, forces mate. Principle: in a king hunt, don't chase him. Instead, encircle and cut off the flight squares.

17 c7!

The pawn's summons are commands, not to be tossed off lightly. Moves like this tend to hand our sense of propriety a bit of a jolt. The deadly point of the combination: the c-pawn lures Black's queen to a tactically unfavourable square.

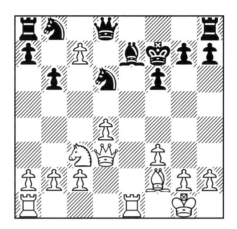

17...♕xc7

When we arrive at hopelessness, we intuitively realize that we can't think our way out of our troubles. So our only recourse is to embrace the irrational. Clearly, emotions inflame past the point of fearing consequences. 17...♕d7 18 cxb8R (who among us doesn't crave the sweet bliss of underpromotion?) 18...♖axb8 leaves Black two pawns down, and hopelessly busted.

18 ♘d5 ♕c4 19 ♖xe7+ ♔f8 20 ♕xc4 ♘xc4 21 ♖c7 ♘d6

21...♘xb2?? 22 ♖c8+ pops the h8-rook.

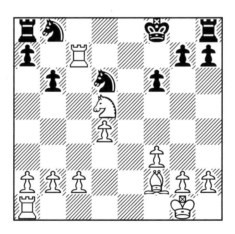

> *Exercise (combination alert):* White to play and win material:

Answer: Removal of a key defender.

22 ♗g3 1-0

22 ♗g3 ♘e8 23 ♖c8 ♔f7 24 ♗xb8 wins a piece.

Summary: 4...♘f5 may be Black's weakest fourth-move option.

Chapter Eight
The Pseudo-Tromp: Second Move Alternatives

1 d4 d5 2 ♗g5

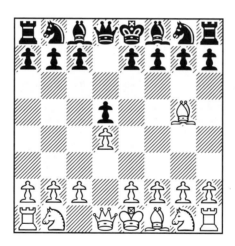

We take a look at some of Black's lesser played second-move options, just in case some of our opponents, unwilling to pit their feeble theoretical wiles against ours (yes, we Trompers are that cocky within our realm of expertise), decide to get sneaky and throw us off the main lines. In this chapter, we deal with opponents who wish to steer clear of Trompowsky theory and insist on some other opening. The trouble is they never quite make it to their intended line, because we invariably contaminate the position with Tromp propaganda, within other systems. On our second move, once again we proudly fly our regimental colours.

It's no easy task to collect one's wits in a position with such a staggering array of off-beat choices. After the second-move main lines, the position sub-divides further:

a) With 2...♞d7 Black seeks to remain within Queen's Gambit Declined lines. Instead, we force our opponents into a slightly favourable (for us, of course) Exchange Slav, where Black's knight doesn't really belong on d7.

b) 2...♝f5. Black probably intends a Slav-like position, but we make life uncomfortable after 3 c4!, intending ♛b3, going after b7.

c) 2...c5. Our opponent is probably one of those initiative-first QGD Tarrasch players, who toss in a quick ...c5 to all double queen's pawn games. We surprise him or her with 3 e4!?, entering an Albin Countergambit a full move over normal, which most certainly removes our opponents from their intended game plan.

d) 2...g6 sees Black insist on a Grünfeld, but our move order won't allow a real Grünfeld after 3 c4, which retains a Tromp twinge, despite Black's efforts to avoid it.

e) With 2...f5 Black plays in Stonewall Dutch style. We meet it with a Veresov, with 3 ♞c3!, or 3 e3! intending 4 c4.

Game 49
J.Hodgson-A.Del Mundo
World Open, Philadelphia 2000

1 d4 d5 2 ♝g5 ♞d7

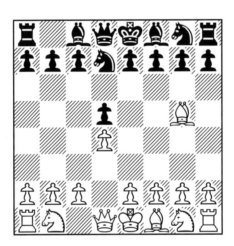

One of Black's most popular second-move responses in the Pseudo-Tromp.

Question: What is the point of 2...♞d7?

Answer: Black wants to avoid the 2...♞f6 3 ♝xf6 line. So he or she precedes the idea with ...♞d7, intending ...♞gf6 and ...e6, essentially circumventing Trompowsky theory and forcing the game into normal Queen's Gambit Declined waters.

Answer: Yes and no. We can't quite force a true Trompowsky position. However, we can perhaps trick Black into a slightly inferior version of an Exchange Slav, with our next move. **3 c4!**

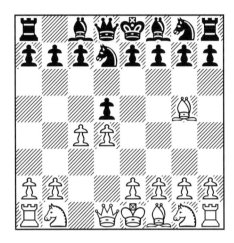

Answer: Normally in the Exchange Slav, Black's b8-knight is developed to the superior c6-square. In this instance, we trick Black into a premature d7 version, which isn't the end of the world, but also keep in mind that most 2...♘d7 players seek to reach QGD positions, not Slav ones. So this is an added bonus for our side as well.
3...c6

Okay, let's forget about the QGD. Black abandons his original intention at its threshold and grudgingly enters Slav territory.

Answer: Black did manage to avoid Slav, but I question the wisdom of the 'free' ...h6 and ...g5, which provides us tempting prying targets later on.

Black can also go for a Queen's Gambit Accepted-style game (albeit a lousy version for him) with 3...dxc4 4 e4 ♘gf6 5 ♘c3 ♘b6 6 ♘f3 c6 7 a4 a5 8 ♗e2 g6 9 b3! cxb3 10 ♕xb3 (White gets massive compensation for one measly pawn sac'ed, since the b6-knight and b7, behind it, are both wobbly) 10...♗e6 11 d5! cxd5 12 exd5 ♗f5 (if 12...♗xd5?? 13 ♗b5+

♗c6 and now the double attack 14 ♘e5! is crushing) 13 0-0 ♗g7 14 d6! (in such positions Hodgson is completely unrepentant, continuing to spend, as if tapping into a bottomless supply of investment funds) 14...♘bd7?! (Black had to try 14...♕xd6 15 ♘b5 ♕b8 16 ♘fd4 0-0 17 ♘xf5 gxf5 18 ♗f3, which gives White a monstrous initiative, for the two pawns invested) 15 dxe7 ♕xe7 16 ♘d5 ♕c5 17 ♘xf6+ ♗xf6 18 ♗xf6 ♘xf6 19 ♗b5+ ♔f8 20 ♘g5 ♘d5 21 ♗c4 ♖d8 22 ♖fd1 ♗e6 23 ♕b2 ♔g8 24 ♗xd5 ♖xd5 25 ♘e4 ♕b4, J.Hodgson-S.Videki, Kecskemet 1988. White wins a full rook after 26 ♘f6+.

4 cxd5 cxd5 5 ♘c3 ♘gf6

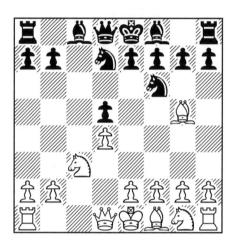

6 e3

After 6 ♖c1 a6 7 e3 ♕a5 8 ♗d3 e6 9 ♘ge2 ♗e7 10 0-0 0-0 11 f3 ♖e8 12 ♗b1 ♘f8 13 ♗h4 ♗d7 14 ♗g3 ♗c6 15 ♘f4 ♖ac8 16 ♘d3 ♗b5!? 17 ♘xb5 (I realize this is his bad bishop, but it still hands White the bishop-pair) 17...♕xb5 18 ♕d2 I admit this is nothing like a Hodgson game, but your dullard writer did manage to attain a slight but enduring edge due to the bishop-pair, and the sense of mild oppression is difficult for Black to lift, C.Lakdawala-P.Graves San Diego (rapid) 2010.

6...♘e4!?

Black isn't satisfied with defending a slightly inferior Exchange Slav, and decides to muck it up and go with the more aggressive ...♘e4 version. 6...e6 7 ♗d3 ♗e7 8 ♖c1 a6 9 ♘f3 0-0 10 0-0 is the safer, if more tedious method of playing the position, I.Miladinovic-S.Medghoul, Cap d'Agde 2003.

7 ♗f4!?

This looks better than 7 ♘xe4 dxe4 8 ♕d2 ♘b6 9 ♘e2 f6 10 ♗h4 e5 11 ♘c3 where Black looks okay.

7...♘df6

After 7...♘xc3 8 bxc3 g6 9 ♕b3 ♕a5 10 ♘f3 ♗g7 11 ♗d3 0-0 12 0-0 ♘b6 13 ♖fc1 ♗e6 14 a4 Black has nothing to do but wait for White to try and make progress on the queenside.

8 ♗d3 e6 9 ♘f3

A more strategically-minded player would perhaps pick the flexible 9 ♘ge2.

9...♗d6 10 ♘e5

More ambitious than 10 ♗xd6 which gives Black a bad remaining bishop.

10...0-0 11 0-0 a6 12 ♖c1 ♘xc3

Otherwise an eventual f3 forces the trade.

13 ♖xc3 ♕e7?

Black should try 13...♘e4 14 ♗xe4 dxe4 15 ♕c2 f6 16 ♘c4 ♗xf4 17 exf4 with a nagging strategic edge to White. Here Black can't play 17...♕xd4? 18 ♖d1 ♕a7 19 ♘d6, since he is busted and unable to develop: for example, 19...♗d7? 20 ♖c7 ♗c6 21 ♕b3 is decisive.

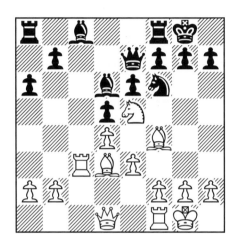

> **Exercise (planning):** We can't afford to squander a precious opportunity.
> Come up with a clear plan which proves Black's last move was a strategic error.

14 ♗g5!

Answer: The pin issues a challenge and forces Black into unpleasant structural concessions. White threatens ♘g4 and ♕f3, so Black's next two painful moves are forced.

14...h6 15 ♗h4 g5 16 ♗g3 ♗d7 17 f4

The human move. Also strong is the counterintuitive 17 ♘xd7! ♘xd7 (Black is also in desperate trouble after 17...♕xd7 18 f4) 18 ♗xd6 ♕xd6 19 f4!. The correct timing. After the coming ♕h5, Black's king will never feel secure in such proximity to White's queen.

17...♗b5

The bishop, atrophied from disuse, takes an initial, painful step. Black logically rids himself of one of White's best attackers, yet it fails to slow White down.

18 fxg5 hxg5 19 ♗xb5 axb5

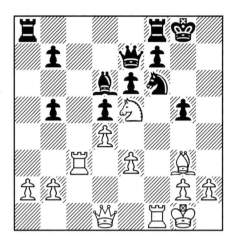

> **Exercise (combination alert):** Continue White's attack:

Answer: Elimination of a key defender/fork. The defensive foundation splinters and collapses.

20 ♖xf6!

White concentrates his fire on the defenders of the dark squares around Black's king.

20...♕xf6 21 ♘d7 ♕f5

Others:

a) 21...♕e7 22 ♗xd6 ♕xd6 (22...♕xd7 transposes to 'b') 23 ♕h5, and if 23...♕xd7 24 ♕xg5+ ♔h7 25 e4 forcing mate.

b) 21...♕d8 22 ♗xd6 ♕xd7 23 ♕h5! ♖fc8 24 ♕xg5+ ♔h7 25 ♕h5+ ♔g7 26 ♗c5! and the threat of e4 followed by ♖g3+ is decisive.

22 ♗xd6

Bishop and knight weave themselves inextricably, deep within the position's fabric, so that dislodging both becomes a near-impossibility for Black.

22...♖fd8

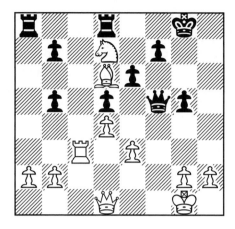

Answer: 23 e4!

Clearance. White's last move allows the decisive participation of his rook.

23...dxe4

23...♕g6 24 ♘e5 is also crushing.

24 ♖c5!

The moody lateral/horizontal menace roams at large and decides to enter from the other angle.

24...♕g6 25 ♘e5 ♕g7

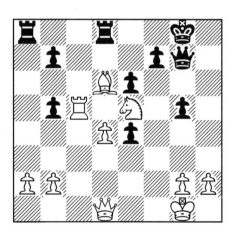

Answer: Demolition of the king's cover. The most ineffective – one could safely say moronic – war strategy of all time is to attack in human waves, World War I style, where hundreds of soldiers were inexplicably ordered to charge an enemy's single-man machine-gun nest. 300 lives would be sacrificed to take out a single enemy soldier and gain 100 yards. Yet here we see Hodgson do just that and all his human-wave attackers magically survive to live happily to a ripe old age. Moral: there are exceptions to everything.

26 ♘xf7! 1-0

If I ever decide to bargain away my soul, the very first clause I would insist upon in my contract with the devil is Hodgson-like tactical ability and attacking instincts, so that I too produce games like this one. It's remarkable how often Hodgson rains down a fusillade of shots upon his often bewildered opponents, so that games like this feel almost routine.

There is no defence to be found. For example:

a) 26...♖xd6 27 ♖xg5.

b) 26...♔xf7 27 ♖c7+.

c) 26...♕xf7 27 ♖xg5+ ♔h7 28 ♕g4! forces mate. The queen smiles as beatifically as her acting skills can muster.

Summary: 2...♘d7 allows us to force a slightly favourable Exchange Slav, since Black's knight may be misplaced on d7.

Game 50
A.Chernin-A.Kundin
Biel 1997

1 d4 d5 2 ♗g5 ♗f5

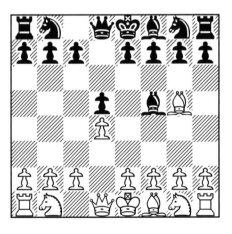

Question: Shouldn't this move be an equalizer, since it will lead to Slav-like positions we looked at last chapter?

Answer: I'm not so sure about either claim. Black may experience difficulties defending b7. Also, the fact that Black can't easily play ...e6, still plagues him, similar to Black's difficulties last game.

3 c4!

Just like last game, this combative move places maximum pressure on Black.

3...c6

Question: Can Black escape troubles with the e7 pin if he plays 3...♗xb1 4 ♖xb1 e6?

Answer: A clever developing idea, yet White retains an edge if he avoids simplification with the unplayed 5 ♗d2!, hanging on to the bishop-pair.

Question: How does the Queen's Gambit Accepted version work out for Black?

Answer: Not well. White gets a clear advantage after 3...dxc4 4 ♘c3 ♘f6 5 f3! (White forces e4, with tempo) 5...h6 6 ♗h4 g5 7 ♗f2 ♗g7 8 e4 ♗g6 9 ♗xc4. White dominates the centre and also induced kingside pawn weakness in Black's camp, L.Nedimovic-S.Stanic, Postojna 2009.

4 ♘c3

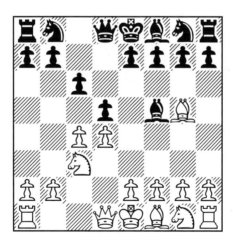

Threat: cxd5, followed by ♕b3, which double attacks d5 and b7.

4...h6

Black decides he has had enough of the annoying pin and goes for the aggressive but potentially weakening ...h6 and ...g5. Alternatives:

a) 4...♘f6 5 ♗xf6 gxf6 6 ♕b3 (6 e3 leads to a position we discussed in Chapter Four) 6...dxc4 7 ♕xb7 ♕b6 8 ♕xb6 axb6 9 e4 ♗d7 10 ♗xc4 b5 11 ♗b3 ♘a6 was B.Abe-M.Grah, Slovenia 2010. Maybe this is stylistic bias, but I prefer White's strong centre over Black's bishop-pair after 12 ♘ge2.

b) 4...f6 5 ♗f4 (played in every game in the database, but *Houdini* prefers 5 ♗d2! e5 6 ♘f3 e4 7 ♘g1, with a strange-looking reversed Advanced French structure where I prefer White's game), and at this point, Black can play the untried 5...e5!? 6 e4!? dxe4 7 dxe5 ♘d7 8 ♘ge2 fxe5 9 ♗e3 ♘c5 10 ♘g3 ♗g6 11 ♗e2 ♘d3+ 12 ♔f1 ♘f6 13 h4. Indeed, here I don't trust White's position and would go for the 5 ♗d2! *Houdini* suggestion.

c) 4...dxc4. This move never seems to work out well for Black if the bishop is already posted on f5, since it entails tempo loss after 5 e4.

d) With 4...♕b6 Black pre-empts ♕b3 by tossing in a quick ...♕b6. At this point White can try 5 cxd5 ♕xb2 6 ♕c1 ♕xc1+ 7 ♖xc1 ♘f6 8 ♗xf6 exf6 9 e4. Now if 9...♗g6?! (the depressing 9...♗c8 may actually be Black's best move) 10 f4! f5 11 e5 ♗b4 12 ♔f2 ♘d7 13 d6 with a clear structural plus for White in the form of the entrenched and passed d6-pawn.

5 ♗h4 g5 6 ♗g3 e6

After 6...♘f6 7 e3 ♗g7 8 ♕b3 ♕b6 9 c5 ♕xb3 10 axb3 ♘bd7 11 b4 White stands better since b5 is coming, J.Bonin-S.Foisor, U.S. Online League 2011.

7 ♕b3

The queen is accustomed to applause when she enters a room.

7...♕b6 8 c5!

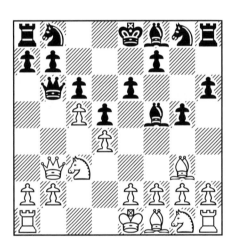

Thematic. The ending is slightly in White's favour.

8...♕xb3 9 axb3

I accumulated a lot of London System experience in such structures and feel White stands slightly better, since the coming b4-b5 is a serious problem for Black.

9...♘d7 10 b4

Now b5 is in the air. White also stands better after 10 e3 ♗g7 11 b4 e5 12 ♘f3.

10...e5!?

Played on principle, and when I figure out just what principle it is, I will let you know. Black displays a deep seated antipathy to dull defence and lashes out. Initiative lust is a kind of temporary madness which at times afflicts us all. Its nature is to hop in the car and drive off, without taking the destination's address, or directions of how to get there. This move, which fails to act as a restorative, smacks of over-optimism and I'm not sure it is a necessary adjunct. Black may well be exaggerating his difficulties and overreaching by establishing a central break, even if it costs him a pawn.

Black keeps disadvantage to a minimum with 10...♗g7 11 e3 ♘e7 12 ♘f3 ♗g4 13 h4 ♗xf3 14 gxf3 e5 (this looks like the correct timing) 15 dxe5 ♘xe5 16 f4!? gxh4 17 ♗xh4 ♘f3+ 18 ♔e2 ♘xh4 19 ♖xh4.

11 ♘f3

Cautious. Chernin avoids 11 dxe5 ♗g7 12 ♘f3 ♘e7 13 e3 0-0 when Black eventually regains the sacrificed pawn, but White may still retain an edge due to control over d4.

11...♗g7!?

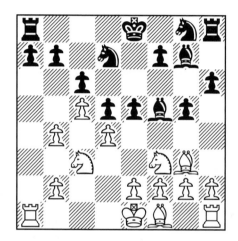

I insist! Black refuses the final chance for 11...exd4 12 ♘xd4.

12 ♘xe5 ♘xe5 13 ♗xe5 ♗xe5 14 dxe5 d4?!

White faces a payback-seeking, revenge-hungry wave of aggression. We soon discover its effects are merely temporary. He should settle for 14...♘e7 15 e3 ♘g6 16 ♘e2 ♘xe5 17 ♘d4 ♗d3 18 ♔d2 with just an edge for White.

15 ♘b1?!

In such positions of abstract manoeuvring, it's easy to allow our forces to go leaderless and rudderless. We begin to speculate: 'this may happen' or 'that may happen', all without really understanding what will really happen. The knight has eyes for d6, but it looks too positional and too slow for the needs of an open game. Better was 15 ♘d1! ♘e7 16 h4 g4 17 e3 0-0-0 18 ♖xa7 ♔b8 19 ♖a3 with an edge for White.

15...♘e7?!

A serious inaccuracy. White's unassuming knight soon takes on enormous authority once it reaches d6. Black foils White's intention with 15...♗xb1! 16 ♖xb1 ♘e7 17 g3 ♘g6 18 ♖d1 ♖d8 19 b5 cxb5 20 ♗g2 b6 21 cxb6 axb6 when he should be okay.

16 ♘d2

Threat: ♘c4 and ♘d6.

16...♘d5 17 ♘c4 0-0

17...♘xb4 18 ♘d6+ ♚d7 19 ♖a4 ♘c2+ 20 ♚d2 ♗g6 21 g3! looks rough for Black as well.

18 b5!

After 18 ♘d6 ♗e6 19 0-0-0 a5 20 b5 f6 21 ♖xd4 fxe5 22 ♖d2 ♖xf2 23 e4 ♖xd2 24 ♚xd2 ♘f6 25 ♘xb7 cxb5 26 ♗xb5 ♘xe4+ 27 ♚e3 ♘f6 28 ♘d6 Black stands worse, but may be able to hold the draw due to the reduced material count on the board.

18...♘b4 19 ♚d2

No more knight fork. White's king is surprisingly safe in his new home.

19...cxb5

If Black chips away at the central bind and activates with 19...f6 20 h4 cxb5 21 ♘d6 fxe5 22 hxg5 hxg5 23 g4! ♗h7 24 ♗g2 ♖xf2 25 ♗xb7 ♖af8 26 ♖xa7 ♗d3 27 ♖e1 even here *Houdini* claims he is hard pressed to hold the game, since White's passed c-pawn threatens to surge forward.

20 ♘d6

White's knight dominates, attacking b5 and b7, and also keeping Black rooks away from c8 and e8. It becomes obvious that Black's intended rebellion ebbed quickly.

20...♗g6?

Black had to try 20...♗e6.

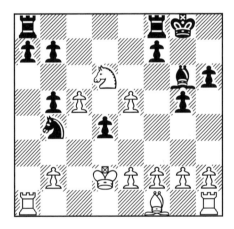

> *Exercise (planning):* White is up on positional trumps, but lags in development. Find a crucial consolidating idea which initiates a Draino-like unclogging effect.

Answer: 21 g3!

Consolidation. Order begins to emerge from disorder:

1. White prepares to back up e5 with f4.

2. f5 may follow, smothering Black's disconsolate bishop.

3. The coming ♗g2 completes development, while taking aim at b7, c6 and d5.

White's newly freed forces break out like a rash on Black's position, which morphs into a grey study of despair, a character from a Dostoyevsky novel, who finally gets around to hanging himself after 899 pages of musing life's suffering. And speaking of suffering, I played GM Alex Chernin twice and can tell you from painful experience that he is a scary strong strategist. I got strategically squeezed in the first game and held a draw by the narrowest of margins after six miserably exhausting hours of defence in the second.

21...♘c6 22 f4 a6 23 ♗g2 ♖ab8?!

White's pressure proves to be overwhelming. The bottom drops out of the market and Black's stock plummets. His last move drops pawns, but also hopeless was 23...♖a7 24 ♗xc6 bxc6 25 f5! ♗h7 26 g4 a5 27 h4 f6 28 e6 a4 29 hxg5 hxg5 30 ♔d3.

24 ♗xc6 bxc6 25 f5 1-0

The f-pawn puts the question to the bishop, who at this stage regards the prying, the way Yoko likes being asked: "So why do you think the Beatles broke up?" After 25 f5 ♗h7 26 ♖xa6 Black's bishop is entombed and c6 hangs as well.

Summary: I don't believe 2...♗f5 equalizes, since Black experiences trouble defending both b7 and d5 after 3 c4!. In fact, Black's second move may actually deserve a '?!' mark.

Game 51
J.Hodgson-G.Roeder
Bad Wörishofen 1995

---

1 d4 d5 2 ♗g5

The positions we reach are similar to this one:

a) 2 ♗f4 c5 3 e4!? dxe4 4 d5.

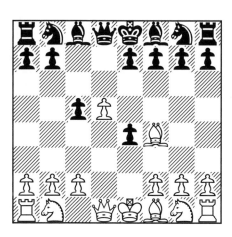

This position is covered in *Play the London System* (your best bet is to immediately order this excellent book, recognized by many to impart the wisdom of the ages). White gets an Albin Countergambit with the free move ♗f4 as a bonus. The only difference between this line and the Tromp version is that in the Tromp, our bishop is posted on g5, rather than f4.

Here is an example of a high-level Albin Countergambit outing: 2 c4 e5 3 dxe5 d4 4 ♘f3
♘c6 5 ♘bd2 ♘ge7 6 a3 ♗e6 7 g3 ♕d7 8 ♗g2 ♗h3 9 0-0 ♗xg2 10 ♔xg2 0-0-0 11 b4 ♘g6 12
♗b2 h5 13 b5 ♘cxe5 14 ♗xd4 ♘xf3 15 ♘xf3 h4 (Black has sufficient compensation for the
pawn; White now goes astray) 16 ♗xa7? (16 e3 ♕f5 is just unclear) 16...♕g4! 17 ♕c2 hxg3
18 fxg3 b6 19 a4 ♗d6 20 e3 (20 a5?? walks into 20...♖xh2+! forcing mate in three moves)
20...♖h3! 21 ♔h1 (or 21 ♕f2 ♗xg3! 22 hxg3 and now the beautiful deflection shot
22...♖d2!! is crushing; 23 ♘xd2 ♘h4+ 24 ♔g1 ♖xg3+ mates) 21...♖dh8 22 ♖f2 ♗xg3 23 ♖g1.

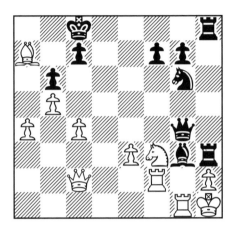

Exercise (combination alert): It's Black to play and force mate.

Answer: Removal of a key defender/queen sacrifice: 23...♕xf3+! 0-1, L.Van Wely-
A.Morozevich, Nice (blindfold) 2008.

2...c5

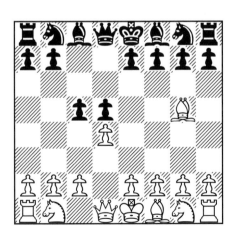

For many years I feared this line and never really liked the positions White got – until I saw the way Hodgson dealt with the move.

3 e4!?

If an addict is clean, we must always factor in the possibility of relapse. There is no way a player like Hodgson is going to turn down a gambit like this.

> *Question:* Oh, no! You certainly seem to be gambit-happy on behalf of your readers in this book?

Answer: The Trompowsky is a bit of an anachronism, harking back to the Romantic era, when largesse was the societal norm.

> *Question:* Is the gambit sound?

Answer: In the immortal words of Richard Nixon: "Let me make myself perfectly clear". The gambit is sound. White gets a Reversed Albin Countergambit, but with the free move ♗g5, since an Albin is normally played by Black, not White.

> *Question:* But doesn't the Albin have a shady reputation?

Answer: Perhaps so, but even the shadiest of gambits becomes appealing a full move up from normal. For this reason it's absolutely sound in our Tromp version. White can also chicken out with:

a) 3 e3 ♛b6 4 ♘c3 e6 5 ♛d2 ♘c6 6 ♘a4 ♛b4 7 ♛xb4 ♘xb4 8 0-0-0 ♘xa2+ 9 ♔b1 ♗d7 10 ♘xc5 ♗xc5 11 dxc5 ♘b4 12 ♗f4 ♘f6 13 f3 0-0 14 c3 ♘c6 15 e4 when I prefer White due to the bishop-pair and control over the dark squares, C.Lakdawala-R.Richard, San Diego 2004.

b) 3 ♘c3 (the Veresov route) 3...♘c6 4 ♘f3 ♘f6 5 e3 a6!? 6 ♗xf6 exf6 7 dxc5 ♗e6 8 ♘a4 ♛a5+ 9 c3 ♗xc5 10 b4!? (10 ♘xc5 was the safe route) 10...♗xb4 (after 10...♘xb4? 11 ♘xc5 ♛xc5 12 cxb4 Black doesn't have enough for the piece) 11 cxb4 ♛xb4+? (11...♘xb4 12 ♘c3 ♗f5 13 ♔d2! is completely unclear according to *Houdini*) 12 ♘d2 b5? 13 ♖c1 ♘e5 14 ♘c5 when Black didn't have enough initiative for the sac'ed piece and White consolidated, C.Lakdawala-G.Singh, San Diego (rapid) 2013.

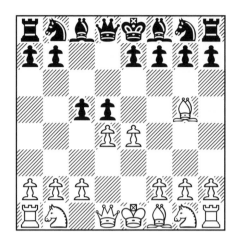

3...dxe4

Black bravely takes up the challenge. Alternatives:

a) After 3...h6 4 ♗h4 ♘c6 5 dxc5 d4 6 c3 g5 7 ♗g3 ♗g7 8 e5!? ♗f5 9 ♗b5 ♕d5 10 ♘f3 ♗xb1 11 ♕xb1 dxc3 12 0-0 ♕xc5 13 bxc3 White's massive development lead proved to be more dangerous than Black's extra material, L.Winants-H.Jonkman, Haarlem 1998.

b) 3...cxd4 4 ♕xd4 ♘c6 5 ♕xd5 ♕xd5 6 exd5 was E.Heyken-C.Schmidt, Travemuende 2002. Play might go 6...♘b4 7 ♘a3 f6 8 ♗d2 ♘xd5 9 ♘b5! a6 10 c4 e5 11 cxd5 axb5 12 ♗xb5+ when Black is left struggling.

c) 3...♘f6 4 ♗b5+ ♘c6 (White looks slightly better after 4...♗d7 5 ♗xd7+ ♘bxd7 6 exd5 ♘xd5 7 ♘f3) 5 ♗xf6 gxf6 was P.Pizarro-M.Grassi, Internet (blitz) 2003. It becomes a battle of development lead versus the bishop-pair after 6 dxc5 dxe4 7 ♕xd8+ ♔xd8 8 ♘c3 f5 9 0-0-0+ ♔c7 10 f3.

4 d5 h6 5 ♗f4

5 ♗h4 ♕b6 6 ♘a3 ♕xb2 (brave!) 7 ♘b5 ♕b4+ 8 c3 ♕a5 9 ♗g3 ♘a6 was E.Torre-P.Roca, Makati 2002. White gets full compensation for the material after 10 ♗c4.

5...♘f6 6 ♘c3 a6

6...e6?! is a known Albin trap. White can play 7 ♗b5+ ♗d7 8 dxe6 fxe6 ripping apart the integrity of Black's structure.

7 a4

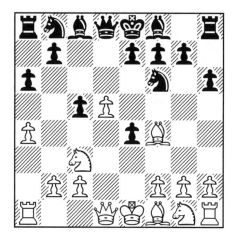

White shouldn't allow the undermining ...b5 and eventually ...b4.

7...e6!?

Black wants to unravel, but this move violates the principle: don't open the position when lagging in development.

> **Question:** What is Black's alternative developing scheme?

Answer: Something like this: 7...♘bd7 8 f3 g5 9 ♗g3 ♕a5 10 ♕d2 exf3 11 ♘xf3 followed by ...♗g7 and ...0-0.

8 ♗c4 ♗d6 9 ♘ge2!?

A more technical player like me would cop out with 9 ♗xd6 ♕xd6 10 dxe6 ♕xd1+ 11 ♖xd1 ♗xe6 12 ♗xe6 fxe6 13 ♘ge2 ♘c6 14 ♘g3. White regains the sac'ed pawn and remains with the slightly superior structure.

9...exd5 10 ♘xd5 ♗xf4 11 ♘exf4 0-0

More accurate was 11...♘c6 before castling.

12 ♘g6!

Hodgson finds a sneaky way to interrupt the natural narrative with a violation of the demilitarized zone.

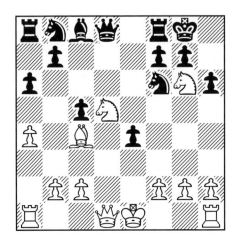

12...♘xd5!

Black retains his bearings and finds the best defence:

a) 12...fxg6 13 ♘b6+ ♔h7 14 ♕xd8 ♖xd8 15 ♘xa8 ♗f5 16 ♘b6 e3 17 fxe3 ♗xc2 18 ♖c1 ♗f5 19 ♗e2 and Black doesn't quite have enough for the exchange.

b) 12...♖e8 13 ♘de7+ ♔h7 14 ♗xf7 sees White regain the lost pawn and stand better.

13 ♘xf8 ♕a5+ 14 c3 ♘b6?

But this was not best:

a) 14...♘f4! 15 g3 (15 ♕d6 ♘xg2+ 16 ♔f1 ♗h3 17 ♖g1 ♘c6 18 ♕g3 ♘f4+ 19 ♔e1 ♘g2+ forces a draw after 20 ♔f1 ♘f4+) 15...♘d3+ 16 ♗xd3 exd3 17 ♕xd3 ♔xf8 18 ♕h7 ♘c6 19 ♕h8+ ♔e7 20 ♕xg7 is completely unclear.

b) 14...♘xc3 15 ♕d2 ♘c6 16 ♕xc3 ♕xc3+ 17 bxc3 ♔xf8 18 ♗d5 with advantage to White.

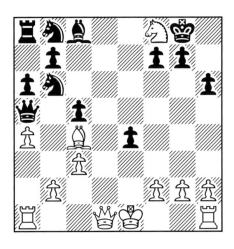

> ***Exercise (combination alert):*** Black's knight lands on b6 with
> that nauseating 'plop' sound a misdirected golf ball makes when
> ending up in the lake, rather than on the intended green.
> It allows White a surprising combination. What did Hodgson play?

Answer: Queen trap.

15 ♗xf7+!

The bishop flies into a rage, the way I do when a student dares to interrupt one of my fascinating, yet lengthy stories during a chess lesson, with a cavernous yawn.

15...♔xf7 16 ♕h5+ ♔xf8?

Black can reduce his pain a bit with 16...♔g8, but I can't give you the rest because I would give away the answer to the exercise.

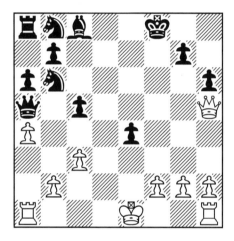

This capturing path leads to capitulation.

> ***Exercise (combination alert):*** Hodgson envisions an outcome, the way a
> sculptor views a shapeless chunk of marble. Black, in obvious shock,
> compounds the problem and does actually lose his queen. How?

Answer: Queen trap (and this time I really, really mean it!). White's queen despises her sister with the stored up malice accumulated over a lifetime. She conspires with her b-pawn to construct an escape proof prison.

17 b4!

After walking headlong into a trap, we endure the dazed incredulity which surrounds us in an uncomfortably soggy mist. This move is made all the more shocking, since it arrives in the silent watches of the night. Who would have guessed that Black's woes fall on the other side of the board?

17...♗g4 18 ♕e5! ♕xa4

A path to reconstruct the majestic ruins of Black's position isn't easy to plumb, but when expectations fall short and we are deprived of the real thing, the substitute always disappoints us. 18...♘8d7?? is met with 19 ♕d6+ followed by bxa5.

19 ♖xa4 ♘xa4

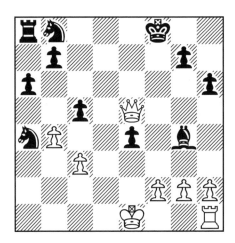

Exercise (combination alert): White to play and win more material.

Answer: Double attack.

20 ♕f4+ ♔g8 21 ♕xg4 ♘c6 22 ♕xe4

The aftermath leaves Black down a queen for only two knights.

22...♔h8

22...♘xc3?? drops another piece to 23 ♕c4+.

23 ♕e3!?

Hodgson prefers to sacrifice a pawn to secure his king. A greedier man, like your writer, would possibly play 23 ♕c2 ♖e8+.

23...cxb4 24 cxb4 ♘xb4 25 0-0 a5

Destination: a1. Black prays for a future headline, reading: 'Miracle occurs; 100 to 1 shot wins race by a nose'.

26 h3

First things first. No back-rank cheapos.

26...b6 27 ♖d1 ♘c5 28 ♖d6 a4

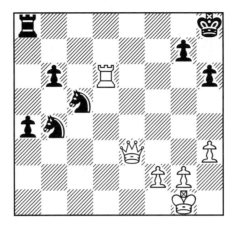

Exercise (combination alert): It feels as if White has no worlds left to conquer, but we would be mistaken in that assumption. Black hopes to make a fight of it with his passed a-pawn. However, White's counterattack is too swift. White has a tactic in the position which wins even more material.

Answer: Double attack. Both b4 and h6 are en prise.

29 ♕d4!

The sight of White's tyrannical queen is enough to send otherwise courageous black pieces diving for cover under furniture.

29...a3

Why not? Black lunges with his a-pawn, hoping for a promotion miracle. 29...♔h7 fails to 30 ♕xb4 a3 31 ♕b1+ ♔g8 32 ♖xb6 a2 33 ♖b8+ ♖xb8 34 ♕xb8+ ♔h7 35 ♕a7.

30 ♖xh6+ ♔g8

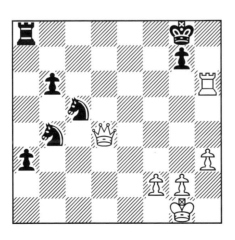

> ***Exercise (combination alert):*** One need not be a clairvoyant, a palm
> reader, or an adept in Tarot cards to foretell the result of the game
> anymore. How did White win material and halt the a3-passer for good?

Answer: Attraction.

31 ♕c4+! ♔f8

The king's clumsy attempt at escape painfully reminds us of the time Tiger's Wood's enraged ex-wife chased him down the driveway with a nine-iron, for cheating on her with 23 other blondes.

32 ♖h8+

Oops. Black's Zen master rook sits motionless on a8, contemplating the infinite.

32...♔e7 33 ♖xa8 1-0

Summary: 2...c5 can be met with 3 e4!?, which leads to a move-up Albin Countergambit.

Game 52
C.Lakdawala-R.Bruno
San Diego 2004

1 d4 d5 2 ♗g5 g6

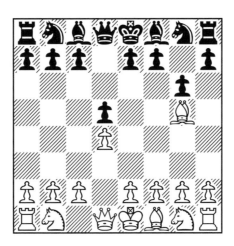

Black opts for a Grünfeld structure.

3 c4!

White's sharpest and also highest-scoring move:

a) 3 ♘f3 may lead to the Torre Attack versus Grünfeld structure.

b) 3 e3 ♗g7 4 c4 ♘f6 5 ♘c3 ♘e4 6 ♗f4!? (6 ♗h4 is normal) 6...♘xc3 7 bxc3 c5 8 cxd5 cxd4 9 ♗b5+ ♗d7 10 ♗xd7+ ♘xd7 11 cxd4 ♕a5+ 12 ♕d2 ♕xd5 13 ♘f3 saw Black emerge

with a satisfactory Grünfeld position, J.Hodgson-S.Fairbairn, Winnipeg 1997.
3...dxc4

Question: Why did Black give up the centre like this?

Answer: ...dxc4, at some point, is common in Grünfeld structures. Also, it may be Black's best move since alternatives tend to land Black in inferior versions. For example:

a) 3...c6 4 cxd5 ♕xd5 (4...cxd5 leads to an inferior Exchange Slav for Black, where the bishop, once fianchettoed, hits a pawn wall on d4) 5 ♘f3 ♗g7 6 ♘c3. White reached a favourable Grünfeld/Slav position since he gained a tempo on Black's queen, R.Hasangatin-V.Volodin, Cartak 2003.

b) 3...♗g7 4 cxd5 ♕xd5 (or 4...♘f6 5 ♗xf6 ♗xf6 6 ♘c3 c6 7 ♖c1! 0-0 8 dxc6 when I don't believe in Black's compensation, no matter which way he recaptures; here 7...cxd5 is met with 8 ♘xd5!) 5 ♘f3 ♘f6 6 ♘c3 and once again, White gains a move over normal Grünfeld lines, A.Schirbel-J.Newald, German League 1998.

4 e3

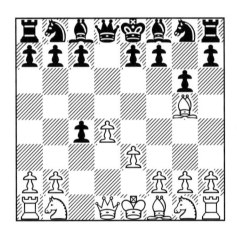

This is actually a pawn sacrifice on your very brave writer's part.
4...c5?!

Question: Why criticize when ...c5 is such a natural move in the Grünfeld?

Answer: ...c5 should only be played in a Grünfeld after Black catches up in development. In this instance Black violates the principles: don't open the game and create confrontation when behind in development.

Question: Can Black win a pawn with 4...c6, since it threatens the cheapo ...♕a5+, followed by ...♕xg5, and also ...b5, hanging on to the extra pawn?

Answer: Correct. However, White gets loads of play for the pawn after 5 ♘f3 b5 6 a4 when the undermining b3 is in the air. *Houdini* analysis runs: 6...♕a5+ (Black's greediest move) 7 ♘c3 b4 (Black gets into trouble after 7...♕b4?! 8 ♕d2 ♗b7 9 axb5 cxb5 10 b3!) 8 ♘e4 ♗f5 9 ♘ed2 c3 10 ♘c4 ♕d5 11 bxc3 bxc3 12 ♕b3 and White regains the pawn with a development lead.

5 ♗xc4 cxd4

A new move. Previously seen was 5...♗g7 6 ♕b3! ♕a5+ 7 ♘c3 and now Black backed down with 7...e6 in E.Meduna-G.Dizdar, Trencianske Teplice 1985, since 7...cxd4? is met with 8 ♗xf7+ ♔f8 9 ♗xg8 e6 (9...♖xg8?? loses to 10 ♗xe7+!) 10 exd4 ♕xg5 11 ♗xe6 when Black is in deep trouble.

6 ♕b3!

The god/queen breathes life into the c4-bishop's corpse reanimating a once dead creature into something very different from what it was before. White's development lead reaches alarming proportions. Neither player knows what the future holds, yet one senses that White is in a position to take advantage of any situation which arises.

6...♕a5+ 7 ♘d2

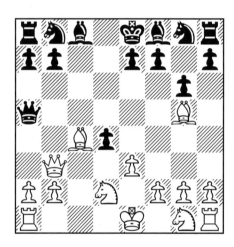

7...e6

This reminds me of a man who proposes to the love of his life, then getting cold feet, retracts the proposal and asks for his ring back.

> **Question:** Why the vacillation? Can't Black get away with 7...♕xg5?

Answer: Self-preservation is not vacillation. White gets a wicked attack after 8 ♗xf7+ ♔d8 9 ♘gf3 ♕c5 10 ♗xg8 dxe3 11 ♘e4! ♕a5+ 12 ♔e2 ♘c6 13 ♖ac1. I have grave doubts about the black king's ability to survive the coming wave.

8 ♘gf3 ♗b4?!

The bishop turns to his queen with the air of a man in secret pain. If you are going to suffer, then at least get paid for it. Now Black doesn't even have a single pawn to compensate for his sub-optimal position. He should enter 8...dxe3 9 ♗xe3 ♘f6 10 0-0 ♘c6 (10...♗g7 is met with 11 ♗b5+ ♗d7 12 ♘c4 ♕c7 13 ♖ac1) 11 ♗b5 ♗d7 12 ♘c4 ♕b4 13 ♕d3! ♘d5 14 ♖ad1 ♖d8 15 ♖fe1 ♗g7 16 a3 ♕e7 17 b4 (threat: ♗c5) 17...♘xe3 18 ♘d6+ ♔f8 19 ♕xe3 when White still enjoys huge compensation for the pawn, since Black's out-of-play pieces linger on the outskirts, away from all the fun.

9 exd4 h6 10 ♗f4 g5?

Unfaltering resolve to seize initiative when the position clearly doesn't call for such measures is synonymous with suicide. The charitable explanation for this move is exasperation; the unsympathetic one would be temporary madness. Why is it so easy to make the most awful moves with the most pure motives in our hearts?

Black finds it difficult to restrain his enthusiasm by banging out a move born from frustration. So he takes a wild gamble, and his king's health and welfare tremble in the balance. This attempt to seize the initiative is a form of hara-kiri and a violation of the principles: don't provoke the opponent or create confrontation when lagging in development.

It's important to remain calm in a rotten position. Black desperately attempts to unearth a resource to meet the emergency, which only makes matters much worse. Lashing out is exactly what the better developed side wants. Black demands a second chance at a good first impression. The move is based on the philosophy: if a novelist inserts a gun into the hero's hand in Chapter I, then it should be used in Chapter II. Now what was once hope of counterplay becomes a travesty of its former self.

11 ♗e5 ♖h7

11...f6 12 ♗xe6 is also hopeless for Black.

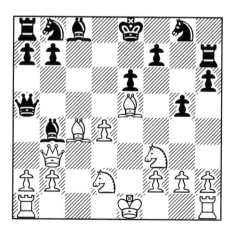

> **Exercise (combination alert):** White's initiative amplifies and his entire army is out and about, while Black's wanders about aimlessly, afflicted by a malaise of the spirit. So it isn't surprising that White has a forcing method to win material. Find one key idea and Black's resistance snaps like an old shoelace.

Answer: Trapped piece. Black's rook isn't as secure as he thinks.

12 ♗d3 g4

Here Black realized that 12...f5 is met with the crushing 13 ♗xf5!.

13 0-0-0 gxf3 14 ♘c4 ♕d5 15 ♗xh7

The bishop decides to trample on the knight's corpse for good measure. 15 ♕xb4 was also tempting and just as strong.

15...fxg2 16 ♖hg1

This isn't quite the tomorrow Black envisioned a few moves ago. He can resign, since g8 and b4 hang, which means White will soon be up a full rook for zippo compensation.

16...♘c6

Hey, I said: "He can resign!"

17 ♗xg8 ♔e7

The captain shoves and tramples his way past the women, children and elderly, in a race to be the first one in the lifeboat.

18 ♗h7 f6 19 ♗f4 ♗d7 20 ♗c2

Home sweet home.

20...♖c8 21 ♘e3 ♕h5

21...♕f3?? is met with 22 ♘f5+.

22 d5

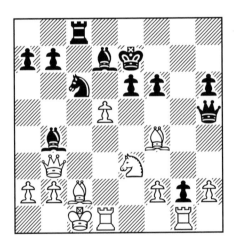

Prying open the centre.

22...exd5 23 ♘xd5+ ♔f7

The incoherent king attempts to impart a final message, drowned out by the sound of gurgling blood in his mouth. 23...♔f8 24 ♘xf6 isn't of much help.

24 ♘xb4+ 1-0

Summary: It looks like White gets a nice-looking Grünfeld after 2...g6 3 c4!.

Game 53
Y.Shulman-Wen Yang
Ningbo (rapid) 2013

1 d4 f5

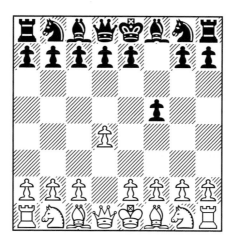

Question: Didn't you earlier advise us against playing the Trompowsky against a pure Dutch?

Answer: Correct. Our position would be reached from the move order 1...d5 2 ♗g5 f5. This move may well deserve a dubious mark, in view of 3 ♘c3, as we shall see. Also quite pleasant for White is simply to switch to Queen's Gambit style with 3 e3! ♘f6 4 ♗xf6 exf6 (this is similar to structures we looked at earlier in the book, except in this case, Black's ugly f6-pawn gets in the way of ...♘d7 and ...♘f6 ideas) 5 c4 ♗b4+ 6 ♘c3 0-0 7 ♕b3 ♗xc3+ 8 bxc3 dxc4 9 ♗xc4+ ♔h8 10 ♘e2 with advantage to White, who leads in development, controls the centre and owns the superior pawn structure, V.Moskalenko-L.Karlsson, Sitges 2009. White can even invert the move order with 3 c4! followed by 4 e3.
2 ♘c3!
   I think the Veresov/Tromp is one of the best ways to meet a pure Dutch move order. It's all explained in that excellent book, *A Ferocious Opening Repertoire*, a book many have called...oh, wait, never mind, I think I already used that line when describing one of my other books.
2...♘f6 3 ♗g5 d5

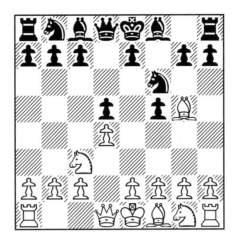

There we go, back to Tromp territory.

4 ♗xf6

The pure Tromp is over. In this position I normally play in Veresov style with 4 f3! c5 (Black probably shouldn't be opening the position when lagging in development; more accurate is 4...♘c6 5 ♕d2 e6 6 0-0-0 ♗b4 7 ♘h3) 5 e4 ♘c6 6 ♗b5 fxe4 7 fxe4 ♗g4 8 ♘ge2 cxd4?! (8...♘xe4 was necessary) 9 ♕xd4 dxe4 10 ♗xf6! gxf6 (10...exf6?? hangs a bishop to 11 ♕xe4+) 11 ♕xe4 ♗d7 12 0-0-0 (Black fell too far behind in development) 12...♕c8 13 ♔b1 a6 14 ♗a4 b5 15 ♗b3 ♖b8.

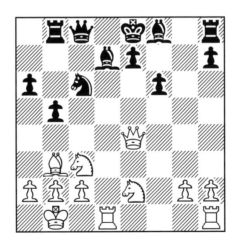

Exercise (combination alert): Continue White's attack.

Answer: Elimination of a key defender, which decimates Black's light squares: 16 ♖xd7! ♕xd7 17 ♖d1 ♕c7 18 ♕e6 (threatening mate on the move) 18...♘e5 (Black has no hope of surviving 18...♘d8 19 ♕g4 e6 20 ♗xe6) 19 ♘d5 1-0, C.Lakdawala-B.Baker, San Diego (rapid) 2007 This game is annotated in *A Ferocious Opening Repertoire*.

4...exf6 5 e3 ♗e6

After 5...c6 6 ♗d3 ♗e6 7 ♕f3 g6 8 ♘ge2 ♘d7 9 0-0-0 ♕c7 10 h3 0-0-0 11 g4 fxg4 12 hxg4 ♗e7 13 ♘f4 ♗f7 14 ♖h6 White exerts kingside pressure and, for now, Black's bishop-pair doesn't mean much, A.Grischuk-P.Svidler, Riga (rapid) 2013.

6 ♗d3 ♕d7 7 ♘ge2 ♘c6

Question: Why block his c-pawn?

Answer: This line is a slightly different pigment from earlier chapters with similar structures. The c6-development for the knight is actually Black's most common set-up in the position.

8 a3

Preventing ...♗b4, ...♘b4 and maybe thinking about b4.

8...g6

8...g5!? seems unwise, since White turned the structure rigid with 9 f4! ♗d6 10 ♕d2 h6 11 0-0 g4 12 ♖fc1 a6 13 ♘d1 ♘e7 14 b3 ♔f7 15 c4 c6 with advantage, since he can expand on the queenside, while the kingside remains closed to Black, E.Iturrizaga Bonelli-H.Nakamura, Istanbul Olympiad 2012.

9 0-0 ♘e7 10 b3!

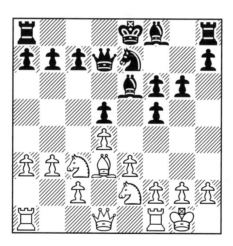

Question: White's last move almost looks like a random gesture. What is the intent?

Answer: Well, I wouldn't quite describe White's plan exactly as the dawning of the Age of Aquarius, but at least it's a start. White plans ♘a4 and c4, expanding on the queenside, similar to what we saw in the Catalan Tromp lines of Chapters Four and Six.

10...♗h6

Hoping to finagle ...f4 at some later date.

11 ♘a4 b6 12 c4

There we go.

12...c6

Black isn't so tempted to capture on c4 if White can recapture with his b-pawn, which in turn increases White's central control.

13 cxd5

Shulman looks for central counterplay but this looks premature. Instead, 13 c5 b5 14 ♘b2 a5 doesn't offer much for White, but 13 ♘ac3 before capturing on d5 looks correct.

13...♘xd5 14 ♘ac3 0-0

Black can also speculate with 14...♘xc3 15 ♘xc3 f4!? 16 exf4 0-0-0! (16...♗xf4? works out horribly for Black after 17 ♕f3 ♗g5 18 ♗b5! ♖c8 19 d5! with a winning position) 17 ♘e2 ♖he8. I think Black gets full compensation for the pawn, with his active pieces, bishop-pair, and the d4-target.

15 ♘xd5 cxd5?!

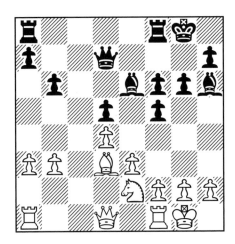

Up until now, each side managed to neutralize the other's strengths. After this decision, heavy defensive work lies ahead for Black, who must mend what is broken and tighten that which has grown slack. As I mentioned earlier in the book, this kind of isolani rarely works out well for Black, yet is commonly played – even by GMs.

> **Question:** Why did he deliberately hand himself an isolani?

Answer: Black wanted to avoid 15...♗xd5 16 ♗c4, which eliminates his bishop-pair, but by taking on an isolani, Black also gives himself a somewhat bad light-squared bishop.

16 ♕d2

I would play the immediate 16 ♗a6.

16...♖fe8

16...a5! does weaken b5, but prevents White's coming grip.

17 ♖fc1 ♗f8

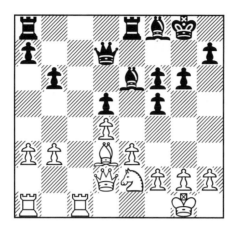

> *Exercise (planning):* One might feel as if the fruitless internecine battle of the queenside depletes resources without either player improving his position. This is just not the case. The d5-burden continues to impede Black's hoped for recovery. How would you continue as White?

Answer: Seize control over c8, and therefore the c-file.

18 ♗a6!

Ordeal by light squares. The bishop settles in with a proprietary air. White's last move offers him a clear field on the queenside.

18...♗d6 19 ♕d3 ♖f8 20 b4 ♖ad8 21 ♖c3 ♗b8 22 ♖ac1 ♗f7 23 ♖c6 ♕e7 24 g3 h5

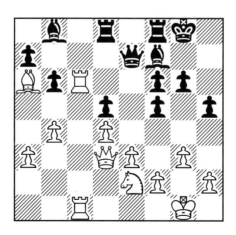

Exercise (planning): Shulman now came up with a simple yet
effective plan to better his position. What would you play here?

Answer: 25 ♖c8!

White probes the defensive barrier from another angle. Shulman essentially gives away
his control over the c-file. He realizes that with rooks off the board, d5 will be very difficult
to hold, since White can attack the pawn three times.

25...♔g7 26 ♖xd8 ♖xd8 27 ♖c8! ♖xc8 28 ♗xc8 ♕c7 29 ♕c3 ♕c4?

This attempted extenuation fails. So far, the defence has been tossed about like a sail-
boat in a squall, which hasn't yet capsized – until now. Black's last move calls into question
his ability to successfully defend. He puts up greater resistance by keeping queens on the
board, hoping to stir something up against White's king, with 29...♕e7 where the queen's
body may reside on e7, but her mind rests near g1, with obsessive thoughts of checkmate.

30 ♕xc4! dxc4 31 ♗a6!

The scheming bishop thinks to himself: "This isolated spot is perfect for a murder."
Shulman presses his argument against c4 with single minded devotion.

31...♔f8 32 ♔f1 h4 33 ♔e1 g5 34 ♔d2 ♔e7 35 f4!

Time to recite a catechism. Principle: if your opponent owns the bishop-pair, it is in your
best interest to force a rigid structure.

35...♗h5 36 ♘c3 ♗f7 37 ♘d1 1-0

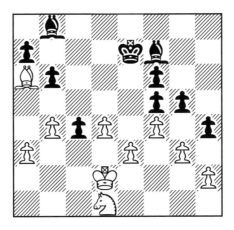

White's plan hangs upon a simple point: attack and win c4. It's very rare to see a decisive game between two GMs which is completely devoid of tactics. The Tromp can be a
technical opening as well.

Question: An empiricist would cringe at such a leap of faith.
I realize that for the c4-pawn, there is imminent doom, but
that's only one pawn. Isn't this a premature resignation?

Answer: It may have been a time loss. *Houdini* assesses at +0.48, only half a pawn. White's win isn't so easy. One example: 37...♗d5 38 ♔c3 ♔d6 39 ♗xc4 (nourishment is slowly absorbed into White's bloodstream) 39...♗f3 40 ♘b2 hxg3 (not 40...h3? 41 ♘d3 g4 42 ♘e1 ♗b7 43 ♗d3 ♗c8 44 ♘c2 ♔e6 45 d5+! ♔xd5 46 ♘d4 a5 47 ♘xf5 axb4+ 48 axb4 ♗d7 49 ♘h6! ♗d6 50 e4+ ♔c6 51 ♗e2 winning more pawns) 41 hxg3 ♗c7 42 b5 ♗b8 43 ♘d3 ♔d7 44 ♘b4 ♗d6 45 ♗d3 (Black is tied down to f5) 45...♔e6 46 a4 ♗b7 47 ♔c4 (threat: d5+, followed by ♗xf5) 47...♗xb4 48 ♔xb4 ♗f3 49 ♗c4+ ♔d6 50 ♗b3 ♗e4. From this point, I couldn't beat *Houdini*, who defended Black and always held the draw.

Summary: If Black plays 1 d4 d5 2 ♗g5 f5, just take the knight when it reaches f6, to reach positions of familiarity we examined in the earlier part of the book. However, White's best shot at an edge may lie in 4 f3, as mentioned in the notes, playing in pure Veresov fashion. If, instead, you want to keep it simple, then play 3 e3 and 4 c4, to achieve a good version of lines we looked at in Chapter Four.

Game 54
B.Finegold-J.Gonzales
World Open, Philadelphia 2001

Chess, like chickenpox, measles and mumps, is better caught in our early youth. Players who take up the game at a later age somehow miss the required wiring, the missing imprints to become top level players. I met kid-Ben Finegold at the 1983 U.S. Open and played a few blitz games with him. I realized that my then annoying kid-opponent (but a very kind adult in this present day and age) was destined to become a GM.

1 d4 ♘c6

Our move order usually runs: 1...d5 2 ♗g5 ♘c6.

2 ♗g5

Question: So it's okay to play Trompowsky on 1...♘c6?

Answer: Yes, the Tromp works out okay on 1...♘c6.

2...d5

Black plays the Reversed Veresov versus our Trompowsky. We cover 2...♘f6, the Two Knights Tango versus the Trompowsky, in the final chapter of the book.

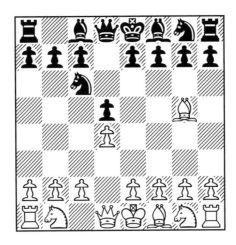

3 e3

Answer: By stalling the g1-knight's development, Finegold denies Black the standard Chigorin plan: ...♗g4 and eventually ...♗xf3. Your plan is also possible: 3 ♘f3 ♘f6 4 ♗xf6 gxf6 5 e3 ♗g4 6 ♗e2 e6 7 0-0 ♘e7 8 c4 c6 9 ♘c3.

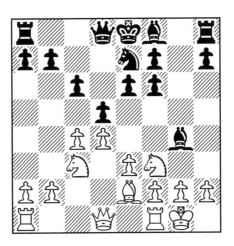

I prefer White's structure and extra space over Black's bishops, J.Ehlvest-J.Dubois, French League 1991.

Answer: Maybe we should, but I trust White's king safety, based on the principle: the side with less space shouldn't launch a direct attack upon the opponent's king. I think White should generate excellent central counterplay with a coming e4.

3...♗f5 4 ♘f3 f6

4...♘f6 5 ♗xf6 exf6 was A.Kartsev-J.Mundorf, Recklinghausen 2005. I would play 6 a3 intending c4 next.

5 ♗h4

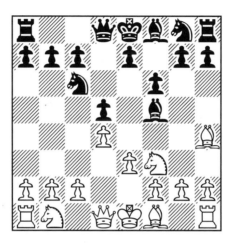

5...e6

> ***Question:*** Black's last move looks like he gave up on
> ...e5 too soon. What if he plays 5...♕d7 intending ...e5?

Answer: Your plan can be met with 6 a3 e5 7 ♗b5 e4 8 ♘fd2 ♘ge7 9 c4 with a reversed French situation which looks favourable for White, since his 'bad' French bishop is on the outside of his formation on h4.

6 a3 ♘ge7 7 c4 ♗g4

A new move. This represents a tempo loss for Black, yet the move is somewhat logical, since he intends ...♘f5 hunting down White's bishop. 7...♕d7 8 ♘c3 was played in J.Bellon Lopez-J.Furhoff, Stockholm 1993.

8 ♘c3 a6 9 cxd5

Turning it into a Queen's Gambit Declined Exchange structure, but with Black's knight on the awkward c6-square.

9...exd5 10 ♗d3 ♕d7 11 ♖c1 ♗f5?!

The bishop wavers in mid-air, not knowing in which direction to land. Black's resolve begins to stray from the original purpose – whatever it was. The third move with the same piece in the opening and a violation of principle. Black should settle for 11...♘f5 12 ♕c2 ♘xh4 13 ♘xh4 g6 14 h3 ♗e6 15 ♘a4 with an edge to White.

12 ♗g3 ♗g6!?

Move number four with the same piece in the opening. White's d3-bishop sighs toler-antly at his strange g6-brother, thinking: "I'm open minded of his unorthodox beliefs, but that pointy hat with moon and stars has got to go!" Clearly Black loses his sense of direc-tion in the trackless wild. Preferable was 12...g6 hoping to someday castle kingside.

13 0-0 ♘f5 14 ♗xf5!

Excellent judgement. Finegold realizes his dark-squared bishop contains more latent power than the light-squared model.

14...♗xf5 15 ♕b3!

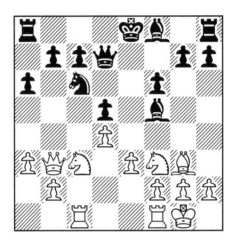

White requires a pretext to go to war, forcing Black to castle queenside, into an open c-file.

15...0-0-0

Black's unfortunate king transfers to flammable living quarters. He hopes to broker a peace to which his white counterparts take a dim view.

16 ♘a4 ♖e8

> **Question:** Black keeps goofing around. Since we are in an
> opposite-wings castling situation, why not go for 16...g5?

Answer: I have doubts about the feasibility of a direct race, since Black's earlier time-wasting manoeuvres ensure that White's attack comes first: for example, 17 ♖c3 h5 (threat: ...h4) 18 ♖fc1! (hey, I said "threat ...h4!"; to Black's king, the c-file persecutors feel like an invariant fixture, destined to intrude upon his peace of mind, forever and ever) 18...h4 19 ♘b6+! cxb6 20 ♕xb6 hxg3 21 ♖xc6+ bxc6 22 ♖xc6+ ♕xc6 23 ♕xc6+ ♔b8 24 ♕b6+ ♔c8 25 ♕xf6 and the final double attack wins.

17 ♘c5 ♗xc5 18 ♖xc5 ♖d8

Hi, I'm back again. 18...♗e6 19 ♖fc1 ♖e7 20 ♘e1 g5 21 ♘d3 h5 22 ♖xc6! bxc6 23 ♘c5 wins.

19 ♖fc1 ♖he8

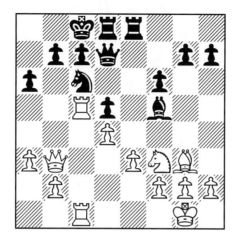

> **Exercise (planning):** Black's queenside is a stage crowded with hopeless actors in some amateur production, who continually botch timing, lines and their delivery. The black king's illness is permanent and incurable. Finegold came up with a powerful winning plan. How would you continue with White?

Answer: Load up on the c-file, and prepare b4, a4 and b5. Black can't do much about this, and his previously well-ordered life soon turns upside down.

20 ♕c3!

Threat: b4, a4 and b5. The ugly shape of White's intent is revealed. White's major pieces are the annoying downtown street corner nuisances, who endlessly preach the coming of Judgement Day to the sinners who pass by. The only difference is in this case they are right and the Apocalypse really is just around the bend.

20...♕f7

20...♖e7 21 b4 ♚b8 22 a4 ♖c8 23 b5 axb5 24 axb5 ♘d8 25 ♕a5 forces mate with the coming ♖a1.

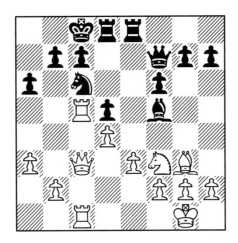

Exercise (combination alert): Black's teetering structure threatens to come crashing down from the disturbance generated by the breeze of a butterfly's wings. All which is required is to give one tiny nudge. Continue the attack.

Answer: Removal of a key defender/demolition of the king's structure.

21 ♖xc6! bxc6 22 ♕xc6 ♖e7 23 ♕xa6+

"Have the traitor drawn and quartered," Black's queen orders. Then she reconsiders her command, adding: "Wait! Have him drawn and eighthed!"

23...♔d7

Inevitability is written on the exhausted king's face as he trickles out of his bunker. I realize now that Marcus Aurelius was talking through his toga when he wrote: "Nothing happens to anybody which he is not fitted by nature to bear." To that I respond: "Ha!". Whenever I lose in particularly horrible fashion, I leave the tournament hall shuffling like a clinically depressed Frankenstein, desperately in need of at least a 25 milligram (if I lose in under 20 moves, then 50 milligrams are required) dose of Zoloft, which clearly disproves Aurelius' theory.

24 ♗xc7 1-0

Summary: I think our Tromp extracts an opening edge against a Chigorin set-up.

Chapter Nine
Unfinished Business

1 d4 ♞f6 2 ♗g5

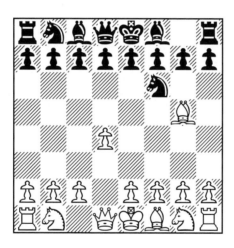

I normally title the final chapter to an opening book 'Odds and Ends', covering not-so-critical sidelines, but not this time. In this chapter we cover lines to which I normally would devote an entire chapter, but the Trompowsky is so vast in scale that I ran out of room, and so smuggle them in here.

After 2...♞e4 3 ♗f4 c5 4 f3 ♞f6 5 dxc5 ♞a6 6 ♞c3 ♞xc5 7 e4 ♞e6 8 ♗e3 d6 9 ♕d2 g6 it can quickly feel like the editor accidentally cut and pasted in material from *The Dragon: Move by Move*. Relax, we are still in Trompowsky territory. This is the Tromp/Dragon, a dark changeling, disturbingly similar to a normal Dragon, except for these differences:

1. Black's clunky knight somehow ended up on e6, rather than on c6, the normal Dragon square. On e6 it gets in the way of Black's bishop when if White plays ♞d5 and there follows ...♞xd5, then exd5 gains a tempo on the e6-knight.

2. Black is slightly behind in development when compared to a normal Dragon, mainly because he took so much time transferring his knight to e6. Now it's one thing to fall behind in a blocked position, and quite another in a Sicilian Dragon structure.

Conclusion: White reached a favourable Dragon and we must adjust our faculties to the altered course of events.

Black can play the Dragon/Tromp with many different set-ups. This is simply one example.

Bravery, when pushed too far, mimics suicidal behaviour, but not in the case of 2...♘e4 3 ♗f4 c5 4 d5 ♕b6 5 ♘d2.

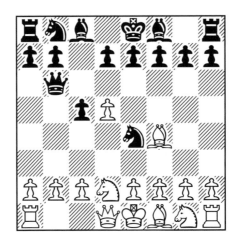

We see at our final gambit of the book. Black can either take first on d2, or even play the immediate 5...♕xb2, since a following ...♕b4+ regains the temporarily sac'ed piece. I always considered this gambit somewhat fishy – perhaps a level below the other gambits in the book. Yet in working on this book, I acquired faith in this one as well, and on scout's honour (yes, in his youth, your writer was a dutiful, if short-lived, member of the Cub Scouts of Canada), I promise to engage the gambit at the next chance in a tournament game. And hopefully you will give it a go as well.

Game 55
C.Lakdawala-B.Cuarta
San Diego (rapid) 2011

1 d4

Compare the position White got in the game to the mainline Sicilian Dragon: 1 e4 c5 2 ♘f3 d6 3 d4 cxd4 4 ♘xd4 ♘f6 5 ♘c3 g6 6 ♗e3 ♗g7 7 f3 0-0 8 ♕d2 ♘c6. I think White gets a better version in our Tromp.

Question: Is the non-Dragon-playing reader able to navigate a
Dragon position over the board, just based on study of this game?

Answer: I realize that reading a book on some opening line and then immediately playing it
in a tournament game is the equivalent of the non-swimmer reading a 'How to Swim'
book and then immediately jumping off the dock into the ocean. This line, however much
it resembles a Dragon, simply isn't a real Dragon. Instead it's Dragon-like, and all we need
is a basic understanding of a few key Dragon ideas, which hopefully are included in the
notes to this game.

1...♘f6 2 ♗g5 ♘e4 3 ♗f4 c5 4 f3 ♘f6

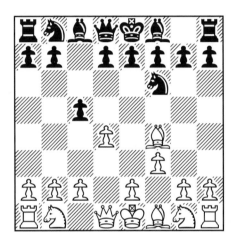

5 dxc5

This move veers toward Sicilian Dragon territory.

Question: This doesn't sound so great to me. Can we opt out with 5 d5?

Answer: Sure, if you want to enter more familiar realms then play it: 5...♕b6 (or 5...g6 6 e4
♗g7 7 ♘c3 0-0 8 ♕d2 d6 9 ♗h6 a6 10 ♗xg7 ♔xg7 11 ♘ge2 b5 12 ♘f4 ♘bd7 13 h4 h5 14 a4
b4 15 ♘d1 ♘e5 16 ♘e3 with balanced chances, G.Kamsky-J.Polgar, Monaco (blindfold)
1994) 6 ♗c1 (6 ♘c3 ♕xb2 7 ♗d2 ♕b6 8 e4 is a Vaganian Gambit with the extra move f3,
which probably doesn't mean much since White may play f4, transposing to a real Vaganian Gambit) 6...e6 7 c4 leads to the Benoni with Black's queen on b6, which we looked
at in Chapter One.

5...♘a6

Rather than waste time with the queen, Black wants to continue developing and recapture c5 with a knight. The trouble is Black's knight isn't particularly well placed on c5, since
it temporarily blocks the open c-file lane for Black's rooks, and also Black is more vulnerable

to e5 tricks, because his knight is AWOL from the normal c6-square, as in the Sicilian Dragon.

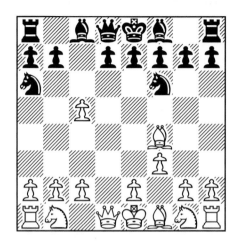

Alternatives are:

a) 5...g6 6 ♕d2 ♗g7 7 ♘c3 ♕a5 8 e4 ♘a6?! 9 a3 0-0? (now White just gets to keep the extra pawn; Black had to play 9...♕xc5) 10 ♗e3! ♖d8 (10...♘xc5?? drops a piece to 11 e5! ♘e8 12 b4 ♕c7 13 ♗xc5 ♕xe5+ 14 ♘ge2) 11 ♘b5! ♕xd2+ 12 ♔xd2 ♘e8 13 ♖b1 ♘ac7 14 ♘xc7 ♘xc7 15 ♗d3 d6 16 cxd6 ♖xd6 17 ♘e2 ♘e6 18 ♖hd1 b6 19 ♔e1 ♗b7 20 ♗c4 ♖ad8 21 ♗xe6! ♖xd1+ 22 ♖xd1 ♖xd1+ 23 ♔xd1 fxe6 24 ♗d4 e5 25 ♗e3 ♔f7 26 a4 ♔e6 27 c4 ♔d6 28 b4 ♗f8 29 ♘c1 e6 30 ♘d3 ♗c6 31 b5 ♗b7 1-0, C.Lakdawala-J.Humphrey, San Diego (simul) 2007.

b) 5...♕a5+ 6 ♕d2 (6 ♘c3 ♕xc5 7 e4 is White's most common move order) 6...♕xc5 7 e4 d6 8 ♘c3 ♘c6 9 ♗e3 ♕a5 10 ♗c4 g6 11 ♘ge2 ♗g7 12 ♗b3 ♗d7 13 0-0-0 0-0 14 ♔b1 ♖fc8 15 h4 h5 16 ♗g5 ♘e5? (16...♔f8 was necessary) 17 ♗xf6! ♗xf6 (he was better off playing 17...exf6 when at least Black hangs on to his dark-squared bishop) 18 ♘d5 (remember this trick; Black's structure gets shredded) 18...♕a6 19 ♘xf6+ exf6 20 ♘f4 and Black found himself strategically (and soon tactically as well) busted, C.Lakdawala-K.Griffith, San Diego (rapid) 2011.

6 ♘c3 ♘xc5 7 e4

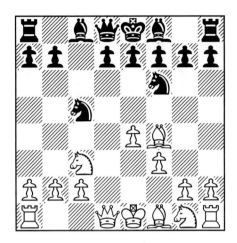

7...♞e6!?

A strange square for the knight, but it isn't easy for White to exploit it.

> *Question:* Can Black hunt for b2, as in the Vaganian Gambit with 7...♛b6?

Answer: 7...♛b6 is a mistake since taking b2 allows White's attack/initiative to spiral out of control. And if he doesn't take b2, then the queen gets in the way of Black's thematic ...b5 push. For example: 8 ♛d2 ♛xb2? 9 ♖b1 ♛a3 10 ♞b5 ♛xa2 11 ♞c7+ ♚d8 12 ♖d1 ♖b8 13 ♞b5 d6 14 ♛c3! and White's initiative is out of control, since he threatens to take on c5 and also opens possibilities of ♖a1 and ♝c4.

> *Question:* Can Black avoid a Dragon set-up and play for ...e5 instead?

Answer: That is also possible, but it hands White a big hole on d5. For example: 7...d6 8 ♛d2 e5 9 ♝b5+ ♞cd7 10 ♝g5 a6 11 ♝xf6 ♛xf6 12 ♞d5 ♛d8 13 ♛c3! ♖b8 14 ♞c7+ was J.Hodgson-D.Reinderman, Leeuwarden 1993. I don't like Black's position after 14...♚e7 15 ♝xd7 ♝xd7 16 0-0-0 ♖c8 17 ♞d5+ ♚e8 18 ♛b3 b5 19 ♚b1 ♝e7 20 ♞e2. Advantage White, since Black lost castling privileges. White owns d5, and d6 remains a sitting target. Also, White's knights for now outshine Black's lethargic bishop-pair.

8 ♝e3 d6 9 ♛d2 g6 10 ♞ge2

A new move. Normal is 10 g4 ♝g7 11 g5!? (11 0-0-0 is more common) 11...♞h5 (11...♞d7 12 f4 0-0 13 ♞ge2 b5! looks unclear) 12 ♞ge2 ♛a5 13 a3 ♝d7, as in M.Gurevich-A.Yap, Jurmala 1985, where Black stands worse: for example, 14 0-0-0 0-0 15 ♞d5 ♛xd2+ 16 ♖xd2 ♖fe8 17 ♝h3! (threatening to take on e6, followed by ♞c7, forking) 17...♖ac8 18 ♝xa7.

10...♝g7 11 0-0-0 0-0

The challenge to the duel has been issued. The only question remaining: pistols or rapiers?

12 ♔b1

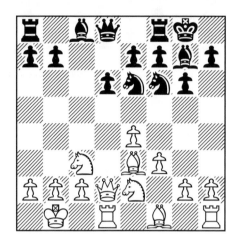

12...b5!?

The goal of delivering mate moves from the stage of whimsical daydream to a potential reality. This pawn sacrifice idea is borrowed from the Chinese Dragon lines. Black dispenses with ...a6 or ...♕a5 and offers the b-pawn to open lines.

After 12...a6 13 g4 b5 14 h4 ♗b7 15 h5 and while I'm no Dragon expert, White's attack looks faster to me. Instead, 12...♕a5?! is met with the trick 13 ♘d5 when Black simply loses time after 13...♕d8.

13 e5!?

Jittery nerves are often the precursor to outright fear. I had only played my Cuban Master opponent once before, didn't know his repertoire, or strengths and weaknesses, and suffered paranoid visions that I had inadvertently stumbled into this position versus a Dragon expert. Still, I should accept the challenge: for example, 13 ♘xb5! ♖b8 14 ♘ed4 (threatening to fork on c6) 14...♗d7 15 ♘xe6 fxe6 16 ♘d4 ♕c7 17 c4 a6 18 ♖c1 I don't believe in Black's full compensation, although I do cede practical chances, especially in a game/40.

13...b4!?

Black attempts a linear solution to a constantly shifting, multi-dimensional problem. Attack-lust is that place where we entertain mad speculations, which would be rejected with a laugh when in a more sober mood. This riotous attempt at upheaval falls short according to the comps, yet is quite dangerous within the human realm. Black decides to take the pace of a mad gallop, when he would be better served with a steady march. Black is determined to follow his risky inclinations to the letter. Sometimes a move can produce 'Ooohs' and 'Aaahs' from the spectators and still not be a good move.

The desire to attack, by itself, is often an insufficient vehicle for the delivery of ambitions. My opponent has a disconcerting habit of endeavouring to concoct new problems for me, rather than take time out to solve his own troubles. This decision teeters between opportunity and pain. He engages in another sharp – but this time somewhat unsound – pawn sacrifice which admittedly does offer Black practical chances. He should settle for 13...dxe5! 14 ♕xd8 ♖xd8 15 ♖xd8+ ♘xd8 16 ♘xb5, which the comps say is an approximately even ending.

14 exf6 bxc3 15 fxe7

This zwischenzug wins a pawn but allows Black open lines to my king.

15...♕xe7 16 ♘xc3 ♖b8

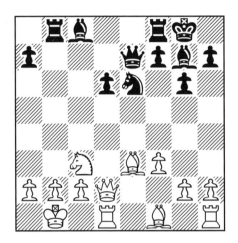

> **Exercise (planning):** There is nothing like an existential threat to rouse us into vigorous action. Black generated a dangerous attack for his pawn (and structural) investment. At this point I considered two plans: a) 17 ♗c4, intending to gum up Black's b-file pressure with 18 ♗b3. b) 17 ♗h6, intending to eliminate Black's most potent attacker. Only one of the plans works for White. Which one?

Answer: Removal of a key attacker.

17 ♗h6!

The mysterious h6-guardian with flaming sword in hand must first be challenged and defeated, before Black is allowed passageway to White's king. Now Black's previous contradictions begin to manifest. The g7-bishop's doppelganger, a dark presence, suddenly makes his existence known on h6. In such Dragon positions, Black's dark-squared bishop is the emblem of his or her power and must be forcibly removed (or at least be made to pay a steep fee for its continued existence).

Why is it that nothing ever unfolds the way you imagined it earlier? I originally intended 17 ♗c4?, but then saw that White drifted into a gigantic tangle after 17...d5! threatening the c4-bishop, and also ...d4. After this move the activity gap between Black and White widens to dramatic proportions:

a) 18 ♗xd5 ♖d8 (White's pocked, ugly pieces, trip into the centre in a vast tangle of pins) 19 ♘a4 ♗d7 20 ♗xa7 ♗xa4 21 ♗xb8 ♖xb8 22 ♗b3 ♕f6 leaves White in deep trouble.

b) 18 ♗b3 d4 19 ♘d5 ♕d8 20 ♗h6 ♗xh6 21 ♕xh6 ♖xb3 22 axb3 ♕xd5 also clearly favours Black.

c) Suicidal is 18 ♘xd5?? ♖xb2+ 19 ♔c1 ♕a3 20 ♕e1 ♖b4+ 21 ♔d2 ♖xc4.

17...♗h8!?

Well, I guess I didn't remove the key attacker after all. This is the human move, since attempting to attack White without the services of the all-important g7-bishop is a bit like being a colour-blind painter. Black engages radical measures to eradicate growing fears that his initiative is on a downward spiral. I was afraid of this thematic exchange sacrifice at the board, yet the comps laugh it off as unsound. It's difficult to fault Black for playing such a move, which signs a binding agreement: he is willing to pay a steep price for the privilege of retaining attacking rights.

After 17...♗xh6 (abandoning the attacking project like this is similar to the religious farmer, who after seeding his fields, refuses to water the soil, stating: "Why bother when the Apocalypse will come upon us any day now?) 18 ♕xh6 ♕f6 19 ♕e3 Black lacks compensation for the pawn.

18 ♗xf8

There go my dark squares. Luckily I have a huge material advantage to console me. Black's king demands to know the whereabouts of his beloved rook. As an answer, my guilty bishop can only stare at the ceiling and whistle through his teeth.

18...♔xf8 19 ♗c4 ♕c7?!

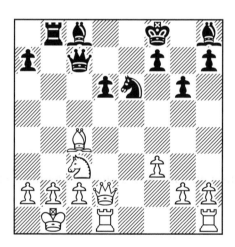

> *Exercise (combination alert):* The queen, a blind woman attempting to
> fend off an attacker with her cane, slashes out randomly in all directions.
> Black's last move was an error. Can you find the trick that I missed at the board?

20 ♗b3?!

We both missed the comp trick.

Answer: 20 ♘b5! ♕e7 21 ♕xd6 ♕xd6 22 ♖xd6 a6 23 ♗xe6! ♗xe6 24 ♘d4 ♗e5 25 ♘xe6+ fxe6 26 ♖xa6 ♖xb2+ 27 ♔c1 leaves Black down too much material and with his initiative at an end.

20...♗e5 21 ♘d5 ♕c5

The queen continues to move about with a stage actor's dramatically exaggerated motions.

22 ♖he1

I wanted to eliminate the e5-pest in the worst way.

22...♗g7

22...a5 23 ♖xe5! (after the removal of this key piece, Black's king finds himself in an un-enviable position, as his kingside is left rotting, without defenders) 23...dxe5 24 ♕h6+ ♔e8 (the king hopes to elude the vigilance of his would-be jailers and makes a run for it; 24...♔g8?? 25 ♘f6+ ♔h8 26 ♕xh7 is mate) 25 ♗a4+ ♔d8 26 ♕h4+ g5 27 ♕xh7 is crushing for White.

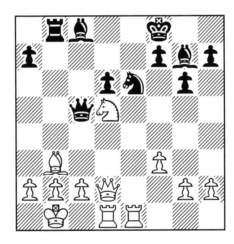

> ***Exercise (planning):*** The passage of time, mixed with Black's violent intentions, still leaves White's king untouched. Come up with a clear plan to consolidate and take over the initiative.

Answer: Principle: centralize when attacked on the wing.

23 ♖e4!

The colony revolts against the mother country.

> ***Question:*** What is the idea behind your last move?

Answer: The ideas behind White's multipurpose move:

1. White eliminates ...♘d4.

2. White keeps an eye on the a4-square, which is important, since Black intends ...a5 and ...a4.

3. White opens possibilities of ♖b4, challenging Black's control over the b-file.

4. White, pushing hard to reclaim lost central domain, opens possibilities of ♘f4.

23...a5

Preventing ♖b4.

24 ♘f4!

Challenging e6 and threatening d6.

24...♔g8

The nervous king decides to absent himself from the proceedings. After 24...♘xf4 25 ♖xf4 ♗f5 26 ♖c4 ♕b6 (26...♕a7 27 ♕xd6+ ♔g8 28 ♖c7 is hopeless for Black as well) 27 ♕xd6+ ♕xd6 28 ♖xd6 Black can't play ...a4, since White's fourth-rank rook prevents it.

25 ♕xd6 ♕b5

25...♕xd6 26 ♖xd6 ♘xf4 27 ♖d8+ ♗f8 28 ♖ee8 is game over.

26 a4

No more ...a4, and no more back rank mate threats.

26...♕b7

The queen removes herself with a noticeable glow of righteous indignation.

27 ♘xe6 ♗xe6 28 ♖xe6

This effervescent rook buzzes about, taking a nibble here and a sip there, like a feeding humming bird. Principle: opposite-coloured bishops favour the attacker. In this case White, who now holds the initiative, along with his extra material.

28...fxe6 29 ♕xe6+ ♔h8 30 ♖d7 ♕b4

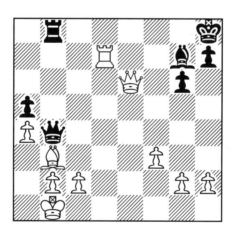

Exercise (planning): The eye aches in sympathy with Black's numerous difficulties. It's clear that the fever of Black's attack passed, burning itself out. In a winning position, our main task is to stay clear of intrigue and upheaval. The pursuit of clarity is our pathway to consolidation. Find White's easiest path to the win.

Answer: Simplification. The queen, having arrived at the end of her great journey, plants the flag and kisses the ground.

31 ♕e7 1-0

Queens come off the board and Black is left three pawns down after 31...♕xe7 32 ♖xe7.

Summary: The Tromp Dragon looks like a favourable version for our side, when compared to a normal Dragon for White.

> *Game 56*
> **S.Mamedyarov-T.Nedev**
> Dresden Olympiad 2008

1 d4 ♘f6 2 ♗g5 ♘e4 3 ♗f4 c5 4 f3 ♘f6 5 dxc5 b6!

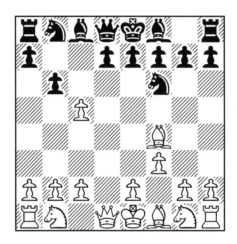

There is no stimulant as restorative as offering your opponent an opening gambit. This pawn offer allows the Tromp/Dragon lines back into realms of playability for Black.

> **Question:** Why an exclamation mark? Isn't Black just giving away a pawn?

Answer: Black offers a promising pawn sacrifice, which if accepted, offers strong Benko Gambit-like pressure along the newly opened b-file.

6 e4

Our best bet is to decline, making Black waste time recapturing.

> **Question:** What happens if White goes for it with 6 cxb6?

Answer: Black gets loads of compensation after 6...♕xb6 7 e4 (not a single player has dared to try the super-greedy 7 b3 ♘c6 8 ♘c3 e5 9 ♘a4 ♕d8 10 ♗g3 d5 11 e3 when Black obtains lots of compensation for the pawn, with a strong centre and White's awkward postings) 7...e6 (7...♕xb2 is unplayed, yet perhaps playable: 8 ♘d2 e5 9 ♖b1 ♕c3 10 ♘e2 ♕c7 11 ♗g5 ♗e7 12 ♘g3 g6 13 ♗h6 ♗f8 14 ♗xf8 ♔xf8 15 ♘c4 ♗a6 16 ♕d6+ ♕xd6 17 ♘xd6 ♗xf1 18 ♘xf1 ♔e7 19 ♘c4 ♘c6 20 ♘fe3 looks approximately even) 8 ♘c3 ♘c6 (8...♕xb2?! 9 ♘ge2 ♗b4 10 ♖b1! ♗xc3+ 11 ♔f2 ♕a3 12 ♖b3 ♕c5+ 13 ♗e3 favours White, who regains the piece with control over the dark squares and bishop-pair) 9 ♕d2 e5 10 ♗g5 ♕xb2 (at last, Black decides to reclaim his previous investment) 11 ♖b1 ♕a3 was D.Collier-V.Gashimov, Gibraltar 2009. I prefer White due to his grip on d5, after 12 ♗c4 ♗b4 13 ♘ge2.

Instead, 6 ♘c3 bxc5 7 e4 ♘c6 8 ♕d2 e5 9 ♗g5 (I would play the immediate 9 ♗e3) 9...♗e7 was D.Fridman-V.Gashimov, Mainz (rapid) 2010. Chances look even after 10 ♘h3 0-0 11 ♘f2 d6.

6...bxc5

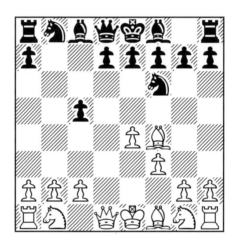

This is dangerous for us since Black may generate future b-file pressure, because we essentially swapped away our d-pawn for Black's b-pawn.

7 e5!?

White's most ambitious try. 7 ♘c3 leads to positions from the Fridman-Gashimov note, above.

7...♘g8?!

Such an incongruous retreat is a strange way to transact business. Structure aside, after this move White's development lead becomes a serious concern for Black. 7...♕c7! is the critical test of White's ambitions: 8 ♕d2 ♘h5 was E.Torre-E.Ghaem Maghami, Manila 2010. At this point White can speculate with the unplayed 9 ♗e3! ♕xe5 10 ♘c3 e6 11 0-0-0 when his development lead should offer full compensation for the pawn, since the coming g4, g5 and f4 gains even more time.

8 ♘c3 ♘c6 9 ♗b5 ♘d4 10 ♘ge2! ♘xb5 11 ♘xb5

In case you didn't notice, Black is distressingly behind in development.

11...♕a5+?!

Black had to try 11...♖b8 12 ♕d3 g5!? 13 ♗xg5 ♕a5+ 14 ♘bc3 ♖xb2 15 0-0 when White remains with a daunting development lead.

12 ♘ec3! a6

Around here, I bet Nedev almost certainly had a chilling presentiment that his opponent was up to no good, and that dirty deeds had passed the planning stages, to full implementation.

13 ♘d6+!

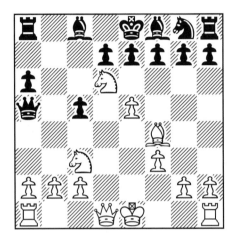

Genius is a principle impossible to teach. Either one has it, or doesn't. Mamedyarov is king in the realm of pure chaos and represents the Tal of our era. This is the move of a gambler who places every one of his chips on red eight on the roulette wheel, and then murmurs a prayer as the white ball tumbles into the correct slot.

Question: Is this sacrifice sound?

Answer: Circumstantial evidence can still convict and shouldn't be discounted as unscientific. At first impression it appears as if White's supposition, a moth trying to reach the stars, has no underlying independent reality. At first the comps frown upon the idea, but when you go a few moves deeper they all change their minds, apologize and hail the sacrifice as brilliant. For the sac, White gets:

1. One pawn, but what a pawn: d6 chokes Black's kingside piece coordination and eternally endangers his king.

2. Black's king remains in grave danger. He seeks to cling to something – anything – solid, in what has become an impermanent, shifting existence.

3. White hopes to mine rich potentialities along the newly opened e-file.

Conclusion: The sacrifice is sound and from a practical standpoint, Black's survival odds remain low.

The simpler and safer 13 ♘a3! looks objectively best, though: 13...♕b4 14 ♗d2! e6 15 g3! (threat: ♘cb5) 15...♕xb2 (15...♕b8 16 ♘c4 is clearly better for White, who didn't even need to sacrifice a pawn to achieve strategic dominance) 16 ♘c4 ♕b7 17 ♖b1 ♕c7 18 ♘e4 when White dominates the dark squares and leads overwhelmingly in development. Black looks busted, despite his extra pawn.

13...exd6 14 exd6

The entrenched d6-pawn isn't merely a random unit in a crowded warehouse. It chokes Black's ability to bring out his kingside pieces.

14...♕b4?

"I will not remain silent, shunned and ignored!" screams Black's queen, who is about as scary as a villain in a Disney movie. Black's counterplay is late and growing later with each passing move:

a) 14...f6?? 15 ♕e2+ ♔f7 (or 15...♔d8 16 0-0-0 ♗b7 17 ♖he1 ♔c8 18 ♕e8+ ♕d8 19 ♕f7 when there is no answer to the threat of ♖e8) 16 ♕c4+ ♔e8 17 ♕e4+ pops the a8-rook.

b) 14...♗b7! (Black's best chance of survival) 15 ♕e2+ ♔d8 16 0-0-0 ♘f6 17 a3 ♖b8 18 ♖he1 ♗c6 19 ♕c4 and *Houdini* rates this position at dead even. I still like White's attacking chances since Black's kingside remains constipated.

15 ♕e2+ ♔d8 16 ♗d2!

The other Vaganian Gambit!.

16...♗b7

Otherwise:

a) 16...♗xd6?? 17 ♘e4 ♕b6 18 ♘xd6 Threat: ♘xf7, and if 18...♕xd6 19 ♗a5+ ends it.

b) 16...♕xb2?? 17 ♖b1 ♕a3 18 ♖b3 ♕a5 19 ♘d5 ♕xa2 and now White wins with the surprising transfer 20 ♖e3!, with a devastating threat on e8.

c) 16...♕b7 17 0-0-0 ♘f6 (after 17...♗xd6 18 ♘e4 ♗c7 19 ♖he1! ♖b8 20 b3 White has too many threats; if 20...d5 21 ♘xc5 ♕c6 22 ♗g5+ f6 23 ♖xd5+ ♗d6 24 ♖ed1 is crushing) 18 ♗g5 ♖b8 19 b3 and now what? White threatens ♖he1, winning.

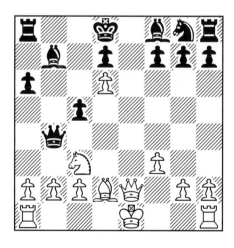

17 0-0-0?!

The complications spin out of control and shoot past the limits of human comprehension – at least over the board. This natural move allows Black back into the game. Mamedyarov missed a discovered attack.

Answer: 17 ♘d5! ♗xd5 (or 17...♕a4 18 b3 ♕a3 19 ♘e3! ♕b2 20 ♗a5+ ♔c8 21 ♘d1! when Black's delicately nurtured queen gasps before the knight's coarse proposal; double attack, with a mate threat on e8 and against Black's hanging queen on b2) 18 ♗xb4 cxb4 19 ♕d2 ♗e6 20 ♕xb4 ♔e8 21 ♕b7 ♖d8 22 ♕xa6 with queen and way too many pawns for three minor pieces. *Houdini* evaluation: +2.93 – losing for Black.

17...♘f6 18 ♖he1 ♗xd6?

Now the defence wilts like oversteamed asparagus. Black had to enter 18...♕b6! 19 ♘a4 ♕b5 20 ♕e5! ♕xa4 21 ♕xc5 ♕c6 22 ♗a5+ ♔c8 23 ♕e5! (threatening a back-rank mate; the queen is accustomed to the finest seat in the house and makes her way to the front row) 23...♗xd6 24 ♖xd6 ♕b5 25 ♖d5! (double attack/discovered attack) 25...d6 26 ♖xd6 ♕xe5 27 ♖xe5 ♔b8 28 ♖e7 ♖f8 29 ♗c7+ ♔a7 30 ♗b6+ ♔b8 31 ♗d4 ♔c8 32 ♗xf6 gxf6 33 ♖dd7 ♗c6 34 ♖c7+ ♔d8 35 ♖xf7 h5 when White stands better, but Black still retains hopes of saving the game.

19 ♘e4 ♗f4!

The only move. After 19...♕b6?? 20 ♘xd6 Black can't recapture due to the discovered check on a5.

20 ♗xf4 ♘xe4 21 fxe4

White regained his piece and his attack rages on.

21...♖e8

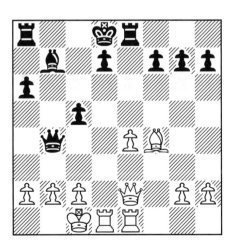

Exercise (combination alert): How would you continue White's attack?

Answer: Double attack.

22 ♕g4!

White's queen, although of a genial nature, grows darkly dangerous when even mildly offended.

22...♖e6

Neither can Black survive 22...♗c6 23 ♕xg7.

23 ♕xg7 ♗c6 24 ♕f8+ ♖e8 25 ♕xf7 1-0

Summary: 5...b6! presents us with our biggest theoretical challenge in the Tromp/Dragon lines. I would decline and continue as Mamedyarov did in this game, which leads to messy positions, often requiring bold sacrifices on our part.

Game 57
T.Radjabov-A.Areshchenko
Moscow 2005

---

1 d4 ♘f6 2 ♗g5 c5 3 d5 ♘e4

3...♕b6 4 ♘c3 enters the Vaganian Gambit.

4 ♗f4 ♕b6 5 ♘d2!?

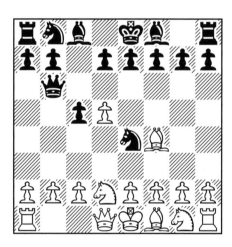

Question: Another gambit?

Answer: Correct, but a voluntary one for our side. If you don't feel comfortable gambiting b2, then simply enter 5 ♗c1 e6 6 f3 ♘f6 7 e4 which enters territory similar to what we looked at in Chapter One. Here the line 7 c4!? exd5 8 cxd5 c4! 9 e3 ♗c5 10 ♔f2 0-0 11 ♗xc4 ♖e8 is no longer popular for White, and with good reason: two decades of analysis have proven that Black obtains more than enough compensation for the pawn.

5...♕xb2

Next game we look at 5...♘xd2.

6 ♘xe4 ♕b4+

Black regains the lost piece and remains up a pawn, at cost to development.

7 c3

7 ♕d2 ♕xe4 8 e3 e6 9 c4 e5 10 f3 ♕f5 was J.Hodgson-M.Chandler, Hastings 1991/92. Here White should hold full compensation for the pawn after 11 ♗g3 (in the actual game, our hero, perhaps not having ingested his normal dose of caffeine that day, flubbed things with 11 ♗d3?? which hung a piece to 11...♕f6 12 ♗g3 e4! – oops, bishop and rook hang simultaneously; Hodgson fought on, but it's tough to begin a game offering your GM opponent piece odds) 11...d6 12 ♗d3 ♕f6 13 ♖b1.

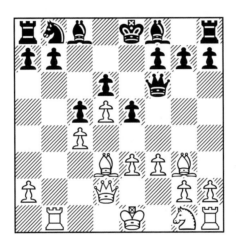

Question: Is this enough for a pawn?

Answer: I believe so. For the pawn, White receives:

1. A development lead.
2. A territorial advantage.
3. An open b-file.

7...♕xe4 8 e3

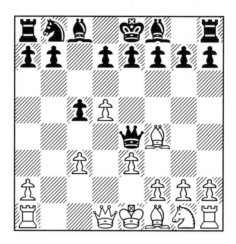

Question: This particular gambit looks pretty shaky
to me. Is this line as sound as the Vaganian Gambit?

Answer: I retain faith, even when surrounded by heretics. An attack's virtues don't always correspond with its present levels of viciousness. Have faith. The viciousness is yet to come. My wishy-washy answer is: probably but perhaps just slightly less so than the Vaganian Gambit. I still believe White gets enough: we receive space, an open b-file, a development lead and a vulnerable black queen for the pawn – enough for an enterprising gambiteer.

8...b5?!

Behind every deliberate theoretical novelty, comes the astoundingly presumptuous thought: "What if they are all wrong and I am the one who is right?" A new move, but be warned: clever doesn't always equate with good. Black utilizes a clever tactical expedient to seize queenside space while he can. The trouble is it violates the principle: avoid confrontation when lagging in development. Other options:

a) 8...g5.

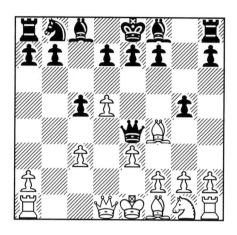

Question: Why is Black offering to return the material?

Answer: It's a faux sac, since taking g5 is met with ...♕e5, double attacking g3 and c3. In reality, Black gains time with the move, but at the price of loosening his kingside pawns: 9 ♗g3 ♗g7 10 ♖c1 d6 11 h4 (Radjabov immediately tries to take advantage of the kingside pawn target to open lines) 11...g4 12 ♘e2 ♘d7 13 ♘f4 ♘b6 was T.Radjabov-M.Vachier Lagrave, Moscow (blitz) 2010. At this point White should continue 14 c4! ♕f5 15 ♗d3 ♕d7 16 ♘h5 ♗h6 17 0-0 0-0 18 ♗f4 ♗xf4 19 exf4 when his attacking chances and superior development easily make up for the missing pawn.

b) 8...e5 9 dxe6 (principle: open the game when leading in development) 9...♕xe6 (played in every game in the database; Black hopes to remove his queen from harm's way).

Question: How do we proceed if Black plays 9...dxe6?

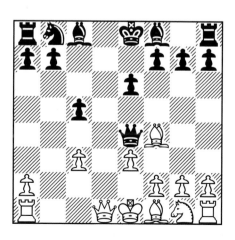

Answer: Something like this: 10 ♘f3 ♘c6 11 ♗d3 ♕d5 12 ♕c2, and if 12...h6?! (Black should try 12...♗e7 13 ♖d1 ♕h5 14 ♗e4 0-0 15 h3!, although White looks better since Black has trouble developing his queenside and his queen doesn't look all that safe either) 13 ♗e4 ♕d8 14 ♖d1 ♕a5 (14...♕b6? 15 ♕a4 ♗d7? 16 ♖xd7! ♗xd7 17 ♘e5+ gives White a winning attack) 15 ♗xc6+ bxc6 16 ♘e5 Black may well be strategically busted.

After 9...♕xe6 10 ♘f3 ♗e7 11 ♗d3 ♘c6 12 0-0 d6 (Black probably avoided 12...d5!? to dodge game-opening ideas from White; still, this is how I would play it as Black) 13 ♗c2 ♗d7 was R.Pert-M.Hebden,M Hastings 2005/06. White earns full compensation for the pawn after 14 ♗b3 c4 15 ♗c2 0-0 16 ♕d2.

c) 8...e6 9 dxe6 transposes to the last note.

d) 8...d6 9 ♘f3 (threat: ♗d3, winning Black's queen mid-board) 9...♕f5 10 a4 g6 11 ♗d3 ♕f6 12 ♕b3 ♘d7 13 ♘d2 ♗g7 14 ♘e4 ♕h4 (the poor queen is getting chased all over the place) 15 0-0 0-0? (15...h6 should be played, when White gets ample compensation for the pawn, in the form of Black's insecure queen's position, along with the normal compensations) 16 ♗g5 ♕h5 was M.Popovic-D.Bojovic, Senta 2009. Black is the one who goes down a pawn after 17 ♗xe7 ♖e8 18 ♗xd6.

Returning to the dubious 8...b5:

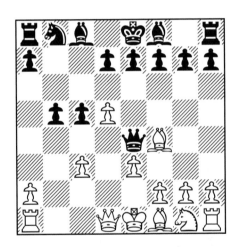

9 ♘f3

Now b5 really is hanging.

> **Question:** I don't get it. Why not just 9 f3 and then pick off the b5-pawn?

Answer: Black continues to hang on to b5, since White's bishop must guard g2 after 9...♕g6!.

9...c4

A move like this does little to inspire confidence in Black's survival chances. Areshchen-ko navigates his precarious position with the grim concentration of a tightrope walker,

walker, who for authenticity, performs the act without the security of a net below. White extracts a huge concession from his opponent since this move opens d4 for White's pieces and also enables a4, prying open the position. Black's options:

a) 9...♕a4!? 10 ♕xa4 bxa4 11 ♗b5 looks depressing since White soon regains the pawn, while retaining his development lead.

b) 9...a6? 10 a4 b4 11 ♘g5! ♕f5 12 cxb4, and if 12...cxb4? 13 g4! ♕f6 14 ♖c1 ♗b7 15 ♖c7 ♖a7 16 ♕c1 when Black can resign, since both ♖c8+ and ♖xb7 are simultaneously threatened.

c) 9...♗a6! (without this indispensable necessity, Black can't survive White's withering assault) 10 ♖b1 d6 11 ♗xb5+ ♗xb5 12 ♖xb5 ♘d7 13 0-0 ♕c4 14 ♖b7 h6 15 e4 ♘b6 16 ♕b3 ♕a6 (Black would love to swap queens, but I don't think he survives the opening of the a-file after 16...♕xb3 17 axb3) 17 ♖c7 g5 when Black is just barely hanging on.

10 ♗e2

Radja prefers to increase his development lead before undertaking action. Also strong was 10 a4. Principle: create confrontation when leading in development. Indeed, 10...b4 11 ♘g5! (perhaps he only analyzed 11 cxb4? e5! when it is Black who stands better) 11...♕f5 12 ♗xc4 looks pretty awful for Black.

10...d6 11 0-0!

11 a4 is met with 11...♗b7.

11...♗b7 12 ♘d2! ♕f5

12...♕xd5?? hangs everything to 13 ♗f3.

13 ♖b1 ♕d7 14 ♗g4!

Hoping to entice Black into further weakening.

14...♕c7

Black just couldn't stomach either:

a) 14...f5? 15 ♗h3 ♗xd5 16 e4 e5 17 exd5 exf4 18 ♖e1+ ♔d8 19 ♘f3 winning.

b) 14...e6 15 e4 ♗e7 16 a4 a6 17 ♘f3 when ♘d4 is threatened and Black collapses.

15 ♖xb5 a6 16 ♖b4 ♗xd5 17 ♗f3!

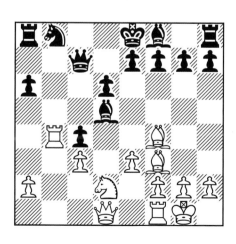

White tailors the position to his changing needs, the way a rapidly growing teenager needs new clothes each year. Brutal efficiency. White eliminates Black's only developed piece.

17...♗c6

Black won't survive 17...♗xf3? 18 ♕xf3 ♘c6 19 ♖fb1.

18 ♘xc4 ♘d7 19 ♗xc6 ♕xc6 20 ♘a5! ♕xc3

Once our eyes are exposed to a truth, it's impossible to close them again. No need for lengthy explanation. One glance tells us Black is busted. Gulp. More open lines for White, while Black remains woefully behind in development, to the point of non-existent. It's pretty safe to declare: that which came about bears little resemblance to Black's original intent. Do you still think the gambit is unsound?

21 ♕a4 g5!?

The mind of desperation works in ingenious, conniving ways. Why not? A dying man doesn't think much about wealth, however if your wobbly position is in dire need of repair, then going on the attack fails to absolve you from defensive obligations. In this case Black judges that his urgency demands swift action.

22 ♗xg5

Even stronger is 22 ♖c4!. A combination lies before Radjabov, but in a language he doesn't speak: 22...♕b2 23 ♕c6 ♖d8 24 ♘b7 ♕b6 25 ♘xd8 ♕xc6 26 ♘xc6 gxf4 27 ♖xf4 and White is winning. I suspect Radja saw this line and quite reasonably desired to keep queens on the board.

22...♖g8 23 ♗h4 f5 24 h3

Perhaps to avoid future back-rank cheapos.

24...♖a7?!

24...♖c8 was forced.

25 ♘c6

White misses the devastating 25 ♖c4! ♕g7 26 g3 ♔f7 27 ♘c6 ♖a8 28 ♘xe7! ♗xe7 29 ♕xd7.

25...♖c7 26 ♘d4 ♔f7

26...♕d3 27 ♘e6 is crushing.

27 ♘xf5 ♘c5 28 ♕a5

When you attempt to set your opponent up in a sneaky trap, your forces should appear non-threatening and sincere. In this instance, White's forces look about as honest as Richard Nixon, when he delivered his teary-eyed Checkers the dog speech.

28...♖d7?!

28...♘b7 is Black's best shot to resist. White wins anyway after 29 ♕d5+ e6 30 ♕f3 ♖xg2+ 31 ♔xg2 ♕xb4 32 ♘d4+ ♔g8 33 ♘xe6 ♖f7 34 ♗f6 ♘c5 35 ♘g5.

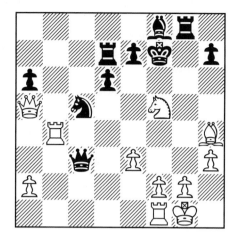

Exercise (combination alert): Find White's breakthrough combination.

Answer: Discovered attack.

29 ♘xd6+!

There follows a deep sense of betrayal at walking into a cheapo, as when we lovingly pat the bug-eyed head of the neighbour's Chihuahua, and the obnoxious bugger repays our act of kindness by biting our hand and then gloating about it with a yapping bark.

29...♔e6

Black's defenders interpret it as a bad sign that their king begins softly singing: "Hello darkness my old friend, I've come to talk to you again." Defenders weave and undulate in perplexing patterns. To what end, no one can say.

29...♖xd6 30 ♖f4+ nets Black's queen.

30 ♘e4!

Winning a piece, since the discovered attack remains.

30...♖d5

It is the nature of time pressure that we see through a distorted lens and interpret aberrations as normal. This hangs a queen, but 30...♕g7 (the queen's eyes are ablaze with the fury of a woman scorned) 31 ♘xc5+ arrives with check.

31 ♘xc3 1-0

Summary: I always considered the 5 ♘d2!? gambit a tad more risky than the Vaganian Gambit. But having studied it in writing this book, I am suffused with new faith in its inherent soundness. So I resolve to abandon formally chickenish ways and vow to play it the next chance I get – even if it's in the final round and a draw earns first place.

Game 58
T.Gareev-V.Mikhalevski
National Open, Las Vegas 2012

Timur Gareev is one of the strongest pure positional players (and also strongest players, period!) in the U.S. today. When I told Timur I was writing a book on the Trompowsky, he emailed me this game, which is a model example of White's play when the gambit is declined.

1 d4 ♘f6 2 ♗g5 ♘e4 3 ♗f4 c5 4 d5!?

This is another move order to reach our gambit position. 4 f3 ♕a5+ is covered in Chapter One, while 4...♘f6 5 dxc5 leads to the Tromp/Dragon lines we looked at earlier in this chapter.

4...♕b6 5 ♘d2 ♘xd2 6 ♗xd2

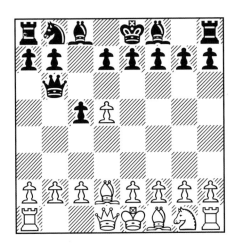

This is the same gambit, part II.

6...e5!?

Mikhalevski declines the gambit and enters a kind of Czech Benoni formation.

> **Question:** What happens after 6...♕xb2?

Answer: We get Vaganian Gambit-like compensation after 7 e4:

a) 7...g6 8 ♖b1! ♕e5 (8...♕xa2?? 9 ♗c3 ♖g8 10 ♖a1 traps the queen) 9 ♗d3 c4 (or 9...♗g7 10 c4 ♕c7 11 h4 d6 12 h5 ♘d7 13 f4 0-0 14 ♘f3 ♘f6 when White gets dangerous attacking chances for a pawn, due to the open h-file, J.Hodgson-B.Jonsson, Reykjavik 1989) 10 ♘f3 ♕c7 11 ♗e2 ♗g7 12 0-0 d6 13 ♖b4 ♗g4 (Black would be better off playing 13...♘a6 14 ♖xc4 ♘c5 15 ♗e3 with approximate equality) 14 ♖xc4 when White, having regained his previous investment, stands better due to his extra space and development lead, S.Ernst-

C.Scholz, German League 2007.

b) 7...♕e5 8 ♗d3 ♕c7 was D.Gormally-J.Hawkins, Hastings 2009/10. At this point we can launch our Vaganian Gambit plan with 9 ♕e2 e5 10 f4 d6 11 f5.

c) 7...♕b6 8 f4 e6 9 ♖b1 ♕c7 10 c4 ♗e7 11 ♘f3 0-0 12 ♗d3 d6 13 0-0 exd5 14 exd5 ♘d7 15 g4!? (I like it!) 15...♗f6 16 ♕c2 g6 17 f5 ♗g7 18 a4 ♕d8 19 ♔h1 ♘e5 20 ♘xe5 dxe5 21 ♗e4 by when White earned full compensation for the pawn and chances may be about even, S.Conquest-A.Kolev, Vrnjacka Banja 1990.

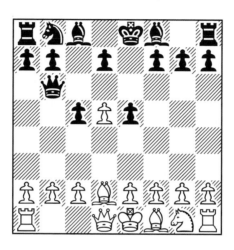

7 ♗c3

Answer: Sure, you can play 7 e4, but if Black didn't take it the first time, he or she probably won't on the second offering: 7...d6 (I wouldn't want to take on Black's side after 7...♕xb2!? 8 ♖b1 ♕a3 9 ♘e2 d6 10 ♖b3 ♕a4 11 ♘c3 ♕a5 12 ♗b5+ ♘d7 13 ♗xd7+! ♔xd7!? 14 0-0 with a monstrous development lead and obvious attacking potential for White for the pawn) 8 ♘f3 ♗e7 (no thanks; 8...♕xb2?? 9 ♖b1 ♕a3 10 ♖b3 ♕xa2 11 ♕c1! traps the queen, since there is no defence to ♖a3) 9 ♗d3 ♗g4 (after 9...♕xb2? 10 ♖b1 ♕xa2 11 ♗c3! c4 12 ♖a1 ♕xa1 13 ♕xa1 cxd3 14 cxd3 Black doesn't have enough for the queen) 10 b3 (at long last, White protects b2) 10...♕d8 11 h3 ♗xf3 12 ♕xf3 ♗g5 13 ♗b5+ ♔f8 14 ♗c3 a6 was L.Winants-M.Turner, French League 2001. White's extra space and light-square control give him the edge after 15 ♗d3.

7...d6 8 e4

Or 8 f4!? f6 (maybe 8...exf4 9 ♕d2 ♘d7 10 ♕xf4 f6 11 ♘f3 ♘e5 12 e4 ♗e7 when Black's position looks passive but playable) 9 e4 exf4 10 ♘e2 ♗g4 11 ♕d3 ♘d7 12 ♘xf4 ♘e5 13 ♕g3 ♗d7 14 ♗e2 and White's space gives him the edge, W.Bode-H.Anhalt, German League 1991.

8...♗e7 9 ♘f3 0-0 10 ♗d3

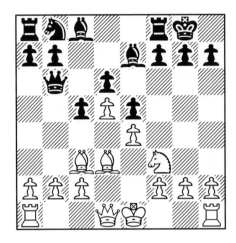

Hoping to suppress ...f5.

> *Question:* How does this suppress ...f5? Black can play it right now.

Answer: Sure, Black can play it ,but it hands White the e4-square after 10...f5 11 exf5 ♗xf5
12 ♗xf5 ♖xf5 13 ♘d2. White may stand a shade better since he controls the e4-square.
10...♘a6 11 a3 c4!
   This move ruffles White's dignity, more than inflicts harm. Mikhalevski indulges in a bit
of extemporaneous speculation and sacrifices a pawn (I believe soundly) to increase piece
activity and take over the initiative. 11...f5 12 ♘d2 ♗g5 13 0-0 ♗xd2 14 ♕xd2 fxe4 15 ♗xe4
c4 is a safer alternative.
12 ♗xc4 ♘c5 13 ♕e2 f5 14 0-0!
   White's worries may outweigh the benefits if accepted: 14 exf5 ♗xf5 15 b4 ♘a4 16
♗xe5 ♖ae8 17 ♗b5 dxe5 18 ♗xa4 e4 19 ♘d2 e3! 20 0-0! exd2 21 ♗xe8 ♖xe8 22 ♕xd2 ♖c8
which *Houdini* rates at dead even.
14...fxe4!
   14...♘xe4? is met with the tactic 15 ♗xe5.
15 ♘d2

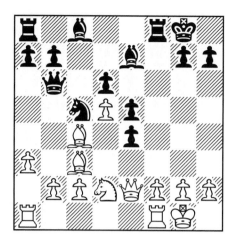

15...♗h4

Multipurpose: Mikhalevski targets f2, while sidestepping White's annoying ♗xe5 cheapos by removing his bishop from the tactically vulnerable e7-square. 15...♘a4? walks into 16 ♗xe5!.

16 a4

Preventing ...♘a4. After 16 ♘xe4?? ♘xe4 17 ♕xe4 ♖f4 18 ♕d3 ♗f5 19 ♕e2 ♗g4 20 ♕d3 ♗xf2+ 21 ♔h1 e4 White is crushed.

16...a5

This halts a5 at the price of creating holes on b5 and c4.

17 ♗b5 ♗f5 18 ♘c4 ♕c7 19 b4!

Gareev seeks to turn the focus to the queenside.

19...axb4 20 ♗xb4 ♖ac8

This move may not be correct. Perhaps better is the queenside blockading plan 20...♗e7 21 a5 ♘a6! 22 ♗a3 when it's hard for White to make progress on the queenside.

21 ♖a3!

Thinking about swinging to c3, increasing the pressure on Black's knight.

21...♕e7 22 ♖c3 ♖c7?!

Black had better options in:

a) 22...♗g6 23 a5 when Black remains under pressure.

b) 22...♗g5 23 a5 ♖f6 24 ♘e3 ♗xe3 25 ♕xe3 ♘a6 26 ♖xc8+ ♗xc8 27 ♗xa6 bxa6 28 c4 ♖g6 29 g3 ♗h3 30 ♖c1 ♖f6 31 ♕xe4 ♕f7 32 ♗e1 also looks tough for Black to hold, despite his light-square attacking potential.

In both cases, though, his position looks better than the one he got in the game.

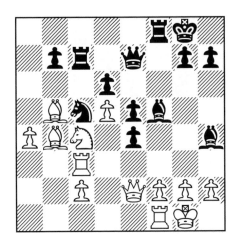

> **Exercise (planning):** Mutual initiatives progress along parallel
> trajectories – until now – but in this universe there is only room
> for one. How did Gareev inflict damage to Black's position?

Answer: 23 ♘e3!

This move damages Black's structure and endangers Black's e4-pawn.

23...♗g6

23...♘a6 24 ♖xc7 ♘xc7 25 ♘xf5 ♖xf5 26 g3 ♘xb5 27 axb5 ♗g5 28 ♕xe4 leaves Black
down a pawn for no compensation.

24 ♗xc5 ♖xc5 25 ♖xc5 dxc5

In the aftermath, Black ends up with doubled, isolated e-pawns and possibly a weak b7-
pawn, while White gained a powerful, protected passer on d5.

26 ♕g4

Better is 26 ♘c4!, intending d6.

26...♗g5?!

Black had to try 26...♕f6 27 ♕e2 ♖d8 when admittedly his position looks passive, but
still better than the game continuation.

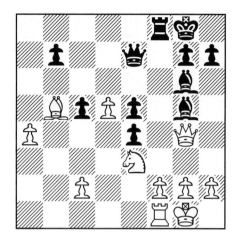

***Answer* 27 d6!**

Black's queen must move aside, since she must continue to protect her g5-bishop. White's passed d-pawn forces its way to the seventh rank, where it ties Black down to fatal levels.

27...♛f6 28 ♗c4+ ♚h8 29 d7

The d8-point is the portal through which White hopes to achieve his ends.

29...♜d8

A blockader is paged, urgently needed on d8. Black's would-be kingside attack evaporates, since his pieces busy themselves dealing with the d7-pest.

30 ♛e6

The queen's awkward stare at her f6-sister surpasses the bounds of proper manners.

30...h5 31 ♜b1!

Going after b7, which forces yet another concession from Black. White won't swap on f6 and allow Black ...gxf6.

31...♗xe3 32 fxe3 ♛g5

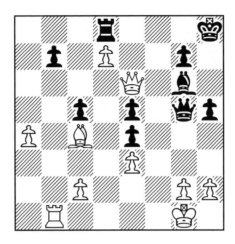

33 ♖e1?!

Unnecessary. White wins immediately with the more vigorous:

Answer: 33 h4!, and if 33...♕xe3+ 34 ♔h1 ♔h7 35 ♕e7 Black drops a rook. When looking for a combination, a key factor for success is to keep our mind free from preconceived notions. In this case 33 h4! is difficult to spot, since e3 hangs with check and we just tend to stop our analysis there. The sure way to miss the combination is to fit the circumstances to the idea, rather than the other way around. Of course, this is very easy for me to say, and odds are, I would have played 33 ♖e1?! myself, for exactly the reasons just described.

33...♔h7

Neither can Black save himself after 33...♗f5 34 ♕e8+ ♔h7 35 ♕xe5 ♕f6 (35...♖xd7?? hangs material to 36 ♗e6) 36 ♕xf6 gxf6 37 ♗b5 ♔g6 38 ♖d1 h4 (38...♔f7 39 ♖d5 ♗g4 40 ♖xc5 wins) 39 ♖d5 b6 40 ♔f2 when he is in zugzwang.

34 ♕d6 h4 35 ♗e6

Halting ...h3 cheapos. Control over the light squares remains a fruitful source of White's domination.

35...♕f6?

A glum mood prevails through Black's position. He had better survival chances after 35...♗h5! 36 ♕d5 ♗f3 37 ♗h3 ♗xg2! (the bishop, long since considered as no more than a worthless appendage, suddenly proves himself quite useful) 38 ♗xg2 h3 39 ♕xe4+ ♔g8 40 ♖d1 hxg2 41 a5 when White's bind begins to release its hold and this isn't going to be so easy to convert.

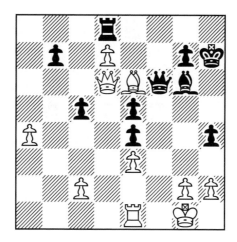

If you have only one arrow in your quiver against a heavily armed enemy, you better not miss your shot. After 35...♕f6?, Black's kingside dreams represent discouragingly unremunerative labours.

Exercise (combination alert): White to play and win material:

Answer: Removal of a key defender.

36 ♖f1!

One by one, Gareev gradually undermines his opponent's hopes.

36...♕g5

Now White's queen is free to take c5.

37 ♕xc5 ♖a8 38 ♔h1 ♖d8

38...♖xa4?? 39 ♕f8 forces the pawn through, and, almost as an incidental, also forces mate!

39 a5 ♔h6 40 h3 ♔h7

Black can do nothing but await events.

41 ♗g4 ♔g8 42 ♕b6 ♔h7 43 c4

A simple winning plan. White intends c5, a6, and then when Black takes on a6, c6, with a pair of unstoppable passers.

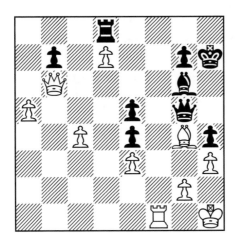

43...♕e7 44 ♖d1 ♕g5 45 c5 ♗h5!?

Hmm. I admit that Black's last move doesn't quite fit with the Platonic ideal of defence. The long suffering bishop's prayers become less sincere with each passing day. Wow, this is what I call desperation! Is it possible that Black's long fermenting frustration rises to the surface? Well, I don't quite get this move, and other than describing it as absolute madness, I find no fault in it.

46 ♕xd8!?

"Remove that vile excrescence from my presence," demands White's queen. The guilt-ridden Lady McBeth-like queen scrubs her body with soap and water, yet her ablutions fail to wash away the conscience-stain of her murder. A little joke from Timur, who sacrifices a queen rather than eat the en prise h5-bishop with 46 ♗xh5! when Black can't recapture.

46...♕xd8 47 ♗xh5 1-0

Black's queen is paralyzed and can only watch helplessly as White promotes one of his queenside pawns: 47...♔h6 48 ♗g4 ♔g6 49 a6 bxa6 50 c6 with c7 to follow, when his d-pawn's exhausting ascent finally comes to a conclusion.

Summary: As in the declined version of the Vaganian Gambit, White achieves a steady space advantage if Black declines the 5 ♘d2 gambit.

Game 59
J.Bonin-H.Stenzel
Nassau 2009

1 d4 ♘c6

Our move order runs 1...♘f6 2 ♗g5 ♘c6!?. Here are a few more oddball second move options we should be aware of:

a) 2...d6 3 ♗xf6 exf6 (if 3...gxf6 4 g3 e6 5 ♗g2 d5 Black took two moves in this version to play ...d5; 6 ♘f3 was J.Hodgson-M.James, Ebbw Vale 1997, when play might continue 6...c5 7 0-0 ♘c6 8 c4 dxc4 9 ♕a4 ♗d7 10 ♕xc4 ♕b6 11 dxc5 ♗xc5 12 ♘c3 with Catalan-like play, favourable for White) 4 c4 g6 5 ♘c3 ♗g7 6 g3 0-0 7 ♗g2 f5 (or 7...♘c6 8 e3 ♖e8 9 ♘ge2 and Black's knight looked slightly misplaced on c6, C.Lakdawala-B.Baker, San Diego (rapid) 2013) 8 e3 ♘d7 9 ♘ge2 and we transpose to the King's Indian versus Tromp chapter.

b) 2...c6 3 ♗xf6 exf6 (3...gxf6 4 c4 d5 5 e3 gets us back to Chapter Four) 4 e3 d5 5 c4 (5 g3 is the Tromp Catalan version) 5...dxc4 6 ♗xc4 ♗d6 7 ♘c3 transposes to Chapter Four.

c) 2...h6 3 ♗xf6 and thanks for the tempo! Either recapture likely reaches Chapter Four positions a move up for us.

d) 2...b6 3 ♗xf6 exf6 (or 3...gxf6 4 e4!? – of course, White can also play the more conservative 4 e3 – 4...♗b7 5 ♘c3 e6 6 ♘ge2 d6 7 ♘g3 ♕e7 8 d5 ♘d7 9 ♗e2 0-0-0 10 a4 and advantage White, who dominates the light squares and also retains the faster-looking attack, A.Zlochevskij-A.Riazantsev, Moscow 1996) 4 e3 ♗b7 5 ♘f3 ♘c6!? 6 a3 g6 7 c4 ♗g7 8 ♘c3 0-0 9 g3 ♘e7 10 ♗g2 d5 11 cxd5 ♘xd5 12 ♘xd5 ♗xd5 13 0-0 ♕d7 14 ♖c1 when White looks better with a clearly superior structure and potential pressure down the c-file, I.Miladinovic-P.Vernhes, French League 2004.

e) After 2...b5 3 ♘d2 (of course, for consistency's sake, we can also take on f6) 3...♗b7 4 ♘gf3 a6 5 a4 b4 6 c4 e6 7 e4!? h6 8 ♗xf6 ♕xf6 9 ♗d3 d6 10 0-0 ♘d7 11 ♖e1 e5 12 c5! dxc5 13 dxe5 ♘xe5 14 ♘xe5 ♕xe5 15 ♘c4 White's dangerous development lead and iron blockade of c4 gave him a clear advantage, despite Black's extra pawn in B.Chatalbashev-T.Todorov, Krynica 1998.

2 ♗g5 ♘f6

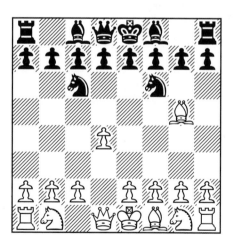

The Two Knights Tango versus our Trompowsky.

Question: What is Black's idea?

Answer: Black seeks to confuse us, keeping us up in the air, if he or she will play ...d5 or ...e5.

The Two Knights Tango doesn't work all that well versus Tromp, since we essentially get the structure we – not the opponent – seeks.

3 ♗xf6 exf6 4 e3 d5

4...f5 5 ♘e2 g6 6 c4 ♗g7 7 ♘bc3 0-0 8 g3 reaches Trompowsky versus King's Indian structures, which we covered in Chapter Six. But in this version Black's knight would be better off on d7, where it can transfer to f6. So, in this case we get a good version.

5 c4

Essentially, we reach a Chapter Four position but with Black's knight possibly misplaced on c6.

5...♗e6

5...♗b4+ 6 ♘c3 ♗e6 transposes.

6 ♘c3 ♗b4 7 cxd5 ♗xd5

I also prefer White after 7...♕xd5 8 ♘ge2 0-0-0 9 a3 ♗xc3+ 10 ♘xc3 ♕d6, J.Bonin-D.Brown, Parsippany 2005, although Black may be okay here due to his development lead.

8 ♘ge2 ♗c4

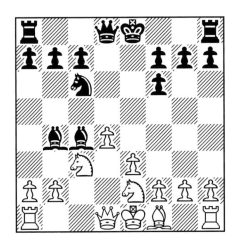

Question: What is Black's idea?

Answer: When White's e2-knight moves, Black chops on f1, disrupting White's castling. However, as the game shows, this plan doesn't seem to give White much trouble.

9 ♘f4 ♗xf1 10 ♔xf1 ♕d7 11 ♖c1 0-0 12 ♘cd5?!

This and White's coming move look premature. He should secure his king first with 12 h4 ♖fe8 13 h5 h6 14 ♖h3 when White stands better, due to his superior structure and king-side potential.

12...♗d6 13 ♘h5

Threatening a pair of dirty cheapos on f6.

13...♕e6?

13...♕f5! pretty much forces a draw after 14 ♕f3 ♕d3+ 15 ♔e2 (I don't trust White's position after 15 ♔g1 f5 since the h1-rook remains out of play, and White can't play 16 g3?? ♘xd4) 15...♕f5 16 ♕f3.

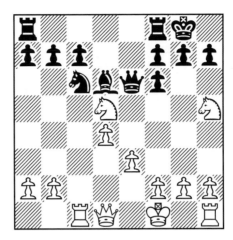

14 ♕f3?

Answer: Both sides overlooked 14 ♘dxf6+! gxf6 15 d5 ♕f5 16 dxc6 which blows Black's structure to smithereens.

14...♔h8

After 14...f5? 15 ♘df6+! ♔h8 16 d5 ♕e5 17 dxc6 ♕xb2 18 ♖d1 ♕b5+ 19 ♔g1 bxc6 20 ♘xg7 ♔xg7 21 ♘h5+ ♔h8 22 g3 White, although down a pawn, holds an edge, since Black's structure is in shambles and his king looks unsafe.

15 g4!

We saw this same clamping idea in a few games from Chapter Four, so let's store it in our mental database.

Answer: The move clamps down on Black's ...f5 counterplay and increases White's hold on the light squares.

15...♖fe8 16 h4 ♕e4

White's attacking potential gets Black nervous, so he takes queens off the board. However, White retains advantage in the ending as well, due to his light-square control and superior structure.

17 ♔g2 ♖ac8 18 ♕xe4

Both parties are agreeable to this accommodation.

18...♖xe4 19 ♔f3 ♖ee8 20 ♖c2

20 g5 f5 21 ♘g3 ♗xg3 22 ♔xg3 also looks quite favourable for White.

20...♘b4 21 ♘xb4 ♗xb4 22 ♖hc1 ♗d6 23 ♘g3 ♗xg3

No choice since e4 would be a powerful post for the knight.

24 ♔xg3

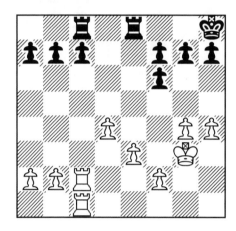

Externally, it feels as if Black is worse but not losing, but this might not be the case. We feel an underlying unease, like a man who can't enjoy himself on vacation, due to the anxiety of a critical and unfinished business deal back home. Black's game is worse than it looks on the surface. Watch how Bonin methodically improves his position:

24...♖e7 25 d5

Threat: d6.

25...♖d7 26 e4 ♔g8 27 g5! fxg5 28 hxg5

Otherwise the defence of h7 will be a perpetual worry for Black.

28...f6 29 gxf6 gxf6 30 ♔f4 ♔f7 31 ♔f5

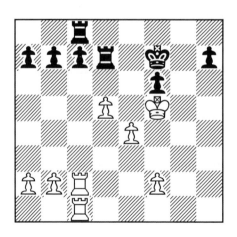

Let's organize our thoughts and break down the position:

1. White's king enjoys overwhelming superiority over his f7-counterpart.

2. Black's rooks are tied down to defence of c7.

3. Both h7 and possibly f6 are potential targets.

4. White can play f4 and eventually e5, producing a passed e-pawn.

5. White's e and d-pawns are both architect and foundation of his fortunes. After that, d6 follows, due to the pin. This creates two deeply passed pawns which paralyze Black.

Conclusion: It's difficult not to view Black's sagging position with a deprecatory eye, since the evidence of decay mounts to such a degree, that we can pronounce Black busted with unalterable conviction. The factors of numbers 4 and 5 are decisive, and Black can do nothing about this plan.

31...罝e7 32 f4 罝d7 33 e5! fxe5 34 fxe5 當e8

34...罝xd5 35 罝xc7+ 罝xc7 36 罝xc7+ is hopeless for Black.

35 d6 c6 36 當e6?

Combinations, by their very nature, are geometric aberrations. It's difficult to put our finger on it, but something is aslant in White's position – a painting hung slightly askew on the wall. White's foundation, once believed to be so firm and solid, mysteriously transforms into an unstable substance. His last move walks into a diabolical trap. Instead, the unnatural 36 當e4! leaves Black in a resignable position.

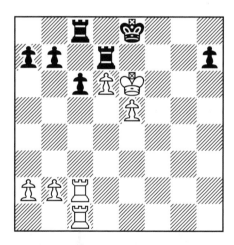

Exercise (combination alert): Through some mysterious force of alchemy, Black manages to forge haphazard elements in his position into a viable saving idea. Find a stunning idea which exhibits Black's deeply hidden strength, while suppressing the inherent defects. Time to ruffle the laws of precedence with a bizarre geometry where Black may well save himself. How?

36...罝g7?

Indifference in a bad position can be as fatal as premature desperation. Black (and White, for that matter) simply didn't believe there could possibly be a combination in such a wretched-looking position. But as we all realize, Caissa is a notorious practical joker. **Answer:** The miracle shot 36...♖f7!! may save the day. There is no greater uplifter of our sagging spirits than when fate gifts us with an unexpected combinational opportunity (of course, we still must find it), in what would otherwise be described as an arid environment. Suddenly, White's king feels out of place, a bit like an ancient Christian vacationing in pagan Rome. But the story doesn't end here. *Houdini* now went on to find an equally difficult win for White.

We must cast off the doubly misleading facade in order to reveal the underlying truth of the position. To win, White must find the humanly impossible-to-find continuation: 37 ♖f1!! (37 ♖d1? Is the human move and the one we all would play, but actually allows Black to draw after 37...♖d8 38 ♖cd2 ♔f8! – with a nasty threat – 39 d7 ♖e7+ 40 ♔f6 ♖f7+ 41 ♔g5 ♔e7 42 ♖e2 ♖g8+! 43 ♔h5 ♖fg7! 44 e6 ♖g5+ 45 ♔h4 ♖5g6 46 ♖e5 ♖g2 47 ♔h3 ♖8g3+ 48 ♔h4 ♖g8 is drawn) 37...♖xf1 38 d7+ ♔d8 39 ♖g2! ♔c7 (not 39...♖c7?? 40 ♖g8+ mate) 40 dxc8♕+ ♔xc8 41 ♔e7 h5 42 e6 h4 43 ♖g8+ ♔c7 44 ♖h8 ♖f2 45 ♖h7! ♔c8 46 ♔e8 ♖xb2 47 ♔f8 ♖f2+ 48 ♖f7 ♖xa2 49 e7 ♖e2 50 e8♕+ ♖xe8+ 51 ♔xe8 h3 52 ♔e7 ♔c7 53 ♔e6+ ♔b6 54 ♔e5 h2 55 ♖h7 ♔c5 56 ♖xh2 a5 57 ♖c2+ ♔b4 58 ♖b2+ ♔c3 59 ♖xb7 a4 60 ♖a7 ♔b3 61 ♔d4 a3 62 ♔d3 a2 63 ♔d2 ♔b2 64 ♖b7+ ♔a3 (64...♔a1 65 ♔c3 c5 66 ♖h7 c4 67 ♖h1 is mate) 65 ♔c2! a1♘+ 66 ♔c3 ♔a2 67 ♖b8 c5 68 ♖c8 ♔b1 69 ♖xc5.

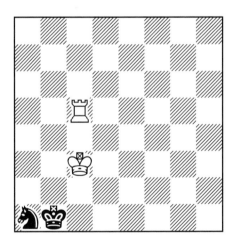

This book seems to be loaded with king and knight versus king and rook endings. In this case as well, the rook beats the knight side, since Black's king and knight suffer asphyxia in the corner: 69...♔c1 70 ♖a5 ♔b1 (70...♘c2 71 ♖a2 wins) 71 ♖h5 ♔a2 72 ♖b5 is zugzwang. White wins.

From a practical standpoint, I don't believe there is a single human on earth who can come up with this 3100-rated *Houdini* technique over the board.

37 ♖f2 ♖d8 38 ♖cf1 ♖g6+ 39 ♔f6 ♖g8

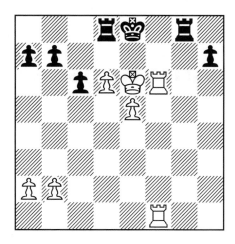

Exercise (combination alert): How did White convert his overwhelming advantage?

Answer: Deflection/pawn promotion. There are many other ways to win as well. This one looks the most clear.

40 d7+! ♖xd7 41 ♖f8+ ♖xf8 42 ♖xf8+ ♔xf8 43 ♔xd7 1-0

There is no taste as vile as futile effort. Nothing can stop the e-pawn's march to e8.

Summary: In the Two Knights' Tango, we reach positions we looked at in Chapter Four, except in this case Black's knight sits on c6, a more awkward square than the traditional d7.

Index of Variations

Quasi-Benoni Lines

1 d4 ♘f6 2 ♗g5 ♘e4 3 ♗f4 c5 4 f3 ♕a5+ 5 c3 ♘f6 6 d5 ♕b6 7 ♗c1

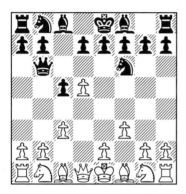

7...e6

8 e4 exd5 9 exd5

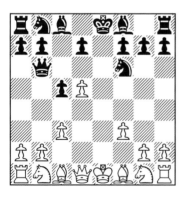

9...♗d6

2...♘e4 3 ♗f4 d5

1 d4 ♘f6 2 ♗g5 ♘e4 3 ♗f4 d5

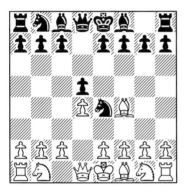

4 f3

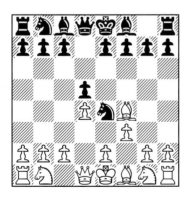

4...♘f6

5 e4 dxe4

    5...e6 6 e5 ♘fd7 7 ♗e3 c5 8 c3

        8...♘c6 – 101

        8...♕b6 – 94

6 ♘c3 exf3 7 ♘xf3

    7...♗g4 – 81

    7...g6 – 88

2...e6 3 e4 h6 4 ♗xf6 ♕xf6

1 d4 ♘f6 2 ♗g5 e6 3 e4 h6 4 ♗xf6 ♕xf6

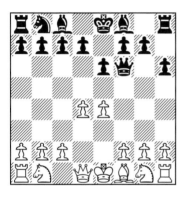

5 ♘f3

    5 c3 d6 6 ♗d3

        6...e5 – 172

        6...♘d7 – 178

5...d6 6 ♘c3 ♘d7 7 ♕d2

7...a6

    7...♕d8 – 151

    7...c6 – 166

2...d5 3 ♗xf6

1 d4 ♘f6 2 ♗g5 d5

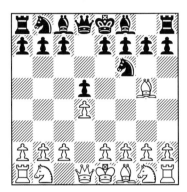

3 ♗xf6 exf6

4 e3

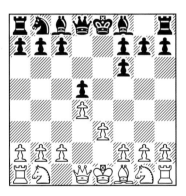

4...c6

5 ♗d3 – 203

The Vaganian Gambit

1 d4 ♘f6 2 ♗g5 c5 3 d5

   3 ♗xf6 – 16

3...♕b6 4 ♘c3

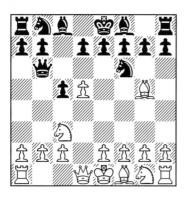

4...♕xb2

   4...e5 – 265

5 ♗d2 ♕b6 6 e4 d6

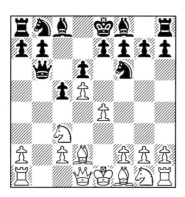

7 f4

   7...e5 – 237
   7...e6 – 246
   7...g6 – 252
   7...♗g4 – 260

Trompowsky versus King's Indian
1 d4 ♘f6 2 ♗g5 g6 3 ♗xf6 exf6

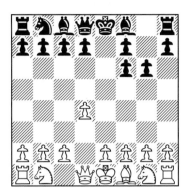

4 e3 ♗g7 5 h4 h5
6 ♘e2

The Pseudo-Tromp
1 d4 d5 2 ♗g5

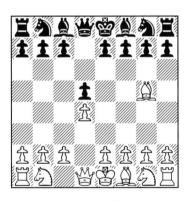

2...h6

3 ♗h4 c6 4 ♘f3 ♕b6 5 ♕c1

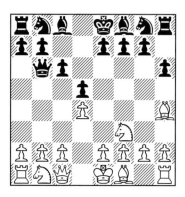

5...g5

5...♗f5 6 c4 e6 7 ♘c3 ♗e7 8 ♗g3 ♘f6 9 c5 ♕d8 10 e3 0-0 11 h3 ♘bd7 12 b4 ♘e4 13 ♘xe4 ♗xe4 14 ♘d2 ♗g6 15 ♕c3

15...♖e8 – 321

15...♗h4 – 328

6 ♗g3 g4 7 ♘e5 ♕xd4 8 c4

8...♘d7 – 303

8...♘f6 – 315

The Pseudo-Tromp: Second Move Alternatives

1 d4 d5 2 ♗g5

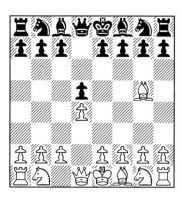

2...♘d7 – 362

2...♗f5 – 368

2...c5 – 373

2...g6 – 382

2...f5 – 387

2...♘c6 – 393

Unfinished Business
1 d4 ♘f6 2 ♗g5

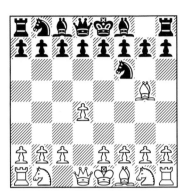

2...♘e4
   2...♘c6 – 430
3 ♗f4 c5

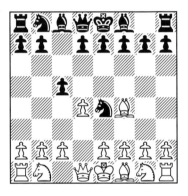

4 d5
   4 f3 ♘f6 5 dxc5
      5...♘a6 – 400
      5...b6 – 409
4...♛b6 5 ♘d2
   5...♛xb2 – 414
   5...♘xd2 – 422

Index of Complete Games